Ancient Persia

JOSEF WIESEHÖFER

ANCIENT PERSIA
from 550 BC to 650 AD

TRANSLATED BY
AZIZEH AZODI

I.B. Tauris *Publishers*

LONDON • NEW YORK

Reprinted in 2011 by I.B.Tauris & Co Ltd
6 Salem Road, London W2 4BU
175 Fifth Avenue, New York NY 10010
www.ibtauris.com

In the United States of America and in Canada distributed by Palgrave
Macmillan, a division of St Martin's Press,
175 Fifth Avenue, New York NY 10010

First published in 1996 by I.B.Tauris & Co Ltd
New edition 2001; reprinted 2004, 2005, 2007, 2010

The publishers wish to thank Mr Saeed Barkhordar, whose interest and
support for this edition has made its publication possible.

The translation of this work has been supported by Inter Nationes, Bonn

ISBN   978 1 86064 675 1

A CIP record for this book is available from the British Library
A full CIP record is available from the Library of Congress

Library of Congress catalog card: available

Typeset in Monotype Ehrhardt by Ewan Smith, London
Printed and bound in the UK by
CPI Antony Rowe, Chippenham and Eastbourne

CONTENTS

ILLUSTRATIONS

Figures

Plates

Sources

The following plates were obtained from the German Archaeological Institute, Berlin: I, IV, V, IX, Xb, XII, XVc, XVIIIa, XX.

The following plates are by the author: II, VI, VIII, Xa, XIV, XXI, XXII, XXIII, XXIV, XXV, XXXb, XXXIa.

The other illustrations come from books about which there are detailed discussions in the 'Bibliographical Essays'.

All maps were newly drawn for this book. They are based on S. Sherwin-White/ A. Kuhrt, *From Samarkhand to Sardis*, London 1992 (maps 1–3); and R. Gyselen, *La géographie administrative de l'Empire sassanide*, Paris 1989 (map 4).

PREFACE

When we now turn our attention to a peaceful, civilized people, the Persians, we must – since it was actually their poetry that inspired this work – go back to the earliest period to be able to understand more recent times. It will always seem strange to the historian that no matter how many times a country has been conquered, subjugated and even destroyed by enemies, there is always a certain national core preserved in its character and, before you know it, there re-emerges a long-familiar native phenomenon.

In this sense, it would be pleasant to learn about the most ancient Persians and quickly follow them up to the present day at an all the more free and steady pace.

Goethe, *Noten und Abhandlungen zu besserem Verständnis des West-Östlichen Divans* (1819)

I am blind. But I am not deaf. Because of the incompleteness of my misfortune, I was obliged yesterday to listen for nearly six hours to a self-styled historian whose account of what the Athenians like to call 'the Persian War' was nonsense of a sort that were I less old and more privileged, I would have risen in my seat at the Odeon and scandalized all Athens by answering him.

But then, I know the origin of the *Greek* wars. He does not. How could he? How could any Greek? I spent most of my life at the court of Persia and even now, in my seventy-fifth year, I still serve the Great King as I did his father – my beloved friend Xerxes – and his father before him, a hero known even to the Greeks as Darius the Great.

The Persian ambassador Cyrus Spitama in the Athens of Pericles, in: Gore Vidal, *Creation* (1981)

Even if our definition of the continuities of Persian history and culture differs from Goethe's, or if we find Cyrus Spitama's criticism of Herodotus's view of the Persian Wars exaggerated, although perhaps understandable, these two quotations illustrate the basic aims of this book about ancient Persia: to present a reliable overview of pre-Islamic Iranian culture, and wherever possible to allow Iran its own voice through its own testimonies.

The timing of this publication is not accidental. While it is true that ancient Persia fascinates Europeans and Iranians alike, it has aroused increasing interest over the last few decades. In Europe we have come to recognize that our Western civilization is only one among many others; and that although culturally – and above all, economically and politically – successful and astonishingly versatile, it has no claim to be exemplary. The attempt to break free from an exclusively European outlook and to gain new spiritual perspectives on other foreign cultures has broadened the study of ancient cultures to embrace those on the 'margins' of the Graeco-Roman world, among them that of early Iran.

In Iran itself, especially during the years 1935 to 1942, there was a redefinition of the idea of Iran in the sense of a 'supra-historical continuity of the Iranian spirit and the Iranian identity' (Fragner), which culminated in the version put forward by the Pahlavi dynasty when it proclaimed a 2,500-year-old consecutive history of Iranian royalty, or created the historicized title šāhanšāh āryāmehr ('King of kings, light of the Aryans') for the last Shah. The special promotion of early Iranian studies pursued by the Shah with Western assistance until the late 1970s had conflicting results. On the one hand, it had repercussions in Europe and America, where museums held more and more shows of Iranian cultural treasures brought to light by excavations, thus giving fresh impetus to 'research on early Iran'. On the other hand, the propagation of distorted or false continuities exposed the study of pre-Islamic Iranian history and culture to the danger of being disregarded in post-Shah revolutionary Iran.

Yet the fact remains that there are areas of Iranian culture and social life that cannot be understood without their roots – that is, without exploring traditions which go back to pre-Islamic times. There are, for example, the realms of language and literature, there are Iranian concepts adopted by Islam, there is the role of religious minorities (e.g. Zoroastrians, Christians, Jews or Mandaeans), there is the survival of the nomadic element in Iranian society, there are cultural–geographical traditions and developments (settlements and infrastructure, irrigation systems, agricultural produce), and so on.

For the European interested in the classical world, the study of ancient Iran offers a way to avoid the pitfall of regarding Greece and Rome as the centres of the world, a way to stand back from certain standards of value, ethnic typologies and prejudices that were already established in antiquity and are still in circulation to this day. This different perspective enables us instead to acquire an eye for the characteristics of the strange and the unfamiliar. To Iranians, the realization of historical and cultural continuities and breaks with tradition, as well as the impartial study of the cultures of ancient Iran, might reveal their country's pre-Islamic past in the light by which the Graeco-Roman world appears to many Europeans, namely as the 'the foreign[ers] closest to them' ('*das ... nächste Fremde*') (U. Hölscher). With its supposed or even real proximity on the one hand, and its difference and 'exoticism' on the other, 'ancient Iran' provides Iranians and Europeans alike with ample food for thought, enabling each to gain a better understanding of their own and their neighbours' cultures.

Although the title of this book is 'Ancient Persia', we have so far mainly referred to 'ancient Iran'. Both terms have their own history and justification. It is historically established that the name 'Iran' was derived from the Sasanian concept of *Ērānšahr* ('Empire of the Aryans'). The early Sasanians created this political concept in the third century AD, because in order to legitimize their own power they wanted to appear as the heirs of the already long-vanished earlier Iranian empire (of the Achaemenids), as the descendants of the ancient mythical Iranian kings, and also as followers of the Zoroastrian faith, with its deep roots in Iran. In its ethno-linguistic and religious aspects, the word *ariya*, which forms the basis for the Middle Persian *Ērān*, can be traced back to the Achaemenid period (and even earlier times). In their inscriptions, Darius and Xerxes not only emphasize their 'Aryan' origin, but also speak of Ahura Mazda as the 'God of the Aryans' and call their language and their script 'Aryan'. The Achaeminds, it is true, put greater emphasis on the 'Persian' than on the 'Aryan' component of their empire. They focused on their belonging to the 'tribes' of Persians (rather than Medes, Bactrians and other Iranian-speaking peoples), and stressed the fact that they came from the south-western part of present-day Iran, to which they had given their name (Old Persian *Pārsa*; Greek *Persis*). The Sasanians, instead, created a new 'identity' for themselves and their subjects through the concept of *Ērānšahr* as the political, cultural and religious home of all who lived there, and through anchoring this idea in a distant past. In the context of the Nazi perversion of the word 'Aryan' into a racial concept and its interpretation as 'of German and related stock' it is worth recalling that the word 'Aryan' has meaning only as a linguistic term denoting 'Indo-Iranian' and designating the eastern part of the Indo-European family of languages, and that it should be used exclusively in this sense.

It is not surprising that, with the fall of the Sasanian empire, the political concept 'Iran' also disappeared. Islamic geographers and historiographers (and even the great Iranian epic poet Firdausi) used it merely as a historicizing label for the Sasanian empire. It was only with the rise of the

Mongolian partial Khanate of the Ilkhans that the official name 'Iran' was used again, and their political concept of Iran (capital city Tabriz, acceptance of the north-eastern border opposite Transoxiana, certain administrative and fiscal traditions, and so on) remained valid until well into the nineteenth century. As an official designation of the state, however, the name 'Persia' was used for centuries and was not replaced by 'Iran' until 1934.

The overall picture of 'ancient Persia' presented here is based on a broad concept that is not confined to the territory of today's national state of Iran, but takes in all the areas that were inhabited in ancient history by Iranian peoples within the borders of the Achaemenid, Parthian and Sasanian empires. Some of these areas are now part of the state territories of Afghanistan, Pakistan, Turkmenistan, Uzbekistan, Tadzhikistan and Kirghizistan. Examples are Bactria (today in Afghanistan), which was so significant in the Achaemenid empire; the early territory of the Arsacids in Parthia (today in Turkmenistan); and Arachosia (also in present-day Afghanistan), which played a particularly important role in the history of Zoroastrianism. In order to understand the specific features of early Iranian cultures, it is essential to refer to these territories and to evaluate the research – above all archaeological – that is currently being devoted to them.

Unlike most present-day accounts of Iranian history and culture, which are based primarily on chronological data and events, we are here attempting an analysis of a rather systematic kind. This book will take account of the very latest problems, methods and findings that have left their mark on investigations about ancient Iran and compelled scholars to discard or modify many common misconceptions. Its aim is to address a fairly wide public, and at the same time to retain its claim to scholarship. While 'classically' educated readers will feel at home in these pages, students in other fields may also welcome a survey of the new trends, problems and results of research. And if non-specialists interested in the cultures of the ancient Near East find it a rewarding account of modern research, the book will have achieved its objectives. The author attaches special importance to ancient traditions and concepts, as the only way to focus on the essential otherness of this culture, and to avoid applying European and Western categories and adopting an outward rather than an inward approach to the description and interpretation of ancient Iran.

The structure of this book derives both from the scientific advances produced by recent inscriptional and archaeological discoveries, and above all from new evaluations and interpretations of many familiar traditions. These have led the author to provide a survey of the relevant testimonies at the beginning of each of the main parts, which follow in chronological order. Another reason for doing so is that readers familiar with classical, i.e. Graeco-Roman, traditions may have a more limited acquaintance with the Iranian tradition and its unfamiliar languages and scripts. The organization of the parts according to the three great Iranian dynasties, the Achaemenids, the Arsacids (Parthians) and the Sasanians (with the brief interlude of the Macedonian domination of Iran), requires a chapter each about the royal and imperial ideology, or the relationship between king and subjects (and therefore also about the social structure of the Iranian territories of the empire). These are followed, in each respective period, by chapters about the administrative and economic systems, as well as religious conditions. Special attention is paid to what may be called 'everyday life', with notes about chronology and the calendar, the army, the organization of labour, as well as, as far as possible, the family and gender relations. The Conclusion covers the 'survival' of ancient Iran; it deals with native and European knowledge about ancient Iran before its 'rediscovery' by the earliest modern travellers, with the accounts of these travellers themselves, and with the history of scientific disciplines connected with Iran.

Although for these thematic reasons no historical survey is provided in the text itself, a complete chronological table, genealogies of all mentioned dynasties and extensive bibliographical essays appear at the end of the book. A list of abbreviations identifies those used both in the main text and in the bibliographical section.

An effort has been made to render names and concepts in Oriental languages with the greatest possible phonetic precision; for this purpose, the following diacritical or phonetic signs have been used:

TRANSLITERATION	PRONUNCIATION
ʾ	glottal sound, as in *flow in*, rather than *flowing*
ʿ	explosive glottal sound
č	ch as in *child*
ç	s as in *mason*
ð	th as in *there*
ə	short e as in *matter*
ǧ	j as in *jet*
ḥ	emphatic h sound (no equivalent in any European language)
ḫ	approximately ch as in Scottish *loch*

q	guttural sound
ṛ	ar
ṣ	sharp s as in *less*
š	sh as in *shall*
ṯ	th as in *thing*
ṭ	emphatic, unpalatalized t
x	approximately ch as in Scottish *loch*
z	as in *maze*
Ω	voiced g, as in *loge*

The following royal Sasanian names have been given in their modern more familiar form in order to assist in their recognition by general readers: Bahram, Bahram Chubin, Ardashir, Khosrow, Shapur. The consistent Middle Persian form of these names would be: Ardakhshir, Yahram, Yahram Chobin, Husrav, Shabuhr. Some toponyms, in which one component is a Sasanian king, are given in their Middle Persian form – e.g. Veh-Andiyok-Shabuhr, Veh-Ardakhshir, Rev-Ardakhshir and Ardakhshir Khvarrah.

The bibliographical essays in the Appendix, now enhanced in this paperback edition with a bibliographic postscript, reveal the great debt owed by the author to many of his colleagues, whose contributions have appreciably marked his views and the opinions expressed in this book. This acknowledgement particularly applies to the participants in the 'Achaemenid History Workshops' in Groningen/London/Ann Arbor (see the conference volumes *AchHist* I–VIII), especially P. Briant, P. Calmeyer, A. Kuhrt, D. Metzler, M. C. Root and H. Sancisi-Weerdenburg, but also Ph. Gignoux, R. Schmitt and W. Sundermann in the realm of Iranian philology, Gh. Gnoli and J. Kellens for the history of Iranian religion, R. Boucharlat, J.-F. Salles and K. Schippmann in the field of Near Eastern archaeology, and E. Dąbrowa, R. Descat, E. Kettenhofen, D. M. Lewis, S. Sherwin-White and Ch. Tuplin for ancient history.

For assistance in providing the maps, I am grateful to A. Haffner, A. Kuhrt and A. Link; for help in the choice and preparation of the tables and illustrations to P. Calmeyer, B. Grunewald and A. Gebhardt. Thanks also to Maria Brosius and Azizeh Azodi. Without the computer skills of my son Thomas, this book would probably never have been finished.

This study of ancient Persia is dedicated to Fritz Gschnitzer, for whom its subject has always been a special concern, and to whom the author is greatly indebted on professional as well as personal grounds.

INTRODUCTION

THE BEGINNINGS OF IRANIAN SUPREMACY IN THE ANCIENT NEAR EAST

How did it happen that in the sixth century BC a Persian dynasty was able to establish a world empire on the soil of the ancient Near East – an empire that stretched as far east as the Indus and as far west as Egypt, and was to become a model for future Iranian dynasties? Since the ninth century BC, Assyrian testimonies have yielded the names of Iranian tribes and places in the territories on the eastern border of their empire, among them the name of the 'Medes', whose 'tribes' with their apparently loose political ties were later repeatedly subdued by the Assyrians, but were only partially controlled by them. By the end of the seventh century, the Medes even proved capable of a counterattack; they fell upon the territory east of the Tigris, conquered Assur (614 BC) and – in league with the Babylonians – Nineveh (612 BC), and subsequently extended their 'empire' westward at the expense of the Scythians, the Mannaeans and the Lydian empire. After 585 BC, the common border of the Lydians and Medes was the Halys in eastern Anatolia. In the absence of any written traditions of their own, and given the uncertain archaeological evidence, the territorial, political, social and cultural profile of the 'empire' of the Medes as yet remains unclear.

Babylonian sources report that in the third or sixth year of the reign of King Nabonidus (554/53 or 550/49 BC), Cyrus of Anshan, a 'vassal' of the Medes, 'destroyed' the troops of the Medes; evidently they mostly deserted to him. The victor was able to capture the Median 'king' Astyages, take over his residence in Ecbatana, plunder his treasury and send the booty to Anshan. Anshan is the old Oriental name for the centre of the eastern part of the

Elamite empire on the south-western Iranian upland, and is thus situated in a region that roughly covers the territory to which the Persians later gave their name, calling it *Pārsa* (Greek *Persis*). It was from here that Cyrus started his war against Astyages. Assyrian sources record that as early as the ninth century BC, tribute was received from tribes of a country called *Pars(u)a* between the territories of the Medes and the Mannaeans in north-western Iran, and it used to be assumed that this name may be compared to that of the later homeland of the Persians in the south-west, and that the Persians had accordingly 'transferred' their residence and its name on a southward migration. Cogent doubts have since been cast on this assumption, but what is established is that Persis was temporarily under Elamite domination, and that some time after the destruction of the Elamite empire at the hands of the Assyrians (639 BC), it had to yield to the Medes, until Cyrus turned the tables with his victory over Astyages.

As successor to the Medes, the Persian king then extended his kingdom westward. In 547 he succeeded in conquering the Lydian capital of Sardis, where – according to Herodotus – the impressive spectacle of the capture and reprieve of the Lydian King Croesus was supposed to have taken place. Subsequently, the Greek cities along the coast and other territories of Asia Minor came under Persian domination. Whether Cyrus followed up his western campaign by first conquering Syria and Palestine, or whether he immediately turned to eastern Iran, is a debatable question. About the early political history of the eastern regions and the way they were incorporated into the empire, we can hardly do more than speculate. In 539 BC, the (remaining?) territories of the Neo-Babylonian empire fell into Persian hands after only a brief resistance. The 'capital', Babylon, was surrendered to Cyrus without even a fight, thanks to the assistance of influential Babylonians who were dissatisfied with King Nabonidus. Nine years later, according to Herodotus's report, Cyrus fell in a battle against the Sakai Massagetae while attempting to extend the territory of his empire eastward beyond the River Oxus (Amu Darya).

In 525 BC his son Cambyses managed to conquer Egypt, where he had himself enthroned as Pharaoh of Upper and Lower Egypt and appeared as a worthy successor of the preceding Saïtic dynasty. However, the priests of certain temples had suffered from looting (and possibly also a curtailment of privileges) during the early phase of the Persian occupation. They did not welcome the king's efforts, and it was in these circles that the image of an ailing and mad Cambyses was fostered – an image Herodotus was later to describe so vividly. There were also tensions between the king and the Persian aristocracy, so that a rebellion of the Median Magus (and 'vice-gerent') Gaumata in the heartlands caught both king and aristocracy completely unawares. Through popular measures such as temporary exemption from military service and taxes, and by openly confronting the tribal aristocracy, the usurper found considerable support from below, until he was removed by the *coup d'état* of a small group of aristocratic conspirators. Cambyses had died on the way back from Egypt, so the conspirators elected Darius – who claimed to belong to the 'family' of Cyrus – as the new king, in exchange for certain privileges for his accomplices.

After putting down a number of rebellions against his new reign, which many people evidently considered as usurped, Darius managed not only to pacify his empire, but also to push its territorial expansion eastward up to the Indus valley and westward to Thracia and Macedonia. However, both army and fleet failed in 490 BC in a punitive expedition against Athens, which – violating a treaty with the Persians – had supported the Ionian cities in their unsuccessful effort to break away from the empire. As for his internal policy, this most famous of Achaemenid rulers carried out administrative, fiscal and military reforms destined to lend the empire stability and leave their mark on everyday procedures under his successors.

In its Iranian parts, the empire of Darius was geographically and climatically so various that the topographical and regional division of its territory, the development of its agriculture and infrastructure, as well as its political control, can only be understood after proper consideration of Iran's geography. The national territory of present-day Iran can be geographically described as a central upland consisting of valleys and partial basins surrounded by border ranges. In the north, this frame is formed by the Elburz mountains (including the once volcanic 5,604m-high Demavend) bordering on the Caspian Sea, and the northern Iranian mountainous rim extending over the more than 7,000m-high Hindu Kush to the Pamirs. In the south, in the regions of Luristan, Khuzistan and Fars, the Zagros chains stretch southeast in several parallel ranges (with altitudes sometimes exceeding 3,000m) and shield Iran from Mesopotamia and the Persian Gulf. The interior of Iran is subdivided by mountain ranges like the Kuhrud and the chains running diagonally along the eastern Iranian border into undrained valleys and basins; inside are extensive deserts partially filled with saline clay by the rivers and turning into salt marshes during the rainy season. The northern Dasht-i Kavir, for example, is the largest salt desert in the world. Saliferous residual lakes are also characteristic of Iran's uplands. The eastern border is formed by the mountain chains stretching northward from Baluchistan and joining up in the Hindu Kush.

Afghanistan might be considered as the north-eastern continuation of the Iranian upland, a country of which the Hindu Kush chains running towards the Pamirs appear as the central axis. Most of its regions are between 600 and 3,000m high, so that Afghanistan can almost be called a 'pass' between the Indus valley and Central Asia or the valley of the Amu Darya. The country's water flows mainly through the Amu Darya to the Aral Sea and through the Hilmand and Harrut to the Hilmand salt lake, while lesser waters drain off, if at all, through the Indus complex to the Indian Ocean.

Climatically, the Iranian world can be described as continental and dry (with considerable daily and seasonal fluctuations in temperature). While its rainy season occurs in the winter and the mountains in the east receive a little rain during the Indian monsoon season, only the mountains bordering on the Caspian Sea receive regular and substantial precipitation. Obviously this scarcity of rain manifests itself in the kind of plants growing in the country, as well as in the need for artificial irrigation in most of the regions that are at all arable. Rainwater farming is limited to sites on the border ranges, the north-western part of the country and a few small areas in the south. Particularly fertile are the regions on the Caspian Sea.

Afghanistan's climate is even more extreme and markedly continental, with precipitation delivered by westerly winds in the winter and spring. Chronic lack of water has made artificial irrigation vital to this country's agriculture. In this connection, millennia-old techniques and traditions can be observed.

If contemporaries were impressed by the 'land of the thousand cities', as Diodorus (after Ctesias) called eastern Iranian Bactria, if the Alexander historians described Persis as extremely fertile and densely populated, and if archaeological findings have unearthed countless traces of intensive settlement, irrigation and cultivation, then all this speaks eloquently for the technical and organizational capacities of the great Iranian kings and their subjects in dealing with the country's natural features.

There follows a detailed study of the history and culture of Iran under Cyrus and his successors. We will begin our survey and analysis with a look at the testimonies.

PART ONE

IRAN FROM CYRUS TO ALEXANDER THE GREAT: THE REIGN OF THE ACHAEMENIDS

MAP 1
The Achaemenid Empire

CHAPTER I

THE TESTIMONIES

1. Royal dictates and accounting, letters and historiography: languages, writing systems and written traditions of the Achaemenid empire

The 'universal empire' of the kings of the Achaemenid dynasty embraced numerous ethnically, socially, legally and politically separate 'tribes', population groups and administrative units. For some time, at least, it extended, as Darius himself emphasizes in his inscriptions, 'from the Sakai beyond Sogdia to Nubia, and from India to Lydia' (OP *hacā Sakaibiš tayaiy para Sugdam amata yātā ā Kūšā, hacā Hiⁿdauv amata yātā ā Spardā*). No wonder that in such an empire many different languages were spoken and many different scripts were used to record the spoken or dictated word. As we shall see, the testimonies from this period display a correspondingly diverse palette. It should be noted, however, that the ability and practice of writing varied in different parts of the empire, and that in many regions, for instance in the central Iranian lands, the spoken word outranked the written. This is the only explanation for the fact that the reign of a Cyrus or a Darius is most comprehensively and vividly recorded by foreigners, especially by the Greeks.

In its importance to the coherence of the empire as a whole, one language stands out above all others: the official language in many central and regional administrative centres was, as it had already been in the preceding centuries, Aramaic. In comparison, the local written languages also used for administrative purposes, such as Elamite in the early affairs of the court in Persepolis, Babylonian in Babylonia, Egyptian in Egypt, and Greek, Lydian or Lycian in western Asia Minor, were much less important. At the same time, the rivalry of languages in the empire led to mutual influence. Thus traces of the Old Iranian idiom found their way into other linguistic

7

traditions, while Old Persian also adopted formulae and turns of phrase from other languages.

The kings themselves and their Persian – that is, south-western Iranian – subjects spoke Old Persian. Thanks to the royal inscriptions, this is the best-documented Old Iranian language we know; in its written form, it essentially represents a south-western Iranian dialect. It should be pointed out, however, that in its attested form as 'the king's language', the language of Old Persian inscriptions, although based on the mother tongue of the kings, appears as a representational language containing archaic forms, un-dialectal words and other peculiarities that lend it the character of an artificial language.

For a reconstruction of the conditions prevailing in Achaemenid Iran, the royal inscriptions (together with archaeological relics and the tablets with Elamite cuneiform inscriptions found in Persepolis, which will be discussed below) have the advantage of being both contemporary and Iran-oriented. For that reason they should take precedence over all other sources, even if these with their sometimes astonishing wealth of detail and literary quality not only fascinated scholars of earlier generations, but also strike many a modern observer as particularly convincing. Most of the royal inscriptions – which are chiefly trilingual, but sometimes bilingual or monolingual – come from Persis (Persepolis, Naqsh-i Rustam, Pasargadae), Elam (Susa) and Media (Bisutun, Hamadan). From outside the central regions of the empire, we also know of three inscriptions by Darius from the Suez Canal, inscriptions on objects (e.g. vases) from Egypt and other countries, a fragment of a clay tablet with an architectural inscription found in present-day Romania, a rock inscription by Xerxes from Lake Van in Armenia, seal impressions with legends from Dascylium on the Propontis, and fragments of inscriptions from Babylonia. The regular sequence of the texts on the trilingual inscriptions (Old Persian, Elamite, Babylonian) is clearly an expression of Achaemenid respect for tradition and has proved vital in the history of deciphering cuneiform writing, the form used for the inscriptions. Far more than half of the royal inscriptions date from the reign of Darius I and his son Xerxes I – that is, from the end of the sixth to the middle of the fifth century BC. From the reign of Artaxerxes I (465–425/24 BC) they distinctly diminish, are often written in a single language and seem to follow set formulae and models. Linguistically, the period after Xerxes shows a gradual development towards the Middle Persian idiom. Evident grammatical mistakes and a poor command of the language are characteristic of this period.

Phonic signs (in alaphabetical order)

𐎠	𐎲	𐎨	𐏂	𐎭	𐎮	𐎯	𐎳	𐎥	𐎦	𐏃	𐎡
a	bᵃ	cᵃ	çᵃ	dᵃ	dⁱ	dᵘ	fᵃ	gᵃ	gᵘ	hᵃ	i

𐎩	𐎪	𐎣	𐎤	𐎫	𐎶	𐎷	𐎸	𐎴	𐎵	𐎱	𐎼
jᵃ	jⁱ	kᵃ	kᵘ	lᵃ	mᵃ	mⁱ	mᵘ	nᵃ	nᵘ	pᵃ	rᵃ

𐎻	𐎿	𐏁	𐎾	𐏀	𐎰	𐎢	𐎺	𐎻	𐎧	𐎹	𐏃
rᵘ	sᵃ	šᵃ	tᵃ	tᵘ	θᵃ	u	vᵃ	vⁱ	xᵃ	yᵃ	zᵃ

Logograms

XŠ	DH₁ DH₂	BG	BU	AM₁ AM₂	AMha
xšāyaθiya-	dahyu-	baga-	būmī-	Auramazdā-	Auramazdāha
'King'	'Land'	'God'	'Earth'	(GN)	(GN, gen. sing.)

Word dividers

◄ (DB only)   ◥ (others)

Figure 1 List of Old Persian signs

Surveys of the Old Persian cuneiform script show that its beginnings are as yet obscure. All we know for certain is its first application in the great account of Darius's exploits found on the Bisutun (Behistun) rock in Media, with which we shall deal later. The Old Persian cuneiform script is not a development of the Mesopotamian cuneiform, which was already more than two millennia old by that time, but a new creation influenced by the Aramaic consonantal script and consisting of a mixture of syllabic and consonantal signs (see Figure 1). Despite some definite rules of writing, its 36 phonic signs, 8 logograms (ideograms), and its numerals and two word separators admit of different possible readings, and these can be clarified only by resorting to etymology, linguistic history or philology. Having already become obsolete and unreadable in classical antiquity, the Old Persian cuneiform script was 'rediscovered' by early modern travellers and has acquired immense importance in the history of scholarship, due to its application in the context of Achaemenid royal inscriptions that display three versions of an identical content. Its decipherment in the nineteenth century led not only to the unlocking of other cuneiform systems, and so to an understanding of the languages they concealed, but also to the emergence of entirely new branches of learning (such as Ancient Near Eastern studies) and ultimately to a departure from the views about the ancient Orient presented by the Bible and classical (Greek) authors. The now legible contemporary and native texts (as well as the non-written testimonies brought to light by archaeological field research since the mid-nineteenth century) eventually paved the way for a new insight into Ancient Near Eastern cultures, laying greater stress on their characteristic features and on the specific traditions of each. These findings will be amply described and discussed.

The second version of the royal inscriptions, the one in Elamite, bears witness to the last phase ('late Elamite') of a language that has hitherto eluded attribution to any other language or group of languages and thus sets special problems to the philologist. The written language of the Elamites – those old opponents of the Assyrians and Babylonians whose empire was destroyed in their war against the Assyrians in the seventh century BC, and whose ancient territory was settled by the Persians – was the official administrative language of the Achaemenids in Persis until about 460 BC. No Elamite records of a later period have come down to us. Apart from the versions of the royal inscriptions written in this language, the finds particularly relevant for the historian are the clay tablets with Elamite writings from Persepolis, which were saved in the 1930s by the Persepolis excavators Ernst Herzfeld and Erich F. Schmidt and classified, in accordance with their place of discovery, as Persepolis Treasury Tablets (PTT) and Persepolis Fortification Tablets (PFT). While the former (114 pieces) are datable to the period between 492 and 460 BC – after which they must have converted to Aramaic 'bookkeeping' (on parchment) in Persepolis – the latter, of which more than 2,000 have so far been published and thousands of further fragments await publication, are attributable to the granary management of the court of Darius I and belong to the period between 510 and 494 BC. It is assumed that this was when the royal commissariat was transferred from the terrace to the plain. The clay tablets were evidently shaped by hand before they were used, and inscribed while the clay was still damp. One end was smoothed down and often served to receive the seal impressions (see Plate XIIIa). These unusual documents, which can throw light on the geography, administration and economy, as well as the religious and social conditions, of the heartland of the Persian kings from Darius to Xerxes, and are also significant from a prosopographic and onomastic point of view, have reached us – like other testimonies of the kind – by mere chance. Though wind and rain would otherwise have reduced them to dust, the political end of the Achaemenid reign, symbolized by Alexander's setting fire to Persepolis, paradoxically enough contributed to their survival. Baked and hardened by the fire, they bear witness today to the organizational talent of their creators.

It is equally true of the third, the Babylonian, version of the royal inscriptions, that its deciphering opened up other texts in this Akkadian dialect spoken in Babylonia (as far as our subject is concerned, texts written in a late Babylonian idiom). Among the outstanding testimonies for the period concerned are the monolingual Babylonian royal inscriptions from Babylon, Ur and Uruk, the historical data in chronicles, astronomical 'diary entries', lists of kings, prophecies and poems, as well as economic documents, including the particularly significant archival records of the temples of Uruk and Sippar and of the 'commercial firms' of the Egibi and Murashu families. However, the economic testimonies have as yet been sparsely published, unevenly covered from a chronological and regional point of view, and their provenance often poorly documented. Comprehensive historical evaluations of the material have nevertheless shown Babylonia's special significance within the empire as a whole.

Next come the documents in the Aramaic language and script, the papyri and ostraca (clay sherds) from Egypt, and also some from Palestine, as well as inscriptions from Asia Minor and Persepolis. Thanks to its easily acquired alphabetic script, Aramaic had, since the eighth century BC, increasingly become a language of 'international' communication in this region and was eventually made the official (imperial) administrative language of the Achaemenids in a more evolved and independent form of Old Aramaic. In this form, which scholars refer to as imperial or official Aramaic, a great many documents have come down to us from the Jewish military colony of Elephantine in southern Egypt (acting on behalf of the Persian kings), as well as letters written on leather from the Achaemenid prince and Egyptian satrap (governor) Arshama (Arsames), epitaphs from Dascylium, and the Aramaic version of the trilingual inscription from Xanthus in Lycia.

With its Lycian version, the latter document constitutes a transition towards the written documents of the Persian period in Asia Minor, the Lycian inscriptions on tombs, sarcophagi and coins, and the Lydian inscriptions from western Asia Minor.

The fact that the particularly familiar sources in the Greek language have not yet been mentioned calls for some justification. Although outstandingly significant for Graeco-Persian relations (especially when describing the wars or pointing out the contrast between Hellenes and 'barbarians'), these sources, with the exception of some of the Alexander historians, provide too little information about Iran itself. If we nevertheless attempt to make a list of authors and works according to their contribution to reconstructing Iranian history, the following names and titles (in chronological order) stand out: Aeschylus (with his *Persians* as a contemporary document about the Xerxes campaign); Herodotus (with his description of the 'Persian wars', and also his Persian *logos* in Book III); Xenophon (especially with his description of the march of Cyrus the Younger's mercenaries before and after the fight against Artaxerxes II [*Anabasis*]; his *Cyropaedia,* on the other hand, is not a piece of historiography nor very intelligible as regards his Iranian reminiscences); and – as Roman subjects – Strabo (with his geographical and ethnographical observations in the 15th Book), Plutarch (with his 'Life of Artaxerxes II'), and Arrian as perhaps the most important representative of the secondary Alexander tradition. A particularly scrupulous analysis has to be devoted to the Greek authors of the fourth century BC (e.g. Plato, Aristotle, Isocrates, Ctesias, Dinon et al.), who have provided us not only with their verdict about certain characteristics of the 'barbarian' (read: Persian) nature, but also with their view of the steady decline of the empire after Xerxes's abortive campaign in Greece. Nor should we neglect some significant epigraphic testimonies in the Greek language, such as a copy preserved in the Louvre of a letter Darius I addressed to his official Gadatas from Magnesia, or an inscription from Sardis reporting that an Iranian called Baradates had established a filial version of an original Zeus (i.e. Ahura Mazda) cult. The undoubtedly apocryphal Greek inscription on the tomb of Cyrus mentioned in the Alexander tradition is a particularly interesting example of the Greek world's admiration for Cyrus on the one hand, and Greek interpretation of foreign ways of life on the other.

Before the discovery of the testimonies concealed in Iran itself, the history of the Achaemenid empire was not only told by the Greek tradition, but also substantially laid down through the texts of the Old Testament, and above all by the Books of (Deutero-)Isaiah, Ezra and Nehemiah, Esther and Daniel. Research on the Old Testament is even today concerned with finding out both the 'historical' facts in these texts, and the significance of the Persian empire in the history of the Jewish communities in Palestine, Babylonia and Egypt, their theological convictions and religious and ritual establishments, as well as the evolution of their literature (the 'Old Testament').

It is hardly possible to tell which texts of the Avesta, i.e., of the earlier part of the religious literature of the Zoroastrians, go back to the Achaemenid period. This corpus was first committed to writing in the Sasanian period, and the earliest manuscripts go back only to the thirteenth century.

2. The model: a king justifies himself. The *res gestae* and relief of Darius I on the Bisutun rock (DB)

Between Kirmanshah and Hamadan, or ancient Ecbatana, the capital of Media, rises the Bisutun mountain, known in the Achaemenid period as *bagastāna* ('place of the gods'). Here on a rock about 60m above a spring-fed pool, there is a great monument to Darius I, the most famous Achaemenid king. It was no accident that Darius chose this site for his monument. A very ancient caravan route leads past it, which even now connects the Mesopotamian lowland, that is, the area around Babylon and Baghdad, with the Iranian upland (Ecbatana), and then runs further east, where it has become known as the 'Silk Road'. As its name indicates, the Bisutun mountain evidently possessed religious-cultic significance in early historical times and later under the Achaemenids. Herodotus's report that the Persians made sacrifices to their gods on the tops of mountains (they actually also made them to the mountains themselves) may illustrate the kind of prestige it had. Lastly – and this must have been the main reason why Darius had his relief and inscription placed here – it was somewhere near this site that he and his fellow conspirators succeeded in killing the usurper Gaumata in his summer residence and assuming control themselves. In an inscription, Darius describes how this overthrow occurred and also how the rebellions of the following year (522–21 BC) were put down, rebellions that had broken out in many parts of the empire and that he was able to subdue only with the utmost cruelty. Incidentally, Darius found the model for his relief in north-western Iran, in the rock relief of a Lullubi king near Sar-i Pul, dating from the beginning of the second millennium.

The inscription is doubtless a form of royal self-portrayal and propaganda, and in this respect it has been rightly compared with the *res gestae* of Augustus. Both Darius and the Roman princeps were eager to advertise the legitimacy of their reign and to present their own regime as a remedy against chaos, disorder and insecurity. And both used the same methods to do so. An 'official' announcement in the first person singular, with its original version displayed in a significant place – here a mausoleum, there the site of a victory – was to be distributed in numerous copies all over the empire. Thus the *res gestae* of Augustus have come down to us – at least fragmentarily – in a bilingual (Greek and Latin) version from Ankara (*Monumentum Ancyranum*) and in monolingual copies from Apollonia in Pisidia (Greek) and Antiochia in Pisidia (Latin). And the Darius inscription survives not only in its trilingual cuneiform version, but partially also in short monolingual fragments from Babylon, and in an equally fragmentary Aramaic version dating from a hundred years later and stemming from the above-mentioned Jewish military colony of Elephantine in southern Egypt.

On the whole, however, the differences between these two narratives outweigh their similarities. While the *res gestae* of Augustus were conceived as a kind of summary of his reign, the Bisutun inscription was planned, dictated, written down or carved and then distributed directly after the events described in it. The quest for legitimacy must have exerted considerable pressure on Darius. Not everyone clearly realized and admitted that he was the rightful successor of Cyrus and Cambyses. This is how it sounds in Darius's own words:

§ 60 Proclaims Darius, the king: Now let what [has been] done by me convince you. Thus make [it] known to the people, do not conceal [it]! If you shall not conceal this record, [but] make it known to the people, may Ahura Mazda be friendly to you, and may offspring be to you in great number, and may you live long!

§ 61 Proclaims Darius, the king: If you shall conceal this record, [and] not make [it] known to the people, may Ahura Mazda be your destroyer, and may offspring not be to you!

Elsewhere Darius expressly warns anyone who sees the inscription and the images not to destroy them, but to preserve them.

This implies yet another difference with the *res gestae* of Augustus: Darius's effort at legitimation in Media is expressed in both word and image. In Bisutun there stands, at the centre of the entire monument, the relief of the victorious king and his vanquished opponents, whom scholars, following Darius's own expression, call the 'liar kings'. And replicas of the relief were evidently circulated, as witnessed by a chance find from Babylon.

A glance at the relief (Plate I) shows that it was carved into a flattened rectangular rock surface measuring about 3 x 5.5m. Darius is portrayed standing and facing right, wearing a Persian garment, the 'royal' shoes, a bracelet and a crenelated crown of a specially elaborate design. In his left hand he holds a bow, a sign of sovereignty often portrayed in this form. His right hand is raised at face level. With his left foot Darius is treading on the chest of a figure who lies on his back before him and, according to the legends, represents Gaumata, the Median Magus and pretender to the throne whose assassination led to Darius's reign. Gaumata, who is also dressed in Persian attire, which is no indication of any specific ethnic group, is raising his arms as a sign of submission.

From the right-hand side, a group of rebels is walking towards the king. Their hands are tied behind their backs and a long rope is bound around their necks, attaching them to each other. These figures are distinctly smaller than the king, measuring only 1.17m against his 1.72m. Each of these prisoners can be identified not only by his legend, but also by his specific ethnic costume, while the variations in physiognomy and headdress are no doubt also meant to convey a semblance of individuality or of a definite ethnic type. The first eight standing figures represent the leaders of the rebellions that broke out in the year after Darius came to power – rebellions about which the king himself says that he had to smother them in a sea of blood. The last captive, the Scythian Skunkha with the pointed hood, was added to the scene at a later time, after Darius had successfully concluded his Scythian campaign of 519 BC. With the help of the inscription, it has been possible to establish that the pretenders to the throne are depicted in the order in which their rebellions had been quelled.

Behind the king stand two armed figures who have been assumed to represent two of Darius's fellow conspirators, but the inscriptions do not identify them. Above the scene hovers the 'winged' man, who for a long time was believed to depict Ahura Mazda, the god frequently invoked by Darius in the inscription, but perhaps this image should rather be interpreted as the *daimōn* of his royal ancestors.

The next two illustrations (Figures 2 and 3) clarify the spatial relations between relief and inscription – or rather inscriptions. At the same time, they serve to provide information about how – i.e. in what order – the inscription and relief were carved into the rock face. The relief was evidently created first, that is, with the first eight 'liar kings', but without Skunkha, the Scythian with the pointed hood. The only text at the end of this phase was the Elamite legend for the king (DBa[sus.]), for its beginning differs in several minor but significant formulations from that of the royal protocol of the large Elamite inscription produced later.

A second phase saw the creation of the older Elamite version of the inscription in four columns with 323 lines on the right-hand side of the relief and the Elamite legends for the rebels (DBb–j). The asymmetrical

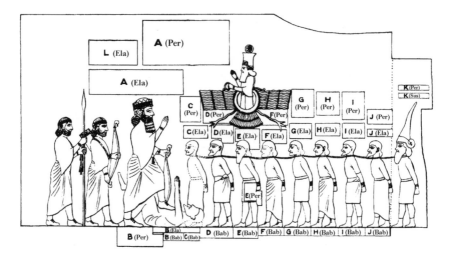

Figure 2 Bisutun, Darius relief. Drawing marking the position of the brief Old Persian (Per.) Elamite (Ela.) and Babylonian (Bab.) inscriptions (legends DBa-l (here A–L)

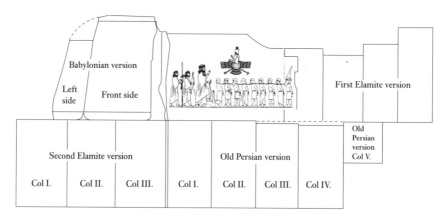

Figure 3 Bisutun, Monument of Darius I (drawing)

placing of the large inscription next to the relief and the above-mentioned changes in the wording of its first section point to a revision or elaboration of the text and the monument as a whole.

The third phase marks the creation of the 112 lines in the Babylonian version of the inscription on the left of the relief, as well as the Babylonian legends (DBb–j). Since this version had evidently not been planned to start with, room had to be found on the ledge to the left of the relief. Similarly unplanned were the Babylonian legends. So it was necessary to omit that of the king and to cram those of the rebels Gaumata and Açina together under Gaumata's Elamite legend.

In the particularly important fourth phase, Darius had the Old Persian version of his *res gestae* placed in four columns below the relief. Compared with the earlier versions, this contained one additional passage (§ 70), and the same passage was simultaneously added to the Elamite inscription (above the Elamite legend for the king). Apart from that, the relief figures (with the exception of the king) were now also provided with Old Persian legends whose lack of harmony with the rest of the relief confirms that they were created later. It is obvious that § 70 was already part of the initial design of the Old Persian version, while the Elamite version did not contain it to start with, and the Babylonian version omits it altogether for lack of space. This proves that the Old Persian script, and hence the Old Persian inscription, did not yet exist at the time when the Elamite version was conceived. And in fact in this § 70, Darius actually states that he had the Old Persian cuneiform script 'made' for the purpose of composing this inscription:

By the favour of Ahura Mazda, this [is] the form of writing [OP *dipiciça*] which I have made, besides, in Aryan. ... And it was written down and was read aloud before me. Afterwards I have sent this form of writing everywhere into the countries. The people strove [to use it].

In the next phase, starting around 518 BC, the figure of the Scythian Skunkha, who was captured in the third year of Darius's reign, was added to the relief and given a Persian and an Elamite legend. Because of this addition, the original Elamite version had to be eliminated, and its text was carved anew word-for-word on the left-hand side of the Old Persian and underneath the Babylonian version (later Elamite version).

Shortly afterwards, a sixth phase saw the addition of a fifth column (§§ 71–76) to the Old Persian version, containing information about the second and third years of Darius's reign. Lack of space prevented an extension of the Elamite and Babylonian versions to contain this part of the *res gestae*. At the very end, the Old Persian legend for the king was created, already following the protocol of the Elamite version instead of the older and more personal formulation of the Elamite legend.

What could have been the royal *conception* of the inscriptions and the relief? Philological and historical analyses of the different versions of the inscription prove beyond all doubt that the Elamite and Old Persian versions on the one hand, and the Aramaic and Babylonian ones on the other, are closely connected. However, the apparatus of variants in the existing versions of inscriptions, the impossibility of immediately translating an oral dictation and carving it into stone, as well as other factors, show that the editorial work must have been considerably more extensive and varied than the surviving (written) versions would have us believe. This rules out drawing up a simple stemma. Among the peculiarities of certain versions, some are especially striking – for example the mention of the numbers of fallen opponents in the Aramaic and Babylonian versions; and supplementary statements and clarifications in some versions, evidently with a view to contributing to a better understanding of the content by the respective groups of populations addressed. In the Old Persian version produced last of all, some statements included in the Elamite version that could hardly be flattering to Darius, for instance regarding the troops of Persian guards who had deserted him, were simply omitted, which shows that the content of the text had been re-examined.

Questions such as how the composition of the relief relates to the rest, whether it was designed prior to the text, as the genesis of the monument would lead us to believe, or whether the first thing planned was to instruct the population about its contents, in which case the text would have been produced first, can hardly be decided. And in view of the rapid creation of both parts of the monument, they are of minor significance.

The earliest Aramaic versions or copies, which have not survived, were no doubt made for the speedy instruction of different parts of the empire and must have been reproduced for this purpose, that is, copied, dispatched, and again recopied, perhaps at the courts of the satraps. All this may be explained by the location of the monument, making it impossible for the passer-by in Bisutun to understand the reliefs or to decipher the inscriptions. It is hardly surprising that later ancient historians attributed the monument to the legendary Queen Semiramis.

The way in which the various versions of the inscription were distributed in different parts of the empire is unknown. Copies of the cuneiform versions were no doubt less common than those of the Aramaic version, which was easier to read and to copy. For one thing, the Aramaic language was spoken and understood by many of the inhabitants of the empire, and for another, 'the Aramaic script, which, unlike all cuneiform scripts, was most suitable for papyrus, leather, etc., eminently met the requirements of the administration and propaganda service' (Borger). If we think of the distribution of the content in terms of the area covered, as suggested by the copy from Elephantine, this would mean that the text may also have been translated into other regional and local languages, for instance Greek, although no such versions have actually been found.

Oddly enough, the papyrus from Elephantine contains, probably in lieu of § 55 of the Bisutun inscription, a passage from the lower epitaph of Darius in Naqsh-i Rustam (DNb); this might be connected with the origin of the Aramaic copy more than 100 years later, although nothing is known of the surrounding circumstances. On the other hand, the epitaph is interesting because, like the reliefs outside Bisutun, it describes the qualities of the Achaemenid rulers in an indeterminate time, so that unlike the Bisutun inscription, it presents no *res gestae*.

Little is known about the places where the copies of the inscriptions were set up, or about the ways in which their content was circulated (through readers, town-criers, etc.?). Considering the limited literacy of the population in the regions where cuneiform script was used, and even in those where Aramaic, Egyptian or Greek was written, the proclamation of the *res gestae* would in fact only have made sense by word of mouth. And indeed, the great king explicitly declares in § 70 that the text of the Old Persian version, for which a system of writing had just been created, was 'read' to him after completion.

In this connection, the reproduction of the relief – which, as already mentioned, has been established only once, in the copy from Babylon – might perhaps yield a new meaning of its own. Was it really so important to publish or re-enact the exact course of events, to mention the names of the usurpers or to know them, or was there a different purpose? That is, for the king to drive home to his subjects the futility of rebellion, to present his own position as unassailable, and for the 'subject' spectator to assimilate the symbolic force of the image and grasp the gist of the message?

We have seen that a widespread distribution of the image is not established, but had there been numerous copies of it, the reproductions of the text would have lost in significance. On the other hand, might not the reproduction of the image have involved too great a financial as well as artistic extravagance? Or could it have been copied in other materials that have not been traced?

With the renewed question as to how image and text relate to each other, we are on more solid ground. For it has been observed that there are two different kinds of royal portraits in the art of the Achaemenid period: those that were reproduced several or many times and those that are – as far as we know – unique. The former are found on coins, palace walls, textiles and a shield, and we cannot go wrong in assuming that textiles and weapons may be interpreted as royal gifts. The unique images are found on gems, cylinder and stamp seals, and less frequently as effigies on the tombs of local princes. 'Thus it is not a question of the difference between "large" and "small-scale" art, rich and poor, court and provinces, or the like, but of unique images serving as individual distinction versus images of royal representation' (Calmeyer). Within the latter group, the Bisutun relief also owes its particular significance to the fact that 'its iconographic legibility and iconological position within the framework of monarchic propaganda' (Calmeyer) is most effectively secured by the inscription.

As already pointed out, the relief represents the 'liar kings' in the order in which they were defeated. The inscription provides the appropriate dates, though not chronologically, but in a sequence following the rank of the different countries involved. While the type and volume of the information it provides make it a historical – even if officious – report, the relief with its 'chain' of captives is a pseudo-historical scene welding together times and places. With its familiar Ancient Near Eastern motifs of the victorious sovereign trampling his opponents underfoot, and the display of prisoners, it is meant to convey to the spectator a specific, easily comprehensible message: This is what happens to those who oppose me. In later Achaemenid art, say in the Persepolis reliefs, the topical reference which is still present in Bisutun, even if it merges places and times, is abandoned for constantly repeated ahistorical compositions, which are not to be understood as un-inspired copies of pre-established themes, since they also convey a certain 'meaning'. The king conducts himself as he is portrayed in the reliefs, though by no means always at the place where he is portrayed, but wherever he may be. This change in imagery corresponds with the change in the content of the inscriptions; they, too, become timeless and can thus be copied by all kings to convey a kind of 'kingly ideology'. The great king is the representative of law and order, the protector of landed property and farmers. He rewards those who are loyal to him and punishes those who seek to revoke this loyalty. Parts of this 'ideology' are already established at Bisutun. In column IV of the Old Persian version, Darius addresses his successors:

§ 55 Proclaims Darius, the king: you, whosoever shall be king hereafter, be on your guard very much against Falsehood! The man who shall be a follower of Falsehood – punish him severely, if thus you shall think: 'Let my country be consolidated!'

Elsewhere he refers to his own exemplary conduct in this connection.

§ 63 For that reason Ahura Mazda brought me aid and the other gods who are, because I was not disloyal, I was no follower of Falsehood, I was no evil-doer, neither I nor my family, [but] I acted according to righteousness, neither to the powerless nor to the powerful, did I do wrong [and] the man who strove for my [royal] house, him I treated well, who did harm, him I have punished severely.

Reliefs and inscriptions of the second kind lead us to Persepolis, the most famous residence of the Achaemenid kings, which the Persians themselves called *Pārsa* ('Persia').

3. Persepolis, city of kings: heart of Persis and the empire

Persepolis (Plates II and III), which Darius started building around 515 BC, symbolized Persia and was at the same time a projection of the Achaemenid concept of empire. It played a part as an administrative centre, was used for great festivities, and had been built with materials and manpower from all parts of the empire. At this place, reliefs and architecture were to contribute to a sense of universal order based on the unanimous support of the king by his subjects. The gift-bearing representatives of the empire's peoples and the dignitaries gathering for banquets portrayed in the reliefs are all presented as participants in ceremonies which, whether they are understood as unrelated to time and place, or as referring to real festivities in Persepolis itself, symbolize the joint effort and mutual support of king and subjects.

A short tour through Persepolis (see Figure 4) gives an idea of the expressiveness and monumentality of its layout. At the foot of the Kuh-i Rahmat mountain, the vast terrace with its palaces extends over an area of 450 × 300m, at an average altitude of 12m above the plain. The façade consists of large, irregularly shaped blocks of limestone, which, joined together without mortar and with the minute precision of a jigsaw puzzle, accentuate the impression of extraordinary architectonic achievement. Originally accessible from the south, the site was provided by Xerxes with a grand double-stairway near the north-west corner. It leads to the 'Gateway of All Lands', which is the actual access to the buildings on the terrace. The huge composite creatures guarding the gates (winged and human-headed bulls) are based on prototypes from the Assyrian palace of Sennacherib in Nineveh and possess a certain symbolic meaning in their function to ward off evil. The gateway gave embassies, courtiers and other personalities access

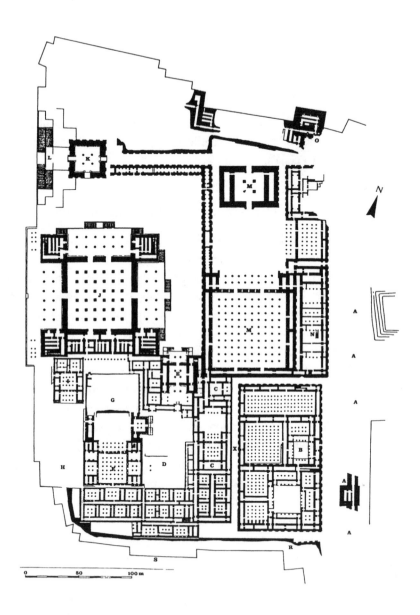

Figure 4 Persepolis (plan) (A) Eastern fortifications; (B) Treasury; (C) Residential section ('harem'); (E) Tripylon; (F) Palace of Xerxes; (I) Palace of Darius I; (J) Throne-hall (Apadana); (K) 'Gateway of All Lands'; (L) Staircase; (M) 'Hall with a Hundred Columns'; (R) Southern wall; (S) Foundation inscription of Darius

to the square audience hall (*apadana*) 60.5m long, 25m high, and with its imposing roof construction resting on 36 columns – an edifice which, according to its excavator Ernst Herzfeld, could accommodate 10,000 people. The side walls of the stairway north and east of the *apadana* and leading up to it contain meticulously executed bas-reliefs depicting representatives of all the peoples of the empire and members of the court.

On the south-western part of the great terrace are the residential palaces of Darius (OP: *tačara*) and Xerxes (*hadiš*), as well as the remains of other palaces. The 'harem' south of this complex, which is accessible through a front wing of a residential palace and consists of a long flight of uniform two-room units, might suggest connotations of 'Oriental decadence' in view of its modern title, but the reader is emphatically warned against such fanciful ideas. The eastern part of the terrace also displays pillared buildings, the 'Hall with a Hundred Columns' of Artaxerxes I and the 'Treasury'. The latter structure with its large rooms owes its name to the fact that its access is narrow and that its rooms contained a great number of small relics, mostly of stone, that were presumably scorned by Alexander's pillaging soldiers. The eastern and western part are connected by a gateway building, the 'Tripylon'.

Despite the imposing aspect of its remains, Persepolis today preserves only a faint impression of the splendour its buildings possessed in the fifth and fourth centuries BC. The gigantic timbered ceilings, the gateways and portals with their golden fittings, the sumptuous curtains, tiles, wall-paintings, coloured pillars, capitals and reliefs, as well as the luxurious contents, must have dazzled the ancient visitor. Modern attempts at reconstruction provide at least a suggestion of its grandeur.

It is interesting to note that in Persepolis, all construction and stone masonry work was stopped after Artaxerxes I, although much of it was as yet unfinished. The whole site became the 'old palace', and as such was also used as the burial ground for the dynasty (the tombs of Artaxerxes II and III are located on the Kuh-i Rahmat slope within the ramparts). It was not until a third phase towards the end of the Achaemenid period that Persepolis grew more populated, and there are traces of renewed building activity at this period (especially under Artaxerxes III). The significance of the site in those days, as well as the condition of its buildings and those of the residential city lying at its feet, are described in an eyewitness account from the time of Alexander handed down by Diodorus:

Persepolis was the capital [*mētropolis*] of the Persian kingdom. Alexander described it to the Macedonians as the most hateful of all cities of Asia, and gave it over to his soldiers to plunder, all but the palaces. It was the richest city under the sun and the private houses had been furnished with every sort of wealth [*eudaimonia*] over the years. ... The citadel [*akra*] is a noteworthy one and is surrounded by a triple wall. ... At the eastern side of the terrace at a distance of 4 plethra is the so-called royal hill [*oros basilikos*], in which were the graves of the kings. ... Scattered about the royal terrace [*akra*] were residences of the kings and quarters for the great generals [*katalyseis basilikai kai stratēgikai*], all luxuriously furnished, and buildings suitably made for guarding the royal treasure [*thēsauroi*].

Some particular aspects of Persepolis are worth pointing out: in architecture, the symmetrical, detached buildings, often porticoed, and having rows of pillars of equal height inside; in the sculpture, the striking images of 'gift-bearing subjects' and the king on his throne, supported by his subjects. Other themes known from Mesopotamian art, such as hunting and warfare, are completely absent. The royal hero fighting composite creatures does appear; but, having just been subdued on the reliefs, these fabulous creatures become supporters of the royal palace as capital figures. The monsters guarding the gates and doors are increasingly replaced in Persepolis by Persian guardsmen with their typical weapons.

The reliefs require rather more detailed consideration. The king as recipient (and distributor) of gifts is admittedly not a uniquely Achaemenid phenomenon, but one well known to historians and ethnologists. In Persepolis, however, the bringing of gifts (not the paying of tribute) is actually a characteristic of Achaemenid kingship (see Plate IV): typical products of each of the peoples, or luxury goods, are brought to the king and thus symbolize the solidarity between sovereign and subjects, whether this is felt as genuine or prescribed by the monarch. The king, whose subjects support him, i.e. the sovereign sitting on his throne, a huge piece of furniture (Greek *diphros*, OP *gāθu*) supported by representatives of the empire's peoples (Plate V), is another eye-catching theme of Persepolis relief art and, like the 'gift-bearers', symbolizes royal authority in the empire as a whole. At the same time, this image is intended to evoke other associations of ideas in the observer, as is proven by the epitaph of Darius I:

If now thou shalt think: 'How many are the countries which King Darius held?' look at the sculptures [of those] who bear the throne [*gāθu*], then shalt thou know, then shall it become known to thee: the spear of a Persian man has gone forth far; then shall it become known to thee: a Persian man has delivered battle far indeed from Persia.

Both themes raise the question of their reference to real feasts and occasions. While the 'throne-carrying' is believed to portray real processions with specific pieces of furniture, scholars have not yet reached agreement about the 'gift-bearing'. Although today it is hardly any longer associated with the celebration of the Iranian New Year (*Nō Rōz*) in Persepolis, it is still debatable whether the procession of these people represents a meeting between king and subjects at some indeterminate time and place, or whether it refers to specific festivities (e.g. the king's birthday, Mithrakana or similar occasions – in Persepolis or elsewhere).

Two legends are certainly false. In the first, Persepolis is seen as a 'holy city' which was always closed to foreigners (especially Greeks). This is out of the question, even if it does appear that in the period before Alexander, the destination of Greek embassies was usually Susa. If no one else, the Ionian artists and builders taking part in constructing Persepolis must have talked about the splendour of the residence when they returned west, and some scholars indeed tend to believe that the ideas carved in stone in Persepolis were adopted in parts of the Acropolis building programme in Athens (the Parthenon frieze). The second misjudgement concerns the fate of Persepolis after Alexander's conquest. The idea of the 'destruction' of the place by Alexander is a literary device – the place as the symbol of Persian hegemony had to 'perish' as the conclusion of the punitive campaign – and has not been confirmed by archaeological research. Only certain parts of the terrace were burnt down, and Persepolis remained inhabited after 330 BC, even though a few centuries later, no one knew the names of its builders or the purpose of the buildings.

To sum up, in Persepolis the themes and motifs of the images complement one another to form a new blueprint for a specific concept of Persian kingship and empire. Whether we are dealing with gift-bearing delegations or throne-carrying subjects lined up according to their ethnic origins, with the royal hero fighting against composite creatures or portrayed in an attitude of adoration and prayer, as on the burial façades, for the early Persians all this was the expression of a timeless idea of universal and cosmic order upheld by divine assistance and mutual loyalty between king and subjects. This same idea is reflected in the trilingual inscriptions, whether through their emphasizing the qualities of the king or the importance of the subjects' loyalty to the stability of the empire, or through their references to divine support for the king or to the vast expansion of the empire. The Achaemenids, and above all Xerxes, were for a long time criticized for producing stereotyped copies of models established by their predecessors, for arbitrarily mixing the most dissimilar artistic traditions and motifs, and even for stylistic 'stagnation'. What really underlies the Persepolis programme of buildings and imagery is the conscious attempt to impress upon all subjects and visitors alike the Persian imperial order with its claim to universal and 'eternal' validity. It is only very recently that this point of view has re-emerged.

4. Pasargadae, Susa and Naqsh-i Rustam: coins, seals and jewellery. Other archaeological sites and testimonies of Achaemenid art and culture

When Cyrus founded the Persian empire, he had his first residence built in Pasargadae, which lay 30km north-east of Persepolis and was presumably the site of his decisive battle against the Medes. Only remnants of buildings, not the general ensemble, have survived to suggest how beautifully this site must once have blended into the landscape. Strewn, as it were, around an irrigated garden (Greek *paradeisos*) at an altitude of 1,900m were the citadel (*Tall-i Taxt*), a complex of palaces and garden pavilions, a building for royal investiture (*Zindān-i Sulaimān*, see Plate VI), the 'sacred district' with two fire altars, and the tomb of Cyrus himself, shaped like a house with a saddle-roof standing on a stepped plinth (Plate VII). Even after Persepolis was founded, Pasargadae remained an important ceremonial centre of Persis.

In Susa, the old metropolis of Elam (*Xūzistān*), Darius I had a palace built on an artificial terrace (the Apadana hill). With its 72 columns in the main hall, this was to serve as a model for Persepolis. Further Achae-menid remains at this site, which had already been inhabited in prehistoric times, are a citadel on the acropolis, the 'artisans' quarter' east of the 'royal city', and the palace of Artaxerxes II on the west bank of the Sha'ur, which flows past Susa. Particularly well known are Susa's glazed tile reliefs depicting lions, composite creatures and guardsmen. Stone reliefs, like those in Persepolis, are rare.

In his 'charter of foundation' for the citadel (DSf), Darius enumerates the artists and workers who contributed to the construction of the residence and also mentions the materials used:

This palace which I built at Susa, from afar its ornamentation was brought. Downward the earth was dug, until I reached rock in the earth. When the excavation had been made, the rubble was packed down, some 40 cubits in depth, another [part] 20 cubits in depth. On that rubble the palace was constructed.

And that the earth was dug downward, and that the rubble was packed down, and that the sun-dried brick was moulded, the Babylonian people – it did [these tasks].

The cedar timber, this – a mountain by name of Lebanon – from there was brought. The Assyrian people, it brought it to Babylon; from Babylon, the Carians and the Ionians brought it to Susa. The *yakā*-timber was brought from Gandhara and from Carmania.

The gold was brought from Sardis and from Bactria, which here was wrought. The precious stone lapis-lazuli and carnelian which was wrought here, this was brought from Sogdiana. The precious stone turquoise, this was brought from Chorasmia, which was wrought here.

The silver and ebony were brought from Egypt. The ornamentation with which the wall was adorned, that from Ionia was brought. The ivory which was wrought here, was brought from Ethiopia and from Sind and from Arachosia.

The stone columns which were here wrought, a village by name Abiradu, in Elam – from there were brought. The stone-cutters who wrought the stone, those were Ionians and Sardians.

The goldsmiths who wrought the gold, those were Medes and Egyptians. The men who wrought the wood, those were Sardians and Egyptians. The men who wrought the baked brick, those were Babylonians. The men who adorned the wall, those were Medes and Egyptians.

In the early 1970s, an oversized headless statue of Darius was found near the east court of the palace of the king in Susa, the first statue in the round of an Achaemenid that has ever come down to us (see Plate VIII). Created in Egypt, the statue – and a matching piece (?) – must originally have stood in the temple of Heliopolis in Egypt. There is a brief trilingual cuneiform inscription on the right-hand side of the king's garment, and a longer Egyptian one in hieroglyphs on its left-hand side, on the dagger, the bow of the belt and the four sides of the plinth. The latter also contains, above the corresponding cartouches with the names of subject peoples, illustrations of the representatives of these peoples with their hands rendered palms-up. Scholars have puzzled over the occasion and reasons for setting up the statue(s) in Egypt and later transporting them to Susa.

A last centre of Achaemenid kingship to be described is Naqš-i Rustam ('picture of Rustam'). The name of the place, which derives from a much later tradition, alludes to reliefs from the Sasanian period (see below), which were believed to represent Rustam, the great hero of Iranian folklore. In the Achaemenid period, this rock face (see Plate IX), about 6km north-north-west of Persepolis, which had already been used for reliefs by the Elamites, was the burial place of kings who had themselves entombed in monumental cruciform rock graves decorated with reliefs. Only the grave of Darius I is safely identified by its inscription (through Darius's epitaphs DNa and DNb); the others are usually attributed to Xerxes (see Plate Xa), Artaxerxes I and Darius II. In front of the rock face stands the Ka'ba-i Zardusht (Plate Xb), a building presumably erected by Darius, and similar both in its aspect and probably also in its function to the Zindan in Pasargadae. Although the Sasanians seem to have had no more than a rudimentary knowledge of their Achaemenid 'ancestors', they nevertheless underlined the special significance of this place for the history of their country and for their sense of identity by adding their own reliefs to it. We shall return to this subject.

Apart from such monumental Achaemenid works of art, certain specimens of minor art are also particularly expressive, for instance the gold (*dareikoi*, see Plate XIa) and silver coins (*sigloi*) which the Greeks called *toxotai* ('bowmen') because they portray royal heroes armed with bows. These were not only the coveted reward of the great king's Greek mercenaries and the dreaded instruments of Persian politics in Greece and Asia Minor, but – like the royal inscriptions – they are lasting reminders of the military prowess of these sovereigns. The images on the seals (Plate XIIIb, c), mainly known from their impressions on Elamite tablets from Persepolis, display the Achaemenid artist's ties with Ancient Near Eastern traditions in this genre, but they also show a deliberate tendency towards innovation and the introduction of new ideas into the imagination of the kings and their subjects.

What remain to be mentioned are objects pertaining to the royal and aristocratic lifestyle, such as bracelets and anklets, pearls, pendants, earrings, diadems, accessories for garments, fibulas, pins and belts, whether they have come down to us as such or are known only through reliefs. Other features are examples of metalwork and fine textiles, as well as precious weapons and other objects, which served their purpose within the framework of 'the presentation of gifts to' and 'the distribution of gifts by' the king, a system of establishing or confirming friendly relations or mutual dependence between king and subjects.

And finally, the works of art of regional or local provincial provenance, quite often inspired by great models, the Graeco-Roman 'images' of Achaemenid kings and their subjects, as well as the 'Perserie' in attire and finery in fifth-century Athens, provide an idea of the Persian lifestyle.

CHAPTER 2

THE KING AND HIS SUBJECTS

1. 'I am Darius, the great king, king of kings, king in Persia, king of the countries/peoples, son of Hystaspes, grandson of Arsames, an Achaemenid': kingship in the Achaemenid empire

A closer look at this introductory passage of Darius's great Bisutun inscription enables us to recognize some characteristics of Achaemenid kingship. Darius first calls himself xšāyaθiya (literally, 'distinguished by a kingdom'), a title believed to be borrowed from the Median language; he frequently enhances this self-designation by the epithet vazṛka ('great'), which is also of Median origin, and thus follows a Mesopotamian example (cf. Akkadian šarru rabû). And thirdly, he assumes a relationship with the kings of the preceding empires of Babylon, Assur, Urartu and Media, whose sovereignty he subordinates to his own (xšāyaθiya xšāyaθiyānām). Thus in the course of history, the title 'king of kings' – Middle Persian šāhān šāh, New Persian šāhanšāh – which is probably also of Mesopotamian origin, but which the Persians borrowed from Urartu, became the title par excellence of Iranian sovereigns. The belonging of many 'countries' or 'peoples' to the empire is emphasized through the combination 'king of the countries/peoples' (x. dahyūnām), a new creation of Darius's, and a set of titles which may also include the variants x. d. vispazanānām ('king of the countries containing all races' or 'king of the peoples of every origin') and x. d. paruzanānām ('king of the countries containing many races' or 'king of the peoples of many origins'). A last variant is represented by the formula xšāyaθiya ahyāyā būmiyā (vazṛkāyā) (dūraiy apiy) ('king on this [great] earth [even far off]').

Royal protocol, however, insists on one other point: that kingship is firmly rooted in Persia, or more precisely Persis, and requires descent from one 'family', that of Achaemenes (*Haxāmaniš*). It appears to have been this stumbling-block that caused Alexander, who was thoroughly familiar with Achaemenid conduct, to fail in his attempt to assume the sovereignty of the empire and gain the support of the Persians for himself (against Darius III) until the death of his antagonist. The successor to the throne was apparently chosen by the ruling monarch. Usually it was the first-born son, and perhaps only in exceptional cases the 'first son born in purple', when the father was king. The conflict between the two thus characterized sons of Darius II, Artaxerxes II and Cyrus the Younger, is introduced by Plutarch in his 'Life of Artaxerxes' in the following words:

For Parysatis [the mother, who preferred the younger son, Cyrus] had a specious argument (the same that Xerxes the Elder employed on the advice of Demaratus), to the effect that she had borne Arsicas [name of Artaxerxes before his coronation] to Darius when he was in private station, but Cyrus when he was a king. However, she could not prevail, but the elder son was declared king, under the new name of Artaxerxes, while Cyrus remained satrap of Lydia and commander of the forces in the maritime provinces.

This quotation also proves that the kings (at the latest, since Darius) adopted throne-names that appear as precise programmes of their reign. Thus the name Darius (*Dārayavauš*) may be translated as 'holding the good', Xerxes (*Xšaya-ṛšan*) as 'ruling over heroes', and Artaxerxes (*Ṛta-xšaça*) as 'whose reign is through truthfulness'. The Achaemenid empire has incidentally been assumed to have admitted something like a joint rule between father and son (synarchy), but this theory is not tenable.

The Achaemenid king was not worshipped as a god in Iran, nor was he attributed divine descent. Nevertheless, his special relationship with the gods counted, together with his extraction and his personal valour, as a fundamental element of his legitimacy as a sovereign. Ahura Mazda 'and the other gods that are' bestowed the kingdom on Darius (*xšaçam frābara*); 'by the favour of Ahura Mazda' (*vašnā Auramazdāha*) he was elected and installed, and – successfully – ruled the empire, as his 'representative', so to speak. In this respect, those who referred to the 'divine right' of the Persian sovereign were justified. As the representative of the gods on earth, he is vested with *farnah (Avestan xvarᵊnah), a kind of divine radiance or royal charisma.

In relation to the members of the Persian tribal aristocracy, there has been a tendency to conceive the Achaemenid king as *primus inter pares*. However, that kind of informal leadership, even supposing it might be applied to more evolved societies, is quite incompatible with the real position of the king, and all the more so with his propagated one. Even if, to establish his sovereignty, Cyrus had to urge the Persians to rise against the Medes, as Herodotus insists, even if Darius had to concede certain privileges to his six fellow conspirators against Gaumata (and their families), neither of them could have succeeded in those situations without wielding power and authority. Both the inscriptions and the reliefs lack any allusions to certain dependences or certain considerations, apart from the fact that the men who stand around the king on the relief are clearly separated from the representatives of the subject peoples. The Achaemenid king as the supreme master, 'legislator' and 'judge' in times of peace and war nominally united all authority and power in his hands and stood far above all his subjects, whom he called his *bandakā* ('dependants'; 'those who wear the belt [*banda*] of dependence'). His divine right and his personal qualities legitimized this nominally outstanding position. In conflicts about the succession, in the royal approach to loyalty and disloyalty and in the efforts of certain dignitaries to acquire more power and authority, there can nevertheless be detected an at least temporary contradiction between the 'ideological programme' and the 'political reality'. Such cases, however, concerned only the relations between central and partial power or struggles for influence at court, while the institution of kingship itself or its attribution to the house of the Achaemenids were never called into question.

The brief interval between the death of a king and the beginning of his successor's reign was particularly significant for all Achaemenid kings (and for those who intended to have their say in the attribution of this authority), as reported especially by the Alexander historians. The successor who had been appointed by his father did not start his reign immediately, but only after a given period of mourning and 'cessation of legal conditions' (*anomia*), as well as the fulfilment of certain duties (burying his predecessor and executing the provisions of his 'will') and the observation of certain rites, among which the ceremonies in Pasargadae stood out. An episode handed down by Ctesias in a fancifully embroidered version may throw more light on the 'critical atmosphere' of such periods. After the death of Artaxerxes I, Crown Prince Xerxes (II) ordered Bagozaros, an official, to convey the corpses of his father and mother to Persepolis. The procession had not yet started moving when Xerxes was killed at the hand of his brother Secyndianus. The mules that were to draw the parents' catafalque refused to do so and did not start until the corpse of Xerxes was also brought there. Secyndianus thereupon had Bagozaros executed 'under the pretext', as Ctesias emphasizes, 'that he had abandoned the corpse of his father [Artaxerxes] without the king's [Secyndianus's] approval'. Secyndianus obviously had good reason to interpret the attitude of Bagozaros as opposition to himself and criticism of his legitimacy. He had refused to carry out the transportation of the dead ruler in the name of his successor, whose right to the throne he contested.

The actual investiture of the kings took place in Pasargadae, the ancient residence of Cyrus, and started with a kind of 'royal initiation' (*basilikē teletē*), as Plutarch reports in his 'Life of Artaxerxes II':

A little while after the death of Darius [II], the new king made an expedition to Pasargadae, that he might receive the royal initiation at the hands of the Persian priests. Here there is a sanctuary of a warlike goddess whom one might conjecture to be Athena [Anahita?]. Into this sanctuary the candidate for initiation must pass, and after laying aside his own proper robe, must put on that which Cyrus the Elder used to wear before he became king; then he must eat of a cake of figs, chew some terebinth, and drink a cup of sour milk.

The king is thus reminded of the old Persian way of life and, by putting on the clothes of Cyrus, assumes his power and authority too. The 'consecration' in the temple of Anahita and the invocation of Ahura Mazda in the course of the ceremonies are seen as the ritual expression of the idea of the divine right of sovereignty, as recorded in the inscriptions. In a further phase of royal investiture, the new ruler apparently received the insignia of his power (certain royal garments and shoes; the upright purple tiara; the sceptre in his right hand and the lotus blossom in his left; lance and bow) and showed himself thus to his subjects. It has been assumed that this took place on the roof of the Zindan-i Sulaiman (see above), the building in which these regalia were possibly preserved. The new king then had to perform a series of symbolic acts (acceptance of the official seal, confirmation of privileges, confirmation or new conferment of offices and functions), thereby assuming his 'official duties'.

How did the king actually see himself? What sovereign qualities did he claim for himself (or did he need in order to preserve his reign) and what qualities did he demand from his subjects? Having recognized the timeless, programmatic character of the royal inscriptions and reliefs, we now have a clearer picture of the fundamental patterns of royal self-identification. In one of his two epitaphs (DNb), Darius specifies what distinguishes him and his reign:

By the favour of Ahura Mazda I am of such a sort that I am a friend to right, I am not a friend to wrong. It is not my desire that the weak man should have wrong done to him by the mighty; nor is it my desire that the mighty man should have wrong done to him by the weak.

What is right, that is my desire. I am not a friend to the man who is a lie-follower. I am not hot-tempered. What things develop in my anger, I hold firmly under control by my own thinking power. I am firmly ruling over my own [impulses].

The man who cooperates, him according to his cooperative action, him thus do I reward. Who does harm, him, according to the damage thus I punish. It is not my desire that a man should do harm; nor indeed is that my desire, if he should do harm, he should not be punished. ...

As a horseman I am a good horseman. As a bowman I am a good bowman both afoot and on horseback. As a spearman I am a good spearman both afoot and on horseback.

Already at Bisutun, Darius had proclaimed his endeavours towards justice, but had at the same time made it clear that he expected unconditional loyalty from his subjects. Unlike the followers of Zarathustra, for whom 'truth' (OP *rta*) and 'lie' (*drauga*) were moral concepts according to which they tried to organize their lives, Darius indeed considered *drauga* as anything directed against his own god-given and dynastically legitimized reign – that is, any kind of rebellion or usurpation. To him even *rta* was ultimately what he himself proclaimed as truth.

With his own military qualities, Darius expressed the idea that the personal test (at the hunt and in war) distinguished a good and legitimate king, and this idea, combined with that of the king's 'love of truth', emanated into the non-Iranian parts of the empire and was declared a characteristic of Persian education (see below). With these qualities – in addition to divine protection – the king was in a position to ward off the dangers threatening his empire and thus to become the defender of farmers and fields. This is how Darius describes it in the DPd inscription:

May Ahura Mazda protect this land from a hostile army [*hainā*], from famine [*dušiyāra*] and from the Lie [*drauga*].

As an outstanding warrior, he can ward off invasions (and protect the Persian soil), as mediator between the world of the gods and that of men, he can invoke divine assistance and blessings, and as a good farmer (and gardener) he personally contributes to the prosperity of the country.

2. *Prōtoi, autourgoi* and *kurtaš*: ethnic, genealogical and social 'stratification' in Achaemenid Persis

On the contrary, [God's work must be imagined in accordance with] that which has been reported of the great king. For the court of Cambyses, Xerxes and Darius was splendidly adorned for ceremonious and brilliant eminence. He himself, as it is heard, sat on the throne in Susa or Ecbatana, invisible to all, in a wonderful royal castle and palace domain sparkling with gold, electrum and ivory; many successive gateways and entrance halls, separated by a distance of many stades, were secured by brazen doors and mighty walls. And outside there stood, decked out and ready, the first and most distinguished men [*andres hoi prōtoi dokimōtatoi*], some destined to serve the king himself as bodyguard and attendants [*doryphoroi te kai therapontes*], some as guardians [*phylakes*] of the different courts, so-called door-keepers and listeners [*pylōroi te kai ōtakoustai*], so that the king himself, who was addressed as sovereign and god, might see everything and hear everything. Apart from these, others were posted as administrators of revenues [*proshodōn tamiai*], as generals in wars and in hunting expeditions [*stratēgoi polemōn kai kynhēgesiōn*], as receivers of gifts [*dōrōn apodektēres*] and as providers of other services required from time to time [*tōn te loipōn ergōn hekastoi kata tas chreias epimelētai*]. The entire empire of Asia, however, bordered as it was by the Hellespont on its west and by the Indus on its east, had been divided up into peoples [*kata ethnē*] by generals [*stratēgoi*], satraps [*satrapai*] and princes [*basileis*], dependants of the great king [*douloi tou megalou basileōs*], [who were in their turn obeyed by] day couriers [*hēmerodromoi*], scouts [*skopoi*], messengers, [*angeliaphoroi*] and observers of fire signals [*phryktōriōn te epoptēres*].

This quotation from the pseudo-Aristotelian *de mundo* shows great familiarity (except for its statement about the 'divinity' of the great king) with the organization of the royal court and the empire, as well as the people surrounding the sovereign and occupying pivotal positions, whom it classifies according to their prestige and influence. In parts, it reads almost like a description of the Persepolis reliefs. Those who interest us for the present are the 'dependants' (OP *bandakā*) of the great king. While we are quite well acquainted with the king and his 'house' (*viθ*) through testimonies by the kings themselves and the Greek historiographic tradition, information about the kings' *bandakā* is rather scarce. There have therefore been attempts to see the social 'stratification' of Persians in a larger – ancient Iranian – context, and perhaps to grasp it within the conceptual system of the Avestan (Zoroastrian) texts, in which the three 'functions' of priest, warrior and farmer are believed to be discernible. It is in this sense that the passage presented from DPd has been interpreted. Darius as the supreme priest, warrior and farmer is in a position to meet the respective dangers.

For the ethno-genealogical structures of Persis, the heartland of the Persians, Herodotus is our chief witness, for want of any detailed information in Old Persian:

There are many tribes [*genea*] in Persia, and the ones which Cyrus assembled and persuaded to revolt from the Medes were the Pasargadae, Maraphii, and Maspii, on whom all the other Persians rely. Of these the Pasargadae are the most distinguished; they contain the clan [*phratria*] of the Achaemenids from which the kings of Persia are drawn. Other tribes are the Panthialaei, Derusiaei, Germanii, all tillers of the soil, the remainder – Dai, Mardi, Dropici, Sagartii – being nomadic.

If we express this classification in Avestan and – as far as linguistic evidence allows us – in Old Persian categories, then *genea* would presumably correspond with Avestan *zantu*, *phratria* with Avestan *vīs*, OP *viθ*, and as the smallest unit one might consider the 'family' (OP *taumā*), as the largest the 'country'/'population' (Avestan *danghu*, OP *dahyu*) of Persis. The special quality and outstanding position of this land is often emphasized by Darius in his inscriptions. He himself is proud to be a 'Persian' and invokes the special protection of Ahura Mazda for his native country.

No wonder that with this altogether meagre information, we know only little about the social stratification of Persian society. Both our Greek informants and the royal inscriptions and reliefs go little further than broad dichotomies or distinctions. In some inscriptions, there are adjectives such as *āmāta*- ('noble', 'of noble birth', 'aristocratic') and *tunuvant*- ('powerful') to qualify the 'top layer', and *skauθi*- ('poor', 'weak') to describe the rest of the free population of Persis. The Greek sources distinguish between groups according to criteria such as wealth, clothes, food, educational levels or forms of social intercourse. The latter can be illustrated by the following quotation from Strabo:

When they meet people on the streets, they approach and kiss those with whom they are acquainted and who are of equal rank [*gnōrimoi kai isotimoi*], and to those of lower rank [*tapeinoteroi*] they offer the cheek and in that way receive the kiss; but those of still lower rank [*hoi d'eti tapeinoteroi*] merely make obeisance [*proskynesis*].

While this does not give us much of an idea about the bulk of the population in Persis, who might no doubt rightly be called 'small farmers' (*autourgoi*) – as Aelian does in his *Historical Miscellanies* – something more can be said about the Persian 'aristocracy', even though that too would be almost exclusively 'from a Greek perspective'. First of all, that it was hierarchically structured within itself. Herodotus and other Greek authors allude to these gradations by using comparatives and superlatives. But if asked what the rank of a person in Achaemenid Persia depended on, our informants again let us down. From the fact that membership of the Achaemenid clan is often expressly pointed out, one can deduce that the (other) *prōtoi* ('foremost') Persians must have been the leaders of the most distinguished clans of the major tribes. The patronymic of a protagonist mentioned by Herodotus, and also in the Bisutun inscription, draws our attention to the level of the 'family' or 'house', a level on which the *pater familias* – to use a Roman expression – wielded special authority; he decided about all matters concerning his 'house' (for instance, settling disputes or questions about succession). The downfall of the house of Intaphernes, a fellow conspirator of Darius's against Gaumata, whom the king accused of disloyalty, indicates, however, that an offence committed by the head of a household had fatal consequences not only for the perpetrator himself, but for anyone belonging to the house. The female members of a Persian 'family' will be discussed separately. Suffice it to say here that for the Greeks, polygamy and therefore having a large number of children simply appeared as a characteristic of Persian life. Thus Strabo writes: 'The men marry many women, and at the same time maintain several concubines [*pallakai*], for the sake of having many children. The kings set forth prizes annually for those who have the most children.'

On a par with the 'most distinguished' Persians were, according to Herodotus, Darius's six fellow conspirators against Gaumata, who in addition enjoyed special royal privileges. As the same historian reports, they always had access to the ruler (except when he was with one of his wives), and the future king had to choose his wives from among their daughters. At the same time, all the relations of the 'Seven Persians' could expect high command posts. Special prerogatives for himself and his descendants were granted to Otanes, who was said to have renounced being king of his own free will after the death of Gaumata.

There can be no doubt that at the beginning of his reign, Darius depended on the support of his fellow conspirators, probably because he was not considered as the only potential heir to the throne of his predecessors. The fall of Intaphernes and the marriage policy of Darius and his successors show, however, that the privileges (and powers) of the fellow conspirators must soon have ceased to be as exclusive as they may still have been in 521 BC. There is evidence for six marriages by Darius: with a daughter of Gobryas (before his accession); two daughters of Cyrus, the founder of the empire (Atossa and Artystone); a daughter of Cyrus's son Bardiya (Parmys); a daughter of Otanes (Phaidyme); and a daughter of his brother Artanes (Phratagune). With the exception of Phaidyme, none of the women Darius married as king belonged to the families of his fellow conspirators. However, a distinct effort can be detected (as already with Cambyses and Gaumata, and later with Darius's successors) to bring about a union with the family of Cyrus and in all other respects to arrange the succession within his own royal family. The marriage policy of Darius II and his wife (and half-sister) Parysatis is another example illustrating this principle: Darius had his son Arsices (the future Artaxerxes II) marry Statira, the daughter of Hydarnes (who seems not to have belonged to one of the 'seven families'). At the same time Amestris, the sister of Arsices, married Terituchmes, the son of Hydarnes. There are indications that Darius owed a debt to Hydarnes in connection with his accession to the throne. Once Darius no longer needed his help, all the members of the Hydarnes family – who were at the time occupying key positions – were disposed of one after the other: Terituchmes and his son, Statira and her parents, sisters and brothers. Starting with Artaxerxes II, alliances through marrying into prominent families were no longer made for the sake of establishing loyalty, but rather as a reward for faithful service. In other respects, the kings always endeavoured to follow an endogamous policy, thus keeping the royal house closed to outsiders and securing their reign. No wonder then that the 'king's relatives' (*syngeneis*) were particularly influential.

This policy of the Achaemenids did not prevent the kings from attempting to satisfy the Persian aristocracy, or at least its loyal members. Indeed, shrewd royal politics, perhaps accompanied by the prospect of appointments and sinecures for many a nobleman, made the majority of the aristocracy fall into line with royal interests. Characteristic features of this cooperation were, on behalf of the ruler, the royal *polydōria* ('liberality': titles, offices, property, fortunes, gifts of honour) or the inclusion of loyal aristocrats in the king's circle of 'benefactors' (*euergetai/orosangai*), who were registered by name with their privileges. The resulting dependence of 'noblemen' on the king's favour, a favour that might easily be withdrawn, also led to the emergence at court of a kind of 'service aristocracy', which was open to deserving non-Persians as well. To the members of this group, whose innermost circle was described as the king's 'friends' (*philoi*), loyalty to the king became more important than loyalty to their clan or family (or to the political traditions of their native country), even if these bonds still held good because of the basic requirement of noble birth for a career at court or in the empire.

However, it was not only Persians in the ethnic sense who lived in Persis. Other peoples, such as Ionians, Lydians, Lycians, Egyptians and Babylonians, also worked there on a temporary or permanent basis. If they contributed to the building of Persepolis, if they worked in the royal workshops and treasuries of Persis, as well as in farming, it was not as enslaved war prisoners, but as manpower recruited and paid by the state. These people, called *kurtaš* in the Elamite tablets, will be discussed in more detail below.

3. Presenting gifts to the great king: the ruler meets his subjects

When the great king travels through Persia, every Persian presents him with a gift in accordance with his capacity. But as the Persians practise farming and till the soil with their own hands, they bring no luxurious gifts, not even very precious ones, but a cow, a sheep, or else cereals or even wine. When the king passes by on his journey, everyone offers him such gifts, which are described as presents and accepted by him as such. But those who are even more poorly off bring milk, dates, cheese and fruit, according to the season, and others bring the first fruits of the season grown on their land.

Omises brought King Artaxerxes, when he was travelling through Persia, a huge pomegranate in a basket. Quite amazed by its size, the king asked: 'From which garden did you take the gift you are bringing me?' Omises's answer that he had it from his own land at home gave the king great pleasure. He had royal presents sent to him and said: 'By Mithras, with his diligence this man could, in my opinion, make even a small state great and powerful!'

Among the characteristics of Persian kingship was the ruler's habit, illustrated here in two episodes by Aelian, of travelling around in his empire even when he was not on a campaign. The king's sojourn in his different residences, depending on the season, has indeed often been mentioned and commented upon by observers of classical antiquity. Suffice it here to quote a passage by Xenophon from his *Cyropaedia*:

Cyrus himself made his home in the centre of his domain, and in the winter season he spent seven months in Babylon, for there the climate is warm; in the spring he spent three months in Susa, and in the height of summer two months in Ecbatana. By so doing, they say, he enjoyed the warmth and coolness of perpetual springtime.

Those who are familiar with climatic conditions in Mesopotamia and Iran will see the sense in this. It can therefore be compared, as Aelian does, with the migratory habits of birds, but has nothing to do with the 'effeminacy' of the ruler, as Xenophon would have us believe in another passage.

This custom of the great king has rightly been compared with the sojourns of medieval German rulers in the residences ('*Pfalzen*') of the empire. With this comparison, in fact, a political feature of 'travelling kingship' also becomes apparent. On top of his imperial affairs, in the various parts of his realm the king tackled the specific problems of each region, and at the same time established contact with his subjects (or their representatives). Such actions by Persian kings are recorded in many ancient testimonies, which go into great detail about their journeys, their reception at important places on their itinerary and in the residences themselves, and even about the onlookers in the streets. But although some authors try to convey the impression that the journeys and visits of the kings were direct, spontaneous and improvised, the truth looks different. These journeys were prepared down to the last detail, and the receptions were ceremonials steeped in symbolism and modelled on ancient traditions. The bringing of gifts by the subjects and the distribution of gifts by the king may have occurred spontaneously in certain concrete situations, and may have been a genuine concern if the ruler was popular; but they were always and equally a symbolic expression of the relationship between overlord and subjects. We shall again consult Aelian with a quotation from his *Historical Miscellanies*, a story which was also told by Plutarch in his biography of Artaxerxes II:

This story, too, occurred in Persia. It is said that a Persian called Sinaites met king Artaxerxes [II], who bears the epithet Mnemon, far away from his court. In his embarrassment he was seized with great dismay for fear of the law and out of reverence for the king, for at the time he did not know what to do. As he did not want to be inferior to the other Persians and did not want to lose face because he had no present to give the king, he quickly ran, as fast as his legs would carry him, to the river flowing past nearby, which was called Cyrus. He bent down, scooped up water with both hands, and said: 'King Artaxerxes, may your reign last forever! For the moment I honour you as well as I can; for you shall not, as far as lies within my power, go away without a gift of honour from me. With the water of the Cyrus I show you my respect. But when you go to your camp, I shall honour you with the best and the most precious thing in my house, and I shall certainly not be inferior to any of the others who have already greeted you with presents.' ... When the king arrived in his quarters, he sent the Persian a Persian garment, a golden bowl and thousand dareikoi and told the bearer to give the recipient the following message: 'The king desires you to take pleasure in owning this golden vessel, since you gave him pleasure by not wanting to leave him without a present and a tribute, but honoured him in the way it was possible at the time. He wants you to scoop the same water with this bowl and drink it.'

When the king visited the cities and larger towns of his subject countries on his journeys, it was part of their duty to entertain him and his retinue. The resulting expenditures, which may be seen as a kind of supplement to the tribute (see below), could sometimes put a considerable strain on the financial resources of a community. Banquets were occasions on which the king would distribute the goods he had received among his mostly aristocratic 'fellow banqueters' (*syndeipnoi*), and sometimes among his soldiers.

And so, Heracleides continues, the 'king's dinner', as it is called, will appear prodigal to one who merely hears about it, but when one examines it carefully it will be found to have been got up with economy and even with parsimony; and the same is true of the dinners among other Persians in high station. For one thousand animals are slaughtered daily for the king; these comprise horses, camels, oxen, asses, deer, and most of the smaller animals; many birds are also consumed, including arabian ostriches – and the creature is large – geese and cocks. And of all these only moderate portions are served to each of the king's guests, and each of them may carry home whatever he leaves untouched at the meal. But the greater part of these meats and other foods are taken out into the courtyard for the body-guard and the light-armed troopers maintained by the king.

What it looked like when the king travelled through the country with his retinue is reported by our ancient informants, albeit mainly in connection with the king's campaigns. Particularly illuminating in this connection are descriptions by the Alexander historians of the arrival of Darius III in Cilicia, his defeat at Issus and Parmenio's seizure of the suite and royal household:

Shortly after them followed the 'relatives' [*cognati*] of the king, 15,000 people. ... About 200 of the king's closest relatives [*propinquorum*] attended him [Darius] on his right and left. The rear of this part of the procession consisted of 30,000 foot-soldiers, followed by 400 royal horses. Then, at a distance of a single stade, came a chariot carrying Sisygambis, the mother of Darius, while his wife sat in another. A group of women from the queen's household rode on horseback. There followed 15 vehicles which they call *harmamaxae*; in them were the king's children and their governesses, as well as a group of eunuchs, who are by no means despised among these peoples. Behind them followed the file of the king's 365 concubines, also regally dressed and adorned. After them came 600 mules and 300 camels carrying the king's money, with at their head a guard of bowmen. This detachment was followed by the wives of the 'relatives' and 'friends' of the king and units of canteen-men and servants. Light-armed men with their respective officers brought up the rear. ... Scattered all over the field lay the riches of the king, the money that was to serve as wages for a great army, the adornments of many a person of high rank, of many illustrious women, golden vessels, golden bridles, tents adorned with royal splendour, chariots left behind by their owners and laden with great treasures, a sorrowful sight even for plunderers.

Athenaeus has handed down to us a letter from Parmenio to Alexander, in which he described the servants of Darius who had fallen into his hands when he had captured Damascus, giving even greater details about their numbers and tasks:

I discovered concubines of the king who played musical instruments, to the number of 329; men employed to weave chaplets, 46; caterers, 277; kettle-tenders, 29; pudding-makers, 13; bartenders, 17; wine-clarifiers, 70; perfume-makers, 40.

Our Greek informants often enough construed the luxury of the great king's table as mere opulence and gluttony and considered its 'debilitating' effect as a cause of the fall of the Persian empire. We might compare the warning words which Polyaenus ascribed to Alexander when addressing his Macedonians: 'For so much gluttony and opulence must necessarily lead to much unmanliness. And you can see that those who eat such enormous meals are far too quickly beaten in battles.' The Greeks, however, were only able or willing to recognize one aspect, though doubtless a true one, of this royal display of luxury. The fact that this lifestyle was not merely a sign of the king's paramount position, but that it also played its part in the redistributive system of interchange between king and subject in view of adjusting social and political relations, was something they superficially perceived, but never quite understood.

On his journeys and during his campaigns, the king lived in a 'tent' of enormous dimensions, easily recognizable as his. Because of its size, complexity and equipment, and not least because of its function, it was rightly described as a 'movable palace'. The place where the ruler happens to be is, of course, the centre of his royal power and authority. In the tent, with the king, were the insignia of his power, and it is no wonder that after Issus, Alexander underlined his claim on ruling all Asia by taking possession of the tent and the royal insignia.

The 'travelling kingship' of the Achaemenids can therefore only superficially be considered as a climatically conditioned necessity. Its political function was much more significant: the 'king on the move' reminded his subjects, whatever their social and political rank, of his own dominant and their subordinate position, of their duty to be loyal and to support him materially, of the fact that their offices and functions, as well as their material welfare, depended on the good will and authority of their ruler.

4. The 'good' king and the 'bad': Cyrus and Xerxes

If one were to choose among the rulers of the Achaemenid clan the two kings who, in antiquity as well as in later centuries, had respectively the best and the worst reputations, practically everyone would point to Cyrus and Xerxes. What a wealth of positive impressions we have of the first Persian king! Not only is he said to have led his people from small beginnings to great eminence, not only is he meant to have laid the foundations for the first universal empire of antiquity worthy of this name; but he is also considered to have shown discretion, modesty, tolerance and political sagacity in his day-to-day actions. How different, on the other hand, is our idea of Xerxes. Did his campaign against Greece not prove that his ambition knew no bounds, that he was not prepared to concede freedom and self-determination to a small 'nation' on the periphery of his empire, that he treated his opponents with monstrous brutality and could not be tolerant even in religious matters? And did it not already appear to many an ancient observer that the reign of Xerxes had marked the inevitable decline of Persian power and culture?

By way of a test, we might compare the entries for 'Cyrus II' and 'Xerxes I' in the latest edition of a standard German encyclopaedia. About the founder of the empire it says:

Cyrus II (according to Herodotus C. III), the Great, d. 529 BC, king (since 559). Founder of the great Persian empire: 550/49 shaking off Median supremacy and conquest of Media (see Astyages), 547 conquest of Lydia (see Croesus), 539 Babylon (return of the Jews from Babylonian Exile, q.v.), assumption of the title 'king of the countries' following Ancient Near Eastern traditions of rulers. C. was killed during a campaign against the Massagetae. The type of reign he established was based on tolerance and mercy for his opponents; his historical achievement was depicted in literature and provoked controversies about state theory and ideology (Aeschylus, Herodotus, Xenophon [*Cyropaedia*], Nicholaus of Damascus).

As for the son and successor of Darius, this is how he is presented:

Xerxes I (OP Khshayarsha ... = the one ruling over heroes; in the OT cf. Ahasuerus), b. ca. 519, d. Susa 465, great king (from 486) of the old Persian dynasty of the Achaemenids. Son of Darius (q.v.) and Atossa (q.v.), through whose influence he was preferred to his father's elder sons in the succession to the throne. Soon after his (not undisputed) accession, he forcibly (and lacking the tolerance towards other religions typical of Cyrus II and Darius I) suppressed rebellions in Egypt and Babylonia. Emulating his father, he resumed the huge armament preparations the latter had already begun against Greece, but although he mobilized all the available sources of power, he failed in his attempt to conquer Greece as a result of his defeats at Salamis (q.v.) (480) and Plataea (479) (see also Persian Wars). Vast building projects in later years (above all, enlargement of Persepolis). X., under whom the decline of the Persian empire began, was killed in a palace revolution by Artapanus, the leader of the bodyguard.

If we speculate about the reasons for the good reputation of Cyrus and the bad press for Xerxes, we are again thrown back upon the reports of the ancients, so we shall begin with a glance at the testimonies describing Cyrus as a 'good' and Xerxes as a 'bad' king.

First, Cyrus. Of the founder of the Persian empire there are no known inscriptions or equivalent testimonies from Iran. The Iranian form of esteem for this king inheres solely in the manifest respect and care for his material estate (Pasargadae with his tomb), as well as in the popular lore which, in a markedly oral culture like Iran's, proves particularly conducive to creating traditions. In the works of the Greek authors, this popular lore merely appears in a fragmentary form. And it is precisely these classical sources (see the encyclopaedia entry) that contain the most detailed reports about Cyrus. Aside from them, Old Testament texts as well as inscriptions and (historical) literature from the Babylonian area also play a key part, and are of particular value because of their nearness in time.

If we now turn to each of these testimonies and inquire about the roots of the (mostly altogether positive) picture of Cyrus they bequeath to us, the following facts emerge. Herodotus presented parts of the picture that has prevailed to this day; the Persians under Cyrus were distinguished by their modesty, sober reasoning and courage, and their king, whom his subjects called 'father', excelled in military and statesmanlike skill, friendship, liberality, leniency and kindness, even with regard to enemies such as Astyages and Croesus. The well-known episode about his indulgence towards the Lydian king has become a topos for the 'magnanimous victor'.

Even more historically effective than Herodotus's picture of Cyrus was Xenophon's, which he presented in a kind of 'biography' of this king (*Cyropaedia*). Until the eighteenth century, this work was one of the most widely read books of all time, and there are countless references to Xenophon's Persian king in European literature and art. More than any other work, Xenophon's 'Education of Cyrus' has established the picture of a good, wise and tolerant Cyrus, and the contrast between the ideal early days of the Persian empire and the 'decadent aftermath' described in the last part may have served to accentuate this impression. As an illustration, we shall quote a few lines each from the beginning and the end of the *Cyropaedia*:

Believing this man [Cyrus] to be deserving of all admiration, we have therefore investigated who he was in his origin, what natural endowments he possessed, and what sort of education he had enjoyed, that he so greatly excelled in governing men. Accordingly, what we have found out or think we know concerning him we shall now endeavour to present. ... That Cyrus's empire was the greatest and most glorious of all the kingdoms in Asia – of that it may bear its own witness. For it was bounded on the east by the Indian Ocean, on the north by the Black Sea, on the west by Cyprus and Egypt, and on the south by Ethiopia. And although it was of such magnitude, it was governed by the single will of Cyrus; and he honoured his subjects and cared for them as if they were his own children; and they, on their part, revered Cyrus as a father. Still, as soon as Cyrus was dead, his children at once fell into dissension, states and peoples began to revolt, and everything began to deteriorate.

Aside from the qualities of Xenophon's Cyrus, hardly any factor has so endeared this king to people as the Old Testament texts ascribing to him the repatriation of the Jews (Judaeans) from their Babylonian captivity and the summons to build a new temple in Jerusalem. Who can ignore the words of Deutero-Isaiah, in which he presents Cyrus as the instrument of God:

Thus says the Lord, thy redeemer, and he that formed thee from the womb, I am the Lord that maketh all things; ... That says of Cyrus, He is my shepherd, and shall perform all my pleasure; even saying to Jerusalem, Thou shalt be built; and to the temple, Thy foundation shall be laid.

Thus says the Lord to his anointed, to Cyrus, whose right hand I have holden, to subdue nations before him; and I will loose the loins of kings, to open before him the two leaved gates; and the gates shall not be shut.

Although without much impact on European intellectual history, parts of the contemporary Mesopotamian historical tradition, such as the 'Nabonidus Chronicle', the 'Cyrus Cylinder' and the 'Persian Verse-Account', were decisive factors in the way Cyrus was seen by his Achaemenid subjects in Babylonia. All these texts sing the praises of Cyrus and contrast him with his political and military opponent and predecessor on the throne, Nabonidus. The 'Cyrus Cylinder' from Babylon now in the British Museum (Plate XIb) may serve as an illustration. The contents of this inscription, which comes under the category of royal foundation inscriptions, fall into six parts: 1. a historical introduction presenting and reviling Cyrus's opponent, Nabonidus (Nabuna'id), and explaining the part played by Marduk, the chief god of Babylon, in Cyrus's assuming control of the city (lines 1–19); 2. the royal protocol and genealogical table (lines 20–22); 3. a (positive) assessment of Cyrus and of his restoration policy (lines 22–34); 4. a prayer addressed by Cyrus to Marduk for himself and his son (lines 34–35); 5. the comment that all is well in the empire (lines 36–7); and finally, 6. information about Cyrus's building activities in Babylon (lines 38–45). Here are some particularly characteristic passages of this Cyrus inscription:

The worship of Marduk, the king of the gods, he [Nabonidus] [chang]ed into abomination. Daily he used to do evil against his city [Babylon] ... He [Marduk] scanned and looked [through] all the countries, searching for a righteous ruler willing to lead [him] [in the annual procession]. [Then] he pronounced the name of Cyrus, king of Anshan, declared him to be[come] the ruler of all the world ... I am Cyrus, king of the world, great king, legitimate king, king of Babylon, king of Sumer and Akkad, king of the four rims [of the earth], son of Cambyses, great king, king of Anshan, grandson of Cyrus, great king, king of Anshan, descendant of Teispes, great king, king of Anshan, of a family [which] always [exercised] kingship; whose rule Bel [Marduk] and Nebo love, whom they want as king to please their hearts ... I did not allow anybody to terrorize [any place] of the [country of Sumer] and Akkad. I strove for peace in Babylon and in all his [other] sacred cities. As to the inhabitants of Babylon ... I abolished forced labour ... From Nineveh, Assur and Susa, Akkad, Eshnunna, Zamban, Me-Turnu and Der until the region of Gutium, I returned to these sacred cities on the other side of the Tigris, the sanctuaries of which have been ruins for a long time, the images which [used] to live therein and established for them permanent sanctuaries. I [also] gathered all their [former] inhabitants and returned [to them] their habitations.

Many scholars have read into these last sentences a confirmation of the Old Testament passages about the steps taken by Cyrus towards the erection of the Jerusalem temple and the repatriation of the Judaeans, some even going so far as to believe that the instructions to this effect were actually provided in these very formulations of the Cyrus Cylinder. In any event, the clemency Herodotus ascribed to Cyrus, the aptitudes Xenophon saw in him, his mission according to the Old Testament and his piety as described in the Babylon inscription – all combine in the eyes of many observers to form a harmonious character study of the first Persian king.

But how are we to explain the bad reputation of Xerxes, who is occasionally accused, as in our encyclopaedia article, of expressly departing from the political concepts of Cyrus? Let us first piece together what our ancient informants have handed down to us about the life of Darius's successor. Born as the son of Cyrus's daughter, Atossa, when his father was already king, Xerxes was mainly raised under the care of the women of the royal house, as especially emphasized by Plato:

But Darius was succeeded by Xerxes, whose education had reverted to the royal pampering of old [basilikē kai tryphōsē paideia]. – ('Darius', as perhaps we'd be entitled to say to him – 'you haven't learnt from Cyrus's mistake, so you've brought up Xerxes in the same habits as Cyrus brought up Cambyses.') So Xerxes, being a product of the same type of education, naturally had a career that closely reproduced the pattern of Cambyses's misfortunes.

Under Atossa's influence, his father appointed him to be his successor. Soon after his accession to the throne, he had to put down rebellions in Egypt and Babylonia, according to Herodotus.

Xerxes gave in and allowed himself to be persuaded to undertake the invasion of Greece. First, however, in the year after Darius's death, he sent an army against the Egyptian rebels and decisively crushed them; then, having reduced the country to a condition of worse servitude than it had ever been in the previous reign, he turned it over to his brother Achaemenes.

When there was a second rising in Babylonia in 479, he is said to have suppressed the rebellion with monstrous brutality and even to have 'offended' against the sanctuaries, as Herodotus and Strabo maintain:

In the temple of Babylon there is a second shrine lower down, in which is a great sitting figure [agalma mega] of Zeus [Bel], all of gold ... In the time of Cyrus there was also in this sacred building a solid golden statue of a man [andrias] some twelve cubits high ... Darius the son of Hystaspes had designs upon it, but he never carried it off because his courage failed him; Xerxes, however, did take it and killed the priest who warned him not to move the statue.

Here, too, is the tomb of Belus [Marduk], now in ruins, of which it is said that Xerxes destroyed it ... Alexander planned to restore [this pyramid tomb]; but this would have been an enormous task, requiring a great deal of time ... so he was unable to accomplish what he had sought to do.

After three years of preparation, Xerxes mounted his campaign against Greece, with a gigantic army, to wipe out the humiliation of Marathon. Here one is bound to be reminded of the numerous occasions reported by Herodotus, on which the great king had acted as an unbridled and ruthless despot. We recall the 'punishment' of the Hellespont, the fate of the son of Pythius, the profanation of the corpse of Leonidas and the destruction of the shrines on the Acropolis of Athens. After his defeat at Salamis, the king pulled all the way back to Susa, and a year later learned of the defeat of his general Mardonius at Plataea. He then gave up his plans to conquer Greece and devoted himself to two of his 'favourite pastimes': the improvement of Persepolis and his relationships with the women of the court. About the latter we are well informed, for example about his liaison with his niece, Artaynte, which led to the death of Xerxes's brother Masistes and his family.

In 465 Xerxes and his eldest son and heir to the throne, Darius, fell victims to a palace plot and were murdered. Their portraits on the façade of the stairway leading to the Apadana in Persepolis (Plate XII) were thereupon removed and stored in the Treasury building.

Even today, the words Aeschylus has Atossa say to her husband Darius in *The Persians* seem to sum up the character of Xerxes:

They [the Persians] indeed say: you once acquired great wealth for your children with the spear. But he [Xerxes], since he is not a man, only needs his lance at home, and so he does not increase his patrimony.

Many scholars find the intolerance of Xerxes also confirmed by an inscription that came to light in 1935 in two Old Persian copies as well as in a Babylonian and later an Elamite version in Persepolis (and in 1963 in a third Old Persian copy in Pasargadae). It is generally known as Xerxes's 'Daiva inscription' (XPh). Here is an excerpt from it:

Proclaims Xerxes, the king: When first I became king, there is among these countries/ peoples which are inscribed above [one which] was in commotion. Afterwards Ahura Mazda bore me aid; by the favour of Ahura Mazda I smote that country/people and put it down in its place.

And among these countries/peoples there was [one] where previously false gods [*daivā*] were worshipped. Afterwards, by the favour of Ahura Mazda I destroyed that sanctuary of the demons, and I made proclamation, 'the demons shall not be worshipped!' Where previously the demons were worshipped, there I worshipped Ahura Mazda at the right [ritual] time and in the right way.

Many of the other Xerxes inscriptions, above all the XPc inscription found by a peasant in Persepolis in 1967, which turned out to be a textual copy presented in the name of Xerxes of the lower epitaph of Darius in Naqsh-i Rustam (DNb), have been considered as proofs of Xerxes's 'lack of independence' (Hinz); and morally, his claim to have followed his father's example is more than ever disputed.

But can we praise the son for not shrinking from setting his own name on this unique personal record handed down by his father [DNb]? Could Xerxes, who never fought in a battle himself, but merely watched it from a lofty position, enthroned under a canopy [at Salamis], say like Darius in the inscription: 'As a warrior I am a tested one'? Could Xerxes, who was prone to outbursts of fury, say like his father: 'Even when I am seething inside, I control my anger'? (Hinz)

It is not surprising that even Xerxes's building policy in Persepolis has been considered as hardly independent and described as an imitation of the standards set by his father.

Is not all this a perfect confirmation of the widely held views about Cyrus and Xerxes, as summed up in the encyclopaedia articles? Yet something makes us wonder. We have so far found out little about the temporal background of the testimonies presented, and virtually nothing about the motives behind the historical accounts on the one hand and the royal inscriptions on the other. What is more, the descriptions and evaluations of these two personalities appear curiously colourless and undifferentiated. So the question arises whether other sources might not modify the picture behind the tradition. We shall therefore take a second look at the records, starting again with the founder of the empire.

Herodotus, the 'father of history', attributes thoroughly negative aspects to Cyrus, and these even appear to predominate, although they have had less influence in forming the king's traditional image than his positive features have exerted. Cyrus can also be hard and intolerant, hot-tempered and irascible. His end is almost an illustration of Herodotus's idea of the expansionist ruler who does not realize when he is going too far. Yet it looks as if Herodotus, despite his reservations regarding some of the oral traditions about Cyrus – for instance those of Iranian origin – could not resist being fascinated by the Persian king's personality. If we further bear in mind that many Persian subjects had approved of Cyrus, that in retrospect – Herodotus was writing about 100 years after Cyrus's death – certain things may have seemed 'transfigured', and that the Greek historian was less concerned with the life and politics of Cyrus than with the wars between Persians and Greeks in the days of the great kings Darius and Xerxes, then the positive features of Cyrus may appear more intelligible.

As for Xenophon in his *Cyropaedia*, the fictitious and imaginary nature of this work has long been acknowledged, but to this day it has not been classified within any specific literary genre. Although it certainly reflects Xenophon's own observations of the Persian way of life as a writer, soldier and eyewitness, and although it could also presuppose some knowledge about Persia among its readers, any assessment of the 'Education of Cyrus' as a piece of historical writing must be ruled out. How the 'Greek' and 'Iranian' components of the work are to be evaluated is another question. In the past, its Greek character was rightly emphasized, and it was compared with the 'Mirrors for Princes' which had appeared as a result of the debates about the ideal state (and ideal statesman) that had become so popular in Hellas in the fourth century BC. More recent scholars, however, have also stressed its connections with the Iranian epic tradition and Iranian folklore. As our knowledge stands at present, the question about the relative importance of these two elements cannot be answered. But what is clear is that Xenophon's motives required an attractive picture of Cyrus.

Nor was it without good reason that the Old Testament Cyrus was depicted with such positive qualities. Old Testament exegesis has shown that the texts of particular importance in this connection (the Second Book of Chronicles, the Book of Ezra and the Prophecies of Deutero-Isaiah) are not to be considered as strictly 'historical' records, but as writings promising or describing a 'theological turning-point' (Zenger) for Israel. Cyrus appears as the 'instrument of Yahweh's historical action' (Zenger), ending the period of exile and leading to a new beginning. Scholars even debate whether the order to build the temple, the restoration of the cult in Jerusalem and the repatriation of the deported Jews can in fact be traced back to Cyrus, or whether we are rather to assume a (theological) 'back-projection', attributing deeds to this hoped-for saviour that were only to be authorized or begun at a later period.

The Cyrus Cylinder inscription, for its part (like the other Babylonian testimonies referred to) is not to be considered as a document that has come down to us by chance, but as a kind of *res gestae* composed for the new ruler and presenting his qualities against a background of their ostensibly special appreciation by Babylon's city god, Marduk. It thus fits into the framework of the ideological conflict between the new and the old king, and says less about Cyrus's character than about his efforts at legitimation and his ability to use local traditions and models to serve his own purposes.

We can take one further step towards a more differentiated evaluation of Cyrus's personality and politics by calling on other – so far rather neglected – sources, and by reinterpreting already familiar material. There are indications to the effect that Cyrus did not always distinguish himself by treating his opponents leniently and kindly. Thus the final conquest of Media and its capital city Ecbatana was not achieved as smoothly and non-violently as the classical sources in particular would have us believe. The Nabonidus Chronicle, like the Cyrus Cylinder a piece of propaganda at Cyrus's service, reports that the Persian king had plundered Ecbatana (the Treasury building?) and sent the booty home to Anshan. About the fate of Astyages/Ishtumegu there are different versions. While Herodotus reports that he had remained in Cyrus's entourage until his death, Ctesias says that he had later been killed without the king's knowledge. Herodotus's account is also partially contradicted by the statement in the 'Sippar Cylinder' that the king of the Medes was brought to Cyrus's homeland in chains. Hence the widely held opinion that Astyages was honourably treated by Cyrus after the latter's victory can neither be ruled out nor proved with complete certainty.

To mention another example, although Cyrus's entry into Babylon was managed without difficulty or bloodshed, this was not true of his previous campaign. Thus the 'Nabonidus Chronicle' which was well disposed towards Cyrus, reports:

In the month of Tishri, when Cyrus was fighting the battle of Opis on the shores of the Tigris against the army of Akkad, the people of Akkad [soldiers] retreated. He [Cyrus] had the booty taken away [and] the [captive] people killed.

Nor should we assume that there was a unanimously pro-Persian atmosphere in the country. Nabonidus's reign, and above all that of his viceroy Belshazzar/Bel-shar-usur, had been efficient and sensible according to documental evidence, and certain traditions that were critical of Cyrus were able to persist in Babylonia.

Probably the best-known example of the Persian king's allegedly magnanimous treatment of his opponents, namely his leniency towards Croesus, is totally unhistorical. Not only are there ancient testimonies reporting the death of Croesus when Sardis was conquered, but the pro-Cyrus versions have been proved to be later phases in the elaboration of the Croesus tradition. The result is a chain 'from the report of the catastrophe ("Nabonidus Chronicle": Croesus falls by the hand of Cyrus) by way of the pictorial illustration of the catastrophe (the Myson vase in the Louvre) to the transcendental supplement (Bacchylides: Croesus owes his life to divine intervention) and finally to the pseudo-historical rationalization (Herodotus: Cyrus spares Croesus's life)' (Burkert).

One last example: it has been rightly assumed that Ionian troops had supported Croesus in his fight against Cyrus. Cyrus thereupon denied all of them, with the exception of Miletus, the legal and political status they had held under the Lydian reign, blaming them for having ignored his summons to secede from Lydia. Military conflicts with the Persians started only after the suppression of the Paktyes revolt, which most of the coastal cities had joined. The first victims of the campaign led by the Persian king's emissary, Mazares, were Priene and Magnesia-on-Maeander. The inhabitants of Priene or their city élite were enslaved, which means probably deported, and the city and surroundings of Magnesia were plundered. After the death of Mazares, the supreme command was passed to Harpagus, Cyrus's confidant from the days of the Median wars. Subsequently, not only Caria and Lycia, but all the Ionian cities with the exception of Miletus, which had not joined the insurrection, were forcibly brought under Persian rule. These included Phocaea, Teos, Clazomenae, Lebedus, Colophon, Ephesus, Myus and Eretria, and evidently Smyrna as well. Phocaea and Teos were conquered by means of an artificial mound built by the Persians close to the city walls, but according to Herodotus the inhabitants had left the cities shortly before their fall and had sought new places to settle. For the conquest of Smyrna, there is even archaeological evidence. Many residences, as well as the magnificent, newly built temple building with votive offerings on its terraces, and the terrace walls themselves, were burnt down or destroyed. The allegation that the Persians destroyed temples is substantiated by Herodotus's statement that the Phocaeans had completely emptied their temple before their departure, evidently to forestall its pillage and ravage by the Persians. Little more is known about further sanctions against the conquered cities, except for obligatory induction into the army. The burden of taxation is believed to have been even lighter than under Lydian rule.

As our investigations have shown, the person and politics of Cyrus need to be examined with much more discrimination than is found in those reports that have given rise to the most enduring traditions. But was there in fact such a thing as a political concept behind Cyrus's attitude? Or is the make-up of the king's personality a sufficient explanation for everything? A comparison with Xerxes may lead us further.

We shall start by observing the Xerxes of Herodotus, our principal informant. Though not an eyewitness of the events, Herodotus, unlike many of his compatriots, endeavoured to acknowledge the merits of the opponents of Greece, and thus allotted a significant place in his 'Histories' to Xerxes as a strategist. Contrary to the imputations of modern scholars, his 'psychograph' of the Persian king by no means portrays an autocratic tyrant whose hubris knew no bounds. Even if, as a king, he had greater freedom and greater scope in decision-making, Xerxes did not determine the course of events on his own. He was talked into the war against Hellas, and he also took many decisions under the influence of 'divine' inspiration, which proved fatal to him. We often have the impression that whatever he did, Xerxes always made the wrong choice. That is why Herodotus's Xerxes has sometimes been described as 'tragic', which is not far from the truth. Bear in mind that Herodotus was writing almost two generations after Xerxes's defeat at Salamis, and that he could hardly have had any sources providing unbiased

and competent reports about the events and persons involved; we may therefore expect his 'psychograph' to provide us with an insight into the historian's
opinions about the connection between predestined fate and human potenti-
alities to shape it, rather than with a historically reliable character-study of
the Persian king. This might be illustrated by an example. What does the
'indifference' of Xerxes at the battle of Salamis, so vehemently criticized by
a modern commentator, tell us about the character of the king? Is it really
an expression of incompetence, or might we not see the enthroned Xerxes
within the context of certain ritual, ceremonial or other 'prescriptions' and
ways of behaviour which a Persian monarch was obliged to follow? What
may strike us today (or the Greeks at the time) as incomprehensible, or as a
sign of cruelty and lack of self-control, may have obeyed certain religious or
political guidelines, or even contain a 'deeper meaning'. To provide an example, Herodotus reports that after his retreat from Greece, Xerxes fell in
love with the wife of his brother Masistes. When she refused him, Xerxes
arranged a marriage between his son, Darius, and the woman's daughter, in
the hope that he might thereby achieve his aim. But while in Susa, his love
for his sister-in-law ceased, and he fell in love with his daughter-in-law
Artaynte, who reciprocated his affection. The liaison became known when
Artaynte, who was entitled to ask the king for a present, insisted of all things
on the royal robe woven by Queen Amestris and could not be induced to
change her mind. Amestris, who considered Artaynte's mother as the main
culprit, took cruel revenge:

She waited for the day when her husband the king gave his Royal Supper ... and
then she asked Xerxes for her present – Masistes' wife. Xerxes, who understood the
reason for her request, was horrified, not only at the thought of handing over his
brother's wife, but also because he knew she was innocent. But Amestris persisted –
and, moreover, the law of the Supper demanded that no one, on that day, might be
refused his request; so at last, much against his will, Xerxes was forced to consent.

Xerxes tried to persuade Masistes to separate from his wife in great haste
and marry one of his daughters, but he refused. When he found his wife at
home, mutilated at the behest of Amestris, he tried to go to Bactria to start
a rebellion there. But on Xerxes's order, he was murdered, together with his
sons and his retinue, on the way east.

This 'novella', which is based on oral tradition, is certainly not to be
understood as a kind of eyewitness account; on the contrary, all the elements
of the story have their special meaning in the Iranian context, a meaning that

was evidently not intelligible to the Greeks. Let us explore its symbolism. There is, for one thing, the 'prescription' that the king, as proof of his power, must meet the request of anyone whom he has expressly invited to ask for a present. Artaynte's wish, however, was not simply *a* robe, but *the* robe of the king, a symbol of his sovereignty. By insisting on this robe, Artaynte poses the question of sovereignty; not for herself, but indeed for her family. This makes it easier to understand why Amestris takes revenge (for her son, the crown-prince). She does this, incidentally, in a manner which anyone in Iran would have understood. Here rebels were punished by having their nose, ears or tongue cut off. Masistes, too, ends up paying with his life for his ambition to be king. To uncover the deeper meaning of the story, we might perhaps even go a step further. To some scholars, the name Masistes suggests the Old Persian word **maθišta-* ('greatest, highest' = 'leader'). If this is to be understood as a title ('the greatest after the king'), then Masistes might be identified with Xerxes's eldest brother, Ariamenes, who, according to Plutarch, was said to have 'reigned' in Bactria – like Herodotus's Masistes – but of whose later career our sources do not inform us (because of his assassination?). So without knowing it, Herodotus may have made literary use of accounts about a usurpation attempt on behalf of a family member within the Achaemenid clan.

The following crimes, which some scholars attribute to Xerxes in Babylonia, are also questionable:

Xerxes had the Babylonian 'stable of idols' Esagila so thoroughly razed that, when Alexander later (331 BC) ordered the Marduk temple to be rebuilt, the debris had not yet been completely removed after fifteen years and they had to give up the plan to reconstruct it. Xerxes also had the six-metre-high seated statue of Marduk in massive gold carried off and melted down. (Hinz)

His alleged renunciation of the title 'King of Babylon' after the in-surrections in Babylonia is equally problematic. For one thing, Herodotus does not blame Xerxes for the removal (and melting down) of the Marduk statue; it was not the *agalma* of the city god that he supposedly took away, but an *andrias* (of another divinity? a statue of an Assyrian or Babylonian king?). Besides, there can be no doubt that Esagila and the cult of Marduk continued until the end of the Achaemenid period. The information about the attempt by Alexander to restore the ruined temple then simply means that the Macedonian – like all kings in Babylon before him – promoted the 'restoration' (i.e. repair, etc.) of the sanctuaries to prove himself as the divinely chosen legitimate king whom the gods entitled to build temples. Moreover, according to recent research, the title 'King of Babylon' is repeatedly attested for Xerxes until the seventeenth year of his reign.

But does not the 'Daiva inscription' at least prove the basic intolerance of the king? Here, too, a popular misconception has to be discarded. Why was it that Xerxes did not more clearly indicate the place of the 'idol worship'? The answer lies in the 'timeless' character of Achaemenid inscriptions (and, as we have seen, reliefs). Xerxes had no specific event in view, he proclaimed once and for all: 'Whoever defects from the king will be punished, and the holy places of rebels will be destroyed.' This is an 'ideological and programmatic' declaration, not a reaction of the king that can be historically pinpointed. Seen against this background, Xerxes's imitations of his father's inscriptions and reliefs can also be understood. They were not due to a 'lack of imagination', but were meant to emphasize the validity of generally accepted principles for his own reign as well. Xerxes never demanded that his subjects give up their old gods in favour of Ahura Mazda, but if rebels mingled politics and religion so that gods were invoked to stand by them in a fight, if insurrections were proclaimed to be willed by gods, then insurgents as well as their places of worship could expect severe punishment. The destruction of the Athenian Acropolis is not to be understood otherwise, nor was it without good reason that, as Herodotus reports, as early as the following day, Xerxes ordered that sacrifices again be offered to the (Athenian) gods, though not by the rebels, but by the exiled Athenians in his retinue.

If we now look again at the two encyclopaedia articles, we will realize that the sharp contrast made between Cyrus and Xerxes is not justified. Cyrus's politics – for about his character, as we have seen, nothing reliable can be inferred from the sources – consisted of reflections, aims and methods similar to those of his predecessors in the Ancient Near East. Side by side with his 'tolerant' aspects, such as the restoration of places of worship, the repatriation of exiles and the acceptance of religious diversity, he also committed 'intolerant' acts such as looting temples and deporting people. Cyrus's life and politics managed to acquire an exemplary character because certain political constellations were in his favour and certain factors that might have clouded his image were not – or not yet – operative. Thus, while the Graeco-Persian conflict still lay in the future, there were politically as well as 'ideologically' influential groups or individuals who were interested in his success or wanted to set him up as an example. And how would he compare with his successors, above all with Xerxes? Of course, they had different *tasks*, and the initial situations were also different: here the foundation of an empire under a 'charismatic' leader with the prospect of booty and benefices, there the protection and preservation of the reign once it had been institutionalized and put on a legal basis by Darius. As for the crucial question, the only one allowing a comparison, namely their *methods* of safeguarding their reign, there was little difference between Cyrus and Xerxes. Whoever would not consent to the devolution of 'the fallen enemy's sovereign rights upon the conqueror' (Walser), whoever resorted to arms to regain his independence, could count on the direst punishments from both kings. Even religious policy, as we have seen, was largely determined by this principle of the necessary proof of loyalty. Regardless of their own religious convictions, Cyrus and Xerxes were ready, for political reasons, to accept and respect the creeds of their subjects and to promote their cults, as long as such conduct would consolidate the bond between ruler and subjects. Religious ardour was alien to them, but so was the modern conception of religious tolerance as a humanistic principle. If Xerxes could have submitted his inscriptions to Cyrus, the founder of the empire would not have hesitated to countersign them.

CHAPTER 3

XŠAÇA, DAHYĀVA AND BĀǦI: THE KINGDOM, THE PEOPLES AND THE TRIBUTES PAID TO THE KING

1. 'Darius the king proclaims: By the favour of Ahura Mazda I am king; Ahura Mazda bestowed the kingdom upon me': the Achaemenid empire

In his inscriptions, Darius legitimizes his reign in several ways. First through his birth, that is, his belonging to the Achaemenid clan and furthermore to the Persian people and to the Aryans (*Haxāmanišiya, Pārsa, Pārsahya puça, Āriya, Āriyačiça*); second, through his pre-eminent position and his succession to the kings of the preceding empires (*xšāyaθiya xšāyaθiyānām*); third and last, through his 'divine right' as sovereign (*vašnā Auramazdāha adam xšāyaθiya amiy, Auramazdā xšaçam manā frābara*). Ahura Mazda thus bestows the 'kingdom', and he who possesses the 'kingdom' is king. That *xšaça* in the inscriptions does not have the abstract meaning of 'reign', but the concrete one of 'kingdom' has been established with many good reasons; similarly, the satrap governing a province (OP *xšaçapāvan* – 'protector of the kingdom') is not a king because he possesses no 'kingdom' of his own, but 'only' protects the empire of the king, his overlord. For the same reason, the title 'king of kings' does not describe the relationship between king and 'vassal kings' or the like, but exclusively a relationship to preceding sovereigns. Besides, the 'Persian kingdom' was never mentioned in official statements and only rarely in unofficial usage. The 'Persian country' was Persis, while the empire as a whole was considered as the country of the king, as we learn from the historian Thucydides in connection with the treaty of 412/11 BC between Persia and Lacedaemon: 'All the land and cities that are held by the king and were held by the fathers of the king shall belong to the king.'

Until early modern times, the succession of world empires, one after another, had been considered as a principle governing world history, a principle 'on which not only political and intellectual events were chronologically fastened, but which could also serve as a widely understood vehicle for eschatological propaganda' (Metzler). What Herodotus seems to postulate – though with no projection into the future – is a succession of three empires (Assyrians – Medes – Persians), and in the Book of Daniel dating from the second century BC, a pattern of four is chosen (Babylonians – Medes – Persians – Ptolemies/Seleucids). Cyrus has been regarded as the ruler for whom the concept of the three empires was developed. This makes sense, but it remains to be seen whether the 'creators' of this concept did not run the risk of proceeding contrapuntally, as it were, with the idea of the emergence and rise of world domination, to argue for both the coming and the going of world empires, as was later the case in the apocalyptic literature of the Graeco-Roman period.

When Darius died in 486 BC, the Achaemenid empire embraced the territories of the originally independent kingdoms of Media, Lydia and Babylonia, as well as eastern Iran and parts of Central Asia (conquered by Cyrus), the sovereign domain of the Saïtic dynasty in Egypt (acquired by Cambyses), in addition to Thrace and 'India', which had been won shortly before. The result was the creation of a state structure on an unprecedented scale, characterized by ethnic and cultural heterogeneity. In addition, the Persians had appeared in the great majority of these regions as 'conquerors', and in some of them, namely the territories that had so far remained autonomous, they had even disposed of the 'legitimate' dynasties. Though by previous contacts, for instance with Elam, Babylonia or Media, they may have acquired a certain familiarity with the traditions of these areas and found a better approach to the respective regional problems and political peculiarities, the question still remains what the Achaemenid concept of sovereignty looked like at the imperial level or from a regional and local perspective.

From the example of the policies of Cyrus and Xerxes, we are already acquainted with some of the characteristic methods of government, such as 'tolerance' in religious matters, which might go as far as having kings and satraps expressly promote the cult embraced by their subjects through endowments and sacrifices if the divinities they worshipped had been seen to foster peace and order. On the other hand, these places of worship, unless otherwise exempted, were under an obligation to pay taxes and, of course, to toe the political line. This principle of religious policy was actually observed by all Persian kings.

Yet the Persian concept of ensuring sovereignty differed from the system which, for Rome at the time of the emperors, has been described as 'Romanization' – the integration of subjects into the political and social world of values defined by the Romans, a policy partially desired by the provincial élites themselves, but also positively pursued by Rome. This type of integration is illustrated in the well-known ironical passage by Tacitus describing Britons giving themselves the airs of Romans:

To let people who were scattered, backward, and therefore given to fighting have a taste of the pleasures of a peaceful and untroubled existence, and so to accustom them to it, Agricola gave encouragement to individuals and assistance to communities in the construction of temples, markets and private houses. If they showed willing he had praise for them, if they hung back, a rebuke. In that way, instead of being put under duress they were spurred on by rivalry for marks of his esteem. Not only that: he was having the sons of the chieftans educated in the liberal arts ... so that the very people who a short time before would have nothing to do with Latin were eager for the training of an orator. Then our way of dressing came to be held in regard, and the toga was often to be seen. Little by little they went astray, taking to the colonnades, bath-houses and elaborate banquets that make moral failings attractive. They were naive: they called it 'civilization' when it helped to ensure the loss of their freedom [*idque apud imperitos humanitas vocabatur, cum pars servitutis esset*].

Thus there was nothing in the Persian empire that might compare with the Roman colonies and municipia, in which – or in the surroundings of which – there occurred economic and familiar interchange between conquerors and subjects. Nor were there such Roman phenomena as the granting of citizenship to the élite of the peregrine cities (and later to all inhabitants of the empire), with the opportunity for social advancement or even admission within the *ordines* and official functions. Though it is true that for many a *bandaka* of the great king, the Persian or royal and aristocratic way of life became exemplary and worthy of imitation, this did not go so far as in the Roman world, where such acculturation percolated into the details of daily life, through learning the Latin language and through adopting legal concepts, religious views, forms of work, housing conditions, clothes, etc. The regional and local élites of the Achaemenid empire only very rarely gained access to the highest offices, which were chiefly reserved for the members of the Persian aristocracy. Being a Persian and coming from Persia specially distinguished an inhabitant of the empire. There were, it is true, non-Persians in high political and military positions, such as the Carian dynasts (Mausolus et al.), the only hitherto attested non-Persian satrap Belshunu/Belesys, or the Greek brothers Memnon and Mentor, but such examples are few and far between. Although the *koinonia* between Persians and loyal Greeks was evoked and cultivated, the great king would express his gratitude for proofs of good will and loyalty by granting honorary titles or material benefits, rather than by opening access to the politico-military decision-making level. Besides, even if the Persians tended to tolerate religious, cultural, social and economic autonomy, even if the king tried to adopt the traditions of the subject countries' rulers, or to use local traditions for the proclamation of royal principles, there was, at the same time, an effort on the part of the Persians to form a clear contrast with other inhabitants of the empire. Moreover, unlike those of their Roman counterparts, the script, language and religion(s) of the Persians were hardly attractive or 'open' enough to help in tying closer bonds between Persians and non-Persians.

And yet, numerous regional studies have shown that at least the great majority of the élites of subject peoples, with the possible exception of Egypt, saw the Persian king not as a foreign ruler and tyrant, but as the guarantor of political stability, social order, economic prosperity, and hence ultimately of their own position. Real outside dangers did not threaten the empire until after Macedonia's emergence as a great power, or even after the military victories of Alexander, who moreover availed himself of 'Achaemenid' models of reasoning and politics. The temporary or conclusive loss of certain peripheral provinces or the ambitions of certain satraps were less of a threat to the existence of the empire than were conflicts within the royal house. In the Achaemenid empire, local autonomy and decentralization of jurisdictions led to stabilizing rather than undermining the system, especially since both proceeded under constant and solid supervision from the centre. At no time was the great king's empire a 'colossus with feet of clay' (Bengtson).

2. 'Countries', 'peoples', 'satrapies' and 'fiscal units': the inner structure of the Achaemenid empire

The ethnic, topographical, administrative and fiscal structures of the Achaemenid empire are even today the subject of great controversy. This is first of all due to the fact that there exist various lists of units below the imperial

level, which are moreover interpreted in different ways. The most important
among them can be described as follows:

1 The royal Achaemenid inscriptions mention *dahyāva* that 'devolved
on' Darius (DB-i 13, 18), that 'feared him and brought [him] tribute' (DPe
9–10) or 'did what they ... were told' (DNa 20–21; XPh 17–18). DN Iff.
from Darius's tomb and the list on the plinth of the statue from Susa (DSab)
are legends for the supporting figures on reliefs described above ('This is the
Persian' etc.). The concept *dahyāva* (sing. *dahyu-*) has given rise to a great
many arguments. While some scholars translate it as 'countries', others see
in it a 'word oscillating' between 'countries and peoples' (Calmeyer); yet
others consider that it can only be appropriately rendered by 'people' or
'population'. There is nothing to indicate that the lists in question are those
of administrative units, as for instance lists of satrapies, for they do not cover
the whole empire. If we try to put these inventories in order, the following
can be established. The lists (and reliefs) of Darius I are 'baffling in their
diversity: no record resembles another'. They reflect historical reality (for
instance, the 'loss' of peoples) and follow Assyrian and Babylonian models in
that they are arranged in dynamic, centrifugal rows. Here again, Darius's
successors copied both the inscriptions and the iconography of these set
models, not for lack of imagination but to confirm the structure of the
empire. The only exception is Xerxes's 'Daiva inscription', which tries 'in a
grandiose manner to combine the stock-taking of Darius with an expression
of pride about the gigantic expanse of the empire' (Calmeyer):

Proclaims Xerxes, the king. By the favour of Ahura Mazda, these are the peoples/
countries of which I was king ... [The people from] Persia ... Media, Elam,
Arachosia, Armenia, Drangiana, Parthia, Aria, Bactria, Sogdia, Choresmia, Babylonia,
Assyria, Sattagydia, Lydia, Egypt, the Ionians by the sea, the Ionians beyond the sea,
[the people from] Maka, Arabia, Gandhara, Sind, Cappadocia, the Dahans, the Saka
haumavarga, the Saka tigrakhauda, the Thracians, Akaufaka, [the people from] Libya,
Caria and Kush.

2 In the writings of Greek authors we often find lists of army formations
that are arranged by ethnic groups (*ethnē*), but are not to be understood as
historical descriptions of units of the empire.

3 Particular difficulties are presented by Herodotus's list of 20 tribute-
paying *nomoi* (or *archai*) that often include more than one *ethnos*. The models
for this list are as controversial a subject as the question whether and in what
way it can be reconciled with the other evidence (royal inscriptions, reliefs).

4 In Plato we find descriptions of the Achaemenid empire postulating

its division into seven units and basing this on the number of the conspirators against Gaumata.

5 There have been regular attempts to determine what the Achaemenid system of classifying satrapies and provinces looked like at certain periods, since proper lists of satrapies have only come down to us from post-Achaemenid times. For the period under discussion, the Greek authors often mention names of satraps, but never describe the territory they ruled. This makes it almost impossible to mark in the borders of satrapies in historical maps.

In Western sources, satraps are sometimes referred to by other titles (*praefectus*, *epitropos*, *hyparchos*, etc.). Since these terms have different meanings (and were also used for officials of lower ranks), it is not always easy to identify a person as a satrap. In this field of research, the term satrapies (which is not very often used in the sources) denotes those regions in which satraps are mentioned; at the same time, satraps (without this title) are even believed to be identifiable when their names appear in connection with such regions. This could lead to a circular argument. It should be realized that satraps were not the highest-ranking administrative authorities. Thus a *šākin māti* ('governor of the country') from Babylonia is mentioned for the first years of Cyrus's reign, before the documents from this area refer to the first satrap (*bēl pāḥati*) of 'Babylon and Ebir-nari'. Another known title is that of *karanos*, which was handed down by the Greeks (e.g. for Cyrus the Younger) and designates a military commander-in-chief of western Asia Minor who is vested with special powers. Moreover, certain regions of the empire were temporarily governed by local dynasties (Caria, Lycia, Cilicia), others were under the control of city 'kings'. For certain populations, again, there is no record of the office of satrap, and we are not in a position to make any precise statements about the administrative head. Particularly surprising at first glance is the fact that certain groups of people could evidently maintain very loose connections with the state authorities, and others (especially the mountain people of the Zagros) not only did not have to pay 'tributes' themselves, but would even receive 'presents' from the king. An exceptional status was that of Persis, which will be discussed separately.

On the satrapy level (or that of comparable territorial units), there were other functionaries who were subordinates of the satraps, among them men with no specific title, whose tasks cannot be clearly determined. Relevant here, for example, are the *philoi*, *homotrapezoi* and *skēptouchoi* (the 'friends', 'table companions' and 'staff or sceptre bearers') of Cyrus the Younger, the cavalry commanders of the satrap Pharnabazus, the 'men under the governor' of the Book of Nehemiah, the members of the satrap's 'chancelleries' (*phoinikistēs*, *grammateus* et al.), the 'judges' (*dātabara*) and 'overseers' on the satrapal or provincial level, and those without a special function, the royal informants at the satrap's court (usually called 'the eyes and ears of the king' by earlier scholars).

Below the satrapy level, the administrative structure continued. From several territories we know of hyparchs, etc. (of the satrap), from Babylonia comes the title *pāḫatu* ('governor' of Babylonia), from Ebir-nari (the territories 'across the river', i.e. the Euphrates) the *bēl pāḫati ebir nāri* or the *pḥw'/paḫat yᵉhūdāyēʾ* ('governor' of Judaea/Yehud), each with their apparatus of officials. In Egypt the satrapal and regional system is particularly easy to grasp: under the satrap, the *frataraka* ('superintendent') acted on a provincial level, and under him (for the Elephantine/Syene territory) was the **haftaxvapātā* ('seventh-part protector'), who was called *rab ḥaylā* ('chief of the army') in his military function as garrison commander and *segan* in his legal office.

What remains to be mentioned is the local level. In Armenia, Xenophon's 10,000 mercenaries became acquainted with some (Persian-speaking) kōmarchai ('village heads'), a term evidently designating both the head of a single village and the official who supervised several villages. Subject cities do not appear to have lain under direct Iranian administration, but territories *with* cities were. We are better informed about people in charge of 'treasuries' (e.g. in provincial centres and other places), which were used not only for 'storage' but also as 'working houses'; and we also know more about officials in food depots, village granaries and magazines. Characteristic for the Achaemenid control of subject countries were the garrisons (*phrouroi*), which were supplied (from local resources) by the satrap and had a commanding officer appointed by the king.

At this lowest level of imperial administration we may also place the lands owned by members of the royal family, the properties bestowed by the king on aristocrats and 'benefactors', the 'fiefs' of military settlers in Babylonia or special settlements for deported people who worked for the king in exchange for a subsistence allowance.

3. *Phoros*, *dōra*, *tagē* and *bāǧi*: tribute, taxes and gifts in the Achaemenid empire

Already Aeschylus realized that the power of the Achaemenid empire depended on the payment of tribute and taxes, the observance of the Persian 'laws' and the acknowledgement of the great king's pre-eminent position. Loyalty towards the sovereign might, in addition, be proved by joining the army on a voluntary (or compulsory) basis.

And when he [Darius] had set up the provinces [*archai*] and appointed governors [*archontes*], he established the tributes [*phoroi*] that were to be paid to him, people by people, and to the peoples he adjoined the neighbouring ones and went beyond the adjacent peoples to distant ones, assigning some to one and some to another people. As for the provinces and annual tributes, he arranged them as follows: Those who paid in silver were appointed to render the weight of a Babylonian talent, and those who paid in gold a Euboean one ... During the reign of Cyrus, and later that of Cambyses, there was no fixed tribute, the revenue coming from gifts only. And because of this fixing of tribute and other like ordinances, the Persians called Darius a huckster [*kapelos*], Cambyses a master [*despotes*], and Cyrus a father [*pater*]; the first being out for profit wherever he could get it, the second harsh and arrogant, and the third, merciful and ever working for their well-being.

These remarks by Herodotus about Darius's reform of the administrative and tributary system show how incisive the subjects found this reorganization. We may assume that under Cyrus and Cambyses the payments to the centre followed no regulations or fixed amounts (this appears to be expressed by the word *dōra*), and that Darius's description as a 'huckster' consisted in the observance of this very rigidity. 'Gifts' had now become a prerogative, even if they were brought regularly: 'The following did not have to pay taxes [i.e. tribute (*phoros*)], but brought free gifts [*dōra*]: the Ethiopians ... the Colchians ... [and] ... the Arabs.'

These peoples at the limits of the empire (and of Herodotus's 'view of the world') evidently had tax/tribute exemptions while at the same time acknowledging the great king's suzerainty. Nevertheless, Ethiopians and gift-bearing Arabs do turn up in the inscriptions of the great kings, as well as in the Persepolis reliefs. So we are led to interpret Darius's words: 'These were the peoples who brought me tribute [*bāǧim*]' as implying that the *bāǧi* - bringing included both payment of tribute (*phoros*) by subjects and delivery of presents (*dōra*) by semi-autonomous ethnic groups.

Certain peoples, groups or individuals were treated even more obligingly by the Achaemenids. Thus the South Palestinian Arabs had become 'guests' (*xenoi*) of the Persians because they had supported Cambyses on his Egyptian campaign, and were therefore exempt from any contributions in acknowledgement of sovereignty (i.e. tribute *and* gifts). Similar exemptions or privileges were granted to the eastern Iranian Ariaspians, to the Apollo temple of Magnesia in Asia Minor and to the house of Darius's assistant Otanes. Something that has puzzled scholars to this day is the exemption from duties (*ateleia*) of Persis, as attested by Herodotus, while at the same time, the Persepolis tablets show a profusion of 'payments' from its provincials. Herodotus, however, merely maintains that Persis was free from the payment of *phoros* (i.e. tribute), which applied to dependent, conquered countries. This privilege (among others) may have been granted to the Persians by Darius at a certain juncture of his reign.

The *phoros* appears to have been collected on a provincial level, and – after deduction of the part needed for the province itself (and after conversion into precious metals?) – taken to the heartlands of the empire, where it was hoarded up in 'treasuries' to be used for minting, disbursements and presents. Apart from the tributes and the 'gifts' from semi-autonomous peoples, the king had other revenues as well: the already repeatedly mentioned 'gifts' presented to the great king by his subjects during his journeys, which he distributed to 'friends' and 'benefactors', as well as the *tagē* referred to in Greek sources for the support of the king and his army (as part of the *phoros*?). Since all these contributions were rightly interpreted as a sign of recognition of the great king's sovereignty, the ruler himself must have realized that such revenues were guaranteed only if the land and its inhabitants prospered. The king's efforts to ward off enemies and to take care of the flora and fauna (for instance, by controlling the irrigation system and planting new crops) had their motives here, too.

On the provincial level, the satrap or governor was evidently responsible for levying and collecting the tribute connected with the land, for which purpose he would probably have referred to traditional precedents from pre-Achaemenid times and consulted the available cadastres and registers. Here he would be assisted by hyparchs on the medium taxation level and by chiliarchs and autonomous urban authorities on the lower taxation level. These were aware of the fiscal privileges of various individuals or groups, landed estates, villages and towns. The temples, for instance in Mesopotamia, Syria and elsewhere, counted as 'great landowners' and were usually taxable, while some of their (unfree) staff were liable to conscription; but conversely, they enjoyed royal privileges and received disbursements from the public treasury. A peculiar status belonged to the already mentioned 'military fiefs' in Babylonia; these were inalienable but inheritable allocations of land which the king granted to soldiers in exchange for military service. In the course of time, however, it became common practice for the soldiers to farm out these lands, and military service was replaced by taxation and labour conscription. The problem of how to interpret the individual and/or collective taxes attested in the Persepolis tablets will be discussed in a later section.

The amount of the great king's (annual) revenues cannot be ascertained. The quantities of precious metal that fell into Alexander's hands when he occupied the Achaemenid palaces and administrative centres have been estimated at 180,000 talents (i.e. 4,680 tons of silver or 468 tons of gold), a sum attained at no other occasion in antiquity. But such amounts of treasures hoarded up over decades distort our view of the burden of tributes and other impositions on subjects within a given period, for these do not appear to have been felt as excessively onerous. If it is true that the contributions by the members of the Delian maritime confederacy were based on the Persian model, then it must have been a successful system, since it was even reviewed and improved by the satrap Artaphernes after the Ionian rebellion. Nowhere in our sources is there indeed an explicit reference to the effect that the *magnitude* of the tributes imposed had led to any rebellions by subjects. Of course, the greater systematization of the fiscal relations between king and subjects must needs have influenced the traditional assessment of Darius and his son Xerxes. Darius appeared to Herodotus as a 'huckster' (*kapelos*), and consequently as someone who 'bargained' with his subjects about the price of his sovereignty. Xerxes who, first of all, had to see to it that his father's reform proved successful during his reign, and secondly, must have found it convenient to uphold the system, was branded as a despot for the same reason.

CHAPTER 4

EVERYDAY LIFE IN ACHAEMENID PERSIS

In recent decades, historical interest has rightly focused (again) on the realm of everyday life. What must be realized, of course, is that the microcosm of man's experiences in his narrower daily surroundings is also determined by the macrocosm of 'big politics' and the overall social, economic and legal structures, and that it can only be grasped against this backdrop. Now the daily life of the Achaemenid subjects in Iran, as can be imagined in the light of the available sources, can be apprehended only in a rudimentary way, both in time and in space, and the aristocratic élite of the country plays a much more visible part in it than the 'ordinary' man and woman. That anything at all is known about such people is owing to the clay tablets from Persepolis (see Plate XIIIa), which Alexander's arson helped preserve. 'Of life in the great Persian empire' they have little to say, of course. Dated within the brief period from 509 to 458 BC, geographically they deal above all with Persis, the heartland of the empire, and the adjacent Elymais to the west. Since the interruption of this tradition was exclusively caused by the change in writing material (parchment for clay), the continued recording of these notes and of the practice they illustrate is altogether plausible. These texts are moreover so numerous and so astonishingly eloquent that, though still to be assessed primarily as 'Persian' (i.e. south-western Iranian) 'sources', much of what they say goes beyond the homeland of the Achaemenid clan. The facts they describe may be confirmed, completed or set into a larger context by other types of evidence; but these, on their part, may also partially be corrected by the tablets or 'unmasked' as stereotyped and serving specific interests. It is therefore with good reason that the Persepolis texts have gradually moved into the focus of attention (although despite all the legitimate criticism about the 'biased' views of the classical texts, we must definitely not consider them incapable of providing additional information). The tablets admittedly have their own way of being 'insidious'. Because of its isolated position in the linguistic network, the Elamite language, in which they are almost exclusively written, is counted among the most 'difficult' languages (as is fully proved by the arguments endemic among its experts). In addition, the published texts comprise only a part of the recovered material, so that the conclusions drawn from them are for the most part plausible, yet subject to possible revision.

The reader is reminded that apart from the 114 Persepolis Treasury Tablets (PTT), all of which concern 'payment' to workers in silver from the treasury and date between 492 and 458 BC, what remain to be evaluated are, above all, the over 2,100 published and more than 2,500 read Persepolis Fortification Tablets (PFT) from the years 509–494. Written in the form of brief administrative notes, they concern the supply, transfer and distribution of natural produce in the south-western Iranian heartlands, provisions that were issued as daily, monthly or sometimes extra rations to individuals or groups of workers, and also for the upkeep of animals. Each of the individuals or groups named is 'paid' or supplied in kind, and the 'accounting' is done so subtly that the system of receipts and expenses can only be described as highly sophisticated. It has been calculated that the surviving texts provide information about the maintenance of more than 15,000 individuals in more than 100 localities. An examination of the material in order to detect the activities and walks of life described in them leads to the following impressions:

Members of the royal family appear in them personally by writing letters, giving instructions or endorsing the arrangements made by their subordinates with their seal. A great many officials in their respective positions are introduced by name, and their spheres of responsibility are made known. Major groups of workers as well as individuals are engaged for specific jobs, and their compensations are correspondingly fixed. Taxes paid in kind are collected at certain localities, deposited and again used for the supply of workers. The disbursements of seeds and the ensuing income from harvests are noted down with the greatest precision. So a great many localities are mentioned, and in connection with them, the officials responsible in each case. Priests are provided with sacrifices for the gods they worship. The upkeep of travellers is secured by tablets they can show at the different post-stations. At the same time, the distribution and location of natural produce is scrupulously accounted for, and single, collective and annual settlements are preserved in great quantity. Special officials are engaged to prepare and check these accounts. (Koch)

To turn to questions about everyday life in all its detail: What type and what status of people are we dealing with here? What were the fields of work, the duties and services of those who were active in this system, and how were they remunerated and supplied? How were their fields of activity – among which we are particularly interested in manufacture, farming, and the information and army systems – structured and organized? Where are we to place men and women in this system? What religious ideas, worshipping practices and religious–political conditions determined the life of people in Persis during the reign of Darius I? Starting with the tablets, and complementing them with other testimonies and findings, we may perhaps provide the reader with an idea of what people felt in those days, what was expected of them and what they 'achieved'.

1. Artystone, Artaphernes, Farnaka and 'the boys of Farnaka': people in the administration and economy of Persis

Soon after the tablets were read, it was discovered that some of the personalities known to us from classical sources also appeared in the Persepolis texts: queens, princes and princesses, other relatives of the royal family, satraps and members of the Persian high aristocracy have all left their traces in them. They receive or distribute rations differentiated in accordance with positions, offices and tasks, and – when they themselves are the recipients – far exceeding the amount needed for their own maintenance. They give instructions to their subordinates, who travel on their behalf, or they travel themselves (and are looked after); they are identified as owners of large properties or workers' collectives. Three personalities may serve as illustrations. They are among the Persians we know quite well through Herodotus:

1. The *pater historiae* tells us that Darius I married, among others, Artystone, the daughter of Cyrus, who became his favourite wife. The sons they had together, Arsames and Gobryas, served as commanding officers in the Persian Wars. This Artystone (Elam. *Irtašduna*) is mentioned in 25 Persepolis texts, in two of which she is explicitly described as *dukšiš* (female member of the royal family). On various occasions, she receives wine, beer, cereals and other goods. Thus apparently for a feast in the first month of the nineteenth year of Darius's reign (503 BC):

Tell Yamakhshaita the 'wine carrier' [of Rautanayacha], Farnaka [the head of the entire administrative and economic system] spoke as follows: '200 *marriš* [jugs] of wine are to be issued to the queen. It was ordered by the king.' 1st month, 19th year [of reign]. Anzuka wrote the text. Varaza conveyed the message.

Tell Aryaina, the 'master of flocks', Farnaka spoke as follows: 'King Darius has instructed me: 100 sheep from my property are to be delivered to Queen Artystone.' And Farnaka spoke as follows: 'As King Darius has ordered me, so I order you. Deliver to Queen Artystone 100 sheep, as was commanded by the king.' 1st month, 19th year. Anzuka wrote the text. Varaza conveyed the message.

(In the following texts, 1 *marriš* or jug = 1 BAR = 10 QA, and 1 QA = 0.97 litre.)

Artystone herself was the owner of at least three large properties (palaces?), and in one of them (Kuganaka) she evidently entertained her husband in the year 498 BC. She often sent letters there with instructions to her (Babylonian) bailiff, as shown by copies of these letters from Persepolis. On her numerous journeys through the country, she received food and drink for herself and her retinue, and confirmed their receipt by setting her seal on the disbursement tablets. We know even more about the activities of Artabama, who is not mentioned by Herodotus, and whom we shall encounter later.

2. We are also familiar with Gobryas, one of the assistants of Darius I in his fight against the Magus Gaumata, and a companion of the king's on his Scythian campaign. His son Mardonius (from his marriage with the sister of Darius), who, according to Herodotus, had just married Darius's daughter Artazostra, appears in the 'Histories' as the most important Persian general between 493 and 479. The extent of Gobryas's significance to the king (of which Herodotus was not aware) is proved by his appointment as general when the revolt in Elam was being put down, and by the fact that he was immortalized both by name and pictorially as the king's spear-carrier on Darius's tomb. This same Gobryas (Elam. *Kambarma*) also appears in the Fortification Tablets. Among other things, he belonged to a group of travellers who set out in February 498 BC, presumably to meet Mardonius on his way back from Ionia. Apart from Gobryas, the party included Radushdukka (probably Darius's sister and the wife of Gobryas), a lady called Radushnamuya, and another woman about whom one of the tablets provides the following information:

36 [BAR] of flour was received by the wife of Mardonius, the king's daughter, for rations, 9 BAR a day. [A delivery in] Kurdushum, [one in] Bezitme and 2 [in] Litu were received by her. She had a sealed document from the king. 23rd year, 12th month.

So accompanying Gobryas, who incidentally received the largest rations reported in our sources, was Artazostra, the wife of Mardonius and daughter of Darius. This confirms the marriage reported by Herodotus, but shows that it had taken place long before 493 BC. One final example:

3. Darius's brother Artaphernes is known as satrap of Sardis between 511 and 492 BC. The fact that he was staying there in Asia Minor in November 495 is confirmed by a Persepolis text:

4.65 BAR of flour was received by Tauhma. 23 men [received] one and a half QA each. 12 boys [servants] received 1 QA each. He carried a sealed document from Artaphernes [Elam. *Irdapirna*]. They went forth from Sardis. They went to Persepolis. 9th month, 27th year. [At] Hidali.

The second most important person in the texts after Gobryas, judging by the amount of his rations alone, was the head of the entire economic and administrative system, Farnaka (Elam. *Parnaka*, Greek *Pharnakes*), an uncle of the king's. He received, at any place and at any time, a daily allowance of two sheep, 90 QA of wine and 180 QA of flour. The large rations he received show that they were not intended for the consumption of one person, though they did not include provisions for the servants either, since they had their own rations (see below). It is assumed that Farnaka and his kind exchanged the foodstuffs they did not need on local markets or stored them up as reserves. This roundabout way of exploiting natural produce is thought to have been the reason why it was later decided to make (partial) payments in silver, as documented by the Treasury Tablets. We shall come across Farnaka again in his capacity as chief administrator. The following text also refers to him:

48 BAR of flour, provided by Patiaspa [in] Varataukash, was received by Farnaka for rations. For 1 day, on the 20th year, in ... month. Every day, Farnaka together with his boys receive 48 BAR. Farnaka himself receives 18 BAR, his 300 boys 1 QA each.

With his staff, we have arrived at the lowest rung of the ration ladder: 1 and 1.5 QA of flour were the rule for grown-ups; children and adolescents received less. However, these and other minimum wage earners could also obtain special allowances (*sat, kamakaš*). Above the minimum wage level, graduations or rises in salary can be noticed, evidently based on differences of skill or training.

It has been assumed that the individuals referred to in these tablets, some of whom were employed in family groups or lived together, on the one hand received cereals/flour and wine/beer as staples, as well as figs/nuts and small rations of meat as special allowances, and on the other hand were entitled to private exploitation of land (a garden or field) and to keep small livestock, and were provided with essential clothing.

But who were these 'employees of the crown', as they have been called? Since they included numerous members of subject nations, it was for a long time believed that these people, who were called *kurtaš* (in Elamite), were slaves or enslaved individuals (perhaps prisoners of war). Today they are regarded rather as workers whom the state administration obliged to carry out certain activities, for which they were paid. They were controlled in their doings, and the form of their appointment and banishment to places that were distant from their homeland clearly points to coercion (deportation?) and commitment (to the soil).

2. Functionaries, domestic staff and artisans; royal domains and peasant holdings: administration and economy in Achaemenid Persis

Through the discovery of the tablets, Persepolis has also emerged as an administrative centre. For some time (505–497 BC), Farnaka was at the head of it, with his representative Chiçavahush at his side, and they were both assisted by clerks and an 'office' with 'scribes' and auxiliary personnel in Persepolis and elsewhere. The function of Farnaka (aided by Chiçavahush) consisted of furnishing the necessary documents for people travelling at his behest (such as judges, accountants and auditors, leaders of caravans, as well as escorts for official embassies, catering personnel for the king, etc.), organizing the royal storehouse, looking after the king's stables, seeing to religious matters, hiring additional manpower when necessary, and supervising and controlling payments of taxes and rents. All these tasks required him to travel a great deal, as witnessed by the occasions on which his name is mentioned and his seal is affixed. His actual place, however, was at the side of the king, while his representative kept in touch with both. We have already had a little glimpse of the scope of Farnaka's activities with his order for the 'disbursement' of natural produce to Artystone. His 'spot-checks' are attested by his seal on allowance tablets from Dainuka, Rakha, Baraspa and Runan dating from the nineteenth year of Darius's reign. Here is an example of a project handled by Farnaka:

Tell Syaina the 'wine carrier' [in Rautanayacha]: Farnaka spoke as follows: '1404 *marriš* [jugs of] wine shall be issued to Artamazda ... [for] distribution [to] artisans [in] Persepolis ... Let him take [with him] [the wine for] distribution to them [for]

the 8th and 9th month, thus two months altogether, in the 21st year [of Darius].'
Savanta wrote [the text], the message [with the order] was communicated by Varaza,
he received the order from Raibaya. In the 21st year, in the 6th month, this sealed
document was handed over.

The outcome is the following 'routine'. Two months before the period for
which the wine was actually needed, Farnaka issued an order via Raibaya to
the 'office' saying that they should instruct the 'wine carrier' Syaina to deliver
14,040 litres of wine to Artamazda for the group of artisans in Persepolis.
Through Varaza this order reached Savanta, the 'scribe'. Savanta then prepared two copies of a document (or had them prepared), of which one
remained in the Persepolis archives, the other (as the original) was handed to
Artamazda (this is shown by the name Artamazda written on the duplicate
in Aramaic). In Rautanayacha, Artamazda then apparently showed Syaina
the original order and received the goods, with which he returned to Persepolis on the eighth month, as scheduled.

Below the level of central administration were two 'officials' (their Old
Persian title was *grdapatiš* ['guardians of the house']) with their representatives, each of whom was responsible for hiring and supplying workers in
one half of the areas covered by the tablets (and hence also for farming and
tax payments). Their subordinates were the leaders of the 'boards of management' of an administrative district (six of which have been ascertained),
whose duties included catering for the court whenever it travelled within
their district. The Elamite title for their agents was *ullira* ('procurement
officers'). On the 'district' or local level, the officials were identified by their
accountability for certain products and had their own delegates and store-
keepers. Local officials for the workers, who were themselves grouped
together under 'foremen', formed the bottom end of the hierarchy.

It is only in the Treasury Tablets that we come across a high official
whose Elamite title was *kap.niškira* (OP *ganzabara*, 'treasure-keeper'), and
who was instructed by the successors in Farnaka's office to pay out amounts
of unminted silver to the workers of the crown. He manifestly had under his
control all (so far 19 known) 'treasuries' of Persis and the workers employed
in them. These individuals, of whom there were hundreds, are perhaps best
described as 'skilled artisans', with an emphasis on gold and silver work and
the production of furniture and textiles – in short, the supply of luxury
articles to the king and the court. Some names of activities have remained
undecipherable to this day. In the treasuries, which, as already mentioned,
also served as collecting points for precious objects, 'procurement officers'

and 'scribes' saw to supplying the materials and duly delivering the goods produced. An example of a rather modest group of treasury workers may serve as an illustration:

228 [BAR] of cereals, procured by Bagaicha [the director of the granary of Vrantush] were received by treasury workers ... [in] Vrantush, whose allowances are dealt with by Baratkama [the treasurer], as rations for 1 month, [namely] the 13th, in the 27th year. 2 men, 'tailors of ornamental dress', 4 [BAR] each; 20 men, treasury [workers], 3.5 [each]; 7 men, 'precision craftsmen', 3 [each]; 19 men, 'furniture conservators', 3 [each]; 14 men, 'wood carriers', 3 [each]; 1 man, a 'domestic servant?', 3. (In addition) 3 boys (with each) 0.5 (BAR), 4 women [with each] 3, 3 girls [with each] 0.5 [BAR]. That makes 77 workers.

Apart from the treasury workers, there were many other individuals in the service of the state or the king, who therefore appear in the Persepolis texts. They fill up the medium and lower ranks of the administrative echelons, working in the fields or in cattle-breeding, preparing food or manufacturing tools.

All these people were given rations for 'wages' or 'maintenance', differentiated according to their status, position, training or kind of activity. How were these allowances procured? Although we were able to exonerate Herodotus from the reproach of ignorance when he declared that Persis was exempt from paying *tribute*, it is nevertheless true that people had to pay duties and taxes there (though indeed no tribute). Taxes (Elam. *bāzi[š]* = OP *bāǧi* [the king's part]) (and special taxes?) formed, together with the revenues from the royal domains, the very foundations of the redistributive economy of Persis and appear as such in the tablets. As to who had to pay them and in what amount, the tablets say next to nothing. There are many indications to the effect that free peasants, tenants and great landowners had to make such 'payments', perhaps depending on their income. Several investigations have led to postulating a strictly organized system of levying taxes (with its corresponding functional apparatus), based on the 'tithe', but the philological foundations for these theories have not remained unchallenged.

Let us turn to the large properties and estates owned by the king and the aristocracy, which are mentioned in the tablets, as well as in testimonies from Babylonia and elsewhere:

Tell Shalamanu that Artystone spoke as follows: 'From my property [Elam. *ulhi*] [in] Kuganaka 100 *marriš* of wine are to be delivered to Gaushapana, the head accountant. Irtima [is] the *hirakurra* [?]' [In the] 22nd year [this] sealed document was [delivered].

Aside from Artystone's estates (palaces?), a 'village' owned by the queen is also mentioned. Similar possessions are equally attested for her son Arsames, for Artabama, and for the king himself. Even more numerous than the records from Persepolis are those in classical texts and in documents from Babylonia, to which reference has already been made. As in Babylonia, so in Persis, too, part of this land may have been farmed out against 'interest payments' (or forced labour?). Among the royal (and aristocratic) domains those that were both profitable and 'pleasant' stood out. Xenophon, who knew his way about the Persian empire, writes on this subject:

Yet further, continued Socrates, in all the districts he resides in and visits, he [the king] takes care that there are 'paradises', as they call them, full of all the good and beautiful things that the soil will produce, and in this he himself spends most of his time, except when the season precludes it.

Such gardens, often combined with exploitable plantations and game parks, were copied by the Achaemenid kings from models of their Assyrian and Elamite predecessors. Our modern word 'paradise' goes back via the Greek *paradeisos* to Old Persian *paridaida*, which designates this kind of park, thus bearing witness even today to the impression such 'settings' made on their environment and on posterity. At least fifteen *paradeisoi* (Elam. *partetaš*) are mentioned in the tablets, but here they more generally refer to a royal domain. We may safely assume that in Persis, too, royal agents supervised and controlled not only the properties and parks of the king, but also those belonging to other people.

As for the country, he [the king] personally examines so much of it as he sees in the course of his progress through it; and he receives reports from his trusted agents on the territories that he does not see for himself. To those governors [*archontes*] who are able to show him that their country is densely populated and that the land is under cultivation and well stocked with the trees of the district and with the crops, he assigns more territory and gives presents, and rewards them with seats of honour. Those whose territory he finds uncultivated and thinly populated either through harsh administration or through contempt or through carelessness, he punishes, and appoints others to take their office.

To increase the yield of such lands, the Persians practised artificial irrigation by using the groundwater, which they led to their fields through long subterranean canals (Arabic *qanāts*), exploiting the natural slopes of the landscape. Coffer-dams were also built for this and other purposes (canalization of water, storing up drinking-water).

The landed estates with their surplus production, the practice of payments in kind that sometimes considerably exceeded the self-sufficiency level, as well as the partial conversion of this system to payments in unminted silver – all these factors point to the conclusion that there must have been local markets, where part of the rations could be exchanged (for 'non-perishable' goods or money) and where things could be purchased that people could not manufacture themselves or buy in their own village (from village artisans?).

The daily nourishment [of the Persians] ... consists of bread, barley-cake [*maza*], cardamum [a kind of cress], grains of salt and roast or boiled meat; with it they drink water.

Strabo's report about the eating habits of Persians is confirmed and complemented by the Persepolis tablets. According to these, barley, milled or crushed and then made into bread or mash, was indeed a staple food, while meat (chiefly goat or mutton, but also poultry) formed the exception and, organized similarly to the Roman *pastio villatica*, determined the royal menu in its many variants. In Persis, people drank almost exclusively date or grape wine, and they drank it neat, as the Greeks were surprised to discover. A kind of wine vinegar together with salt served to preserve food. In Elam, as the Fortification Tablets attest, there was a preference for (stout) beer, so that one and the same person was allotted wine in Persis, but the same quantity of beer in Elam. Fruit such as figs and dates, as well as mulberries, plums, apples, pears and quinces, almonds, walnuts and pistachios are also mentioned, but others that were known in antiquity as typical 'Persian fruit' (pomegranates, peaches, citrus fruits, etc.) are known to us only from classical sources. Vegetables, herbs and dairy products are also absent or rare in the Persepolis texts (unless they are as yet concealed behind inexplicable Elamite words), but they are also to be assumed as basic foodstuffs.

3. Roads and canals, towns and villages, messengers and fire signals: infrastructure and communications in Iran

... 3 [*marriš* of wine] were received as allowances by Hambadush [and] his 4 companions, lance-bearers [and] road controllers [?], who previously had gone along the Ramitebe road and measured [inspected?] it, then at his [the king's] command [?] had come to Hadahra and waited there for the king. [For] 6 days [in the] 8th month of the 21st year, they each received 1 QA [per day] ...

A significant part of the texts from Persepolis consists of what their publisher has described as 'travel-ration texts'. They provide information about the numerous individuals who were *en route* (either in an official capacity or privately), communicating messages, transporting goods or money, or travelling on festive occasions, or else as hired labourers or for controlling purposes. Among them were our 'road controllers', but there were also 'travelling companions' who escorted and protected visitors or embassies, 'caravan leaders' and auxiliary personnel. Also attested are 'express messengers' on their way to or from the king:

1.5 [?] QA of flour, procured by Bagadushta, was received by Mushka as express messenger. He was on his way from the king to Chiçavahush [Farnaka's delegate]. He carried a sealed document from the king. In the 10th month.

Road watchmen and express messengers are not only known to us from the Fortification Tablets, for Herodotus also mentions *hodophylakai* (road watchmen) who were outsmarted by the Spartan King Demaratus while he was living in exile in Susa and trying to inform his countrymen of the forthcoming campaign of Xerxes, which he did by hiding a message under the wax of a wooden tablet. Express messengers, too, are familiar from Western testimonies. Placed under an *astandēs* (leader of the 'postal' system) as runners and relay riders, they represented, together with communication by fire signals, calling posts and light or mirror installations, the features of a system that made a great impression on Greeks and Romans, and it is to them that we owe the knowledge of this set-up. The basis for such an elaborate communications system was the infrastructure of the Persian empire, which was equally praised and copied, particularly its network of roads. When the Persians followed on from the Elamite, Median, Assyrian, Babylonian, Lydian and Egyptian kings, they found some well tried structures already in place. There existed ancient – sometimes very ancient – caravan tracks as well as roads. Within or in the vicinity of important cities in the Assyrian and Babylonian lands these roads were already paved with stone or bricks or provided with a bitumen surface. This network of roads and tracks was now developed, extended and surveyed by the Persians. The 'imperial roads' served primarily for the quick transportation of troops and material, as well as to deliver information within the shortest possible time. The best-known among them was the 'royal road', for which ample evidence is found in classical sources, and which linked Sardis (or Ephesus) via Asia Minor and Mesopotamia with Susa. However, overland trade – with the exception of luxury goods – can only have been significant over relatively short distances, in view of the high cost of transportation. In the Fortification Tablets, the 600 km link between Susa and Persepolis is frequently mentioned. Due to contemporary geographical and topographical factors and archaeological findings, as well as ancient references to certain localities along this road, the discovery not only of its route, but even of a sequence of 22 (post) stations along it has been claimed. What Herodotus reports about the road from Sardis to Susa probably applies to this part of the road, too:

At intervals all along the road are royal stages [*stathmoi basilēioi*] with excellent inns [*katalyseis*], and the road itself is safe to travel by, as it never leaves inhabited country.

The protection of men and material was secured by forts and by the road watchmen already referred to. So it is not surprising that royal messages could be communicated within the shortest of times.

There is nothing in the world which travels faster than these Persian couriers ... It is said that men and horses are stationed along the road, equal in number to the number of days the journey takes – a man and a horse for each day. Nothing stops these couriers from covering their allotted stage in the quickest possible time – neither snow, rain, heat, nor darkness ... The Persian word for this form of post is *angareion*.

Further roads known to us are the one leading from Persepolis to Ecbatana and Media, of which a section cut out of the rocks near Pasargadae has been discovered; and the very ancient route from Mesopotamia to Media, where it linked up with the road running via Bactria to India and further on through Central to Eastern Asia, later to become known as the 'Silk Road'. The Persepolis texts mention travellers going from Susa or Persepolis to Media, Egypt, Bactria, Kerman, Aria, Sagartia, Babylonia, Maka (on the northern shore of the Persian Gulf?), Arachosia and Hindush (southern Pakistan?) and vice-versa.

While the routes leading through deserts could hardly have been built roads, but tracks well known to the caravan leaders, those in Asia Minor and Iran, which often had Assyrian, Hittite and other precedents, were in very good condition. Although they were unpaved, Aristophanes already reports that even carriages could easily travel on them. These roads were equally suitable for military purposes such as the rapid transportation of soldiers, military vehicles, material and luggage, and for civilian use including the conveyance of men, animals and goods and the transmission of news.

The major roads were measured in stades and parasangs (1 p. = *c.* 5–6 km), and if Megasthenes's information about 'India' also applied to other roads in the Near East, they were equipped with columns indicating the distances and turn-offs at each interval of 10 stades. That there existed a kind of 'milestone' is proved both by the word parasang, which has been interpreted as 'indicator, announcer' and construed as the term for a milestone, and by the discovery of a marker of this type in Pasargadae, dating from the early Hellenistic period.

Only recently has it become apparent that Darius was also interested in developing Elam into a 'maritime province'. Thus Susa was eventually to be connected with the sea, and – by settling (deported) Greeks and Carians with maritime experience in southern Babylonia and Elam – Persian maritime authority in the Gulf was to be secured.

And what about Persis itself? How are we to imagine its population?

Persis is locked in on one side by a continuous chain of mountains … and where the mountains end, the sea laps against it as a further bulwark. At the foot of the mountains stretches a vast plain, fertile land abounding in many villages and cities … No other region in all Asia is considered to be more beneficial to one's health …

The Alexandrian authors, in this case Curtius Rufus, pointed out the dense population, the fertility of the soil and the climatic advantages of Persis, qualities that can only be imagined today. These authors confirm the impression produced by archaeological surveys in the Persepolis region, which is also conveyed by the tablets:

18 marriš of wine, procured by Huçaya, were received by Bagabadush, the 'travelling companion'. He gave [it] to 547 Egyptian workers. They were on their way to Tauka. He carried a sealed document from Bagapana [the satrap of Elam]. 21st year.

This was the place (probably to be identified with the Taokē mentioned by Ptolemy, the geographer) where hundreds of other kurtaš were summoned as manpower from Thracia, Lycia or Cappadocia. Here, as in the many other places referred to in the tablets, there would hardly have been only individuals of this status living and working, but free Persian peasants, artisans and even landowners (together with the people they employed) are not recorded by our royal administration and economy. That it was not Alexander who urbanized Iran is already attested in a short passage by Eratosthenes, who describes Indians and Arianoi (probably meaning Iranians altogether) as 'city dwellers' (asteioi) among the barbarians. Many individual testimonies for cities founded in Iran by the Achaemenids have been adduced later. Though they also include a great number of settlements in Persis, these residences, which were presumably built of sun-dried clay bricks, have unfortunately disappeared.

Only the monumental residential buildings and administrative centres have survived, thus as an example of a fortified administrative centre with treasury and warehouses, the terrace complex of Pasargadae. In addition, tableware, furniture, garments and finery, almost exclusively of a luxurious type, have come down to us as individual pieces or portrayed on reliefs and other materials.

4. 'Scheming queens' and 'effeminate princes'? On men's and women's roles and on education in Achaemenid Iran. The alleged 'decadence' of the late Persian empire

He [Cyrus] ... did not know, however, that his intended heirs were not being instructed in the traditional Persian discipline. This discipline (the Persians being shepherds, and sons of a stony soil) was a tough one, capable of producing hardy shepherds who could camp out and keep awake on watch and turn soldier if necessary. He just didn't notice that women and eunuchs had given his sons the education of a Mede, and that it had been debased by their so-called 'blessed' status. That is why Cyrus' children turned out as children naturally do when their teachers have never corrected them. So, when they succeeded to their inheritance on the death of Cyrus, they lived in a riot of unrestrained debauchery. First, unwilling to tolerate an equal, one of them killed the other.

In the 3rd book of his 'Laws', his last and longest dialogue, Plato looks back over the historical evolution of existing forms of government and discusses, among others, the Persian empire. To him it embodied a regime that did not, like Sparta or Crete, provide for a well balanced relationship between the understanding, freedom and harmony of its citizens, which would have given it stability, but instead excessively strengthened sovereign power. Thus a monarchy led by an intelligent ruler (Cyrus) became an oppressive despotism, a sequence which was moreover repeated under Darius and his successors. As can be gathered from the quotation above, the partners to the dialogue attribute this disastrous development to the education of the king's sons by the women (and eunuchs) of the royal house, an education that must have turned them into effeminate, undisciplined and dissolute men.

A similar image of the negative influence of women of the royal household and of life at court can be found by the start of the fourth century BC in Ctesias, the Greek physician in ordinary to the Persian king Artaxerxes II. Here, however, the actual reason for the instability of Persian sovereignty is not sought in the education of the king's sons, but in the political intrigues of women and eunuchs. The idea of the degeneracy of the Persian character, which we find in the Greek literature of that period, and of the resulting decline of Persian power at the latest from the reign of Xerxes, is particularly evident in the works of Xenophon and Isocrates. In the last chapter of the 8th book of the *Cyropaedia*, Xenophon compares the customs and usages in Persia during the brilliant period under Cyrus, the founder of the empire, with those of his Persian contemporaries, especially with respect to their educational system, and finds that the causes for their downfall lie above all in the change of the *contents* of education: in the abandonment of genuine instruction in horsemanship and hunting, 'where they could prove themselves and honourably put themselves to the test'. At the same time, Xenophon explains the downturn, which to his mind had already begun with the death of Cyrus and had not ceased since then, by blaming it on the faithlessness of kings with regard to promises they had made, on their godlessness and injustice, but especially on their 'effeminacy' (*thrypsis*). The latter, he maintained, manifested itself in opulent meals, as well as in clothes and palace installations, in the abandonment of physical training and in a lack of fighting spirit. In addition, the orator Isocrates, in his great appeals for an all-Greek venture against the great king, mentioned the military weakness of the Persian empire in the fourth century BC, which he ascribed to the effeminacy and servile character of the Persians.

However, there had already been earlier authors who had seen dangers brewing for the mighty Persian empire. The idea of the great king as a despot to whom even the highest dignitaries appeared like slaves can be traced back to the fifth century BC. In Aeschylus's *The Persians*, certain elementary analogies – unlimited personal power, the feeling of being above the law, the lack of accountability, the display of splendour – serve to identify the image of the great king (embodied specifically by Xerxes) with the negative idea of the tyrant that was in the process of being formed at the time, and left a lasting impression on it. The Persian king was from then on considered as the tyrant *par excellence*. Inquiries into the causes for the astonishing victories of the Greeks found a solution in the idea that the independence and strength of the Hellene sprang from his awareness of his individual and collective freedom.

There was in fact nothing new in the idea that power would lead its possessor to luxury and self-indulgence and thus weaken him, so that a dominant people would sooner or later lose its fighting power and succumb to the unchecked energy of a poor but unspoilt people. In the fifth century

BC, this idea was connected with those socio-medical theories that saw a direct relationship between a region's climate, fertility and human stock, as did the Hippocratic writing 'Airs, Waters, Places'. In so far as it leads to the conclusion that a change in the living conditions of a people will make itself felt in their character and behaviour, this theory is of practical value. Regarding its use in the interpretation of history, Herodotus provides us with an impressive testimony in an anecdote at the end of his work, in which he anticipates Xenophon and Isocrates: Cyrus is pressed by his Persians to let them, as would be appropriate for a dominant people, leave their small, rough homeland and settle in one of the rich countries that they would be able to conquer. The king replied:

that they might act upon it if they pleased, but added the warning that, if they did so, they must prepare themselves to rule no longer, but to be ruled by others. 'Soft countries', he said, 'breed soft men. It is not the property of any one soil to produce fine fruits and good soldiers too.'

The Persians had to admit that this was true, continues Herodotus, 'and chose rather to live in a rugged land and rule than to cultivate rich plains and be slaves'.

Nevertheless, they eventually succumbed to the temptations conjured up by their power, and their defeat at the hands of the Greeks, a poor people in a rough country, marked the decline of their strength: such, at any rate, is Herodotus's interpretation of the deeper meaning of historical events.

So neither the idea of rising or falling empires, nor the thought of the pernicious effect of luxury on victorious peoples, or the identification of the great king with a tyrant or possessor of slaves, was anything new to the Greek literature of the fourth century BC. What was new was Ctesias's description of the royal court as a petticoat government full of immorality, intrigues and toadyism, Plato's judgement about the part played by forms of education in the fall of the empire, and Xenophon's and Isocrates's general contempt for Persian fighting power. In the great orator, various motives combined to lead to an almost commonplace contempt of barbarians. The Greeks' original concept of barbarians, which (according to a pattern shared by many peoples) was meant to demarcate their own culture from the entire outside world, had since the mid-fifth century not only narrowed down to the Persians alone, but also acquired unmistakably pejorative features. Isocrates adopted the resulting – and mainly Attic – hostile attitude of caricaturing the barbarians, and even coarsened and simplified it. The war he contemplated was to be waged against 'enemies by nature' (*physei polemioi*), and thus find its moral justification. Because of their inferior nature, the barbarians deserved nothing better than to become Greek subjects, *perioikes*, as Isocrates said with a pointed hint against Sparta. And while Herodotus had found the cause of the age-old antagonism between the world of the barbarians and that of the Hellenes in the overlapping of their geographical living spaces, and had logically advocated their disentanglement, even if it meant abandoning Asia Minor, Isocrates, for his part, called for the conquest of the barbarian territory in Asia.

How are we to explain such Greek portrayals of 'Persian decadence', and how far are they supported by Persian traditions? The Persian educational system and the relations between men and women may serve as illustrations. We have already mentioned the deeper sense of accumulating treasures, over and above the mere wish for a display of luxury. This sense was either absent in the Greeks or held back for the sake of argument. As for the alleged decline of the Persian fighting morale, we shall have more to say on the subject.

Herodotus stated that the Persians taught their sons 'three things only from their fifth to their twentieth year: horsemanship, bowmanship and telling the truth'. This quotation can be juxtaposed with Xenophon's remarks in his *Anabasis* and in the first book of the *Cyropaedia* about the practice of education under Cyrus. However, in the last chapter of his *Mirror for Princes*, Xenophon describes the decline of the educational system. By abandoning riding and hunting, the sons of kings and aristocrats neglected strengthening and testing their physical forces, and by accepting bribery as a means to settle conflicts, they lost the feeling for justice. It is obvious, however, that the educational themes of early Persia, as reported by Herodotus and Xenophon, reflect a 'code of behaviour', and hence rules that were meant to form the qualities of sovereigns. This was precisely how Darius understood them and claimed to have followed them according to his lower epitaph:

By the favour of Ahura Mazda I am of such a sort that I am a friend to right, I am not a friend to wrong ... What is right, that is my desire. I am not a friend to the man who is a lie-follower ... Trained am I both with hands and with feet. As a horseman I am a good horseman. As a bowman I am a good bowman both afoot and on horseback.

This kind of code, this kind of self-assessment, naturally says nothing about the actual behaviour of the ruler, and justice and truthfulness are determined

Plate I. ABOVE. Rock relief with inscriptions at Bisutun in western Iran represents Darius the Great after his victory over Gaumata and other rebel kings.

Plate II. BELOW. Persepolis, one of the royal capitals of the Persian empire, was built by Darius the Great, embellished by his son Xerxes and grandson Artaxerxes and virtually destroyed by Alexander the Great.

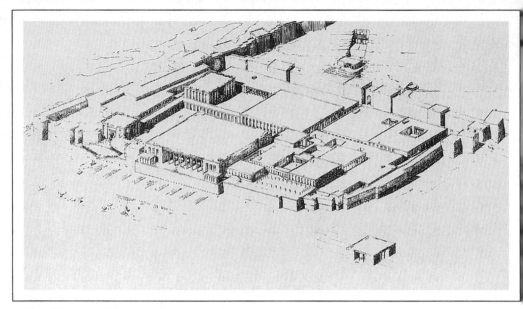

Plate III. ABOVE. The view of Persepolis from the south-west is dominated in the foreground by the Apadana which was the imperial throne room.

Plate IV. BELOW. The Persepolis relief on the eastern staircase of the Apadana shows delegations from the different peoples of the Achaemenid empire coming to present gifts to their king.

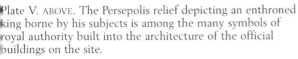

Plate V. ABOVE. The Persepolis relief depicting an enthroned king borne by his subjects is among the many symbols of royal authority built into the architecture of the official buildings on the site.

Plate VI. ABOVE RIGHT. In Pasargadae, early capital of Cyrus the Great, the Zindan-i Sulaiman (Solomon's Prison) was probably used for royal investitures.

Plate VII. BELOW. The tomb of Cyrus the Great at Pasargadae, 30km north-east of Persepolis, was built before the king's death in 530 BC. The monument complemented the nearby buildings, which were part of this early Achaemenid capital before Persepolis was built.

Plate VIII. RIGHT. The headless statue of Darius the Great, excavated at Susa, shows the king wearing the long Persian robe. The base of the statue depicts representatives of the different peoples of the empire in their various national costumes.

Plate IX. ABOVE. Near Persepolis, Naqsh-i Rustam was a complex of Achaemenid royal tombs carved into the mountains; only the tomb of Darius the Great has been positively identified. Other tombs, all robbed in antiquity, are thought to have belonged to Xerxes I, Artaxerxes I and Darius II.

Plate Xa. BELOW LEFT. An Achaemenid royal tomb at Naqsh-i Rustam, possibly belonging to Xerxes I.

Plate Xb. BELOW RIGHT. The Ka'ba-i Zardusht at Naqsh-i Rustam, the purpose of which has so far not been identified, probably dates from the time of Darius the Great. In Sasanian times King Shapur I used one of its walls to record his victories over the Romans.

Plate XIa. LEFT. Gold coin from the time of Darius the Great depicts a royal archer with bow and arrow. Coins of this kind were used by the Achaemenid Royal Treasury for patronage and reward but not for the commercial transactions of the people.

Plate XIb. BELOW MIDDLE. The so-called 'Cyrus Cylinder' from Babylon, written on clay in cuneiform script, was an Achaemenid propaganda document intended to legitimize and glorify Cyrus's rule in Babylonia.

Plate XII. BELOW LOWER. The 'Treasury Relief' in Persepolis, so-called because it was removed after a power struggle from the staircase of the Apadana to the relative obscurity of the Royal Treasury, depicts the Persian king and the crown-prince behind him receiving homage from a high functionary.

Plate XIIIa. ABOVE TOP. An Elamite tablet written in the Elamite cuneiform script and found in Persepolis bears a seal which indicates its purpose as an official document. Administrative records from the different corners of Fars/Persis were regularly stored at Persepolis.

Plate XIIIb. ABOVE MIDDLE. Achaemenid seals such as this often depict women at court, suggesting an active social and political role for them in society.

Plate XIIIc. ABOVE. Hunting scenes were a popular form of Achaemenid seal design. This modern drawing of a seal shows the design chosen by Artabama, a female member of the royal house.

Plate XIV. RIGHT. Figures of King Darius's bodyguard decorated the palace at Susa. This glazed polychrome brick relief is typical of the winged and human figures which embellished the walls of Achaemenid palaces.

Plate XVa. ABOVE LEFT. A coin of the second century BC of the independent prince Vadfradad I. In the Hellenistic period local rulers in southern Iran (Fars/Persis) minted coins both in their capacity as vassals to the Seleucids and as independent rulers. *Obverse:* head of the ruler wearing a satrap's tiara. *Reverse:* coronation scene with a curious mixture of Iranian and Greek motifs.

Plate XVb. ABOVE RIGHT. An inscribed shard *(ostracon in Greek)* from Nisa, an early capital of the Parthians, in today's Turkmenistan.

Plate XVc. BELOW. The Parthian rock relief at Khung-i Nauruzi in south-western Iran shows the Parthian-Elymean inclination to follow Achaemenid traditions of commemorative rock carvings.

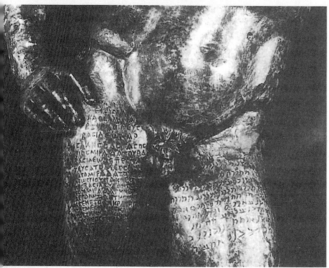

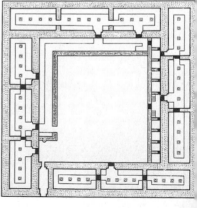

Plate XVIa. ABOVE TOP. Stone relief of a seated King Artabanus IV, handing the ring of power to the standing satrap of Susa, shows that Parthian rulers were no less adept than their Achaemenid precursors at the public manifestation of royal power.

Plate XVIb. ABOVE RIGHT. This statue of the Greek god Heracles found in Seleucia in Mesopotamia was brought there by the Parthian king Vologeses IV to signify his victory over the king of Mesene; from whom he had captured it.

Plate XVIc. ABOVE. Parthian kings would record their victories with inscriptions. On this curiously chosen part of the Heracles statue the inscription appears in Greek and Parthian.

Plate XVIIa and b. RIGHT. Nisa, in present Turkmenistan, was an early Parthian capital. This modern reconstruction and plan depict the so-called 'Mausoleum' or 'Temple' at the New Nisa and the 'Treasury' or 'Spare House' of Old Nisa.

as virtues in terms of their usefulness to him. When in the *Cyropaedia* Xenophon laments the loss of these virtues immediately after the death of Cyrus, he is not doing so in order to report historical facts, but as a man of letters. He is underlining the extraordinary qualities of his ideal ruler and the need for such qualities in his own time. That the Persians always considered military capacities and tenacity during a hunt as the virtues of a ruler, but that the test of weapons and hunting were also features of royal and aristocratic everyday life, is attested – still in the fourth century and later – by the *paradeisoi*, as well as the numerous images on coins, seals and reliefs representing the king as a bowman or on a hunt. We might also point to the influence of such motifs on the artistic and inscriptional self-representation of local princes in Asia Minor during the Persian period. Thus the Lycian dynast Arbinas is praised as follows in a verse inscription from the beginning of the fourth century: 'Everything in which wise men excel distinguishes you: bowmanship, virtue and hunting on horseback.'

Nor are Plato's remarks about the causes of Persian despotism to be interpreted as historical statements or descriptions of Persian reality of the fourth century. They have their place in the political theory of the philosopher, and in his ideas about the best-governed state or – in the 'Laws' – at least a well governed state, in which the most important thing is the morally good life of the citizens. This requires, according to Plato, a radically reformed education, and so it is not surprising that he blames the mistaken education of the king's sons as the main cause for the downfall of the Persian state.

Even the pernicious role attributed to the women of the Achaemenid house, for instance by Ctesias, should not be considered as historical fact, but as a literary cliché. These stories no doubt reflect the misogynistic tendency of some of the Greek literature of the fifth and fourth centuries, which perceived women as a threatening element to the political world of men. If the stories about intriguing women do contain a grain of historical truth, then it is because in a centrally ruled system in a society of tribal origin, political marriages contracted in order to ensure loyalty were particularly important, especially since the question of succession to the throne in the polygamous Persian royal house was liable to assume vital significance. The so-called 'divided loyalties' of women, suggested by Ctesias for the reign of Artaxerxes II and by Herodotus for the women surrounding Xerxes, may have been expressions of such tensions within the ruling system, but they are hardly of historical use in terms of individual portraits of women.

The marriage policy of the Achaemenid rulers, which was first directed towards the families of the high aristocracy (to secure their loyalty), and later on sought to link the dynasty with the family of the founder of the empire (under Gaumata and Darius), had changed under Darius's successors. An effort was now being made to ensure the reign, mainly by alliances within the royal family itself. Unions with the high aristocracy were now formed not so much in order to establish and ensure its loyalty, but to reward it for its proven faithfulness and services. Endogamous unions, such as marriages between brother and sister or father and daughter, particularly preoccupied the Greeks:

This, they say, was the beginning [the assassination of his brother]; and the next crime Cambyses committed was the murder of his sister who had come with him to Egypt. This woman was his sister by both parents, and also his wife, though it had never before been a Persian custom for brothers and sisters to marry. Cambyses got over the difficulty in the following way: having fallen in love with one of his sisters and wishing afterwards to take the illegal step of making her his wife, he summoned the royal judges and asked them if there was any law in the country which allowed a man to marry his sister if he wished to do so ... When, therefore, Cambyses put his question, they managed to find an answer which would neither violate the truth nor endanger their own necks: namely, that though they could discover no law which allowed brother to marry sister, there was undoubtedly a law which permitted the king of Persia to do what he pleased ... Cambyses accordingly married the sister he was in love with, and not long afterwards married another one as well ...

It is clearly Herodotus's intention here to present Cambyses's marriage with his sister as another of his crimes, crimes that are to a great extent unhistorical. We must also be rather cautious with regard to the death of his sister, in drawing conclusions about the involvement of Cambyses. His unions with his sisters, with the one who had remained unnamed and died (Roxane?) and with Atossa, were formed because his marriage with Phaidyme – the daughter of Otanes – had apparently remained childless (or without a son), which would have made his brother Bardiya and the latter's descendants his successors to the throne. Neither Atossa nor Roxane were full sisters of Cambyses, they were his half-sisters, and only this kind of 'brother–sister marriage' was contracted by the Achaemenids, if they did not marry altogether more distant members of the clan or family.

The union between Artaxerxes II and his daughter Atossa, too, which Plutarch so fiercely criticized as incestuous (thereby also censuring the unlimited power of the king), only becomes intelligible at a second glance. If it had taken place at all, and if Atossa did not simply assume the *position* of a 'wife of the king' (the actual 'wife of the king' [Greek *gynē tou basileōs*] was always the mother of the heir to the throne), then the reason for this 'marriage' is to be seen in the king's wish to have a loyal person holding the position of 'wife of the king' after the death of Parysatis, and thus to secure the status of the heir to the throne at court.

Polygamy was a characteristic of Achaemenid marriage practice. The children from these unions were destined to be heirs to the throne (the king chose one of his sons for this purpose), to attain responsible positions in the service of the empire or the court, and – as potential candidates for marriage – contribute to securing the solidarity of the clan and the bond with the aristocracy.

We have already come across female members of the royal house (Elam. *dukšiš*) in the Persepolis tablets. There was Artystone, who owned several estates, Artazostra, the wife of Mardonius, Radushdukka, the wife of Gobryas, and Radushnamuya. For Artabama, who also owned an estate, hundreds of labourers (*kurtaš Irdabamana*) worked in Litu, Hidali, Hunar and Shiraz. She herself was often on the move and received huge quantities of provisions. She issued receipts for all her expenses by using her seal, which is known to us (see Plate XIIIc).

All the women of the royal house, in so far as they are mentioned in the Persepolis texts, appear as positively active, enterprising and resolute. They participate in royal festivities and banquets or organize their own feasts, they travel across the country and issue instructions, they watch over their estates and manpower. The Alexander historians also mention them as camp-followers of the king on his campaigns. It is not surprising that some Greeks who believed in the ideal of the (married) woman leading a secluded, irreproachable life also placed the women of the Persian royal family within the 'house':

As a rule, the barbarian peoples are excessively jealous of their wives, and the Persians outdo all others in this respect. Not only their wives, but also their female slaves and concubines are rigorously watched, and no strange eye is allowed to see them. They live locked up in their rooms, and if they have to travel, they do so in carriages hung on all sides with draperies.

The tablets prove that there was no such seclusion. That to a Greek of that type, Persian women appeared as both attractive and dangerous is hardly surprising. If Persian women – behind the palace walls – were also politically active, then this could only be harmful to the house! This kind of opinion, together with Western ideas about Near Eastern palace life (in the 'harem'), has preserved its influence until recent times.

How are we to explain that the idea of 'Persian decadence', to which the scheming women supposedly contributed a good measure, could have exercised such fascination? Let us open a German textbook of Greek history from 1977:

Despite unmistakable aptitudes, the Persians soon fell victims to the impoverishment of the Orient; the end of Persian culture is levelling, not individualization as in Greece. Hellas, on the other hand, again and again over the centuries supplied the Persian empire with new forces and new life through its artists, physicians and scholars; it received nothing or little in return, and for the most part only material return gifts. But the Greek spirit truly became the leaven of a whole world, both West *and* East.

This judgement certainly has its roots on the one hand in the ancient testimonies just presented, and on the other in the view of antiquity in nineteenth-century Germany. Many readers may be familiar with the fact that with the neo-humanistic rediscovery and idealization of Greek culture and the attempt to correlate its achievements and advantages with the nature of the Hellene, the first step had been taken towards measuring our own period against that of the Greeks. The idea arose that the Germans were particularly close to the Greeks of antiquity because of their spiritual and natural affinity. Romantic theories about the ethnic spirit (*volksgeist*) and German national consciousness here found their point of departure.

An idea promulgated in antiquity, but now in full spate, was that of the unbridgeable contrast between the love of freedom of the highly admired Greeks and the despotism of the Persians. This idea played a decisive role in the subsequent appraisal of the ancient Iranians conducted in Germany. At the same time (or as an alternative), an accent was also laid on the contrast between the cultural achievements of the Greeks – supposedly due to the free expansion of the individual personality – and the development of the mental capacities of their eastern neighbours – allegedly hampered by a theocratic and authoritarian hierarchy of priests. This antinomy did not basically change when the kinship between the Iranian (Aryan) and Germanic languages was recognized, and when soon afterwards – in the wake of the theories about national consciousness – there developed the belief in a culturally highly superior Indo-Germanic people and in a close affinity between different Indo-Germanic peoples as to their character and nature. The altogether more positive assessment of the ancient Persians resulting from this theory singled them out from the community of other Near Eastern peoples, but did not change the previous distinct attitude in favour of the Greek (i.e. mainly Athenian) evolution of art, culture and government. It is precisely this approach that is still reflected in recent textbooks.

While historical reflection in nineteenth- and early twentieth-century Germany unanimously accepted the thesis that Persian greatness and power, as well as Persian morals and productivity, declined in the fourth century BC, there has not always been complete agreement – and this applies to the ancient testimonies as well – regarding the causes and manifestations of this decline. Although to clarify such questions, the inquirer usually turned for guidance to Plato, Xenophon, Ctesias, Isocrates and others, National Socialists claimed to have found a way to elicit the *deeper* causes for the negative evolution of the Persian empire. They found it in the racially and biologically determined negative influences of the 'Semitic' Orient on the 'Aryan' Persians. The result was described in 1942 in the *Lingua Tertii Imperii* (Klemperer) by the well-known scholar of Indo-German and Iranian Walter Wüst, who is remembered as the rector of the University of Munich at the time when the Scholls were arrested:

It leads to a mixture of races and thereby to 'degeneration' [*Entartung, Entnordung*]. The inevitable waste of blood of ancient aristocratic families serving in distant outposts of the empire, the 'eradication through climate' [*Klima-Ausmerze*] the 'counter-selection' [*Gegenauslese*] through wars that gradually have to be led by professional armies, the emigration of resident families from their 'hereditary farms' [*Erbhofgeschlechter*] into the capitals and big cities, Susa, Babylon, Ecbatana, and their civilization, and finally the 'disintegrating' [*zersetzende*] influence of the highly developed money economy in Mesopotamia on the traditional economy of natural produce: all that undermined the position of the ruling race and its foundations, 'blood and soil' [*Blut und Boden*].

After the war there again predominated – and that not only in Germany – the idea of the contrast between despotism and liberal development, and of the political, cultural, military and moral decline of the Persian empire after Xerxes. It is only in the last few years that this Hellenocentric view of the history of the Persian empire and of the relationship between Greeks and Persians has been replaced by an opinion that is commensurate with the diversity and expressiveness of the sources, the strengths and weaknesses of Persian rule and the many-sidedness of Graeco-Persian relations.

To go back to the men and women in Achaemenid Persis, it is not only the leading political, social and economic classes of this province that come into view when we study the Fortification Tablets; they also mention thousands of workers who received rations, and the amount of their allowances apparently depended more on their training and type of activity than on their sex. Among the female staff, the *arassap* (sg. *arassara*) stand out, receiving 5 BAR of grains and 3 *marris* of wine, as well as a meat allowance. It was assumed that they were in charge of all the royal manufactures, for instance of groups of female 'dressmakers' (*kurtas f. pasap*), but even of male workers. But according to a more recent investigation, the *arassara* appears to be rather a 'manageress' (on her own) of what was called *pasap*, that is, mainly female groups of workers in the service of members of the royal house, where *pasap* is not to be understood as describing an ethnic group or an activity, but as referring to a certain 'class' of workers. A further designation of this type is believed to be the expression *kurtas f. harrinup*, the term for another predominantly female group of workers. Unlike the *pasap*, the *harrinup* are not to be associated with members of the royal family. Both *pasap* and *harrinup* are recipients of special rations (Elam. *kamakas*), as mentioned above.

6.5 *marris* of beer, procured by Thripata, were received by Arzabara and his colleagues, and they were distributed to 7 women, who had [just] given birth [Elam. *ratip*]: 6 [with] sons, of whom each [receives] 1 *marris*, and one [with] a daughter, who [receives] 0.5. 23rd year. [At] Drthika. [Workers of] Artabama.

13 [BAR] *mitli* and wheat, procured by Thripata, were received by Arzabara and his colleagues, and they were distributed to 7 women, who had [just] given birth. 6 [who had given birth to sons, received] 2 BAR each, and 1 woman [who had given birth to a daughter] 1 BAR. In Drthika. [Workers] of Artabama. 23rd year.

As these texts show, special rations were given to mothers of newborn babies, and here the mothers of sons were clearly preferred to those of daughters. This encouragement, which no doubt also applied to the free women inhabiting Persis, is also mentioned in classical testimonies. Thus Herodotus reports:

After prowess in fighting, the chief proof of manliness is to be the father of a large family of boys. Those who have most sons receive an annual present from the king.

We are reminded of Darius's words at Bisutun, expressing the following wish for his loyal subjects:

If you shall not conceal this record, [but] make [it] known to the people, may Ahura Mazda be friendly to you, and may offspring be to you in great number, and may you live long!

5. *Athanatoi, mistophoroi* and *phrouroi*: levies, mercenaries and garrisons in the Achaemenid empire

The power of the great king depended on the loyalty of his subjects, which they manifested by paying taxes and complying with the duty to join the army. At the same time, both services were means to the king's end of preserving peace and order within the empire and on its borders. The army of the Achaemenid king is familiar to us through the descriptions of classical authors (Herodotus, Xenophon, the Alexander historians) and through illustrations of soldiers in Iranian and non-Iranian art (reliefs from Persepolis and Susa, the Alexander sarcophagus from Sidon, the Alexander mosaic from Pompeii and so on). Under Cyrus, the founder of the empire, these troops were a militia in which each soldier had to provide his own equipment (which required a certain affluence). In fact, the Old Persian word for 'levy', *kāra*, was also the designation for the 'people' on the whole, although in his inscriptions, the king narrows down this concept to the *kāra par excellence*, that is, the aristocracy. Even after the expansion of the empire, the Persian *kāra* made up the backbone of the great king's army. The latter was now transformed into a standing army in which, side by side with the Persians, there were above all Medes and representatives of eastern Iranian tribes serving and assuming certain responsibilities ('mobile army'). When circumstances required it, contingents of other subject peoples supplemented these central unions ('imperial levy'). Apart from that, the Persians kept a 'border and occupation force' stationed in forts and garrisons, as well as pioneer troops. The standing army was called by the (Median) name *spāda* and consisted of charioteers, as well as 'riders' on horses (OP *asabāra*) and on camels (*ušabāri*), 'lance-bearers' (*ṛ̌stika*) and 'bowmen' (*θanuvaniya*), with the last two groups probably divided into infantry (*pasti*) and cavalry units. Darius (I) sees himself as a 'model' for his soldiers in his lower epitaph:

As a horseman I am a good horseman. As a bowman I am a good bowman, both afoot and on horseback. As a spearman I am a good spearman, both afoot and on horseback.

In the battle of Cunaxa (401 BC) against his brother Cyrus the Younger, the great king Artaxerxes II had his troops drawn up in the formation described below:

It was now midday and the enemy [i.e. the army of the great king] had not yet come into sight. But in the early afternoon dust appeared, like a white cloud, and after some time a sort of blackness extending a long way over the plain. When they got nearer, then suddenly there were flashes of bronze, and the spear points and the enemy formations became visible. There were cavalry with white armour on the enemy's left and Tissaphernes was said to be in command of them. Next to them were soldiers with wicker shields, and then came hoplites with wooden shields reaching to the feet. These were said to be Egyptians. Then there were more cavalry and archers. These all marched in tribes [peoples] [kata ethnē], each tribe [ethnos] in a dense oblong formation. In front of them, and at considerable distances apart from each other, were what they called the scythed chariots.

Right from the start of their hegemony, the Persians also enlisted Greek mercenary units, with each soldier, according to Xenophon, receiving free board and lodging and (401 BC) monthly pay of one gold daric. By the time of Alexander, these troops were fully integrated within the king's army, and their Greek commanding officers had risen – through marriage or admission into the circle of the king's 'friends' or 'benefactors' – to become members of the leading class of the empire. The enlistment of mercenaries should by no means be gauged (as Isocrates did, with a number of people following him to this day) as a sign of the decline of Persian power and strategy; this is contradicted by historical facts, such as the reconquest of Egypt shortly before the Alexander campaign or the so-called 'Great Satraps' Revolt' which had hitherto been regarded as a great threat to the king, but has lately been unmasked as a phantom. The engagement of mercenaries was, moreover, general practice in the fourth century and only speaks for the efficiency and fighting power of the Greek hoplites and their motives for serving the great king. He himself had good reasons and, above all, the necessary means to enlist mercenaries instead of the peasant population, who would otherwise have been prevented from cultivating the land. The mercenaries, moreover, were mainly put into action in the coastal regions of Asia Minor, which already bore the imprint of Greeks, and spent very little time stationed within the interior of the empire. The fact that Isocrates made much of the argument of the Persians lacking fighting strength is not surprising. His aim was precisely to emphasize the weakness of the Persian empire in order to encourage Athens and Sparta, and later Philip of Macedonia, to attack the country of the barbarians. This 'ideology of a Panhellenic war against the barbarians', as it has been called, did not allow for describing the great king as powerful from a military point of view, and his soldiers, including the mercenaries, as being brave and loyal to the Great King.

While some of the classical testimonies show a tendency to minimize Persian fighting strength, others tend to exaggerate it. The army of Xerxes was said to consist of more than 2.5 million soldiers, that of Artaxerxes at

Cunaxa was described as amounting to 900,000, and Darius III was supposed to have led more than one million warriors into the battle of Gaugamela. Through such completely inflated numbers, the victories of the Greeks and of Alexander were meant to appear all the more brilliant and astonishing, while the daring of the Greek mercenaries of 401 BC also acquired a different dimension.

The Persian army was divided according to the decimal system, that is by units of tens, hundreds and thousands with their corresponding 'officers'. A detachment of 1,000 men was led by a *hazārapatiš* ('leader of a thousand'; Greek *chiliarchos*). Higher officers and commanders-in-chief were recruited from the Persian and Median high aristocracy, and some of them were even members of the great king's family. They fought at the head of their units, many of them losing their lives. The king's army also included élite troops, among which that of the 10,000 'immortals' (Greek *athanatoi*) was the most famous. There also existed detachments that can be best described as the king's 'bodyguard'. Herodotus describes these units when Xerxes was leaving Sardis before his expedition to Greece:

Behind him [Xerxes] ... spearmen [*aichmophoroi*], their weapons pointing upwards in the usual way – all men of the best and noblest Persian blood; then a thousand picked Persian cavalry, then – again chosen for quality out of all that remained – a body of native infantry ten thousand strong. Of these a thousand had golden pomegranates instead of spikes on the butt-end of their spears, and marched in two sections, one ahead and one behind the other nine thousand, whose spears had silver pomegranates. The troops mentioned who marched with lances reversed also had golden pomegranates on the butt-end of their weapons, while those immediately behind Xerxes had golden apples ... This corps was known as the Immortals, because it was invariably kept up to strength; if a man was killed or fell sick, the vacancy he left was filled at once, so that the total strength of the corps was never less – and never more – than 10,000.

The 1,000 spearmen with apples on their spears were the 'bodyguard' and stood under the command of a *hazārapatiš* who was, so to speak, the chiliarch *par excellence* of the empire, the first officer of the entire army and a close confidant of the king. Even if Nepos points out that this officer (in this case Tithraustes) controlled the access to the king, he should not be compared with a 'grand vizier' or any similar official, since he had no administrative tasks to perform. The élite unit commanded by a chiliarch is said to have included Darius under Cambyses, and according to Herodotus, all the members of the king's bodyguard were killed in the battle of Plataea.

A majority of scholars are of the opinion that the 10,000 'Immortals' owe their name to a misunderstanding by the Greeks. These are thought to have mistaken their real name (OP) *anušiyā* ('attendants'), for the Old Persian word **anaušā* ('immortals'). This thesis has also had its critics, however. The figures portrayed in Susa (on the brick reliefs; see Plate XIV) and in Persepolis (on the reliefs on the east side of the Apadana) are probably members of the élite units. They wear a long draped robe and Persian shoes, as well as a cord around their head. The guards set the spherical end of their lances on their advanced foot and wear their bow and quiver on their shoulder on the Susa reliefs.

They serve in the army and hold commands from twenty to fifty years of age, both as foot soldiers and as horsemen ... They arm themselves with a rhomboidal wicker-shield; and besides quivers they have swords and knives; and on their heads they wear a tower-like hat; and their breastplates are made of scales of iron. The garb of the commanders consists of three-ply trousers, and of a double tunic [*chitōn*], with sleeves, that reaches to the knees, the under garment being white and the upper vari-coloured. In summer they wear a purple or vari-coloured cloak [*himation*], in winter a vari-coloured one only; and their turbans [*tiarai*] are similar to those of the Magi; and they wear a deep double shoe. Most of the people wear a double tunic that reaches to the middle of the shin, and a piece of linen cloth round their head; and each man has a bow and a sling.

We come across some of these costume details and weapons in Persian reliefs and in the reports of Greek authors about engagements. A foot soldier accordingly carried a short sword (*akinakēs*), a lance with a wooden shaft and metal point, a quiver full of arrows with bronze or iron points, as well as a bow with its ends shaped like animals' heads, which was kept in a box (*gorytos*) together with the arrows. The wickerwork shields were for the most part either small and oval or big and rectangular. For headgear, a felt hood was used; helmets were the exception. The élite units either wore the Elamite–Persian costume with the long draped robe or the Median (equestrian) costume with trousers, upper garment and cape. Coats of mail to cover the chest have also been confirmed.

The Achaemenid cavalry is described by Xenophon as follows:

Cyrus [the Younger] leapt down from his chariot, put on his breastplate, mounted his horse and took hold of his javelins. He gave orders for all the rest to arm themselves and to take up their correct positions. This was done readily enough ... Cyrus and about six hundred of his personal cavalry in the centre were armed with breastplates, and armour to cover the thighs. They all wore helmets except for Cyrus, who went into the battle bare-headed. All their horses had armour covering the forehead and breast; and the horsemen also carried Greek sabres.

This account can be compared with a Babylonian legal document which deals with the duty of an armoured cavalryman to equip himself. He had to furnish himself with a horse with girth and bridle, as well as a helmet, a coat of mail, a bronze shield, 120 arrows, an iron club and two iron spears, and a mina of silver as 'basic allowance'. As compensation for this duty, he was provided by the king, together with soldiers of other parts of troops, with a piece of land (as a kind of 'fief').

The camel riders and combat and scythe chariots have already been described. These, as well as the elephants witnessed at Gaugamela, were sent into action on special occasions or against special opponents. The Persians also had standards, among which the royal one crowned by an eagle with its wings spread out over a shield-like board has been documented by Xenophon (and the Alexander mosaic?).

There were royal garrisons all over the country, divided between city (*akra*) and country (*chōra*) garrisons. Their maintenance was ensured by the satraps from local resources. Their commanding officers were distinguished through their special relationship with the king. The function of the garrisons was the protection of the country and the quick mobilization of detachments in critical periods.

Under the reign of Darius and his successors, the Persians possessed a naval force (*basilikos stolos*) kept in constant readiness and mainly stationed in Cilicia.

We are quite well informed about Persian war tactics. The forces kept a baggage-train with them and supplied themselves from the storehouses along the imperial roads. Expeditions and battles took place almost exclusively in the daytime, and campaigns were started in the spring. Rivers were crossed by means of bridges, rafts and inflated animal skins. Usually a battle was begun by having bowmen and slingers (of stones and lead) discharge their deadly load, so that the disarrayed enemy could then be crushed through a flank attack involving heavily armed men and cavalry. Against the Greek hoplite armies, these tactics did not work, especially since the Hellenes with their armours and shields were strong in their defensive tactics and distinctly superior with close-range weapons, and the Persian action depended far too much on the conduct and instructions of the commander-in-chief. Thus the intentional attacks on the person and life of Cyrus the Younger at Cunaxa and the flight of Darius III at Issus and at Gaugamela became decisive factors in battles whose issue had till then been quite uncertain.

6. 'Ahura Mazda and the other gods that are': on religious conditions in the Achaemenid empire

Hardly any subject has led to as many arguments among scholars as the religious beliefs of the Achaemenid rulers (and their Iranian subjects). In tackling this problem here, we will first of all leave aside the religious policy of the kings, which has already been addressed, and secondly avoid giving any impression that this question is to be resolved here and now. What strikes us at first glance is that discussions on this theme often lead to asking whether or not the Achaemenids were Zoroastrians, i.e. followers of the teachings of Zarathustra (Greek *Zoroaster*), either in their original form or in their gradual transformations. In comparison, much less attention has been paid to the significance attached to religion and worship by the kings, i.e. to the political function of religion. The problems we are dealing with here are perhaps best clarified by asking ourselves the following questions prior to deciding about the main issue regarding the creed of the Achaemenids. Who was Zarathustra and when and where did he live? What are the content and purpose of his hymns (*gāthās*) and to whom are they addressed? How are we to imagine the Zoroastrianism of the Achaemenid period? Of course, there are no definite answers to any of these questions. Zarathustra's dates and origin are as disputable as the content and purpose of his 'message' or the relationship (as far as time and content are concerned) between the texts of his lifetime and those of later periods.

The main testimony regarding Zarathustra, his ideas and the thinking of those who believed in him is the Avesta, the 'holy writing' of the Zoroastrians. In addition to this collection of texts in the Avestan language, there is its translation and commentary (*zand*) in Middle Persian (Book Pahlavi). Scholarly interest in these texts includes both the linguistic–philological field (about Avestan as an Old Iranian language side by side with Old Persian) and the religious–historical domain (about the intellectual world of Zarathustra and the Zoroastrians). The compilation of the texts was due to a collaboration between the Zoroastrian 'priesthood' and government authorities, particularly under the Sasanians, but despite the intervention of the Zoroastrian community in Iran and India (the Parsis), only a part of the original corpus has come down to us. The earliest manuscript dates, in fact, from as late as the end of the thirteenth century. Middle Persian texts present the following history of the 'Holy Writings'. The 21 *nasks* ('books') of the Avesta, created by Ahura Mazda, were handed to King Vishtaspa by Zarathustra; the former or, according to another version, Dara Darayan, had two manuscripts made from them, which were preserved at different places. After the destruction or dispersal (and exploitation) of the Avesta by Alexander, later Iranian rulers, the Parthian King Valakhsh and the Sasanians Ardashir I, Shapur I, Shapur II and Khosrow I undertook the renewed collection, completion, reconstruction and translation of the 'Holy Writings'. Today we know, first, that the texts were created at different periods – the Old Avesta (*Gāthās*, attributed to Zarathustra himself; the *Yasna Haptanghāiti*; the four great prayers from Yasna 27) some time (a few centuries?) earlier than the Younger Avesta; and secondly, it is generally assumed that in the early days, the tradition was handed down by word of mouth. Scholars believe the degree of literality or phonetic fidelity in the transmission of the original texts was highly important and assign this transmission to 'schools of priests'. The theory that the Avesta was written down in the Achaemenid period is there-fore as untenable as that of the destruction and dispersion of the texts by the Macedonians. Nevertheless, there may have been, at this period, a break in the traditional chain (through the death of priests as 'living books'? or through a scission of the followers into different 'schools'?). A written-down Arsacid (Parthian) Avesta is not to be ruled out entirely, but if it existed, it has remained philologically insignificant. The Avestan 'vulgate' is rather the result of a canonization and writing down of the text in the Sasanian period (probably in the fourth century AD), for which purpose a special alphabet was created, one related to Middle Persian in its form and to Greek from a typological point of view. The Islamic conquest of Iran brought about a dispersal of the community, a weakening of the religious tradition and an impairment of its cultic and liturgical management, under which the written transmission of the Avesta also suffered. Today we know that all the manuscripts go back to a 'base manuscript' from the ninth/tenth century AD.

The Avesta that has come down to us was made known in Europe in the eighteenth century by the French Orientalist A. H. Anquetil-Duperron. Used even today by the Zoroastrians as a 'Holy Writing', it does not present a homogeneous collection, but is divided into books and texts without any strict coherence, but with a definite orientation towards liturgical practice. Its separate parts have the following titles: 1) *Yasna* ('sacrifice'), a collection of liturgical texts in 72 'chapters', among which the Gathas and the Yasna Haptanghaiti ('Yasna of the 7 chapters') are the oldest components; 2) *Visprad* (*Vispered*) ('[prayer to] all the patrons'), a collection of supplements to the Yasna with formulary invocations that are relevant on seasonal festivities;

3) *Xorda Avesta* ('Little Avesta'), an excerpt from the whole work for the use of laymen and prayer formulas for different occasions; 4) *Sīrōza* ('Thirty Days'), with the enumeration of divinities patronizing the 30 days of the month; 5) *Yašts*, 21 hymns for the principal deities, among them those that, together with the Gathas, contain most information about the beginnings and evolution of Zoroastrianism; 6) *Vidēvdād* ('law of breaking off with the demons'), 21 chapters, the first two of which explain the genesis of the work, while the rest consist of prescriptions for purification, expiation and penitence (with the exception of chapter 19, which describes 'Zarathustra's temptation'); 7) *Fragments*.

The time and place in which the Avestan texts originated cannot be exactly determined. The dialect of Persis (Fars) is the only one to be ruled out in this respect. As a result, their homeland has been placed both in the north-west and in the north-east, in the region of Mashhad, in Choresmia, in Bactria-Margiana, and also in Sistan. As for the question of dating, a great majority of scholars today tend to believe that the Gathas were created around 1000 BC (which would at the same time establish the lifetime of the prophet Zarathustra), while the most important texts of the Younger Avesta are usually dated a few centuries later, many scholars attributing them to the Achaemenid period. As for other questions, there is no consensus to speak of. This is true of the linguistic and textual comprehension of the Gathas and other parts of the Avesta, and also of their interpretation, their 'place in life' and the figure of the founder of the religion. There are even different theories about the route followed by the message within Iran. Some scholars believe that there may have been a kind of schism between two 'schools', one in the west (under the leadership of the Magian 'clergy' in Media), the other in the east (with an important centre in Arachosia), and that a major part of the Younger Avesta originated in Arachosia/Sistan and made its way into Persis (under Darius I). Here the Arachosian and Median traditions had mixed, but the eastern language had become the authoritative 'church language'. Others assume that the Zoroastrian creed was brought to the west by the Medes and Persians at the beginning of the first millennium BC, in a form that already differed from Zarathustra's ideas; and that it was further modified there by the Magi under the influence of the highly developed Mesopotamian cultures, and subsequently, in order to meet the requirements of the Achaemenid empire in its process of consolidation. Yet others suppose that in the last decades of Median supremacy, which embraced eastern Iran, the Zoroastrianism of the east established itself in the west as well (with the help of 'missionaries' and through the sons and daughters of eastern Iranian princes at the court of Media). According to this theory, the Achaemenids were ardent Zoroastrians from the very beginning. Both the supporters of a late dating of Zarathustra to the seventh–sixth centuries BC – following a Sasanian tradition which held that Zarathustra pre-dated Alexander by 258 years – and those who ascribe an early date to the founder of the religion and to his Gathas, share a crucial problem, that of judging how closely the kings adhered to the message of Zarathustra (or his 'successors'). The answers to this problem vary extensively. While some scholars are of the opinion that all the kings were genuine followers of his doctrine, others believe that this applied only to Darius and his successors, and yet others that it applied to the usurper Gaumata who was overthrown by Darius. At the same time, the promotion of Zoroastrianism by the kings is usually put down to political and practical, rather than to religious motives.

In order either to prove or disprove a connection between the Achaemenid form of religion and Zoroastrianism, it is necessary to point out a few major characteristics of Zoroastrianism and their evolution. The Gathas as the hymns of Zarathustra convey a religious system based on the workings of a single god, Ahura Mazda, the 'wise (or vigilant) lord'. At his side (and as his subordinates) there are an unspecified number of other Ahuras as personified concepts and divine assistants. They are sometimes defined as his sons and daughters. Among them, *Aša* ('truth') has a special position. In the Younger Avesta, things have changed, so that Ahura Mazda is mentioned and, as his 'children', six 'divine entities' called the *Aməša Spəntas* ('prosperous immortals'), whom scholars sometimes describe as 'allegories' or 'archangels'. In contrast to the Gathas, this group is, in the meantime, well developed, and as patron saints of the seven days of the first week of each month, it has its place in the calendar system.

The linguistic similarity of the Gathas to the Indian *Rig-Veda*, which is a major argument for dating the hymns to the end of the second millennium, suggests comparing the two from the point of view of religious content as well. Here we note that in the *Rig-Veda*, an original group of gods called the *Asuras* gradually acquires more and more negative features and is relegated to the state of 'demons', who are in conflict with the good *devas*. In Iran, that is, in the Gathas, the reverse can be observed. Here the *Ahuras* remain divine beings, while the *daēvas* are changed into demons. This class of old divinities is no longer considered as venerable and is removed from the pantheon. As far as cult or ritual practices are concerned, there is some evidence to the effect that Zarathustra disapproved of animal sacrifices (or some of their modalities) and that he prohibited the ritual use of an intoxicating drink, the *haoma* (in a particularly strong, undiluted form?).

In the Younger Avesta, Zarathustra's doctrine is changed (a few centuries later?) – not only through the systematization of the divine 'apex' – but also by the fact that, although the *daēvas* continue to be cursed, part of the Indo-Iranian pantheon is allowed to return into the circle of the divinities marked as positive. Among them Mithra, the Indo-Iranian god of contract, and Vāyu have kept their original names, but others such as Vərəθraγna and Anāhitā are now known under the name that had been their privileged attribute. When, how and why this development took place cannot be decided. While the pantheon of the Younger Avesta can now clearly be described as poly-theistic, although with a dominant Ahura Mazda, a precise characterization of original Mazdaism is much more difficult. 'Ahura Mazda now finds him-self in the company of some divinities who are not yet really gods [Ahuras], and others who are no longer gods [Daēvas], but all of them have their place in the religious sphere' (Kellens). So are we dealing here with an 'unstable polytheism' or an 'unstable monotheism'?

A few words will have to be said about the ethics and eschatology of Zoroastrianism/Mazdaism. In the Videvdad, a late work of the Younger Avestan tradition, the foundation of which may go back to the Achaemenid period, Zoroastrianism clearly shows dualistic features. A god of good, associ-ated with light, Ahura Mazda, and a god of evil, connected with darkness, Angra Mainyu, lead the universe as a whole, a world they have created themselves and in which each of them has his own sphere of activities. From the beginning, both have fought for supremacy. Man is called upon to take sides in this struggle, which will end in a final decision in favour of the good. Plutarch is also aware of this dualism:

The great majority and the wisest of men hold this opinion: they believe that there are two gods, rivals as it were, the one the Artificer of good and the other of evil. There are also those who call the better one a god and the other a daemon, as, for example, Zoroaster the sage, who, they record, lived five thousand years before the time of the Trojan War. He called the one Oromazes and the other Areimanius; and he further declared that ... Oromazes may best be compared to light, and Areimanius, conversely, to darkness and ignorance, and midway between the two is Mithras ... [now Plutarch goes on to describe the mythic ideas of the Persians] Oromazes, born from the purest light, and Areimanius, born from the darkness, are constantly at war with each other; and Oromazes created six gods; but Areimanius created rivals, as it were, equal to these in number. Then Oromazes enlarged himself to thrice his former size, and removed himself as far distant from the Sun as the Sun is distant from the Earth, and adorned the heavens with stars. One star he set there before all others as a guardian and watchman, the Dog-Star. Twenty-four other gods he created and placed in an egg. But those created by Areimanius, who were equal in number to the others, pierced through the egg and made their way inside ... hence evils are now combined with good. But a destined time shall come when it is decreed that Areimanius, engaged in bringing on pestilence and famine, shall by these be utterly annihilated and shall disappear; and then shall the earth become a level plain, and there shall be one manner of life and one form of government for a blessed people who shall all speak one tongue.

The choice between good and evil (for spiritual beings and mortals) is already mentioned in the Gathas. Whether or not the opposition between Ahura Mazda and Angra Mainyu in the Younger Avesta was preceded by a doctrine about two spirits (a good one [Spənta Mainyu] and a bad one [Angra Mainyu] below the level of Ahura Mazda) has been a subject of heated debates among scholars.

To return to our initial question as to whether there are indications of a Zoroastrian form of religion among the Achaemenids, it is clear that should there be any grounds at all to postulate such a connection, only the Younger Avestan form of the creed may be considered. The following points are particularly debated. When Darius mentions Ahura Mazda as the 'greatest of gods' (*haya maθišta bagānām*) in his inscriptions, when he names him together 'with all the gods' (*hadā visaibiš bagaibiš*) or 'the other gods that are' (*utā aniyāha bagāha tayaiy hatiy*), then this religion of his is certainly not to be described as monotheistic. Is his 'Mazdaism' – for he gives great prominence to Ahura Mazda – part of the old Iranian conception of divinities or is it connected with the Younger Avesta? When Darius mentions the other *bagā*, while the Avesta speaks of the venerable divine beings as *yazatas*, does this show a difference between the two concepts, or does *bagā* in the royal inscriptions describe divine beings without any detailed specification, while *yazata* designates the member of a group of gods in a much more restricted sense? Are the Persian educational ideal attested by Herodotus, 'to tell the truth' (*alēthizesthai*), and its negative counterpart 'to tell lies' (*pseudesthai*; see Darius's fight against 'falsehood' [*drauga*]), to be compared with the opposition between *ašavan* and *drugvant* in the Avesta? Are the *daivā* against whom Xerxes fought, according to his inscription, to be seen against the background of the Zoroastrian rejection of the *daēvas*? Does the burial of kings in a house-like tomb (Cyrus) or in rock-cut tombs (Darius and his successors) really contradict the rule laid down in the Videvdad that corpses should be exposed (according to the Magian practice reported by Herodotus), or does it reflect a stage in the evolution of Zoroastrianism when there were as yet different ways of dealing with the dead (or when kings were treated as exceptions)?

We have perhaps managed to show on what difficult terrain we stand when asking the question about the religious confession of the Achaemenid kings. What can be confirmed, however, is that in choosing Ahura Mazda, Darius was on the one hand dealing with something familiar, and on the other hand, hoping to gain legitimacy and support (and justification) for his claim to power by declaring his faith in this god. Whether he associated himself with this god (or the Zoroastrian creed in whatever form) 'merely' for political and opportunistic reasons, or whether he also felt spiritually close to him is a question that can hardly be answered. However, unlike his Zoroastrian subjects for whom 'truth' and 'falsehood' were moral and ethical points of reference according to which they tried to organize their lives, the king considered anything as *drauga* that went against his own god-given and dynastically legitimized sovereignty, hence any form of rebellion or usurpation. *Ṛta* was accordingly anything that the king declared as such, and its observance in the political sphere was a virtue of his subjects.

5 *irtiba* [= 15 BAR] of barley were received by Umbaba, the priest [*šatin*]: 1 [*irtiba*] for the *lan* sacrifice, 1 for [the god] Drva [Zurvan?], 1 for [the god] Hvarira, 1 for the earth, 1 for the Visai Baga.

On the subject of religious practice in Persis, we shall again consult the Persepolis tablets. They prove that the kings – as we already pointed out elsewhere for Cyrus and Xerxes – allowed their subjects to worship a multitude of gods (and even supported them in doing so). There thus appear among Iranian divinities (in strictly circumscribed regions) the Visai Baga, *Drva (Zurvan?), *Hvarira, *Naryasanga, *Ardanafravartish (?), *Spantaragardya, Mizhdushish and Bartakamya, and even mountains and rivers as recipients of offerings, while in Elymais the gods who were worshipped were almost exclusively Elamite divinities, such as Humban and Napirisha and the Babylonian god Adad. For Ahura Mazda there are (so far) only ten evidences, but the sacrifice called *lan* is believed to be the official sacrifice made to this god. This sacrifice was not only supplied by the rations of the king, it was also the only offering that was widespread and received regular allowances.

As for the 'priests', there was a group of them (the *ātṛvaxša) who were only responsible for the *lan* sarifice. The Magi (*maguš*), too, were partly authorized to carry out this sacrifice, but they are also mentioned in connection with the worship of other Iranian divinities. Priests who were designated by the Elamite title *šatin* were mainly active in the cult of foreign gods, but could also sacrifice to Iranian gods. About the Magi there are the most diverse testimonies proving that apart from their religious functions, they also carried out educational, administrative and other tasks. In addition, they played a part in royal investitures and burials and in the interpretation of dreams, and were also considered as upholders of political and religious traditions. What religious orientation they represented at what particular periods remains debatable. Were they responsible for introducing Zoroastrianism in Persis? Or were only part of them converted to Zoroastrianism? Or was it Darius who first appointed the Magi as Zoroastrian 'officials'? These questions will have to be left unanswered.

PART TWO

INTERLUDE

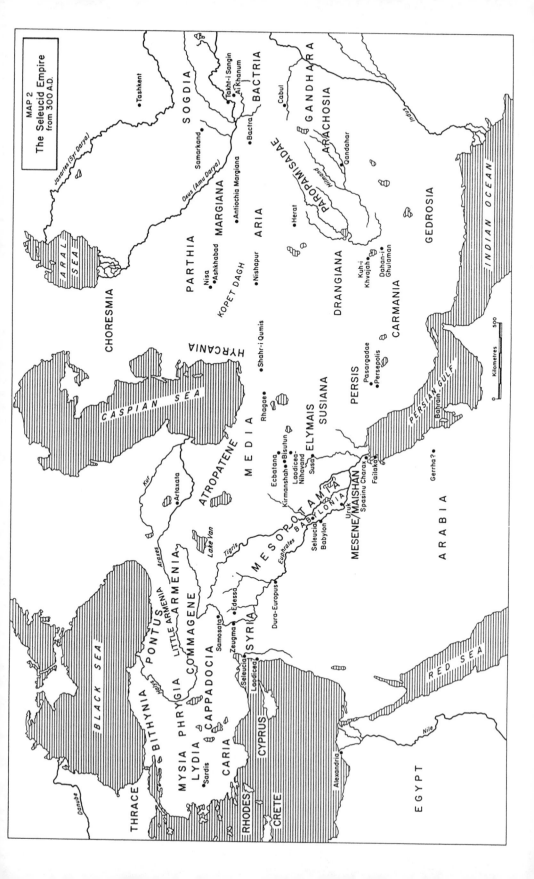

MAP 2

The Seleucid Empire
from 300 A.D.

CHAPTER 5

MACEDONIAN DOMINATION OVER IRAN

The reign of the great kings from the Achaemenid clan came to an end when the Macedonian King Alexander (III) succeeded in taking over the royal residences and, after the death of his opponent Darius (III), broke the eastern Iranian resistance against his reign with great brutality. To the Greeks, he had presented this venture as a punitive campaign to avenge Xerxes's expedition against Hellas; but his true aims, the conquest of the Persian empire and the establishment of his own sovereignty in the regions between Greece and India, only gradually dawned on many a contemporary and participant in the expedition. What a number of people found quite incomprehensible were his efforts to seek support and acknowledgement from the Iranians themselves by passing himself off as the avenger of the murdered Darius, by adopting Iranian customs and usages, wearing local clothes, establishing native military units, marrying Iranian princesses and entrusting members of the Iranian aristocracy with functions in his own entourage or in the satrapies. It has been proved, however, that this 'Achaemenid trend' of Alexander's did not manifest itself after the death of Darius, as has hitherto been assumed, but that it emerged with his arrival in the Achaemenid empire. The discovery of this fact is based on a detailed analysis of the western Alexander history that has come down to us. This history shows that Alexander was not only perfectly familiar with the conditions for the Achaemenid rulers' legitimacy, but did everything to fulfil them himself. In Asia Minor he presented himself as the defender and protector of peace and order, and in his correspondence with Darius after the battle of Issus he declared himself a pretender to the Achaemenid throne. He summoned Darius to fight for his sovereignty (as

befitted an Achaemenid king), took care of the soldiers and the royal Achaemenid household, accused Darius of having unlawfully ascended the throne,
i.e. of being an illegitimate king, and attributed his own success to the will
of the gods, by which he could only mean the divine protectors of the
empire and of the Achaemenid 'family'.

The appeal of Persian kingship to men with great ambitions such as
Alexander (and perhaps even Philip) has often been pointed out. It was based
on its attribution to one family, its concept of divine election and representation, its claim to world domination, its idea of a special relationship
between sovereign and subjects, and its pre-eminent position with respect to
the aristocracy. Alexander's stay in Persis was also proof of his effort not to
mark an 'interruption' in the reign of his predecessors, but by recognizing
Persian grandeur and observing the country's traditions, to win over to his
side the Persian aristocracy and the population as a whole. That was why he
made a point of his personal presence here in the heart of the empire (which
Darius had already abandoned), and it was also why he honoured Cyrus and
openly emulated him and his policies; while by burning down parts of the
Persepolis terrace, he sought to obliterate the memory of Xerxes and also to
prevent potential rivals from taking possession of the valuable objects and
treasures accumulated there. The fact that the fire in the residence was
interpreted by the Greeks as a victorious end to the punitive expedition,
while to the natives it meant that their only advantage lay in a compromise
with the victor, perfectly suited Alexander's purposes.

The assassination of Darius by Bessus made it easier for Alexander to
find general support in Iran as well. Besides, by honouring his dead opponent
and by acknowledging him as his predecessor, Alexander could now present
himself as the avenger of Darius, whose succession he was to assume. So
when Bessus proclaimed himself Artaxerxes (IV), he took charge of Persian
court ceremonial and had his rival executed according to Persian customs. In
so doing, however, he antagonized his old Macedonian entourage, without
being able to prevent opposition to his reign in eastern Iran, an old centre
of Achaemenid power. Indeed, after the débâcle at the Hyphasis and in
Gedrosia, he temporarily had to face resistance in Persis as well. Only in-
exorable brutality and ruthlessness helped him to victory, though they must
also have led to his bad reputation in Iran's Zoroastrian tradition. Tensions
on the Iranian 'front' eased up as a result of his marriage with the Bactrian
princess Roxane, followed by the wedding ceremonies in Susa, the festivities
in Opis, his avowed disapproval of the Persepolis fire and, above all, the

clever policies of his satrap Peucestas in Persis. The latter not only tried to show his affinity with the people by wearing Median clothes, learning the Persian language and adopting Persian customs, but also – with evident success – sought to cooperate with the aristocracy of the region.

While thanks to Peucestas's efforts, Persis remained calm even after Alexander's death, there was unrest in other parts of the empire, starting before or shortly after Alexander's death. In Bactria the native population supported the rebellion of the Greek settlers, apparently with the aim of shaking off the foreign rule of the Macedonians, in India the Maurya ruler Chandragupta eliminated the Macedonian vassal in the Punjab, and in Media Atropatene the previous Achaemenid and Alexandrian satrap Atropates (from 323 BC?) founded a sovereign territory and a dynasty of his own. In 316/17, the governors of the 'Upper Satrapies' (i.e. those of Persis, Carmania [Kerman], Aria/Drangiana, Arachosia/Gedrosia, Bactria/Sogdiana and Paropamisadae) sided with Eumenes in his fight against Antigonus, but their concrete political and military actions were not motivated so much by the idea of supporting the 'just cause' of Eumenes (and the kings), as by the wish to maintain their influence and functions during the conflicts that were raging at the time. Shortly before the decisive battle between Eumenes and Antigonus, Peucestas prepared a sacrificial feast in Persepolis, which Diodorus describes as follows:

... after gathering from almost the whole of Persia a multitude of sacrificial animals and of whatever else was needed for festivities and religious gatherings, he [Peucestas] gave a feast to the army. With the company of those participating he filled four circles, one within the other, with the largest circle inclosing the others. The circuit of the outer ring was of ten stades, and in it were the Macedonian Silver Shields and those of the Companions [hetairoi] who had fought under Alexander; the circuit of the next was of four stades and its area was filled with reclining men – the commanders of lower rank, the friends [philoi] and generals who were unassigned, and the cavalry; lastly in the inner circle with a perimeter of two stades each of the generals and hipparchs and also each of the Persians who was most highly honoured occupied his own couch. In the middle of these were altars for the gods and for Alexander and Philip.

The feast, which followed Persian customs in its sacrificial ceremonies and seating arrangements, manifested a particularly close relationship between Peucestas and the native aristocracy and would have been inconceivable without the active cooperation of the native authorities and population. The gods who were honoured probably included Persian divinities, unless even in

those days Greek–Macedonian and Iranian divinities were already identified
in many of their aspects. The dedicatory plates of altars found in Persepolis,
bearing inscriptions devoted to Zeus Megistos, Athene Basileia, Apollo,
Artemis and Helios, are perhaps connected with these festivities. In the
decisive battle between Eumenes and Antigonus, Peucestas changed sides,
but this did not save him from being dismissed, despite the protestations of
the Persian aristocracy.

Between 312 and 301 BC, Seleucus subjugated the whole of Iran from his
Babylonian base, but failed in his fight against Chandragupta, to whom he
ceded the upper Indus region, Gandhara, Paropamisadae and East Arachosia
in exchange for an alliance (and war elephants). Media Atropatene remained
independent, and so did Choresmia, which had already managed to gain its
autonomy in the late Achaemenid period and had maintained it under Alexander. Of particular significance for the Seleucids (as already previously under
the Persian kings) was the region of Bactria and Sogdia, which was secured
against nomadic invasions by the foundation of settlements and the building
of fortresses. Among early Seleucid establishments in Iran are Rhaga (near
Tehran), Hecatompylus(?) (Shahr-i Qumis), Antiochia-in-Persis, Antiochia-
in-Margiana (near Merv), a city with the same name in 'Scythia', Soteira in
Aria, and above all, Ai Khanum on the Oxus, the archaeologically best-
attested site.

For a long time the policy of the Seleucids in the east was considered
as 'Macedonization', that is, as a break with the traditions and methods of
the Persian rulers who had preceded them (and also with some of Alexander's
policies); during the last few years, however, this approach has been severely
challenged. Today we know that the Seleucids followed Alexander's policies
in this area (through political marriages with non-Greek dynasties, and
through calling upon natives for military and administrative tasks as well as
service at court). We know that they adopted Persian (and Mesopotamian)
models in their choice of residences, their administrative and infrastructural
institutions, their patterns of personal relations, in the court art relating to
the king, and above all in the royal ideology. At the same time, we have
discarded the idea (wrongly applied to the Achaemenid empire as well) that
the diversity of cultures and interrelations between the centre and the
periphery were at the root of the empire's weakness and the germ of decay
within it from the very start. With respect to Iran, a (deliberate) neglect of
these regions and their affairs, to the extent of even excluding their aristocracy from the élite of the empire, was said to be in contrast to the

predominant interest shown by the kings in problems concerning the west of the empire. And it was thought that precisely here in the east, an early weakening of Seleucid supremacy and a breakdown of Greek/Macedonian and Iranian relations could be detected. Today we know that political and military measures enabled the Seleucids to keep major parts of Iran under their control until almost the mid-second century BC, after which simultaneous pressure from the east (Parthia) and the west (Rome) weakened Seleucid authority in this area, as a result of which their Iranian subjects started pursuing their own aims. What has also changed is our concept of the relationship between the Greeks and different groups of natives. In almost all parts of the empire, people of different cultural and ethnic origins lived in close proximity, often since the Achaemenid period. For this reason alone, their relationships must be conceived as much more diverse than has hitherto been imagined. Against this background, such concepts as 'Hellenism' and 'Hellenization', which have a history of their own, must also be redefined.

It is advisable, not least because of the predominantly archaeological nature of the available evidence, to study the history and culture of Iran under Macedonian rule by separate regions. For Media, an inscription from the year 193 BC, found in Laodicaea/Nihavand on the road between Babylon and Ecbatana, not only testifies to the centrally organized dynastic cult of the Seleucids, which is here extended to include Laodice, the wife of Antiochus III, but also bears witness to the existence of a Greek *polis* in central Media (since Antiochus I?) with its connections with Mesopotamia, eastern Iran and Persis.

In the caves of Karaftu on the border between Azerbaijan and Kurdistan, traces have been found of a Seleucid garrison, the likes of which must have existed at other similarly important sites. There is evidence that throughout the third century BC, the Seleucid mint of Ecbatana was in operation, and the Achaemenid palace was used as a residence by the Seleucids.

If the Seleucid reign came up against any native resistance at all in Persis, it can only have been at the very beginning. Although the dynasts holding office there on behalf of the Seleucids from the late third or early second century BC (they called themselves *fratarakā* and are known to us mainly by their coins; see Plate XVa) emphasized their close connection with the Achaemenids by taking over certain ceremonials and symbols, they evidently did not consider themselves as Achaemenids and great kings. It was not until the disintegration of the Macedonian reign in Iran that they gave up their loyalty towards the Seleucids (which is even iconographically tangible), but they again returned to their side when the too powerful Parthians appeared in Mesopotamia. The Parthians, like the Seleucids, had nothing against retaining natives in Fars in their functions as partially autonomous 'kings'. They found this all the more feasible since the Persian dynasts had shown no supra-regional pretensions. No wonder, then, that the later south-western Iranians (Sasanians) added the period of these dynasts to that of the 'petty kings', but at the same time were unable to venture deeper into the past to assume any genuine historical memory of their Achaemenid predecessors. Although the *fratarakā* behaved like devout Zoroastrians, they can hardly be considered as representatives of a religious–nationalistic 'party' or as 'priestly princes' (Magi). During the Seleucid period, their functions must have been mainly of a political, administrative and military nature. In their time, the Magi must have performed tasks similar to those they performed under the Achaemenids. As has been pointed out, the Zoroastrian clergy had negative memories of the Greeks (or perhaps only of Alexander). However, during the Hellenistic period, this tradition did not acquire any political relevance. The long period of unendangered Seleucid rule in Persis not only proves that this province was no 'bulwark of resistance against Hellenism'; it also shows that the foreign rulers were familiar with the traditions of this area. It is hardly possible to find out to what extent Persis was 'Hellenized' during the third and second centuries BC. The existing archaeological evidence seems to point to only a moderate Macedonian–Greek presence; in the absence of written records, however, the example of Antiochia-in-Persis should deter us from jumping to hasty conclusions.

Under the Seleucids, too, Median and Persian units formed the backbone of the army in this area, as witnessed by the Molon revolt. At the same time, Media's strategic position on the routes between Mesopotamia and north-east Iran, and the function of Persis as the connecting link between south-east Iran and Susiana and as the launching-point for operations in the Persian Gulf, rule out any theories about Seleucid indifference in these areas.

In Susa and Susiana, there are many archaeological and epigraphic records of Seleucid presence: the cult of the rulers is testified by inscriptions in the Greek–Macedonian colony of Seleucia-on-the-Eulaeus (Susa), where there also existed a Seleucid residence and garrison, fiscal officers and a gymnasion. Greek presence in Susa and the survival of the Greek language, script and institutions until well into the Parthian period are acknowledged facts today.

While Aria and Drangiana (Sistan) were indisputably Seleucid posses-
sions with hitherto only little archaeological evidence of Greek presence, and
while Hyrcania, too, aside from occasional nomadic inroads, remained
Seleucid until after Antiochus III, when it was definitely captured by the
Parthians, Margiana (southern Turkmenistan with its later centre of Merv)
may have been lost earlier. Here Soviet archaeologists were able to localize
Antiochia-in-Margiana in Gyaur-Kale. This was a 'secondary foundation' of
Antiochus I, which incorporated the old Achaemenid citadel within the
circular city plan intersected by two main streets running at right angles to
one another. Parthia as the region that gave its name to the successors of the
Seleucids in Iran will be discussed in a later section. Here we merely wish
to point out that the early centres of Parthian power were exclusively situated
in the northern part of this province (present-day Turkmenistan, near its
capital city of Ashkhabad) and that it was not until the second century BC
that the Seleucids gradually also lost the regions south of the Kopet Dagh,
Binalud and Elburz mountain ranges.

While the Indus valley, Gedrosia, Gandhara, Paropamisadae (the Swat
valley) and east Arachosia were yielded in the peace treaty of Seleucus I with
Chandragupta, western Arachosia (with its old Achaemenid centre of Qandahar) remained part of the Seleucid empire for a while, but was then lost to
Chandragupta's son Bindusara or to Aśoka. In the rock inscriptions of this
most famous Indian ruler of antiquity (and contemporary of Antiochus II),
there is both linguistic and external evidence in the Greek and Aramaic
versions, and explicit proof in the contents of the Indian version of the
13th edict, as to the presence of Greeks (*Yonas*) and Iranians (*Kambojas*) in
Aśoka's empire. The inscriptions also mention the real (or hoped-for)
influence on these foreigners of the Buddhist orientation of life towards
social responsibility and piety (*dhamma*); conversely, the political and cultural
influence of Achaemenid models on the Maurya rulers has also been pointed
out.

Towards the end of the second century BC, Arachosia and Drangiana
were occupied by Saka tribes, who gave their name to the latter region
(Sakastana > Sistan). The Parthian–Saka–Greek–Indian–Kushan history of
the south-eastern parts of the former Achaemenid empire is one of the most
disputed subjects among scholars of ancient history and will have to be put
to one side.

Bactria, a region already praised for its fertility by the Alexander historians, has been brought into focus particularly by archaeological, numismatic

and epigraphic finds. Bactria and Sogdia formed a single satrapy both under the Achaemenids and under the Seleucids. The border of the uncontrollable steppes of Central Asia and Siberia apparently ran along the Syr Darya (Jaxartes), as shown by the identification of Alexandria Eschate (= Antiochia) with Khodjent. In front of it was a wide zone of contact between the nomadic population of the steppes and the settled oasis inhabitants. Among the newly discovered Hellenistic sites in Bactria, which are often to be interpreted as Seleucid/Greek/Bactrian garrisons on the Oxus, Aï Khanum gives us particular insight into Greek life in eastern Iran (see Figure 5).

Founded in the late fourth century, it reached its apogee under the Graeco-Bactrian kings and deteriorated after the nomadic invasions of the second century BC. Among the buildings found here were a theatre, a *temenos*, a gymnasion, a palace and several imposing 'private residences', a citadel, some temples and areas used for administrative purposes. Gigantic mud-brick fortifications surrounded the settlement. The site displays a mixture of Greek, Bactrian, Achaemenid and Mesopotamian art forms. Its inhabitants must have included a large number of Greeks. This is proved not only by Greek–Macedonian personal names and dedications to Greek divinities, but also by two particularly impressive written testimonies: In 1966, the base of a statue dating from the early third century BC and bearing two inscriptions was found in the Heroon area (the burial place of Kineas, the founder of the city [?]). On the left is an epigram indicating that a certain Clearchus had placed a copy of the Delphic maxims of the Seven Sages there, and on the right are the last five of what must have been twelve sayings, the first seven of which were presumably inscribed on a stele that has not survived. The epigram reads as follows:

These truly wise words of famous men of the past were put up at the most sacred Pytho [in Delphi]. From there, Clearchus has carefully written down these luminous [words] and has set them up in the temenos of Kineas.

The five surviving maxims are:

As a child be well-behaved; as a young man self-controlled; as a middle-aged man be just; as an old man a good counsellor; in death be not saddening.

This Clearchus, long known to us as a peripatetic philosopher from Soli in Cyprus, must have ventured on a journey to the Near East around 300 BC, when he also visited the eastern Iranian regions inhabited by Greeks, including Aï Khanum. The fact that he found an interested audience here is

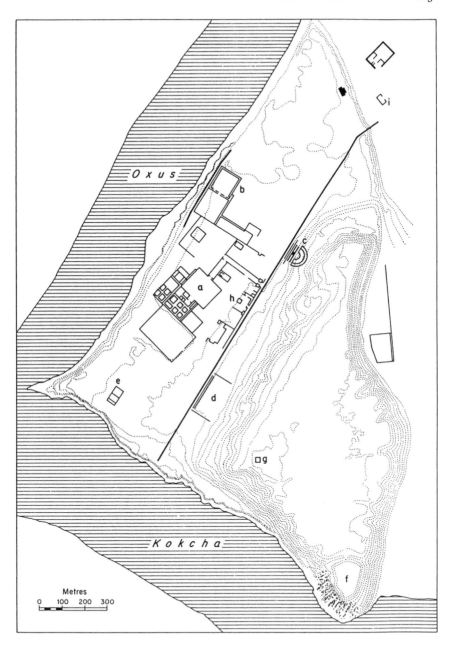

Figure 5 Aï Khanum (plan). The following buildings are marked: (A) Palace buildings; (B) Gymnasion; (C) Theatre; (D) Arsenal; (E) one of the luxurious villas; (F) the citadel on the Acropolis; (G) the temple platform; (H) the temple off the main road; (I) and the temple at the northern gate.

borne out by the maxims from Delphi, as well as the impressions of a papyrus and a parchment – neither of which survives in the original – that can be interpreted as excerpts of a dialogue about Plato's theory of knowledge and as a fragment in iambic trimeters. Further testimonies of Greek *paideia* found in the east are a fragmentary (funerary?) epigram in Jiga Tepe in the Balkh oasis, an inscription by a Bactrian dedicated to the river-god Oxus on a bronze Silenus statuette in Takht-i Sangin at the confluence of the Vakhsh and the Panj, and a fragmentary metric dedication in Qandahar. Similarly, the Greek Aśoka edicts already referred to not only testify to Greek presence in western Arachosia, but also bear witness to the familiarity of the ruler (or of those who translated his edicts from Prakrit [Indic]) with Platonic–Aristotelian terminology.

Meanwhile Sogdia, too, has revealed itself as a region bearing Greek imprints, as shown by various archaeological excavations and surveys. In Maracanda (Samarkand), the ancient Achaemenid centre and residence, traces of a Greek colony (Afrasiab) have been discovered.

After the eastern campaign of Antiochus III, Bactria definitely broke away from the Seleucid empire; the 'Graeco-Bactrian empire' bordering on the Hindu Kush to the south and on the Badakhshan mountains to the east later also included Sogdia, while a southward thrust eventually led to autonomous Indo-Greek kingdoms which survived the collapse of the 'Graeco-Bactrian empire' (around 130 BC) by half a century. Hellenistic influence in these regions mainly continued in the Buddhistic Gandhara art. Towards the end of the second century BC, the Yüeh-chih (Tokharoi?) settled north of the Hindu Kush, and among them, the Kushan clan gradually managed to establish an empire extending from Central Asia to India. Under the rulers of this clan, north-eastern Iran also flourished again. The silk trade proved extremely profitable, farming was intensified and urbanization was promoted. Indian (Buddhist) monks settled in this region. The continued presence of Greek influence is witnessed by the (modified) Greek alphabet, which was used to write down texts in the Bactrian language, as well as by Greek legends and names of gods on the coins of the early Kushans.

PART THREE

IRAN FROM ARSACES I
TO ARTABANUS IV: THE
PARTHIAN REIGN

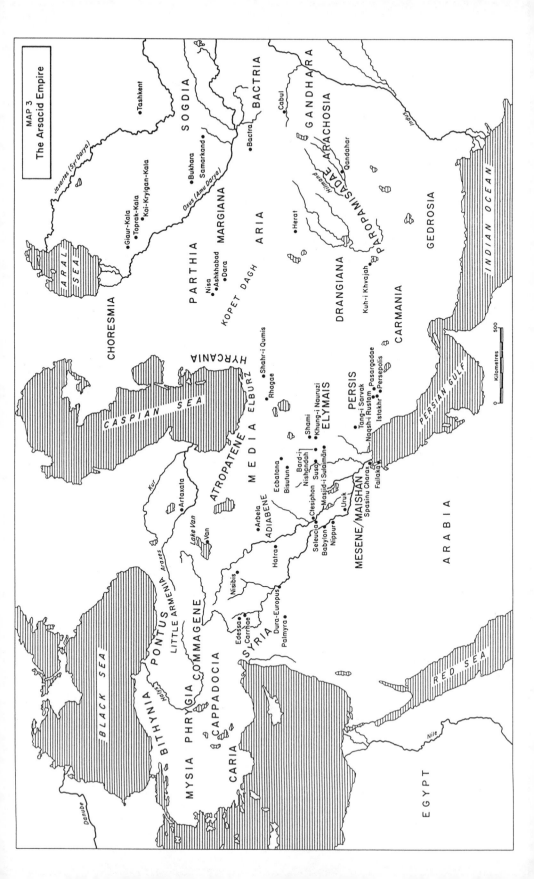

MAP 3
The Arsacid Empire

CHAPTER 6

THE TESTIMONIES

1. Inscriptions, cuneiform texts, Graeco-Roman and Chinese authors: languages, writing systems and written traditions of the Arsacid empire

The Iranian kings called Arsacids after Arsaces, the founder of their dynasty, or Parthians after Parthia, their first centre in Iran, reigned from not later than 140 BC over a great multi-cultural and polyethnic empire. Conquered in their battles against the Seleucids and their allies, it did not have the dimensions of the Achaemenid or early Seleucid empire, yet it embraced the major part of Iran and almost always the whole of Mesopotamia. The Arsacids exercised considerable influence on the history of Armenia, and temporarily also on that of Syria and Asia Minor, both of which led to conflicts with Rome. In their struggle against their western neighbours they were able to assert themselves, on the whole, as successfully as against the nomadic inroads of the Saka in the north-east. The surprising end of the Parthian empire, which had forged the history of Iran for almost twice as long as the Achaemenid empire, came at the beginning of the third century AD, when an extremely ambitious and obsessively power-seeking 'petty king' from Persis, Ardashir, challenged and defeated the Parthian overlord Artabanus (Ardavan).

Like the empire of Darius I, the realm of the Arsacids covered territories in which many languages were spoken. In Iran these were mainly Middle Persian, Parthian, Sogdian, Choresmian and Bactrian; further west they spoke Armenian, various Caucasian languages and Babylonian; in Mesopotamia and other parts of the empire, the language was Aramaic in its different variants, and in the Greek *poleis* such as Susa and Seleucia-on-the-Tigris it was Greek. Before discussing the individual languages, we shall have to say a few words about the Middle Iranian period of Iranian linguistic history, to which the first five above-mentioned languages belong. 'Since there is no continuity in the use of script from the preceding Old Iranian period, Middle Iranian languages can be defined as those that were first written and recorded in the post-Achaemenid, but pre-Islamic period' (Schmitt). It should be added that four of them (Middle Persian, Parthian, Sogdian and Choresmian) were recorded in scripts derived from the Aramaic script, while Bactrian, as already pointed out, was written in a local variant of the Greek alphabet. Aramaic scribes continued exercising their activity as translators and 'editors', as they had done under the Achaemenids, but in many parts of the empire there soon appeared natives who were also conversant with Aramaic.

This led to a separate evolution of the writing systems and to a decline in the command of Aramaic. At first the mother tongue was entirely recorded in Aramaic words, but in the course of time, more and more Iranian words were interspersed with it, and Aramaic forms were gradually reduced to conventionally used symbols, to 'heterograms'. We might also point out that for all Middle Iranian languages, different features or even 'dialects' are known to have existed. While at the beginning of this century, only Middle Persian was known to philologists in detail, research expeditions, digs and linguistic investigations have meanwhile disclosed the entire range of languages for this period. Among the western Middle Iranian languages are Parthian and Middle Persian. They are to be considered as 'two dialects that developed into literary languages out of a multitude of western Iranian languages and dialects that are unknown to us' (Sundermann).

Parthian is the language of the old satrapy of Parthia and was used by the Arsacids as the court and administrative language of their empire. From this period, however, only a few documents in Parthian have come down to us. Poetry and religious tradition were chiefly transmitted by word of mouth, coins for a long time bore Greek legends, and the Parthian script used so many Aramaic words at the time that this alone reduces the attested vocabulary (especially proper names). It is only with records of the period following the reign of the Arsacids that we are on more solid ground. The ability to understand the Parthian versions of royal Sasanian inscriptions from the third century AD and the literary works of the Parthian Manichaean community of the third to sixth centuries from Parthia, as well as the Middle East and Central Asia, have greatly contributed to progress in this field of research.

Middle Persian is the term for the language derived from Old Persian (third century BC to eighth/ninth century AD) and leading, on its part, to the development of New Persian. Until the third century AD, it was merely the local language of Persis (Fars) in south-western Iran, but under the Sasanians, who stemmed from that region, it became the administrative language and lingua franca of their empire. Middle Persian texts of the Parthian period are in fact found only as short, stereotyped legends on the coins of the south-western Iranian *frataraka* (see above) and their successors from the second century BC on; all the others date from the Sasanian period or even later.

As for the eastern Middle Iranian languages, we have already mentioned Sogdia with Samarkand as its chief city; the language of its inhabitants (Sogdian) was spread eastward through merchants on the Silk Road. Most of the written testimonies date from the Sasanian period or even later; from the Arsacid period, there survive only legends on coins from the second century AD. The old Iranian language of Choresmia, that is, the region on the lower Oxus (Amu Darya) and its estuary in the Aral Sea, is called Middle Choresmian and has come down to us in short inscriptions on vessels and bowls, as well as on coins, wood and leather. While in the Graeco-Bactrian and early Kushan empires the Greek language was used in official communications, it was later replaced by Bactrian written in a local variant of the Greek script. This has been documented both numismatically and by a large number of inscriptions.

Apart from Iranian, other languages were also spoken in the Arsacid empire. One of them was Armenian, but as indirect evidence of pre-literary Armenian – the written tradition only started from the fifth century AD – only names (especially toponyms in the Greek parallel tradition) are known to us. As might be expected in view of the close entanglement between Iranian and Armenian history, the Armenian language borrowed countless Parthian words and adopted Iranian proper names during the Parthian period. Iranian was not only spoken and understood by the aristocracy and by the religious or administrative officials, but also by ordinary people.

The influence of the Greeks and of the Greek language in the Arsacid empire is reflected not only in reports about the 'Hellenization' of the Parthian and Armenian court (see below), but also in the fact that the kings 'presented themselves' on their coins in Greek legends and that Greek inscriptions from these times have come down to us from Media, Armenia, Mesopotamia and Susiana.

Aramaic, the lingua franca of the Achaemenid empire, became the vernacular tongue under the Parthians. The lasting effect of this language is witnessed by numerous inscriptions throughout the empire as well as its use as a model for Middle Iranian writing systems and the writings of the Babylonian Jews and Mandaeans.

About Babylonian (Akkadian) the novelist Iamblichus reports in the second century AD that it was still spoken in his time. On the other hand, cuneiform writing had already gone out of use. The latest cuneiform text bearing a date is about astronomy and goes back to the year 74/75 AD. A place that offers a good illustration of this linguistic and ethnic diversity is Dura-Europus. In this city, founded by Seleucus I, conquered by the Romans in 165 AD and definitely captured by the Sasanians in 256 AD, there is almost simultaneous evidence of Graeco-Macedonian, Latin, Babylonian, Palmyrian–Aramaic, Nabataean–Arabic and Iranian personal names.

To appraise the written testimonies of the Parthian period with respect to their content, as well as their relevance to time and place, particular attention must be paid to the documents on clay sherds (*ostraca*) from the ancient Arsacid centres of Nisa in Turkmenistan and Shahr-i Qumis (Hecatompylus?), those on parchment from Avroman in western Iran, and those on parchment and papyrus from Dura. In Nisa (see below), the original Arsacid residence in Turkmenistan (near present-day Ashkhabad), Soviet excavators found more than 2,000 *ostraca* with 2,758 texts from a 'record-office' (see Plate XVb). These mainly provide details about deliveries of wine to the palace (in the first century BC) from the vineyards of various estates, temples or private people, and mention Parthian officials with their names and titles. The *ostraca* are probably to be interpreted as provisional notes which were to be followed up by a summary on some other material (perhaps leather). Here is a typical inscription of the kind:

In this khum [earthenware jug] are 17 *mari* [1 m. = *c*. 11 litres] of wine from the *uzbari* vineyard of the Friyapatikan estate, through the satrap. Delivered for the year 188 [of the Parthian era = 60 BC], brought by Humayak, wine-factor, who is from Artastavanak.

This is followed by the additional note: 'From the store 2 mari 2 k. of wine [added]'. Here it appears that wine from a vineyard in the vicinity of Nisa was delivered – by way of taxes – to the Mihrdatkirt (Old Nisa) fortress, decanted into jugs and later consumed. A small amount was later added to fill up the jar.

The so-called 'Avroman documents', which were discovered in 1913 in a grotto in the Kuh-i Salan in Iranian Kurdistan and are now preserved in the British Museum, consist of two Greek documents and one Parthian on parchment. While the Greek documents from the years 88/87 and 22/21 BC record the sale of half a vineyard named Dadbakan in a place called Kop(h)anis, the Parthian document, dated 53 AD, witnesses the sale of 'a half part of the vineyard Asmak, which [is] by the ploughland' by Pataspak, the son of Tiren from Bod, to Avil, the son of Bashnin, and his brother, for 65 drachmae. Because of the names of the people concerned and the numerous witnesses, these texts have acquired particular significance in the history of research. The same is true of the parchments and papyri from Dura, among which parchment No. 10, an agreement for a loan drawn up in the Greek language and dating from the years 121 or 122 AD, contains not only various names and titles, but also some important information about the internal and external politics of the period. Two less significant *ostraca* in the Parthian script from Shahr-i Qumis conclude this group of records.

Hardly less significant are the records inscribed on stone and bronze. Two rock inscriptions in the Parthian script and language from Khung-i Nauruzi in Khuzistan (*c.* 140 AD) identify the most important figures on the rock relief at that place (see Plate XVc) as 'Mithridates, king of kings' and 'Kabneshkir, [the] governor of Susa'; with this inscription, the title that is so characteristic of Iranian kings is for the first time attested for the Arsacids. Two undated Parthian inscriptions from Sar-i Pul Zuhab in southern Kurdistan on the road from Kirmanshah to Babylon refer to the pictorial representation of a man's investiture by a king called Gotarzes, whose identity is disputed. The last monument with a Parthian inscription that might be presented in more detail is the stele for the satrap Khvasak of Susa from the year 215 AD, on which the 'king of kings' Artabanus (Ardavan) IV hands the ring of sovereignty to his subordinate (see Plate XVIa).

Among the Aramaic inscriptions, that on the reliefs of the Parthian period from Elymais (see below) is particularly worth mentioning. In addition, there are the epigraphic records from Assur (memorial inscriptions) and Hatra, the rich caravan emporium in northern Mesopotamia. Here an Arab dynasty in the service of the Parthians inflicted severe defeats on the Roman emperors Trajan and Septimius Severus; but after going over to the Roman side, this dynasty finally had to submit to the Sasanians.

Greek inscriptions surmount a relief at Bisutun, which represents Mithridates II acknowledging the marks of respect of four dignitaries and – in the immediate vicinity – the figure of an equestrian warrior called Gotarzes, like the above-mentioned king. The Greek inscriptions from Susa have already been mentioned in the previous chapter. The most outstanding of them is no doubt the copy cut in stone of a letter dating from the year 21 AD, addressed by King Artabanus II to the archontes of the *polis*, Antiochus and Phraates, in which he confirms an election at issue within the municipal administration, which was based on the Greek model. It proves that Seleucia-on-the-Eulaeus (Susa) was under the king's jurisdiction, as it had been during the Seleucid period. What has lately caused a particular stir is the Graeco-Parthian bilingual inscription on the upper thighs of a small statue of Hercules from Seleucia-on-the-Tigris (see Plate XVIb, c); the Greek version reads:

In the year 462 according to the Greeks [151 AD], the king of kings Arsaces Vologeses, son of Mithridates the king, campaigned against Mesene, against King Mithridates [Meredates], son of Pacorus, who had been king before, and expelled King Mithridates from Mesene. He became master of the whole of Mesene. He set up this bronze statue of the god Heracles [Parth. *Vərəθrayna*], which he brought from Mesene, in the temple of the god Apollo [Parth. *Tīr*], who sits in front of the Bronze Gate.

The inscription thus proves that after the great eastern campaign of Trajan (117 AD) and the agreements with Hadrian, the Arsacids, though able to dislodge the Romans from the regions they had conquered in northern and central Mesopotamia, had not succeeded in bringing Mesene under their control again. Until the victory of Vologeses IV, this region in southern Mesopotamia, which was of great strategic and economic importance due to its overland routes to Syria (Palmyra) and its contacts by sea to India and beyond, had remained autonomous (as a Roman client state?) under another Arsacid dynast. The statue of Heracles in Parthian Seleucia now proclaimed the restored unity of the empire.

The latest extant Akkadian cuneiform documents have come down to us from Mesopotamia. There are administrative texts from Babylon, almost all of which deal with the Marduk temple in that city, dating from as late as the year 92 BC; as for chronicles, astronomical texts and horoscopes, they even continue until 75 AD. These late Babylonian records also contain references to Parthian office-holders, for instance the *pāḥatu* ('city prefect'), as well as temple officials and members of a council of the Marduk sanctuary Esagila, who were at the same time the supreme civil authority of the city. Dated cuneiform texts have meanwhile also provided more detailed information about the struggle between the Seleucids and Parthians for Babylonia. Babylonia was accordingly under Parthian domination from not later than July 141 until the year 131; it was then reconquered for a brief period

(130–129/28) by the Seleucid king Antiochus VII; after that it was recaptured by the Parthians in 128/27, then occupied for a short time by Hyspaosines (from Mesene), and, from the year 126, it finally became the undisputed possession of the Arsacids. These chaotic years from 141 to 126 BC, which are sporadically reflected in the local records, have long been blamed for the fact that Uruk in southern Mesopotamia gradually lost much of its importance, and that the great temples in it were destroyed and abandoned. A document from the Arsacid period proves, however, that at least until the spring of 108 BC, the sanctuaries of Bit Resh and Irigal were in use and that parts of the temple service or its proceeds were farmed out or sold, respectively. It will be highly interesting to find out what new insights into the Parthian reign in Mesopotamia will be gained by the excavations there and by the recovery of further clay tablet archives. A particular species (from the Seleucid–Parthian period) are the 'Graeco-Babyloniaca', consisting of 16 clay tablet fragments, some of them very small, with Akkadian or Sumerian texts transcribed in the Greek alphabet. Arguments about the scribes, orderers, purpose and interpretation of these writings continue unabated.

This survey of written records ends with the literary tradition of the West (and the Far East), although the fragments by Apollodorus of Artemita and Isidorus of Charax, which we will now discuss, consist of excerpts from two works by Greek subjects of the Arsacids. Apollodorus, whose dates are unknown, was the author of a 'Parthian History' comprising at least four volumes. The only surviving parts are a fragment handed down by Athenaeus and several references by Strabo, who, in addition, emphasizes the accuracy of Apollodorus's reports about the Parthian empire. Aside from his use of secondary sources (Alexander historians, early geographers), Apollodorus is a valuable informant because of his own local investigations, such as the study of the municipal archives of Artemita and Seleucia, and the information he personally collected from his Greek compatriots, as well as merchants and travellers. Isidorus of Charax in the Mesene, who must have lived around the beginning of the Christian era, was the author of the short work *Stathmoi Parthikoi* ('Parthian Stations'), which describes the road crossing the Parthian empire from Zeugma-on-the-Euphrates to Alexandria-in-Arachosia. He evidently combined official information from the time of Mithridates II (124/23–88/87 BC) with experiences of his own. Also remarkable is a surviving fragment of his report about pearl fishing in the Persian Gulf.

Of particular importance for an account of Parthian history are the *Historiae Philippicae* by Pompeius Trogus from southern Gaul, the first 'universal history' of Roman literature, whose 44 volumes date from the end of the first century BC. In this work, the history of the early empires of the Middle and Near East is followed by that of Macedonia (hence the title) and the Parthian empire up to the year 20 BC. The account ends – after a short summary of the early history of Rome – with the victory of Augustus in Spain in the year 19 BC. Unfortunately, Trogus's work was lost in late antiquity and is extant today only as a (Latin) summary by Justin (third century AD), together with brief statements of contents (prologues) of the original books. Trogus's informant for the Parthian section was an unknown author whom some scholars have identified as Apollodorus. Also of great usefulness for our understanding of Parthian history and culture are Strabo's description of Parthia in his *Geographia* and Arrian's account about the rise of the Parthians in his *Parthika*, of which only fragments survive. Additional information has been contributed by the following Western authors: Polybius about the eastern campaign of the Seleucid Antiochus III, which also led him against the Parthians; Flavius Josephus about relations between Jews and Parthians; Plutarch in his biographies of Crassus and Antony, who were both defeated by the Parthians; Appian, Cassius Dio and Tacitus about relations between Romans and Parthians; Pliny the Elder with descriptions of the historical geography of Asia; and finally the Augustan poets, who depicted the eastern neighbours as enemies of Rome to be taken seriously, but at the same time considered themselves as heralds of the successful Augustan policies towards the Parthians.

Much less familiar than these Western views are the reports of Chinese historians. Thus in his *Shi-ji* ('Historical Notes'), Sima Qian, the chief archivist at the court of the Emperor Wu-Di, who is sometimes referred to as 'China's Herodotus', mentions a Chinese embassy that had visited, among others, the regions of Ferghana, Sogdia and Bactria. The brothers Ban Gu and Ban Zhao from the Han period, who followed up the *Shi-ji* with the 'Annals of the early Han', added an account about Parthia. And Fan-Ye, a fifth-century AD historian, whose 'Annals of the later Han' were completed in the eleventh century to form their present version, mentions in chapter 118 about the 'Western lands' that a Chinese official travelled through Parthia (An-hsi) in 97 AD and went as far as the Persian Gulf.

In conclusion, accounts about Iran's Arsacid period have been preserved in the late Iranian tradition (Zoroastrian writings and Perso-Arab authors), but these were abridged and distorted in the latter part of the Sasanian era in order to minimize Parthian grandeur and achievements. On the other hand, the 'Kayani tradition', which tells the story of the ancient mythical kings of Iran, must have acquired its major characteristics during the Parthian period. There will be more to say on this subject.

2. Nisa, Bisutun and Tang-i Sarvak – rhytons and bronze statues: archaeological testimonies of the Arsacid period in Iran

Most Parthian sites in Iran have been discovered in Turkmenistan, Kurdistan and Khuzistan; these are represented by the places named in our chapter heading. Nisa near Ashkhabad, the capital of the state of Turkmenistan, was one of the oldest seats of the Arsacids. Its location proves that the Parni who invaded Parthia only controlled the northern part of this satrapy to begin with, and that they did not at that time break up the Seleucid connections from Media to north-eastern Iran. Soviet excavators found the remains of two old settlements in Nisa, of which one – New Nisa – is to be identified as the city proper, and the other – Old Nisa – as the royal fortress with palace and temple buildings, as well as granaries and treasuries. In the Parthian period, New Nisa was surrounded by a strong fortified wall and had a citadel on its southern side. North of the settlement, next to the city wall, there was a building complex (temple ?; see Plate XVIIa), which had soon fallen into decay, and on the ruins of which burial places (mud chambers) had been built for the Parthian aristocracy. Unlike New Nisa, which survived the downfall of the Arsacid empire, the fortress known as Old Nisa was plundered and razed in the third century AD, and so gave easier access to the excavators. Rising 50 metres above its surroundings on a natural hill, Mihrdatkirt, as it was called, with its pentagonal shape and its 20–25m-high and 5m-thick walls must have made a great impression in antiquity. Inside the citadel, the excavators discovered – as well as the granaries and store-rooms already referred to, which contained most of the *ostraca* – a large, almost square pillared hall believed to have been the throne room. There were also temples and, above all, a windowless 'square building' with 60m-long sides which was presumably the treasury (see Plate XVIIb). This consists of a large inner courtyard surrounded by oblong rooms that can be reached only through the courtyard, and in which were found a great variety of valuable objects and ornaments that the plunderers had ignored, smashed to pieces, carelessly thrown aside or stripped of their most valuable components: precious metals and coins, utensils made of gold, silver and ivory, marble statues, valuable imported articles, clothes and weapons. These objects must have served the Arsacid kings as presents or return gifts, just like the ones the Achaemenids stored in their treasuries. The excavators and art experts were particularly impressed by the more than 50 ivory rhytons (horn-shaped drinking vessels with a figure at their narrow end), which, due to their weight, must have been used only on ritual or ceremonial occasions (see Plate XVIIc). Both the 'classical pieces' with figures of centaurs and an Aphrodite, and the 'Oriental' ones ending in griffins, display friezes with Dionysiac scenes and the twelve Olympic gods, leading to the conclusion that the artists (and those who commissioned them) were familiar with Greek mythical subjects. Where these pieces were made and who ordered them cannot be determined. Apart from Nisa, the archaeologists also found Parthian cities, fortresses and settlements elsewhere in southern Turkmenistan.

A place known to be a later Parthian residence is Hecatompylus ('the [city with] a hundred gates'), which has apparently been rediscovered in Shahr-i Qumis near Damghan south of the Elburz. Here some Seleucid relics and, above all, various forms of Parthian vaulting techniques could be observed.

We shall now have a look at the western part of the empire, at Media, where the Parthian kings had themselves immortalized at the same place as Darius I, namely Bisutun. Whether the Arsacids were actually able to put the *res gestae* and the great rock relief of the Achaemenid king into their proper historical context is doubtful. Already in the fourth century BC, Ctesias attributed the monument (and a *paradeisos* at the same place) to the legendary Queen Semiramis. However the Parthians, like the Seleucids, knew of the 'sacred' character of the site. In the summer of 148 BC, Hyacinthus, the son of Pantauchus, had a Heracles relief with inscription(s) carved here for the Seleucid 'viceroy' Cleomenes; Mithridates II and a king named Gotarzes also had themselves immortalized in Bisutun through rock reliefs with inscriptions (see above); and a relief on a separate rock shows a King Vologeses (?) sacrificing before an altar (with two dignitaries at his sides). The fact that the Parthians considered Media with its capital Ecbatana as an important region in their empire is demonstrated by the relief in Sar-i Pul Zuhab mentioned above and by the discovery of several settlements and burial grounds from their period.

The same is true of the extreme south-western part of Iran, where numerous traces from the Parthian period were found in Susa and its environs, and above all in Elymais (in the Bakhtiari mountains). Particularly famous are the many rock reliefs in this area (with Aramaic inscriptions), among which those from Tang-i Sarvak are devoted to such 'royal' themes as investiture, hunting, marks of respect by local dignitaries and endurance in combat. Their datings debated, they form, with their Iranian style, the connecting link between Achaemenid and Sasanian relief art. It should be borne in mind, however, that even under the Parthians, Elymais was able to preserve much of its cultural and political independence. Since the dynasts of Elymais had themselves represented here without reference to their Arsacid overlords, and since the reliefs have little in common as to their iconography with the Parthian art of Mesopotamia, they had perhaps better be described as 'Parthian–Elymaean'.

As for Parthian art, whoever studies it will observe that most of the works commonly described as 'Parthian' come from the empire's periphery, rather than its centres: from Elymais, and above all, from Mesopotamia (Hatra) and even from beyond the borders of the empire (Dura, Palmyra, Commagene). On the other hand, Iranian sites such as Nisa and Bisutun show a high measure of Graeco-Hellenistic influence (although often applied in a rather independent manner). That the term 'Parthian art' is nevertheless used to cover the area between the Syrian desert and Central Asia for the period between the third century BC and the third century AD is due to certain stylistic characteristics of the art created by the Parthians themselves or developed within the regions under their control or influence. Among these characteristics is frontal representation. Special attention was paid to depicting details, such as the 'Parthian attire' or the jewellery worn with it. The 'invention' of frontal representation of figures in relief art and painting is a subject for heated debate, some scholars attributing its origin to Greece, others to Iranian nomadic tribes and yet others to Syria–Mesopotamia.

The most famous centre of 'Parthian art' is Hatra in northern Mesopotamia, with its characteristic ayvans (large halls roofed with a high barrel vault and having a square ground-plan and opening on one side), its figurative architectural sculpture and stucco ornaments, as well as its variety of stone statues. Since this site lies outside Iran, we shall end this chapter with the description of a Parthian work of art in Iran itself, the famous bronze statue of a 'prince' (?) from Shami in the Zagros mountains (Khuzistan) (see Plate XVIIIa). It is completely preserved except for the arms. The head (which is proportionally somewhat too small) was cast separately from the body, but fits closely at the neck. The face is that of a fairly young man with a set expression. Apart from the moustache, the whiskers and the outswept hair with a band around it, the most striking feature is the man's attire. He wears a tunic that crosses over in front and reveals his bare chest, with a belt clinching the tunic, and wide trousers. Around his neck is a torque, and at his side two polished daggers. The clothes, weapons and ornaments suggest an Iranian (Elymaean?) aristocrat, but since the portrayal lacks any idiosyncratic features, the statue appears to represent a type rather than a definite individual. The aura of authority, composure and strength emanating from the figure does not alter this impression. Augustus could not refrain from celebrating his (diplomatic) victory over the Parthians in the year 20 BC by – among other things – trying to deprive his Near Eastern opponent of this kind of authority by means of a figurative programme extending all over the empire: the many-coloured Roman statues of barbarians on their bended knees carrying objects or standing up supporting things are meant to condemn this opponent to humiliating marks of respect and slavish service.

Not only their legends, but also their pictorial content, have caused the coins of the Arsacids to become important testimonies of their reign (see Plate XVIIIb). Probably introduced shortly after the mid third century BC, the Parthian coinages, which were mainly produced in Ecbatana and Seleucia-on-the-Tigris, are distinguished by special features. The principal metal for coins was silver, copper coins being mainly made for local use. Unlike their Hellenistic predecessors, the Arsacids dispensed with gold coins. The main denomination was the drachma of Attic standard, weighing about 4g; this was followed by the tetradrachm, which – contrary to the drachma – considerably diminished both in weight and in silver content in the course of time. The 4-drachma pieces are also interesting because they bear monograms of mint-masters, dates according to the Seleucid era (starting in the east with the 1st Nisan [April] 311 BC) and names of months of the Macedonian calendar.

The designs follow Hellenistic models, but have a distinctly Iranian character. The obverse shows the head of the king (usually looking towards the left), with the early rulers wearing the typical cap of the nomad warrior, the later ones either wearing the Hellenistic diadem or the Iranian royal tiara. The reverse of the drachma coins has a stereotyped image of Arsaces (I) looking to the right, and seated first on the *omphalos*, later like Zeus on the throne. The tetradrachms show the king on his throne with a bow or as *nikēphoros*, others show a scene with Tyche or the king (during investiture?) on horseback. The copper coins are iconographically more varied. On the reverse of the Parthian silver coins, there are usually Greek legends, which from the mid-first century AD gradually became more and more corrupt and were supplemented by Parthian legends in the genitive case. They are arranged in a square, and always mention the dynastic name Arsaces, describing the ruler in addition as 'great king' or 'king of kings'. Further epithets evidently were at first manifestly political assertions, but were later automatically repeated: *Basileōs Basileōn Arsakou Euergetou Dikaiou Epiphanous Philhellēnos* ('[Coin of] the king of kings Arsaces, the beneficent, just, excellent [ruler] and friend of the Greeks'). Since the real name of the king is at first only mentioned on unusual occasions, for example when rival kings appear, an identification of the ruler portrayed (and thus a dating for the coins) is not always easy. We shall have more to say about the Greek legends and the fact that the rulers called themselves 'friend of the Greeks'.

The 'vassal rulers' of Persis, Elymais and Characene also had the right to strike coins, which they did by following the Parthian models. From the end of the first century BC, there appeared overstruck Arsacid coins in eastern Iran (Sistan); these are believed to be connected with the local Pahlava dynasty (from the Parthian family of the Surens?).

CHAPTER 7

THE KING AND HIS SUBJECTS

1. *Basileus Basileōn Arsakēs Euergetēs Dikaios Epiphanēs Philhellēn*: kingship in the Arsacid empire

Our information about the beginnings of the Arsacid reign is scanty, consisting mainly of testimonies from late Western sources. Authors such as Trogus/Justin, Strabo and Arrian wondered how a dynasty risen to power from small beginnings could become a formidable opponent of Rome. We will first give Strabo a hearing:

and then [at the time of the fratricidal war between the Seleucids Seleucus II and Antiochus Hierax, 240/39 – before 236] Arsaces, a Scythian, with some of the Dahae (I mean the Aparnians [Parni], as they were called, nomads who lived along the Ochus) invaded Parthyaea and conquered it. Now at the outset Arsaces was weak, being continually at war with those who had been deprived by him of their territory, both he himself and his successors, but later they grew so strong, always taking the neighbouring territory, through success in warfare, that finally they established themselves as lords of the whole of the country inside [= east of] the Euphrates ... And at the present time they rule over so much land and so many peoples [*ethnē*] that in the size of their empire they have become, in a way, rivals of the Romans. The cause of this is their mode of life, and also their customs, which contain much that is barbarian and Scythian in character, though more that is conducive to hegemony and success in war.

Trogus/Justin drew a similar picture of the irresistible ascent of the Parthians, but described the earliest developments in more detail:

The Parthians, who hold the east in their hands as if it were their share of the world, were exiles of the Scythians ... Because of internecine wars they were driven out of Scythia, and so they settled stealthily in the barren land between Hyrcania and the tribes of the Dahae, Arians, Sparnians and Margianans. At first since the neighbours on their borders raised no objections, and later despite their attempts to prevent them, they spread out their territory to such an extent that they settled not only in immeasurably wide and low plains, but also on steep and rugged hills and mountains. That is why in most parts of the Parthian territory, there prevails either great heat or great cold, for on the mountains lies heavy snow and in the flat land there is brooding heat ... At this time ['fratricidal war' of the Seleucids] Theodotus [Diodotus], the chief of the 1,000 Bactrian towns, also broke away and had himself named king; and this example was then followed by the nations of the entire east, who broke away from the Macedonians. At this time there lived Arsaces, a man of uncertain origin, but of proven energy. When he, who was used to living as a highwayman and robber, heard the rumour that Seleucus had been defeated by the Gauls in Asia [239 BC], he was delivered from the fear of this king and invaded the Parthian territory with a band of robbers, fell upon their prefect Andragoras and, having disposed of him, made himself chief of the tribe. Shortly afterwards, he also took possession of the kingdom of the Hyrcanians, and thus, endowed with the sovereignty over two peoples, he provided himself with a powerful army for fear of Seleucus and the Bactrian king Theodotus. But the death of Theodotus having soon delivered him from fear, he formed an alliance and made peace with his son, who was also called Theodotus, and a short time later he collided with King Seleucus, who was approaching to persecute the renegades, and defeated him; and this day is ever since celebrated by the Parthians as the beginning of their freedom.

When Seleucus was thereupon called back to Asia because of further unrest, he [Arsaces] was given a free hand to reorganize the Parthian empire; he enlisted soldiers, built fortifications, and made the cities secure. He also founded a city on the Apaortenon mountain with the name of Dara, a place of such a quality and situation that there can be nothing more protected or more pleasing ... So through his both well founded and well organized kingdom, Arsaces became no less memorable among the Parthians than Cyrus was among the Persians, Alexander among the Macedonians or Romulus among the Romans; and when he then died at an advanced age, the Parthians honoured his memory by thenceforth calling all their kings Arsaces.

Arrian, however, whose *Parthika* have survived only in their Byzantine adaptation by Photius and Syncellus, presents a very different version. In it the brothers Arsaces and Tiridates (Syncellus: alleged descendants of the Persian Artaxerxes), together with five fellow conspirators, are said to have killed Pherecles (Sync.: Agathocles), who had been appointed satrap of Parthia by Antiochus Theos (II), to avenge themselves for an insult by the satrap.

Before attempting to answer the question about the political 'ideologies' or traditions behind these reports, a few words will have to be said about the chronology, geography and history of the early Arsacid empire. The Tiridates mentioned by Arrian as the brother of Arsaces is historically doubtful. The early Parthian (Parni) centres Nisa, Dara (burial place of the early kings) and

Asaak (where Arsaces I was crowned) were situated far north of the Elburz, even north of the Kopet Dagh (Nisa near Ashkhabad, Dara near Abivard between Ashkhabad and Merv). The beginning of the Parthian chronology (era), 247 BC, must go back to the earliest period of the Parni, since the actual secession of the Parthians from the Seleucids occurred later than 239 BC. After the withdrawal of Seleucus II, the Parthians may have temporarily occupied places south of the mountain-ranges (Hecatompylus?), but they lost these at the latest to Antiochus III, under whom they appear as 'vassals'. It was only under Phraates I (after 180 BC) that they undertook serious campaigns against the mountain peoples north of the Elburz, and under his successors that they advanced to regions south of the mountains. The Comisene with Hecatompylus was not added permanently to the Arsacid empire until the reign of Mithridates I.

To go back to the legends about empire founding, when Justin compared Arsaces with Cyrus, there was good reason for it. A modest background and a robber's career are similarly attributed to the founder of the Achaemenid empire (and later to Sasan, the eponymous father of the succeeding dynasty). Stories of this kind had deep roots in Iranian popular tradition and were repeatedly adapted to new names. The moral of these stories is that whoever rises to greatness from such lowly beginnings first of all possesses special political and military skills, and secondly will always remember his origins and not let himself be corrupted by wealth and luxury. Honouring the memory of the empire founder, for instance by adopting his name as the official throne-name, is an example of this deliberate creation of traditions. The Iranian 'legends of kings' also lay emphasis on the relationship of such social 'risers' with the old dynasty: Cyrus is said to have been the repudiated son of the Median king Astyages, Sasan to have belonged to the family of Dara, who reigned before Alexander. Was a similar connection with the Achaemenids suggested for Arsaces? To go back to the Syncellus version of Arrian's *Parthika*, it mentions a certain Artaxerxes as the ancestor of Arsaces. He is usually identified with the second Achaemenid king of that name of whom Ctesias maintains that he was called Arsacas/Arsaces/Arsicas before his accession to the throne. Dinon's variant of the name, Oarses (=*ho Arses*), has now been confirmed through the attestation of the name Arses as Arshu in late Babylonian astronomical texts, and so all that remains to be seen is whether the diminutive form derived from Arses – Arsicas (Arsacas, Arsaces) – may not indeed provide the link between the Arsacids and the Achaemenids.

A further remark by Arrian also points to the royal Iranian predecessors. Arsaces and Tiridates are said to have disposed of the Seleucid satrap with five helpers. The fact that the number of conspirators was seven, as in the case of Gaumata's murderers (Darius and his six helpers), can hardly be fortuitous and is probably meant to lend the *coup d'état* a national Iranian gloss. We know of a similar story regarding Mithridates I of Pontus and his revolt against Antigonus. There is no doubt that this legacy and line of descent was construed by the Parthians. Apart from Arrian's Artaxerxes and the seven conspirators, we might mention Artakhshahrakan as the name of an estate on an ostracon from Nisa dated 92 BC, the adoption of Achaemenid royal titles, and the esteem shown by the *mulūk aṭ-ṭawā'if* (the Iranian 'petty kings' after Alexander) for the Arsacids because of their descent from the old Persian royal house, as reported by Biruni, the universal Muslim scholar. There are substantial reasons to believe that in looking back at the successful foundation of the empire, and in their effort to have their sovereignty recognized, the Parthian kings 'discovered' Parthia as their 'homeland' and an Achaemenid king as their 'ancestor'. We may further assume that Mithridates I, the first Parthian for whom the Achaemenid title of 'king of kings' is recorded, played no negligible part in creating this tradition. This makes historical sense as well, for it was after all under him that the sovereignty over Parthia became the sovereignty over a great empire extending beyond the borders of Iran and requiring historical legitimation. That succession to the Achaemenids continued being part of the ideological programme of the Arsacids is proved by the fact that Artabanus II reclaimed previous Persian territories from the Romans in 35 AD, as Tacitus reports:

At the same time, he referred in boastful and menacing terms to the old boundaries of the Persian and Macedonian empires, and to his intention of seizing the territories held first by Cyrus and afterwards by Alexander.

The fact that Artabanus used Alexander's name and thus also acted as the legitimate successor of the Seleucid kings raises the question of the Parthians' attitude towards their Greek heritage. It is certainly out of the question that they had to fall back on it for want of cultural traditions of their own, even if – for quite obvious reasons – the late Sasanian tradition presented the Parthians as foreign rulers and petty kings who began their reign after the unfortunate hiatus in Iranian history (the Alexander campaign). Nor can their philhellenism be altogether explained by existing political demands such as maintaining the loyalty of their Greek subjects.

The Arsacids' genuine open-mindedness to Greek language and culture is illustrated – among other things – by the famous scene which, according to Plutarch, took place at the Armenian royal court after the Parthian victory over Crassus (53 BC):

While these things were doing, Hyrodes [Orodes] had struck up a peace with the king [Artavasdes] of Armenia, and made a match between his son, Pacorus, and the king of Armenia's sister. Their feastings and entertainments in consequence were very sumptuous, and various Grecian compositions, suitable to the occasion, were recited before them. For Hyrodes was not ignorant of the Greek language and literature, and Artabazes [Artavasdes] was so expert in it that he wrote tragedies and orations and histories, some of which are still extant. When the head of Crassus was brought to the door, the tables had just been taken away, and one Jason, a tragic actor, of the town of Tralles, was singing the scene of the *Bacchae* of Euripides concerning Agaue. He was receiving much applause, when Sillaces, coming to the room, and having made obeisance to the king, threw down the head of Crassus into the midst of the company ... Jason handed over the costume of Pentheus to one of the dancers in the chorus, and taking up the head of Crassus, and acting the part of a bacchante in her frenzy ... sang the lyric passages:

'We've hunted down a mighty chase today,
and from the mountain bring the noble prey!'

Of course, royal 'philhellenism' must not be identified with unconditional friendship for the Greeks. The guiding principle was always self-interest.

Though hardly to be interpreted as an anti-Greek movement, the policy of the Parthian kings during the last two centuries of their reign showed a deeper concern with their Iranian heritage. This is witnessed by the appearance of Parthian legends on coins, by the Zoroastrian story about King Vologeses preserving the Avesta, and also by the special furtherance of Iranian traditions. That precise historical knowledge about the Achaemenids and about Alexander was to disappear at the beginning of the Sasanian period (and perhaps already under the late Parthians) (see below) could certainly not have been suspected by anyone in Orodes's time. How is this loss of historical memory to be explained? As we have already pointed out, early Iranian culture had always been predominantly oral. Among the heroic subjects handed down because of their great popularity were epics about the kings of the Kayanid dynasty from eastern Iran, who constantly fought against their Turanian foes. In the Yashts of the Avesta, these 'heroic legends' received a Zoroastrian veneer. In view of its special charm, and perhaps also because of its religious overtones, this eastern Iranian tradition must have been superimposed, during the Parthian period, on the rest of the local or regional traditions of Iran. This led to a loss of authentic remembrance about Medes and Achaemenids in Persis. Although their monuments were in full view at Persepolis, Naqsh-i Rustam and elsewhere, all that the Sasanians knew was that these 'ancestors' had possessed a great empire extending far into the west. At the same time, the epic tradition was enlarged under the Parthians by bringing Arsacid princes and 'vassals' into it through their glorious deeds. This material was made popular by the *gōsān*, a kind of Parthian 'minstrel', 'privileged at court and popular with the people; present at the graveside and at the feast; eulogist, satirist, story-teller, musician; recorder of past achievements and commentator of his own times' (Boyce). Once the memory of Arsacid kings and Parthian 'princely houses' was also erased from the mind of the Iranians (and perhaps even deliberately suppressed by their Sasanian successors), there arose out of the remnants of their epic tradition, combined with other eastern Iranian myths and legends (e.g. the legendary cycle about the hero Rustam from Sistan) and Kayani lore, that particular form of 'Iranian national history' which – having been compiled, completed and written down in the Sasanian period – left its powerful mark on Arabic and New Persian literature. We shall return to this subject.

The tales of heroism, love and adventure told or sung at the royal court of the Arsacids or in the homes of Parthian magnates are reflected in a text that has come down to us as a New Persian poem of the eleventh century and a Georgian prose version derived from it in the twelfth century. The historical substance underlying this work, called *Vis and Ramin*, can be traced back to the Parthian period. Its similarity to *Tristan and Isolde* has often been pointed out. It is the story of the passionate love between Ramin and the bride of his brother, King Mobad, which plunges all the characters concerned into guilt and sorrow, and yet brings the lovers together at the end.

[Fakhr ad-Din Gurgani, who translated the Middle Persian rendering of the Parthian 'original' into a New Persian version, says to the person who ordered it:]

> I said: 'It is truly a beautiful story
> composed by six wise men,
> I have never seen a better one, it is
> like a garden full of flowers,
> But its language is *Pahlavi* [Middle Persian]
> and not all readers will understand the meaning.
> [...]
> But should an initiate take pains with the story,
> then it will grow beautiful like a treasured jewel.

For it is a famous story
that has countless marvels in its details.'
When the master heard me say these words,
he honoured me by putting a crown on my head:
He asked me to adorn the story
as the Nisan [April] adorns the garden.
I was encouraged to tell the story
and do my best to rid it of those senseless phrases
because those words were old-fashioned and the days of their glory were over.

2. *Reges*, *liberi* and *servi*: Parthians, Greeks and Jews: on social conditions in the Arsacid empire

Compared to the situation under the Achaemenids and Sasanians, we know little about social conditions and developments in the Iran of the Arsacids. This is especially true of the early period before the foundation of the great Parthian empire. From Trogus/Justin we learn that the Parni invaded the Parthian regions of present-day Turkmenistan out of need, and that they settled and stood their ground there, not least because their retreat was cut off. We have no idea how the Parni lived before their invasion, whether they were nomads with seasonally changing pastures or already semi-sedentary cattle-breeders (and farmers). Parthia, or rather the part of it they first occupied, was considered by the ancient authors as inhospitable country. That this is clearly an exaggeration – perhaps in order to present the rise of the Parthians as highly unusual, or to emphasize the special 'toughness' and warlike attitude of the Parni – is proved by numerous factors. In the Achaemenid period, Parthia was sufficiently 'populated' to resist Hystaspes after his son, Darius, had come into power, and could only be 'pacified' at the cost of great sacrifices. The Apavortene was the region where Arsaces had founded his new city, Dara, the first burial-place of the dynasty, known to Pliny the Elder as a place of positive *fertilitas* (i.e. self-sufficiency). And the fact that the Parthians could build cities and settlements in these regions (Astauene, Parthyene, Apavortene) must be less due to their special talent than to the conditions they found in them after their invasion. In the region east of Ashkhabad, archaeological surveys have shown evidence of urban settlements that flourished in the late Bronze and early Iron Age; their prosperity, like that of later cities in these regions, must be ascribed to large-scale irrigation schemes and the presence of oases. There have been recent attempts at attributing these early Iron Age settlements and the emergence of a new 'culture' before the middle of the first millennium to the invasion of Saka tribes. These are said to have apparently merged with the auto-chthonous (and equally Iranian) population, while their tribal chiefs are supposed to have formed a kind of 'upper crust' in these regions – a position they had even preserved during the Achaemenid period. If this was the case, then the invasion of the Parni can be imagined as a similar process, leading either to the expulsion of the provincial upper class or to a union with it, and again to a mixture of the original population with the newcomers.

For an idea about the attitude of the Parni (Parthian) aristocracy towards the rest of the Parni population and towards the subjugated Iranian people, we will turn to two classical texts. In one of them, Justin depicts social conditions in the Parthian empire, in the other Plutarch describes the deploy-ment of the Parthian army before the battle of Carrhae against Crassus. Here is Justin to start with:

The administration of the people after their secession from the Macedonian empire lay in the hands of kings. Closest to the kings in rank are the councillors [*ordo probulorum*], and from among them they choose their commanders in war [*duces*], as well as their leading politicians in peace [*rectores*]. Their army does not, like that of other nations, consist of free men, but mainly of slaves [*sed maiorem partem servitiorum habent*], whose masses grow from day to day, because there is no possibility of freeing them, so that they all remain slaves from their birth [*ac per hoc omnibus servis nascent-ibus*], but whom they then regularly instruct in riding and archery with the same care as they teach their freeborn children. The richer someone is, the more horsemen he provides for the king in the event of war. So it happened that Antony, when he took the field against the Parthians, was faced with 50,000 horsemen, but of these only 400 were free men [*liberi*]. In the end this is also the difference between slaves [*servi*] and free men [*liberi*], that the former move on foot, but the latter only on horseback.

In his biography of Crassus, Plutarch describes Surena, the Parthian commander at the battle of Carrhae, and his soldiers as follows:

Nor was this Surena an ordinary person, but in wealth, family and reputation the second man in the kingdom, and in courage and prowess the first, and for bodily stature and beauty no man like him. Whenever he travelled privately, he had one thousand camels to carry his baggage, two hundred chariots for his concubines, one thousand fully armed men [*hippeis de kataphraktoi*] for life-guards, and a great many more light-armed [*pleiontes de tōn kouphōn*]; and he had at least ten thousand horsemen altogether, of his servants and retinue [*eiche de tous sympantas hippeis homou pelatas te kai doulous myriōn apodeontas*]. The honour had long belonged to his family, that at the king's coronation he put the crown upon his head.

It would divert us too far from our subject if we tried either to explain the obvious contradiction in Justin/Trogus (*servi* learn how to ride – *servi* move only on foot) or to find out the true structure of the Parthian army at Carrhae. What does concern us here is the evident existence of groups of people – Plutarch's *pelatai* and *douloi* or Justin's *servi* – who were dependent on the Parthian aristocracy (the *liberi*). There are many indications to the effect that the *pelatai* were the native Parthian peasant population who as 'retainers' had to pay certain tributes or provide certain services to the landowning aristocracy among the Parni immigrants; while the *douloi* were even more dependent people, perhaps 'serfs' who were attached to the soil and had fallen to the lot of the Parni aristocracy when they took over the conquered lands. This does not mean that there were not also slaves (to be bought and sold) in the Parthian empire. Thus Pliny the Younger told Trajan about a certain Callidromus, who was said to have been the slave of King Pacorus, and according to Diodorus, the Parthian satrap Euhemerus (Himerus) enslaved many Babylonians and sent them to Media as war-booty. The complete publication of the *ostraca* from Nisa and their careful analysis will contribute to further disclosures about the non-aristocratic population of Parthia.

The classical sources also suggest social differentiations within the immigrant population. Thus Ammianus Marcellinus distinguishes between aristocracy and the common people (*summatus et vulgus*), and so does Tacitus (*nobilitas et plebs*). While in wartime the latter, like the retinue of the nobility, fought as mounted bowmen, the aristocrats fought as armoured horsemen. Among the aristocracy, the most distinguished were those who – either through their birth or wealth and/or on the basis of certain privileges, enjoyed special powers and a special relationship with the king; Seneca described them as *megistanes*.

Among the *ordo probulorum* (Trogus) of the Parthians were both Surena and Monaeses, but the latter went over to Antony in 37 BC for fear of King Phraates (IV). Certain noble clans, such as the Suren, Karin, Gev, et al., preserved their influence and privileges even into the Sasanian period.

Arrian's reference to the seven conspirators against Pherecles (Andragoras) also reflects this idea of privileged aristocratic clans. Unfortunately, the Parthian period has yielded no such records as the Sasanian royal inscriptions from the third century AD, which contain details about the aristocracy. These tell us that it was divided into four ranks, consisting (in order of importance) of šahrdārān ('kings', 'landholders'), vāspuhrān ('princes'), vuzurgān ('magnates', 'grandees') and *āzādān* ('nobles'). In a parchment from Dura dated 121 AD, Manesus, the son of Phraates, the *stratēgos* of Mesopotamia, is said to have held the rank of *batēsā* and to have counted among the *eleutheroi* ('free men'). Since *āzād* also means 'free', the *āzādān* may probably be identified with the *eleutheroi* (Justin's *liberi*); the *vuzurgān* are perhaps to be recognized as the *megistanes*, whom Seneca describes as the heads of the noblest clans. In the absence of adequate evidence on the subject, the question whether there already existed a proper classification of ranks in the Parthian empire will have to remain unanswered. However, the adoption of the Hellenistic system of court titles speaks for a hierarchy of ranks existing at least at court. The Parthian aristocracy must have been recognizable as such not only in war, but also in peacetime. The 'prince' of Shami with his diadem, torque and belt and his particularly striking clothes is a vivid example.

How are we to imagine the relationship between the king and the nobility? We know that already in the early phase of the Arsacid reign, a change of structure occurred, by which, under the impact of the occupation of Parthia and the simultaneous threat to such 'acquisitions', a 'commander-in-chief' was turned into a 'king' (by crowning). Whether or not Arsaces already enjoyed certain privileges beyond those of a *primus inter pares* before the invasion of Parthia is unknown. The original influence of the chiefs of other Parni clans is illustrated by the right of the Suren 'family' to crown the king, and by the *synhedrion* ('council') mentioned by Strabo (Posidonius), which 'appointed' (*kathistasthai*) the king, and which consisted of *syngeneis* (literally 'relatives' of the king, here noblemen who were close to him), as well as *sophoi* ('wise men') and *magoi* ('Magi', 'priests'). From the fact that in their later altercations with the kings, the nobility hardly envisaged any pretenders to the crown outside the Arsacid clan, it may be concluded that the Arsacids' prerogative to supply kings was not called into question.

He [King Phriapites I] died after fifteen years of reign, leaving behind two sons, Mithridates and Phrahates [Phraates]. The elder, Phrahates, the heir to the throne according to the tradition of his clan, subjected the Mardi, a powerful people, in a war, but not long afterwards he died, and although he left several sons behind, he bequeathed the reign to his brother Mithridates, passing over his sons.

So according to Trogus/Justin, the king himself had the right to appoint his successor, and it was usually the eldest son who became his heir. It was then for the nobility (or their representative council) to confirm the successor.

That this confirmation required carrying out certain formalities is shown by an episode recorded by Tacitus:

Then, as he [Tiridates, the grandson of Phraates IV and opponent of Artabanus II] was debating what day to fix for his formal assumption of sovereignty, he received letters from Phraates and Hiero, holders of the two most powerful satrapies, asking for a short postponement. It was decided to wait for men of their high importance, and in the interval a move was made to the seat of government at Ctesiphon. However, as day after day found them still procrastinating, the Surena, before an applauding multitude, fastened, in the traditional style, the royal diadem upon the brows of Tiridates ... For Phraates and Hiero, with others who had taken no share in the solemnities of the day fixed for the assumption of the diadem, some in fear, a few in jealousy of Abdagaeses (now master of the court and the newly crowned king), went to Artabanus.

It is hardly surprising that after the end of the great conquests which had joined king and nobility in the same aims, the latter, backed by a body of retainers, should make bold to intervene in struggles about the throne in times that were favourable to them, making contacts with foreign powers for that purpose and even deposing the old king.

So because of his cruelty, Mithridates [II], the Parthian king, was ousted from kingship by the senate [senatus] after his Armenian war. His brother Orodes took possession of the empty throne.

The suggestion that this might illustrate an evolution from hereditary to elective kingship must be called into question. It is equally unjustified to ascribe to Parthian history the same process of 'decadence' or 'decline' that was imputed to the Achaemenid empire after Xerxes. The great success of the Parthians at Mesene, of which the statue of Heracles informs us, the victory of the last king Artabanus over Rome, and the long resistance of the Armenian Arsacids against the Sasanians should make us wary of such conclusions. Depending on the personalities of the kings, the resources of power at their disposal – such as mercenary troops – the ambitions of individual heads of clans or members of the royal family, and, to a great extent, on the situation prevailing in foreign affairs, the conflicts between king and nobility were decided sometimes in one side's favour and sometimes the other's. And like the royal family, the Parthian aristocracy was also often enough 'divided' because of rivalries between heads of clans. So the Parthian reign was more than the reign of 'petty kings' which it was made out to be by the late Sasanian tradition.

How a possible transfer or confirmation of rights of property or usufruct was made from king to nobleman and from nobleman to his dependants is difficult to imagine. Similarly, nothing is known about their respective duties and services, and we can merely speculate about their being based on personal allegiance, perhaps solemnly confirmed by an oath. As long as this is so, concepts such as 'feudal system' should be completely avoided, and ones such as a 'vassal status' used only with the necessary discretion.

In the heartlands of the Parthian empire there lived, aside from the aristocracy and the peasant (and artisan) population of different origins and status, a 'middle class' consisting of people whose special knowledge, skills and services could not easily be dispensed with in the royal residences and aristocratic households. These were artists, craftsmen, traders, physicians, eunuchs and other 'personnel', as well as the 'minstrels' (gōsān) already mentioned.

For the population of the conquered regions, the Greeks and Jews may serve as representative examples. After the expulsion of the Seleucids, the Greek element survived not only in its art and culture, but also in its personal and institutional components. This is confirmed by Arsacid coins, as well as archaeological and inscriptional findings from Mesopotamia and Iran. A Greek inscription from the year 110/09 BC provides a list of ephebes and neoi ('young men') as winners at athletic competitions, thus bearing witness to the existence of a Greek–Macedonian 'community' in Babylon (a polis?), which also boasted a Greek theatre, an agora and a gymnasion. From other inscriptions we learn that Greek poleis, probably founded in the third century, also existed in Susa (Seleucia-on-the Eulaeus, see below) and on the Silhu river (Apamea-Silhu). As for Seleucia-on-the-Tigris and Dura-Europus, the most important settlements under Parthian sovereignty, there will be more to say about them. Greeks also influenced the intellectual life of these areas, among them Archedemus the Stoic (presumably a disciple of Diogenes ['the Babylonian' from Seleucia]), who founded a school of philosophy in Babylon in the Parthian period, the geographers Dionysius and Isidorus of Charax, the historians Agathocles of Babylon and Apollodorus of Artemita. Greeks (and Babylonians with Greek names) were also in the service of Parthian overlords like Xenon, a 'messenger' of the governor of Babylonia. Yet the guiding principle of the Parthians in their attitude towards the Greeks always remained self-interest. If these aliens turned out to be the 'Fifth Column' of a foreign power, as at Syrinx in the year 209 BC during the attack of Antiochus III, or in Babylonia after the victory of Phraates II over Antiochus VII, then violence was used against them.

Two Greek *poleis* require more detailed attention. In Susa, archaeological investigations have shown an extraordinary expansion of the city and intensive building activity under Parthian rule. What is interesting is the simultaneous change in the economic structure of the city and of Susiana in general. Susa as a trade centre gave way to Susa as the centre of a region intensively used as farmland. Greek inscriptions witness the interest shown by the Greek city élite in promoting this fundamental element of their wealth, but at the same time point to the limited autonomy of the city in the face of royal superintendence. Regarding Seleucia-on-the-Tigris, which we will exceptionally include in these observations, although it lay outside Iran, a most remarkable record about the relations between the king and his Greek subjects has come down to us. It is a report by Tacitus about the history of this city at the beginning of the first century AD.

The extreme of adulation was shown by the powerful community of Seleucia, a walled town which, faithful to the memory of its founder Seleucus, has not degenerated into barbarism. Three hundred members, chosen for wealth or wisdom, form a senate: the people has its own prerogatives. So long as the two orders are in unison, the Parthian is ignored: if they clash, each calls in aid against its rival; and the alien, summoned to rescue a part, overpowers the whole. This had happened lately in the reign of Artabanus, who consulted his own ends by sacrificing the populace to the aristocrats: for supremacy of the people is akin to freedom; between the domination of a minority and the whim of a monarch the distance is small. They now celebrated the arrival of Tiridates with the honours paid to the ancient kings, along with the innovations of which a later age has been more lavish: at the same time, they poured abuse on Artabanus as an Arsacid on the mother's side, but otherwise of ignoble blood. Tiridates handed over the government of Seleucia to the democracy.

What strikes us in the first place is that Tacitus also uses the cliché of the *degeneratio* (of a city, of a people) through the influence of 'barbarian' customs and usages. Secondly, it is clear that the Parthian pretenders to the throne, Artabanus and Tiridates, supported different 'parties' in Seleucia: Artabanus the Greek upper class (which also controlled the 'council' [*senatus/ boulē*]) of this city with its alleged 600,000 inhabitants, and Tiridates the *populus*, a term usually interpreted to include mainly the non-Greek elements of the population (natives, Jews, Syrians). More plausible, however, is a conflict between the oligarchic and 'democratic' parties, following the model of the *staseis* (internal strifes) in the Greek *poleis* of the classical period, a conflict in which the ethnic factor was not decisive. Seleucia's 'popular party' sided with Tiridates and was able, after his failure, to stand its ground against

Artabanus from 35 to 42 AD. Only afterwards did the city surrender to his son Vardanes, who appeared in it as master of the mint in June 42 AD and had the *boulē* struck on the reverse of coins in both image and legend. For the alleged 'orientalization' of the place after this year, there is neither archaeological nor numismatic evidence. The fact that both Artabanus and Tiridates had only their own interests in mind can be gathered not only from Tacitus, but also from numismatic data showing that in 23/24 AD, royal bronze coins were issued in lieu of the municipal coinage. Artabanus hence encroached on the autonomy of a city which, at the time, was still controlled by the *boulē*; in addition, this king renounced the attribute 'philhellene'.

For a long time the centres of Jewish life in the Parthian empire were also situated in Mesopotamia – for example, in Nisibis and Nehardea. Although nothing is known about the internal and intellectual life of these communities, it is a fact that they enjoyed a period of peace and maintained close and positive contacts with the reigning dynasty. This is proved, among other things, by the participation of the Jews in the rebellions against Trajan in Mesopotamia (116 AD). In addition, the Jews took an active part in organizing the silk trade, an advantage they owed to the evident support of the kings. Not later than in the second century AD, an exilarch of Davidic origin (*rēš gālūtā'*) represented the Jewish minority at court and also carried out functions of a political–administrative nature. With the religious persecutions in Palestine after the Bar-Kochba revolt (135 AD), Tannaitic refugees also brought traditions of the Palestinian academies to Mesopotamia.

CHAPTER 8

SATRAPS, TRADERS, SOLDIERS AND PRIESTS: ADMINISTRATION, ECONOMY, THE ARMY AND CULTS IN ARSACID IRAN

Unlike the Seleucid and Sasanian periods, the Arsacid empire is very poorly documented in terms of its administration. We lack the kind of information from Western sources that enabled us to reconstruct Seleucid administrative institutions, and such data as the inscriptions on seals and bullae which helped us to achieve the same purpose for Sasanian Iran. As for potential evolutions and changes in Arsacid administrative history, they are hardly possible to detect. So we can do no more than speculate about the relationship between well attested early Sasanian territorial units and those of the late Parthian period.

The Parthi possess in all eighteen kingdoms [*regna*], such being the divisions of their provinces on the coasts of two seas, as we have stated, the Red Sea on the south and the Caspian Sea on the north. Of these provinces the eleven designated the Upper Kingdoms begin at the frontiers of Armenia and the shores of the Caspian, and extend to the Scythians ... The remaining seven kingdoms are called the Lower Kingdoms.

If we relate this report by the Roman geographer Pliny the Elder to his period, he must have had in mind the 'principalities' which were dependent on the Parthian king, although their dynasts could be entitled to call themselves kings. Among these we can certainly count Persis, Elymais, Mesene (Characene), Hatra, Osrhoene, Adiabene, Media Atropatene, and probably Hyrcania. From the great inscription of the second Sasanid king Shapur, we find out in addition about the 'kingdoms' of Segan (on the Black Sea), Virozan (on its east), Armen (Armenia), Balasagan (west of the Caspian Sea), Gelan (south-west of the Caspian Sea), Kerman, Makran, Turgistan, Hind (all of them east of Kerman), Sakastan (Sistan), Marv and Choresmia. Most of these must have already existed under the Parthians, whose 'regional kings' were now replaced by 'princes' of the Sasanian royal house.

Regarding Persis, as well as other parts of the empire, there is proof that the Parthians, when establishing their sovereignty in these regions, retained the dynasts who had been acting on behalf of the Seleucids (or had just become independent), so long as they recognized Parthian sovereignty. This recognition was also a condition for the confirmation (or re-establishment) of the regional mintage right and other prerogatives. These 'petty kings', for their part, carried out their own policies under certain political circumstances. They interfered in fights about the throne, like Izates of Adiabene, who supported Artabanus II; they went over to the enemy's side, like the king of Mesene after Trajan's campaign; or else they aspired towards full independence from the empire. Normally these dynasts were committed to go to war for the Arsacids. In particularly important parts of the empire, such as Media or Armenia, members of the Arsacid family were appointed as kings after the reign of Mithridates II. So it is not surprising that to the Romans (Pliny) the Arsacid empire of the first century AD appeared as an association of *regna* rather than as a unified state. However, the weakness or strength of the empire cannot be ascertained from this structure alone.

Aside from the 'kingdoms', there were regions subject to the king alone and administered by 'satraps' (or stratēgoi), for example in Mesopotamia. Tacitus mentions *praefecturae* as territorial units, Isidorus of Charax refers to the provinces by their names (Choarene, Comisene, etc.). On a Greek inscription from Bisutun, there is even a 'satrap of satraps', conceptually a deliberate imitation of the title 'king of kings'.

Important officials are also mentioned in the *ostraca* from Nisa, for instance *hštrpn* ('satraps'), a *mrzwpn* ('margrave', 'warden of the marches') and a *dyzpty* ('commander of a fortress'). From Dura we learn of a **hargbad* (Greek *arkapatēs:* '[chief] tax collector'? 'commander-in-chief of a fortress'?).

The magnates of the empire possessed vast landed properties in Iran: the Suren clan in Sistan and elsewhere, the Karin in the Nihavand area in Media. Whether these properties were registered for tax purposes, and if so how, are questions that remain unanswered.

Our information is equally scant about agriculture in Iran during the

Arsacid period, except for the fact that archaeological investigations in Susiana have shown an improvement in farming techniques and progress in the cultivation of rice under the Parthians. These must have made up for Susa's dwindling importance as a trading centre by having the city remain at least a regional market.

We are more conversant with trade in the Parthian empire, especially long-distance trade, in which Parthians or individuals acting on their behalf controlled the exchange of goods by land from west to east and vice-versa. Seeing that their eastern trade depended on Parthian middlemen, and also that transport by sea was considerably cheaper, the Romans, for their part, tried to choose the sea-route for their contacts with Arabia and India. For a number of reasons, however, maritime trade never completely supplanted overland trade. Apart from the route from Syria over Mesopotamia and Iran to China (the 'Silk Road'), a significant part was also played by the combined land-and-sea trade, leading from Syria to southern Mesopotamia (Mesene) and from there by sea to India (and also overland further east). For this route, the inhabitants of Palmyra in Syria were the 'middlemen', transporting goods between Syria and Mesene as transit traders. Although their success entirely depended on friendly relations between the Roman and Arsacid empires, these two great powers must have been sufficiently interested in such contacts to allow the Palmyrans to exercise their activity for a long time and in relative peace. This interest shared by both Parthians and Romans is illustrated in Caracalla's offer to Artabanus IV, as reported by Herodian:

Furthermore [C. had previously commented upon the political and military advantages of a close cooperation between the two powers, which he wished to establish through a union by marriage], the locally grown spices of the Parthians and their wonderful clothes, and on the other side, the metals produced by the Romans and their admirable manufactured goods would no longer be difficult to get and in short supply, smuggled in by merchants. Instead both sides would have commerce and unimpeded advantage from the unification of their countries under a single rule.

The Palmyrans had their own trading posts in Parthian trading centres such as Seleucia, Babylon, Vologesias and Spasinu Charax. The friendly terms between Rome and the Parthians during the reign of the emperors Hadrian and Antoninus Pius are attested by the abundant Palmyran caravan site inscriptions at this time, and also by the existence of a temple in Vologesias devoted to the cult of the Roman emperors. A Graeco-Palmyran bilingual inscription dated 138 AD from the agora in Palmyra bears witness to the tribute paid by the city council to a widely travelled Palmyran:

... who had at any moment readily cooperated with the merchants who [were] in Spasinu Charax, who was associated with them, and who did not spare personal effort or money, and who volunteered to go as an emissary to Orodes, the king of Elymais ...

The inscription thus bears witness not only to the connections between Palmyra and Mesene (which was independent from the Arsacid empire at the time), but also to those between Spasinu Charax and Susa. Further epigraphic records show that Palmyrans also travelled to Bahrain, the Indus delta and India.

While the Romans bought mainly spices (pepper), aromatics, perfumes, precious stones and pearls from India, they themselves supplied linen fabrics, silver vessels, gold and wine. But India was also an intermediate trading centre for merchandise from China, above all the much-coveted silk, which could also be acquired by way of Iran. Parthian imports from China in addition included the famous 'Seric iron' (steel), as well as apricots and peaches. Goods dispatched in return were pomegranates – the 'Parthian fruit' - vine and lucerne, and particularly the famous Nisaean horses from Media, which became famous in China as 'heavenly horses'. The western part of the 'Silk Road' is described by Isidorus of Charax in his *Stathmoi Parthikoi*. Here we learn that Antiochia-on-the-Orontes and Zeugma-on-the-Euphrates were the western starting-points from which people travelled via Seleucia/Ctesiphon/Vologesias through the Zagros mountains over Bisutun, Ecbatana, Rhaga, the Caspian Gates, Comisene, Hyrcania, Asaak, Nisa, Margiana (Merv), Aria (Herat), Drangiana and Sistan to Arachosia (Alexandropolis). In Iran, there was also an old road leading from Damghan to Herat without passing through Hyrcania and the regions north of the Kopet Dagh. But to Isidorus, who was a Parthian subject, it seemed less important than the one which included the early Parthian residences. The usual itinerary of the 'Silk Road' led from Merv via Afrasiab (Samarkand) further east.

About the Parthian army our information is also insufficient, consisting only of scattered references by ancient authors, archaeological finds of weapons and equipment, and, above all, illustrations of Parthian warriors on reliefs and graffiti. The crucial element of the Parthian military impact was the cavalry, divided into the heavily armoured cataphracts (see Plate XIX) and the lighter, more mobile, mounted archers. These two formations had to complement each other from a tactical point of view. While it was the task of the mounted bowmen to wear down the opponent with a steady volley of arrows, the cataphract cavalry usually carried out a frontal attack on the weakened enemy troops. In comparison, the infantry was evidently of secondary importance, although according to the Christian–Syrian 'Chronicle of Arbela', Vologeses III was said to have sent 20,000 footsoldiers against the Alans in 136 AD. The mercenaries enlisted by the king were not only important from a military point of view, but also politically, as a royal safeguard against the power of the landed aristocracy, from among whose *pelatai* and *douloi* the Parthian army was usually recruited.

The light cavalry were clothed in belted tunics and wide trousers with the lower part stuck in their boots. Their crucial weapon was the compound bow. As for the 'armoured cavalry' (*kataphraktoi*), a unit already known – though with lighter armour – under the Achaemenids, the Parthians had both men and horses protected with mail and plate armour or cuirasses. These fully armoured horsemen were later called *clibanarii* by the Romans. Their weapon was the lance, which, according to Plutarch, 'had impetus enough to pierce through two men at once'. The Romans often had to yield to the tactics and fighting strength of the Parthian army. This was especially the case with Crassus at the battle of Carrhae in 53 BC:

While the Romans were in consternation at this din [the beating of a kind of drum], suddenly their enemies dropped the coverings of their armour, and were seen to be themselves blazing in helmets and breastplates, their Margianian steel glittering keen and bright, and their horses clad in plates of bronze and steel ... But the Parthians now stood at long intervals from one another and began to shoot their arrows from all sides at once, not with any accurate aim ... but making vigorous and powerful shots from bows which were large and mighty and curved so as to discharge their missiles with great force. But when they [the Romans] perceived that many camels laden with arrows were at hand, from which the Parthians who first encircled them took a fresh supply, then Crassus ... began to lose heart ... [After a sally of the Roman cavalry, the Romans were expecting close combat.] But the Parthians stationed their mail-clad horsemen in front of the Romans, and then with the rest of their cavalry in loose array rode round them, tearing up the surface of the ground, and raising from the depths great heaps of sand which fell in limitless showers of dust, so that the Romans could neither see clearly nor speak plainly, but, being crowded into a narrow compass and falling one upon the other, were shot, and died.

Famous and notorious, too, was the 'Parthian shot', a volley of arrows discharged backwards by the mounted bowmen while they pretended to flee. The horses of the Parthians, illustrated on seal imprints from Nisa and early Sasanian rock reliefs and coins, were praised for their beauty and size, and, according to Trogus/Justin, formed the centre of attraction in Parthian life.

They ride horses at all times; they sit on their backs in wartime and at feasts, and on any public or private occasion. Whether moving or stopping, trading or talking, everything is done on horseback.

It is generally assumed that the Arsacids, despite their political 'tolerance' regarding other religions, were attached to the Zoroastrian faith in some form or another. Unfortunately, our main testimonies about the religious conditions of their time do not concern the Iranian heartlands, but Armenia and Asia Minor (or else Mesopotamia with its plethora of different non-Iranian cults and religious ideas). The following may serve as evidence for the Zoroastrianism of the Arsacids: testimonies from Nisa referring to a 'fire priest' ('*tvršpty*) and a 'Magus' (*MGWŠH*), as well as the use of the Zoro-astrian calendar; Justin's statement about their exposing their dead ('Their funerals usually consist of letting their dead be torn to pieces by birds and dogs; only the naked skeleton is then covered with earth'); and the role of the Parthian king Valakhsh (Vologeses) as compiler of the Avesta in the Zoroastrian tradition.

Other characteristics of the Parthian period that made an impression on Western authors were the ever-burning (royal?) fire of Asaak and the marriages between close relatives. Within the purely Iranian context, the Parthians used a chronology of their own, beginning on the 1st Nisan (= 14 April) 247 BC, which was occasionally used together with the chronology of the Seleucid era. Thus the letter from Artabanus II to Susa is dated as follows: 'In the year 268 by the royal chronology, in the year 333 by the old chronology [21 AD].' The stele of Khvasak from Susa, however, only mentions the Arsacid era (and uses Zoroastrian names of months and days): 'Year 426, month Spandarmat, Mihr-day [14 September 215].'

PART FOUR

IRAN FROM ARDASHIR I
TO YAZDGIRD III: THE REIGN
OF THE SASANIANS

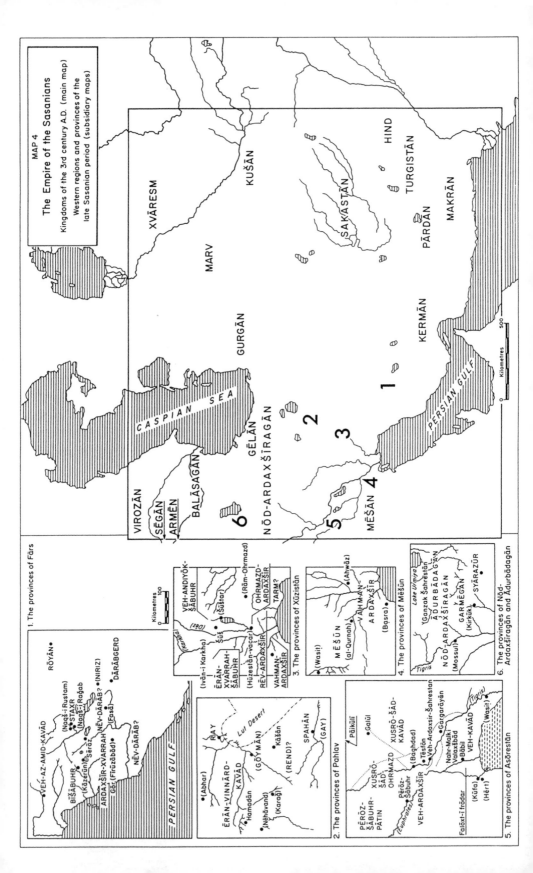

MAP 4
The Empire of the Sasanians

Kingdoms of the 3rd century A.D. (main map)
Western regions and provinces of the
late Sasanian period (subsidiary maps)

CHAPTER 9

THE TESTIMONIES

1. Royal inscriptions, Roman–Byzantine, Christian–Syriac, Manichaean, Armenian and Arabic sources: languages, writing systems and written traditions of the Sasanian empire

When on 28 April 224 the Parthian King Ardavan (Artabanus) IV laid down his life in the battle against his challenger Ardashir, this marked the beginning of the end of the almost 500-year-old Arsacid reign over Iran. The new masters from the 'house' of Sasan, who had begun their ascent as local dynasts of Istakhr near Persepolis and extended their domain since 205/06 at the expense of other 'petty kings' of the south, in the following years came into possession of all the Parthian territories, as well as north-eastern Arabia. From their predecessors they inherited, apart from many initiatives in the economic, social and cultural realms, the foreign and domestic policy problems connected with ruling Iran and Mesopotamia. These included the potential opponents to the west and east (Romans, steppe populations) and rivalry between kings and the landed aristocracy. Despite the major crises of the late third century (fratricidal war and defeat against Rome) and those of the fifth century (defeat against the Hephthalites, famine, popular rebellions), the Sasanians, in their turn, maintained their throne and sovereignty for over 400 years. The culminating periods of their empire were the reigns of Ardashir I and his son Shapur I, and those of Shapur II in the fourth and Khosrow I in the sixth centuries. Thanks to their influence on the development of 'Iranian national history', the Sasanians have taken their place, side by side with the ancient mythical kings and the eastern Iranian Kayanians, as Iranian rulers *par excellence*, living on in the epics of Firdausi and Nizami, as well as in the chronicles of Islamic historians and in popular fiction.

Luckily for present-day inquirers like ourselves, the Sasanians, especially their early kings, felt compelled to lend full written and pictorial expression to their own ambitions and aspirations. Consequently their inscriptions and reliefs, as well as their palaces, fire temples and coins, have come down to us in numerous examples. In addition, contemporary and later writers, Christian and Manichaean subjects, as well as Roman–Byzantine or early Islamic historians, took issue with the Sasanian state, either because they had past or present experiences with it as their religious persecutor or military opponent, or because they tried to insert the history of pre-Islamic Iran into the context of the 'salvation history' introduced by Muhammad's mission.

Even if these 'sources' flow more copiously than those for the Arsacid empire, they should not induce us to fit together all the pieces, no matter what their origin or period, like parts of a puzzle so as to assemble a picture of Sasanian Iran. That would make us lose sight of changes and evolutions and would lead to a grave neglect of the specific circumstances behind the origin of each piece of evidence and the motives of its creator or patron. An alternative is to divide the sources into primary, secondary and tertiary, in accordance with the time and place of their origin, their language and their cultural tradition. The written records will then yield the following result. The primary sources include trilingual, bilingual and monolingual inscriptions, the most significant of which are the *res gestae* of Shapur I on the Ka'ba-i Zardusht at Naqsh-i Rustam (see Plate Xb) near Persepolis (ŠKZ), the inscription of Galerius's opponent, King Narseh, at Paikuli (NPi; see Plate XXXa), and the self-testimonial of the *mōbad* ('priest') Kirdir (see Plate XXXb) at Naqsh-i Rajab.

These inscriptions are important, first of all for our knowledge about the early Sasanian court, since some of them mention the major officials of the empire with their titles and functions; secondly, because the way they present the kings with their titles and speeches embodies a specific idea of kingship as the intercessory authority between the god Ohrmazd (Ahura Mazda) and the royal subjects; and thirdly, because some of them can be considered as *res gestae*, thus acting as a corrective, especially with regard to Roman and Arabic records. It goes without saying that these inscriptions can only be viewed as extremely one-sided evidence of the royal patron's image of himself. In their original versions on rock faces and buildings in 'sacred sites', they were meant to proclaim the king's intimate relationship with his 'ancestors' and gods, and in their copies, none of which has survived, they were efforts to prove his legitimacy to the outside world.

Thus Shapur writes in his *res gestae*:

I, the Mazda-worshipping god Shapur, king of kings of Eran and Aneran ['non-Iran'], whose origin stems from the gods, son of the Mazda-worshipping god Ardashir, king of kings of Eran, whose origin stems from the gods, grandson of the god Pabag, am the ruler of the empire of Eran. And I possess [the following] countries [provinces; Greek *ethnē*]: ... And the people we displaced from the Roman empire, from Aneran, those we settled in the empire of Eran, in Persis, in Parthia, in Susiana, in Mesopotamia and in all other provinces in which we, our father and our ancestors and forefathers possessed crown domains [Greek *ktismata*]. And we searched out (for combat) many other peoples and accomplished a great number of glorious and heroic deeds which have not been recorded here ... Therefore we ordered them to be written down so that he who comes after us will recognize these glorious and heroic deeds and our reign.

Shapur had his *res gestae* placed at a well chosen site, on a building (Kaʿba-i Zardusht) erected in the Achaemenid period (according to Shapur: under his 'forefathers') at Naqsh-i Rustam in the vicinity of Istakhr and Persepolis, in front of the rock face with the tombs of the Persian kings (see below). Following the example of his 'forefathers', he had them inscribed in three languages: Middle Persian, Parthian and Greek. Narseh, who had to fight for his 'throne', describes his conflict with his rival Bahram III and the way he was subsequently acknowledged (and crowned) by the great men of the empire in a bilingual (Middle Persian and Parthian) inscription on the Paikuli monument in Iraqi Kurdistan. And Kirdir, who had become one of the most powerful men of the state in the second half of the third century, chose four eminent 'royal' places to display his account of his social and political rise, his labours for Zoroastrianism (and his spiritual experience on a journey to the other world?). Among other inscriptions from the Sasanian period, the most significant are the commemorative inscription of the 'governor' of the city of Bishapur (Veh-Shabuhr) for Shapur I, announcing a 'Sasanian era' (see Plate XXXIa), and the recently discovered inscription of Abnun, which tells about a victory of Shapur (I) over the Romans in 242 AD, and confirms 239/40 as Shapur's first year of reign.

As for the secondary sources, they can be mainly divided into Greek and Latin documents, which were contemporary, though remote from Iran, and native Syrian and Manichaean testimonies written for the most part later. Though not always entirely reliable, both Dio Cassius and Herodian, who partially depended on him, witnessed the rise of the Sasanians under Ardashir, but only one of them, Herodian, was able to appreciate the full extent of the 'Persian danger'. A further author worth mentioning is Heliodorus of Emesa, to whose *Aithiopika* we are indebted for a precise description of the Persian armoured horsemen, a description that is impressively confirmed in rock reliefs, graffiti and archaeological finds.

The most prominent among the later Western authors are: Ammianus Marcellinus from Antiochia-on-the-Orontes, who, continuing where Tacitus left off, wrote his only partially extant history of the Sasanian–Roman wars of the fourth century from his own point of view; Procopius of Caesaraea in Palestine, a confidant of the Byzantine general Belisarius, who wrote eight books about the wars against the Persians, Vandals and Goths in the sixth century; and Agathias of Myrina in Asia Minor, who in his historical work *On the Reign of Justinian* tried to continue the work of Procopius both historically and formally and claimed to have had access to the royal Sasanian archives.

Within the Christian tradition, numerous 'Acts of Martyrs' provide information about Christianity's early history and self-image in the Sasanian empire, and the religious policy of the rulers. We also owe valuable details to (local) chronicles and church histories with their sometimes astonishingly accurate chronology and reliability. This should be pointed out despite the fact that late publication dates, poor manuscript preservation and hagiographical hyperbole and formularity necessarily call for great care in historical interpretation. Many a chronicler, martyr or hagiographer had acquired a good deal of his knowledge because he was a convert from Zoroastrianism to Christianity and had previously carried out important functions in the service of the 'king of kings', so that he was quite familiar with the institutions, social structures and customs of Sasanian Iran. A great many 'holy' traditions, religious teachings and community rules were committed to writing and have thus been preserved.

Here is a quotation of the first lines of a martyr's story from Adiabene:

In the thirty-seventh year of our persecution [under Shapur II in the fourth century] a cruel command was issued, and the mobads were given power over all Christians to torment them with tortures and pains and to kill them by stoning and execution. The good shepherds who did not hide during this persecution were accused by the servants of evil, who said to the judges: 'The Christians destroy our doctrine and teach people to serve only *one* god, not to pray to the sun, not to worship fire, to pollute water by hateful washing, not to marry, not to beget sons or daughters, not to take the field with the kings, not to kill, to butcher and eat animals without qualms, to bury the dead in the earth and to say that God, not Satan, has created snakes, scorpions and all the vermin of the world. They also spoil many servants of the king and teach them magic, which they call writings.' When the evil judges heard this, they flew into a great rage that burnt in them like fire in wood.

The content of this argument will have to be discussed in more detail.

Within the Manichaean tradition, the original Coptic writings of the Manichaeans from central Egypt – parts of which were unfortunately lost in the wartime troubles of 1945 – as well as the extensive finds, at the beginning of this century, of Middle Iranian, Old Turkish and Chinese texts from the Tarim basin of Chinese Turkistan, have given us a deeper insight into the doctrines of Mani. Thanks to them, we can now approach these teachings, and also the early history of the Manichaean mission and the Manichaeans' relations with the Sasanian political and religious authorities, not only from the point of view of their Christian and Zoroastrian opponents, but also against the background of their own concept of themselves and own body of traditions. Although the writings in question mainly consist of texts (or manuscripts) of a later tradition, they also contain remnants of 'books' composed by Mani, the founder of the religion, himself. Of special significance in this connection is the 'Cologne Mani Codex' (CMC), a tiny Greek manuscript on parchment, presumably from the fifth century, which has given Mani scholarship a new foundation, especially regarding questions about the religious milieu in which its founder was brought up.

Also to be mentioned here are the Armenian historians, whose testimonies are relevant not only because Armenia was closely connected with Iran during the Sasanian period, but also because they contribute a wealth of individual observations about the history and culture of the Sasanian heartlands. However, we must avoid overestimating their reliability or blindly trusting the information they provide, especially about the early Sasanian period. The Armenian – i.e. often anti-Iranian – tendency is evident, and most of the works were written in the fifth century (Agathangelos, the historical epic ascribed to Faustos [Buzandats'i], Eznik of Koghb, Ghasar of Pharph), or even as late as the ninth century (the comprehensive history of Moses Khorenats'i).

On the borderline between secondary and tertiary sources – especially with reference to the early Sasanian period – are the literary testimonies in the Middle Persian language with their religious, Avesta-oriented and epic–courtly character. We must remember that most of these texts were not written down until the late Sasanian and even the Islamic period, and that the earliest extant manuscripts go back only to the thirteenth century. The reason for this late recording lay on the one hand in the predominantly oral character of Iranian culture, and on the other in the reminiscences of the 'good religion', as it called itself, as a result of the Muslim conquest and the times of distress. Of course, the survival of certain historical details from the early Sasanian period cannot be ruled out, but in assessing the reliability of data concerning the remote past, it is better to be sceptical. The tendency to project certain institutions, customs and conditions back into the period of empire founders is as familiar a phenomenon in oral cultures as is the organic, unintentional modification of traditions. Investigations show, however, that this does not apply to religious literature, in which – precisely for the cultic-ritual prescriptions and the 'holy texts' – a closer and more lasting literality can be observed. Particularly well qualified Zoroastrian priests are thus believed to have preserved the tradition as 'living books'.

As already indicated in the section about the Arsacids, the 'Iranian national history' was written down in the late Sasanian period. Its summary in the form of the Khvaday-namag ('Book of Lords') at the end of the reign of Khosrow II (590–628) may have been motivated by the need to remember the glorious past in the face of a rather gloomy present. The result, at any rate, was the long history of Iran from the first world king Gayomard to the period of Khosrow II, by way of the reigns of fifty kings and queens. Despite all the attempts at connecting or unifying the material in it, there are passages in which the original independent and individual 'legendary cycles' can be detected. It is interesting to observe that the 'heroic' times are usually superseded by periods in which seers, men leading holy lives or 'prophets' raise ethical or moral questions, letting the wars recede into the background. As a genre, the 'national history' thus presents a mixture of heroic material, sayings by kings and 'sages', clerical controversies, philosophical reflections, moral prescriptions, royal testaments and speeches from the throne, with questions about justice, piety and the exemplary life again and again being thrown into relief. However, the 'Book of Lords' was not merely a semi-official 'history book', but also a work of literary entertainment and social education. It was intended to proclaim the moral and politico-social ideals or subjects' virtues on which the Sasanian kings based their empire and by means of which it was said to survive. The life stories of kings, heroes and 'sages' formed the background for the illustration of these ideals, and the discrimination between myth, legend and historical fact was of minor importance.

As for the rest of Middle Persian literature, more of it has indeed survived than from the Parthian period; but if we exclude religious and juridical instruction, nothing much remains except the 'poem' *Ayādgār ī Zarērān* ('Memorial of Z.'). Such poems were usually sung to the accompaniment of a musical instrument. The Sasanian court supported poets and singers; thus Bahram V was said to have given them the highest rank at court. Sung poetry survived the fall of the empire and was even practised in the Islamic period, especially in the countryside. Unfortunately, relatively few of the literary works that were produced in the Sasanian period have come down to us. Many were lost at the time of the Muslim conquest of Iran or during later invasions, others were 'put on the index' by religious zealots, and yet others 'neglected' by the conversion from the Aramaic-Middle-Persian to the Arabic script. Arabic and modern Persian translations and adaptations, as well as bibliographical summaries and notes, provide only a poor impression of the wealth and range of Sasanian literature. Middle Persian literature is in fact known to have comprised (apart from religious writings) historical, geographical, didactical and astronomical works, regional studies and travelogues, titles about good behaviour and etiquette, historical novels and romances, popular fiction and other genres.

Although the wealth of information they contain does not appear to justify it, the works of Perso-Arabic historiography must nevertheless be classified as 'tertiary' sources (especially when dealing with the early Sasanian empire). This is because authors of universal history in the Arabic language owe their view of the Sasanians mainly to the late Middle Persian tradition. Their value lies in the transmission of Sasanian material that would otherwise have been lost, but this transmission went through three stages: it was written down and revised or edited in the late Sasanian period, translated and arranged in the early Islamic period, and made to conform with the specific Muslim conception of history. To what extent information about the early Sasanian period was intentionally distorted or organically altered in this process cannot altogether be determined. Only a scrupulous comparison of the Arabic with the contemporary Sasanian tradition on specific questions may lead to improving our knowledge in this field; what is also required is the precise demarcation of the 'actual' meaning of these writings from what present-day research expects of them.

2. Firuzabad, Naqsh-i Rustam, Bishapur and Taq-i Bustan: silver bowls, coins, seals and bullae: archaeological and numismatic testimonies of the Sasanian period from Iran

Closely connected with the epigraphic testimonies as regards both sites and subjects are the reliefs of the Sasanian kings, among which those representing the investiture of Ardashir I and the 'deeds' of his son Shapur are doubtless the most famous. Through their location at the 'sacred' places of their forefathers or at sites of their own great military victories, through their combination of cosmic and worldly events, and their compound and cumulative character, these reliefs are eloquent witnesses of the sovereigns' images of themselves and their effort to establish their legitimacy. They are equally important in terms of prosopography, since they often show the king in the company of his relatives and dignitaries. More than thirty reliefs of Sasanian kings have survived, among them only few from outside their home province of Persis (Fars); moreover, almost all were commissioned by the first rulers of the third and fourth centuries. The predominant theme is the investiture of the king (by the gods); other reliefs show the king triumphing over the enemies of the empire or fighting; the remainder present him on the throne or with his retinue. For these portrayals the Sasanians found prototypes in the earlier relief art of Iran, but their works have rightly been described as the apogee of early Iranian rock-relief art. There have been disagreements about the purport of these works. Is there any unified objective for all the 'themes', or are some of them to be interpreted as idealized testimonies of historical events, others as royal figureheads with generally accepted 'truths'?

Two of the best-known reliefs are carved on the rock face at Naqsh-i Rustam below the Achaemenid tombs. There is first of all the relief of the investiture of Ardashir I (ANRm I = Ardashir [I], rock relief I from Naqsh-i Rustam; see Plate XXI), with the king on horseback on the left-hand side being handed the ring of sovereignty by the god Ohrmazd (Ahura Mazda), who is also on horseback. The figure behind the king represents his page. The two heads under the horses' hoofs are the opponents of the king and the god. Just as Ohrmazd defeated the 'devil' Ahriman, so Ardashir triumphs over the last Parthian king, Ardavan IV.

The second Sasanian king, Shapur, is also portrayed on horseback during his investiture. But here we shall discuss his triumphal reliefs, above all the most famous of them, which 'immortalizes' his victories over the Roman emperors Philip the Arab (peace dictate of 244 AD) and Valerian (capture in 260 AD) (ŠNRm 6; see Plate XXII): Philip bends his knee, Valerian is 'seized' by Shapur; Philip appeals to the *clementia* of the vic-torious Sasanian king, while Valerian adopts the Persian attitude, like a subject of the ruler. There are four reliefs that can be compared with this one. Three of them show another Roman emperor defeated by Shapur, Gordian III, lying with his face to the ground under the horse of the Sasanian. These rock reliefs appear like the timeless and placeless 'perpetuations' in stone of Shapur's victorious reports in his *res gestae* (ŠKZ):

And when I first came to rule in the empire, the emperor Gordian gathered an army from the whole empire of the Romans, Goths and Germans and came to Meso- potamia against the empire of Eran and Us. And at the borders of Babylonia near Mashik [Greek Misiche] a great battle was engaged between us. And the emperor Gordian met his death, and We annihilated the Roman army. Then the Romans proclaimed Philip Caesar. And the emperor Philip came to plead with Us, and he paid Us for Their life 500,000 denars of ransom, and he became Our tributary ... And on the third campaign, when We had marched against Carrhae and Edessa and laid siege to Carrhae and Edessa, the emperor Valerian advanced against Us ... We fought a great battle against the emperor Valerian. And We captured the emperor Valerian Ourselves with Our own hands.

After a long interval without rock reliefs from the fourth to the seventh century – unless this circumstance is due to 'transmission accidents' – relief art was 'rediscovered' by the last great Sasanian, Khosrow II, as a means of royal self-representation. In the 'great ayvan' of Taq-i Bustan in Media (near Kirmanshah), the king presents himself as the divinely elected ruler and good horseman, and in two other scenes he is portrayed in the midst of a wild boar and deer hunt (see Plate XXIII).

Two colossal statues of Shapur I and Khosrow II have in addition come down to us as rare examples of Sasanian sculptural art. As for Sasanian monumental architecture, it is very impressive even today. This is true of urban quarters and palaces, as well as religious buildings, bridges and fortresses. The first city founded by Ardashir was Ardakhshir Khvarrah ('To the Glory of Ardashir'), built in the plain of Firuzabad (Fars) on a circular plan with a diameter of about 2km and two axes crossing one another at right angles. The four sectors thus created were again divided into five parts each, and these smaller units linked together by ring-shaped streets. In a walled centre with a diameter of about 450m there was a terraced religious building and a 30m-high tower, the remains of which are still to be seen today. The conceptual origins of this city layout and the purpose of the tower have remained a mystery.

Bishapur (Veh-Shabuhr: 'the beautiful [city] of Shapur'), built on a rect- angular plan according to the Hippodamic model, was the main residence of the second Sasanian king in Fars. Covering 155 hectares, it leans against the mountain, where a fortress used to protect the city. In its eastern parts were palaces and an underground construction which has been interpreted as a place of worship. Another city founded under this great ruler was Jundai-sabur ('place of Shapur's army'), which was also known by the name of Veh-Andiyok-Shabuhr ('better than Antiochia [has] Sh. [made this city]') or Beth Lapat (in the Syriac testimonies). At this place, situated about 30km east of Susa, Shapur settled artisans and specialists deported from Antiochia (among them many Christians), whereupon it soon developed into a cultural and scientific centre with an academy of its own, and also became famous as the focus of Persia's silk production. We shall come across it again as a Christian centre in Khuzistan.

Further Sasanian cities in Iran have been archaeologically ascertained, and many others are known by name, but quite often cannot be localized or were overbuilt at later periods. Under the Sasanians, the empire's centre and the city where coronations took place continued to be Ctesiphon on the Tigris, which, together with the newly founded Veh-Ardakhshir, became known by the Arabic name al-Mada'in ('the cities').

Among the royal palaces, the two early residences of Ardashir on the route between Shiraz and Firuzabad are impressive to this day. They are Qal'ah-i Dukhtar, a fortified palace on a rocky plateau over a ravine which blocks the access to Firuzabad (see Plate XXIV), and Atashkadah at its feet in the plain. The latter is considerably bigger (55×104m), shaped as an ayvan with large adjoining rooms and three dome chambers. The residential area consisted of suites of barrel-vaulted and domed rooms on the two upper storeys. Shapur's palaces at Bishapur are particularly famous for their mosaics, which follow Roman prototypes, while his residential building (or that of Khosrow I?) in Ctesiphon is renowned for its surviving monumental ayvan arch (Taq-i Kisra; see Plate XXV), which was apparently damaged during the Gulf War. The late Sasanian site of Qasr-i Shirin between Iraq and Iran was destroyed in the 1980s as a result of the war between these two countries.

There are also about twenty known bridges and dams from the Sasanian period (see Plate XXVIa), many of them built by Roman prisoners-of-war, as well as defences such as forts and walls to protect cities and entire territories. Numerous fire temples, for the most part conceived as closed Chahar Taqs ('four-arched buildings'), bear witness to the Zoroastrian creed of the majority of Iranians of that period. The most important sanctuary of the late Sasanian period, the Takht-i Sulaiman in Azerbaijan, was brought to light by German excavators. It is a vast complex of both sacred and secular buildings and has been identified with all sorts of contemporary sites mentioned in ancient literature (see Plate XXVIb).

Among the objects in great demand in the art world are the Sasanian silver bowls representing hunting scenes and other metalwork. Although we are still in the dark about the kind of people who commissioned them, and also about their purpose or use and their possible prototypes, we know that from the reign of Shapur II they featured a central portrayal of the king, who can be personally identified through his crown, and who is shown as an experienced 'hunter' or enthroned amid the notabilities of his court (see Plate XXVIIa). The more political than practical purpose of these pieces, which most probably served as royal gifts in a regular exchange of presents, is supported by the fact that from the fourth to the sixth century, the king apparently had a monopoly on the production of silver bowls. It has been suggested that these metal vessels with their 'message' from the king as the 'heart of the state' and 'invincible warrior against all threats', were taking the place of the rock reliefs in the representational art of the empire, now that the *raison d'être* of these reliefs had been fulfilled by the consolidation of the dynasty.

Much could be said about other products of Sasanian arts and crafts, for instance about the silk fabrics and their influence on the textile art of the West, or about cameos (see Plate XXVIIb), glass and the famous Sasanian stucco ornaments, but we shall content ourselves with simply enumerating them here.

However, a brief discussion of Sasanian seals, bullae and coins is called for, because they have proved to be valuable testimonies to the historian due to their combination of image and inscription. Thus by mentioning the owner and his titles and functions, seals and bullae (see Plate XXVIII) acquaint us with state and religious 'officials' both from the prosopographic and onomastic point of view, and as regards their political, administrative and religious competences. In the case of coins, their images and legends, as well as their style and minting technique, enable us to deduce the names and chronological order of the Sasanian rulers. As for the lumps of clay bearing seal imprints (clay bullae), which date from the late Sasanian period and come from Qasr-i Abu Nasr in Fars or Takht-i Sulaiman, it is not clear whether they served to seal goods or documents. Stamp seals, which for the most part consisted of semi-precious stones and were worn on a string round the neck or as a ring on one's finger, could be of fine workmanship and bear legends as well as male or female portraits, scenes of investiture, hunts and banquets, and illustrations of animals and gods.

Sasanian coins (see Plate XXIX) bear the bust of the king with his personal, unmistakable crown and legend on the obverse, and a fire altar with flames on the reverse, to which may be added two assisting figures and a bust inside the flames. Gold and copper coins were rarely in circulation. Most pieces were coined of (thin) silver. The main denomination was, as with the Parthians, the drachma with a weight of 4g; under Shapur II, this coin was produced in great quantity, probably for the sake of recruiting mercenaries from Central Asia. Mints and names of mintage authorities are occasionally mentioned, but their number and kind are difficult to reconstruct. From the reign of Kavad I, it became canonical to indicate the year. The 'Kushano-Sasanid coins', issued by the Sasanian governors in the regions of the former empire of Kushan, form a problem of their own, and attempts at dating them still produce the most discrepant results.

CHAPTER 10

THE KING AND HIS SUBJECTS

1. *Šāhān šāh Ērān ud Anērān*: kingship in the Sasanian empire

This is the portrait of the Mazda-worshipping god [MP *bay*] Shapur, the king of kings of Iran and non-Iran [MP *Šāhān šāh Ērān ud Anērān*, Parth. *Šāhān šāh Aryān ud Anaryān*; Greek *basileus basileōn Arianōn kai Anarianōn*], whose origin is from the gods [MP *kē čhr az yazdān*; Greek *ek genous theōn*], the son of the Mazda-worshipping god Ardashir, the king of kings of Iran, whose origin is from the gods, the grandson of the god Pabag, the king.

With its characterization of kingship, this inscription on the rock relief of Shapur I at Naqsh-i Rajab near Persepolis succinctly illustrates the king's concept of himself. It establishes Shapur's relationship with the other dynasts of the empire and of the conquered regions, with the territory, with the gods and with the preceding rulers. Let us examine these connections a little more closely. Though it is true that the title 'king of kings' was also characteristic of the pre-Sasanian dynasties of Iran, it was not combined with the word Eran. The Sasanians created the idea of Eranshahr ('Empire of the Aryans') as a political concept, one of whose aims was to establish their legitimacy as heirs of the earlier great Iranian empire of their 'forefathers' (the Achaemenids), as successors to the ancient mythical kings, and as followers of the Zoroastrian creed which had its roots in Iran. A further aim was to create a new 'identity' for themselves and their subjects by using this concept of Eranshahr as the political and cultural homeland for all who lived there and by anchoring it in a very remote past. As 'king of kings', Ardashir set himself above all the other dynasts of Iran, and Shapur even included the newly conquered regions (and their princes).

The fact that the king referred to himself as god (MP *bay*, Greek *theos*) shows that the subjects were to consider their ruler not only as some kind of overlord, but as a king with divine qualities. However, the reference to divine descent indicates that there was to be a difference between the kings and such gods as Ohrmazd (Ahura Mazda) or Anahita, who had invested the Sasanians with their sovereignty. This is not reflected in the Greek version, which uses the word *theos* for both king and god, but it does appear in the Middle Persian (and Parthian) version. Here the king is given the epithet *bay* (< OP *baga*), and Ohrmazd the word *yazd*, which goes back to the Avestic, and hence clerical, *yazata*. For the Iranians of the Sasanian period, there were accordingly two kinds of gods: 'First the great king and his royal father, no matter whether alive or dead, as god-men and consequently material beings. Secondly, however, the remote ancestors, gods in the real sense, who are to be conceived as spiritual beings' (Humbach).

And because of the fact that the gods have thus made Us their 'own property' and We have gone to so many countries and taken possession of them with the help of the gods, therefore We founded a great number of Vahram fires in each country and carried out good deeds for many Magi. And we enlarged the establishments of the gods.

Here Shapur emphasizes his close relationship with the gods, based not only on his descent, but also on his attitude. He acts as their instrument, and they are kind to him in return. As a sign of gratitude he looks after the Zoroastrian cult, like the kings before and after him. He founds fires and thereby multiplies the centres for the worship of gods, he does good deeds for the 'priests' (through donations?), he acts as a promoter of the Zoroastrian religion. But as we shall see, the personal convictions of the ruler and his policies with regard to other religions cannot be so readily derived from statements of this kind, which aim at external effect and legitimation.

Shapur's reference to fires reminds us that a fire is also depicted on the reverse of Sasanian coins. This has been interpreted as the personal 'fire of the king', which was lit at the time of his accession to the throne. The 'king's fire' is referred to in the above-mentioned inscription of Bishapur (see Plate XXXIa), dated 262, which furnishes proof of a 'Sasanian era' (starting in 205/06 AD):

In the month of Fravardin, in the year 58 [of the era]; in the year 40 of the Ardashir fire; in the year 24 of the Shapur fire, the king of fires ...

Therefore Ardashir's proclamation as king (and the lighting of his fire) must have taken place in the Sasanian calendar year corresponding with

223/24 AD, and the investiture of Shapur (and the lighting of his fire) in 239/40 AD. We have already come across 'king's fires' with the Achaemenids and Parthians. The latter had already adopted the custom of founding fires for the benefit of the souls of dead members of the royal family.

On the reverse of the coins (see Plate XXIX), there are attendant figures on either side of the fire, and starting from the reign of Hormizd II, there also appears a bust within the flame. Depending on their headgear, the two figures have been interpreted as the king with his daimon, as the king with the daimon of a dead predecessor (when there was a difference in crowns), as the king with his *xvarrah* ('divine grace', comparable with the Greek Tyche or Roman Fortuna), or as a divinity, and also as priests, as a king and a priest, and as a king with two functions. The bust has also been interpreted as the *xvarrah* of the king portrayed on the obverse. That the idea of the king's *xvarrah* as the necessary requirement for his divine election as a ruler had an enduring effect on Sasanian kingship is illustrated in the Middle Persian 'Ardashir romance', in the episode where Ardavan pursues the fugitive Ardashir:

When he [Ardavan] arrived at another place, he asked the people: 'Those two riders [Ardashir and a girl from the court], when did they pass?' They said: 'At noon they rushed past as fast as the wind, and a ram [constantly] ran along by their side.' This seemed curious to Ardavan, and he said: 'Bear in mind that we know the two riders, but what is the meaning of this ram?' And he asked the judge, and the judge said: 'The divine grace [*xvarrah*] of the sovereignty of the Kayanians has not [yet] reached him, we must ride [further], for we may possibly be able to catch them before this divine grace reaches him.' ... [Later on, Ardavan is told that the ram is sitting on Ardashir's horse.] The judge said: 'May the king live forever! The divine grace of the Kayanians has reached Ardashir, there is no longer any possible way to catch [him].'

Hence, whoever is in possession of the *xvarrah* is the rightful ruler, and any rebellion against him is doomed to fail.

In the inscriptions of the early kings, legitimacy can also be established by reference to preceding rulers, thus in Shapur's case by reference to his father Ardashir and his grandfather Pabag. Like the Parthians, the Sasanians also tried to trace back their ancestry to the founders of the empire. In his *res gestae*, Shapur I mentions the 'crown dominions' (Parth. *dastgird*; Greek *ktismata*) of his father, his 'ancestors' (*niyāgān/pappoi*) and his 'forefathers' (*ahēnagān/progonoi*), implying Ardashir, the earlier chiefs of the Sasanian clan and the Achaemenid kings whose names, it is true, were unknown to him. This concept of kingship is conveyed by Roman authors such as Dio Cassius, Herodian and subsequently Ammianus Marcellinus, when they describe Sasanian demands that the Romans return to them the possessions of the *progonoi* (or *maiores*). In Iran itself there were also such references to the past: to the eponymous founder of the clan, to the time before Alexander and the reign of 'petty kings' he had caused, and to the primeval mythical kings. The already mentioned 'Ardashir romance' from the late Sasanian period reports the following about Sasan, who appears in it as Ardashir's father (and the husband of Pabag's daughter):

Sasan was a shepherd of Pabag's and was always with the small livestock, and he was from the family of Dara, the descendant of Dara [Darius]. And during the evil reign of Alexander, [his] ancestors had gone into exile and seclusion and had associated with Kurdish herdsmen.

Ardashir came to be considered as the son of Sasan, the founder of the clan, who in his turn was linked up with Dara (Darius III), known to the Sasanians through the MP version of the 'Alexander romance'. Tabari goes a step further, after borrowing from the Arabic adaptation of the 'Book of Lords' two genealogies, the second of which is quoted here:

According to another statement, however, his family tree is: Ardashir – Pabag – Sasan – Pabag – Zarer – Behafarid – the elder Sasan – Bahman – Isfandiyar – Vishtasp – Luhrasp. He now rose, as he maintained, to avenge the blood of his cousin Dara, son of Dara, grandson of Isfandiyar, whom Alexander had fought and whom his two chamberlains had murdered. As he declared, he wanted to bring back the reign to the legitimate family, to restore it the way it had always been at the time of his forefathers who had lived before the petty kings, and to reunite the empire under one head and one king.

Here the link with the Kayanians is successfully established (even if Zarer and Behafarid – who are no longer recognized as Arsacids – have also got themselves into the family tree!). How far the early history of the Sasanians was changed by compilers of the late Sasanian period, and how much the story of the rise of the dynasty was transformed by oral tradition, is shown not only by the elimination of the Arsacids from the 'national history' and by genealogical constructions, but also by Ardashir's ostensible aim to turn away from the Parthian reign (rule of the 'petty kings') by 'centralizing' the empire. Today we are aware that the Arsacids and Sasanians had more things in common than otherwise. The Arsacid heritage is conspicuously reflected in characteristics such as: the attribution of kingship to one 'family', the division of the aristocracy into separate classes of nobility depending on their descent, standing and political importance, the government and administration of the empire, the relationship between king and nobility and the continued influence of Parthian clans. This is hardly surprising considering the fact that the Sasanians had risen to power as Parthian 'petty kings', and that only a few decades had passed since the fall of the Arsacids.

After almost 500 years of Parthian sovereignty in Iran, the Arsacid influence on kingship and administration, social structure and 'historical tradition' was too great for the Sasanians to contemplate replacing everything Parthian by something new. On the contrary, internal stability was possible only through continuity in organization as well as personnel. The new elements of Sasanian policy lay in other fields: in the renewal of the vanguard position against Rome; in a greater emphasis on the 'Iranian' character of kingship and religion; and in a stronger reference to the Zoroastrian gods. The wars against Rome and the promotion of Mazdaism were unequivocally motivated by political calculation. The wars were primarily to serve the purpose of consolidation and legitimation, while the advertised nearness to the gods was to lend the reign a religious warrant. The trends towards centralization are a phenomenon of a later period and become particularly obvious in the reforms of Khosrow I. As we shall see, the close ties between 'throne' and 'altar' postulated already for Ardashir's reign by Middle Persian and Arabic records must have been construed at a much later period.

What do we know about the regulations regarding royal succession in the Sasanian period? As with the Arsacids, the heir was appointed by the ruling monarch. When the provisions were not clear or when alleged prerogatives were ignored, disputes about the throne occurred among the Sasanians as well, offering the aristocracy (and the clergy) an opportunity to exercise their influence. A conflict of this kind, which was resolved in his own favour, is described by King Narseh in his inscription on the Paikuli tower (see Plate XXXa), which includes a verbatim record of the letters exchanged before his accession and the speeches held during his acclamation, to prevent any doubts about the legitimacy of the succession.

According to Arabic and Byzantine sources, Khosrow II also took great pains to substantiate his claims to the throne. In a letter to his rival Bahram (VI) Chubin, he is said to have written the following:

Khosroes [Khosrow], king of kings, ruler over the ruling, lord of the peoples, prince of peace, salvation of men, among gods the good and eternally living man, among men the most esteemed god, the highly illustrious, the victor, the one who rises with the sun and who lends the night his eyesight, the one famed through his ancestors, the king who hates war, the benefactor who engaged the Asones [Sasones = Sasanians] and saved the Persians their kingship – to Baram [Bahram], the general of the Persians, our friend ... We have also taken over the royal throne in a lawful manner and have not upset Persian customs ... We have so firmly decided not to take off the diadem that We even expected to rule over other worlds, if this were possible ... If you wish your welfare, think about what is to be done.

For the Sasanian period, something like a 'King's Council' has been inferred, with varying assumptions about its composition. Like its counterpart of the Parthian period, this council is supposed to have carried out certain functions in determining the succession. The records, however, are either very incomplete (Paikuli inscription), or bear a Zoroastrian tinge (the 'letter of Tansar'). For Narseh and his predecessors, we might assume a 'mock consultation' of the highest dignitaries of the empire, documenting an ancient right of co-determination or rather confirmation held by the nobility:

We [i.e. Ardashir I], from [...]ness made Shapur king (?). But whoever may know [that in Eranshahr?] there is someone who may be more righteous than King (?) Shapur and more officious in the service of the gods, or better, and [who] hereafter (may be) able to keep this Eranshahr [better] guarded [and healthier?] and to govern [it better] than King (?) Shapur, let him say [so]!

The investiture and coronation of a new king may be imagined as follows. The new ruler was enthroned at the place where he had been appointed; in the presence of the princes of the royal house, the great personalities of the empire and the men in the service of the court or government, the crown was put on his head. The process is vividly illustrated in the 'Letter of Tansar', although from the view point of the clergy:

That night they will set the crown and throne in the audience-room and the groups of noblemen will take up their position in their own places. The *mobad* [head of the Zoroastrian clergy] with *herbads* [other religious 'officials'] and nobles, the illustrious and the pillars of the realm, will go to the assembly of the princes; and they will range themselves before them and will say: 'We have carried our perplexity before God Almighty and He has deigned to show us the right way and to instruct us in what is best.' The *mobad* will cry aloud, saying: 'The angels have approved the kingship of such-a-one, son of such-a-one. Acknowledge him also, ye creatures of God and good tidings be yours!' They will take up that prince and seat him on the throne and place the crown on his head ...

A second and particularly solemn ceremony, the religious investiture (coronation), is said to have usually taken place in a fire temple. There appear to have been no fixed places for either the sacred or the secular coronation, as had been the case with the Achaemenids.

The question whether the Sasanians, unlike their 'forefathers', practised co-regency has been discussed in connection with the (supposed) synarchy of Ardashir I and Shapur I, and has so far remained controversial. A special admiration or idealization of Ardashir, the founder of the empire, is already recorded under Narseh, but it was enhanced in the late Sasanian period.

2. *Šahrdār, vispuhr, vuzurg, āzād* and *bandag – dūdag* and *kadag*: social conditions in the Sasanian empire

This is the range of the arrow shot by Us, the Mazda-worshipping god Shapur, the king of kings of Eran and Aneran, whose origin is from the gods, the son of the Mazda-worshipping god Ardashir, the king of kings of Eran, whose origin is from the gods, the grandson of the god Pabag, the king. And when we shot this arrow, we were shooting before the kings [landholders; *šahrdārān*], the princes [*vāspuhragān*], the grandees [*vuzurgān*] and the nobles (*āzādān*).

In his inscription from Hajjiabad, Shapur I mentions four 'groups' of aristocrats, in the order following their political significance and prestige and corresponding with the criteria of lineage. King Narseh also refers to them in his Paikuli inscription as the most important personalities for his acknowledgement. The first group, each member of which was called *šahrdār* in Middle Persian and *despotēs tōn ethnōn* in the Greek version of Shapur's *res gestae*, comprised local dynasts as well as those sons of the 'king of kings' whom he had entrusted with the reign of particularly important parts of the empire. The second 'rank' (MP *vāspuhragān*, Greek *hoi ek basileōn*) was composed of members of the Sasanian clan who were not direct descendants of the ruler, and the third (MP *vuzurgān*) included the heads of the most important noble families, above all the Varaz, the Parthian clans Suren and Karin, the 'lords of Undigan' and other members of the high nobility. As for the *āzādān*, they were the rest of the Iranian nobility.

In connection with the common duty to offer sacrifices for the benefit of the souls of the living and the dead, Shapur's *res gestae* lists the contemporary members of these four groups by their names and, if they held offices, also by their functions at court or in the empire. The Narseh inscription, for its part, makes it clear that the 'king of kings' and the aristocracy were linked by a network of mutual obligations, interdependences, and also common interests. The fact that the Sasanians did not create these 'structures of standing' themselves, but took them over from the Parthians – while at the same time enhancing the rank of the Persian, i.e. south-west Iranian, aristocracy – is proved by the end of the 'formula' in which the groups of nobility are presented: 'The landholders and the princes, the grandees and the nobles and the Persians and the Parthians.' The loyal Parthian clans warranted continuity, but were now complemented by Persian clans without having to give up their leading position. At a later period, other 'clans' rose to the ranks of magnates. As already pointed out, the high aristocracy was made to play an advisory and corroborative role in the process of proclaiming the king.

While this was going on at the court of Constantine ... Antoninus [a Roman deserter] was led into the winter residence of the king [Shapur II] and was received there with open arms. He was distinguished with the dignity of the tiara, an honour by which you may sit at the royal table and by which deserving men among the Persians are allowed to give advice and voice their opinions at assemblies.

Apart from a person's own inherited possessions, it was his closeness to the king that reflected his standing, as this account by Ammianus shows, and perhaps also a certain way of dressing. However, prior to the late Sasanian period, for the Iranian aristocracy the real criterion for grandeur was not so much a title or royal distinction as lineage. This is still attested by Procopius for the reign of Kavad (fifth/sixth century).

He [Kavad] was mindful of the rule that did not allow the Persians to transfer any offices [archai] to strangers, but only to such men who were entitled to the respective position of honour [timē] through their lineage.

Among the marks of aristocracy were the tiaras mentioned by Ammianus, on which certain colours and symbols of a heraldic kind could point to particular ranks or distinctions. Belts studded with gems and earrings played a similar part.

Although such signs of distinction could also be bestowed by the king, the rank of a Parthian or Persian nobleman was for a long time independent from the king's favour. This changed only in the late Sasanian period, when the wearing of belts, rings, clasps and other marks of prestige required royal approval. As Theophylactus maintained, the (bestowed) rank now came to be esteemed more highly than name and descent. This strengthening of royal power had become possible after the great crisis of state and empire which began in the mid-fifth century. Crucial factors of the crisis were the disastrous defeats of Peroz I (459–484 AD) against the Hephthalites in the east, leading to tributary dependence on the Hephthalite state, in addition to several years of drought and famine. Meanwhile, the twofold burden imposed on the peasants by landlords and state taxes on the one hand, and the Hephthalite occupation of parts of the country on the other, had led to a rural exodus and revolutionary protests on behalf of the peasant population. The latter had found a religious and ethical motivation for such actions in the social doctrine of Mazdak (see below), especially in his call for communal ownership. The nobility had also grown weaker as a result of war casualties, encroachments by the poor, and quarrels within the aristocracy itself about the proper reaction to this crisis. Whether the main victims of these uprisings were the owners of great estates or the lower nobility, history does not say. In any case, the subsequent reforms by Kavad I and his son Khosrow (I) were of a fundamental nature. They not only extended direct land taxation (see below) to the estates of the landed aristocracy but, by establishing a new order for the nobility and the army, drastically changed the empire's social structure and the position of the ruler with respect to the aristocracy. As Tabari reports on this subject:

Thereupon he [Khosrow] gave orders to behead the leaders of the Mazdakites, distribute their properties to the needy, kill many of them who had taken away the belongings of people [an-nās, i.e. the nobility], and restore these to their owners ... He had the children of distinguished people written down as his own if their providers had died, wedded their daughters to men of their own rank and provided them with a dowry from state funds. As for themselves, he had them marry women from noble families, for whom he paid the bridal-money, and made them rich, but bade them stay at his court, in order to employ them at his high offices ... He also mustered the cavaliers [al-asāwira], and supported those of them who had no property with a gift of horses and equipment, and also fixed regular wages for them ... He chose qualified judges [ḥukkām], officials ['ummāl] and governors [wulāh] and gave each of them strict orders.

This shows that both restoring their old property to the nobility and giving away estates that no longer had owners were measures carried out at the behest of the king. In addition, a kind of 'administrative nobility' was created, and in the case of the 'cavaliers', a military nobility whose duty was to follow the king in his campaigns. The latter was apparently meant to replace the retainer units formed by self-equipped members of the aristocracy, troops that were never really at the king's command. Arab authors also introduce a new (or newly emerged) lower nobility, the *dehkānān*, who took over the administration of a village as its richest landowners and sometimes even owned entire villages. These had been promoted by the king, who had granted them land, money and other assistance. They were to be his partisans on a local level (against members of the high aristocracy who were critical of the king, and the potentially rebellious peasantry), and should also, if necessary, stand by him in military matters.

But already under Khosrow's immediate successors, renewed tensions arose between king and aristocracy. Khosrow had created a group of four *spāhbeds* (commanders-in-chief), to each of whom he had entrusted a quarter of the empire, allowing them, at the same time, to levy and use part of the land taxes so as to maintain their troops. Some of these, as well as other military leaders, now tried to pursue their own policies and even to come forward as pretenders to the throne. The most famous of them was Bahram Chubin from the Mihran clan, who ventured an uprising under Hormizd and to make a bid for the crown (590/91 AD), and whose memory, despite all the efforts to the contrary by his subduer, Khosrow (II), lives on in a romance. Temporarily hindered in their ambitions because Khosrow II had centralized the financial administration, the landed and military aristocracy nevertheless managed to conspire against the king, who was reproached for his tyrannical attitude towards the nobility, his ruinous exaction of land taxes and his bloody wars. After Khosrow's death, kingship remained the instrument of different factions of the aristocracy vying with each other. The rapid advances of the Muslim army and the sudden collapse of Sasanian sovereignty in Iran present a most eloquent testimony to the paralysing particularism of interests among the leading classes of the empire in this last phase of Iran's pre-Islamic history.

The Iranian records of the third century (inscriptions, reliefs, coins), show that the female members of the royal family received an unusual amount of attention and respect. Thus the most important were commemorated with fires 'for their spiritual welfare and posthumous fame', and even with sacrifices. Some bore a distinctive title, for instance Adur-Anahid, the daughter of Shapur I, who was called 'queen of queens' (MP *bāmbišnān bāmbišn*, Greek *basilissa tōn basilissōn*) and is mentioned before the king's sons; or Khoranzem, the 'queen of the empire' (*tou ethnous basilissa*), who preceded Adur Anahid in the enunciation of people commemorated with sacrifices and who is considered as Shapur's wife. Also among the most outstanding women of the early empire were Denag, the mother of Pabag (and grandmother of Ardashir), Rodag, the mother of Ardashir I, and Denag, his sister, who was also called 'queen of queens'. This title has also been interpreted as a connubial relationship between the 'king of kings' and his female counterpart, implying a father–daughter marriage for Shapur and a brother–sister marriage for Ardashir, but there is no evidence for this. The title vouches for the special ranks of these women, which were a result of their birth, rather than being a sign of the very close and incestuous form of 'consanguineous marriage' contracted by the kings, which was quite current in Sasanian Iran (see below). Female members of the royal family appear on the royal reliefs as well as on coins, for instance on those of Bahram II, who has himself portrayed (following Roman examples) with the queen and crown prince(s) (see Plate XXIX). Women are also immortalized on gems, as is Ardashir's sister Denag, and on seals of their own. So it is no longer surprising that shortly before the fall of the empire, women could even ascend the throne, as was the case with Puran and her sister Azarmigdukht, even if this happened for lack of male candidates.

... and I have written this inscription also because I, Kirdir, have from the very beginning sealed testaments and agreements about fire temples and Magi for kings [šahrdārān] and lords [xvadāyān] and have often signed my name at [different] places on testaments, contracts and documents, so that, whoever sees a contract, a document or a testament or another piece of writing at a later time may know that I am that very Kirdir whom Shapur [I], the king of kings, called 'Kirdir, the Mobad and Herbed', and whom Hormizd [I], the king of kings, and Bahram [I], the king of kings, the sons of Shapur, called 'Kirdir, the Mobad of Ohrmazd', and whom Bahram II, the king of kings, the son of Bahram [I], called 'Kirdir, whose soul Bahram saved, the Mobad of Ohrmazd'.

This *cursus honorum* of Kirdir's, which he personally handed down to posterity, leads us to the 'priests' and religious dignitaries of the Sasanian period. It dates from the late third century AD and comes from Naqsh-i Rajab. Elsewhere he expands it by pointing out that Bahram II had conferred on him the position and rank of 'magnate' (*vuzurg*) and appointed him as '*mōbad* and *dādvar* ["judge"] of the whole empire' and as 'director and authority over the fire of Anahid–Ardakhshir and Anahid the lady [in] Stakhr'. The rise of Kirdir, who also perpetuated his own memory pictorially (see Plate XXXb), began with his activity as *hērbed*, a religious official of low or at most medium rank with no precisely determined tasks, and proceeded through the function of *mōbad* to that of *mōbad* and *dādvar* of the empire. Whether he had lawfully worked his way up to becoming the head of the Zoroastrian 'priesthood' is not known. If so, other *mōbads*, the simple *mogs*

(Magi) who served as guardians of the less important fire temples (*ādurān*), and the *mogmards* who were caretakers of the more significant provincial Bahram fires, would have been his subordinates. What we do know for certain is that he became the empire's most powerful religious dignitary.

From the fourth century on, there appears to have been a greater differentiation and – following the example of monarchic power – a greater regionalization of the offices and jurisdictions, for the Syriac (Christian) Acts of Martyrs distinguish between a 'head of the *mōbads*' (*rēš mauḥpātē*), a 'great *mōbad*' (*mauḥpātā rabbā*: < MP **vuzurg mōbad*), and a *mōbad* of a province. The creation of top political, military and religious functions is traditionally attributed to Mihr-Narseh, the powerful general and politician (*vuzurg framādār*) under kings Yazdgird I, Bahram V and Yazdgird II. According to Tabari, he procured the positions of *hērbedān hērbed*, 'supreme farmer' (highest land tax collector: MP *vāstaryōšān sālār*) and 'supreme warrior' (supreme commander of the army: MP *artēštārān sālār*) for his three sons Zurvandad, Mah-Gushnasp and Kardar. Here the more interesting point is not that these titles remind us of the Avestan 'stations' of priest, farmer and warrior, but the fact that even in the religious sphere, the tendency to hierarchize functions and offices had asserted itself.

We know very little about the medium strata of Sasanian society, but they must have included both the lower state officials at a local level and the section of the urban population working as artists, craftsmen and retail dealers (see below), a section that is reflected in the Christian Acts of Martyrs as well as in the products of its work. In addition, there were the 'specialists' such as medical practitioners, astronomers, 'scientists', 'singers', servants at the royal court and on the estates of the nobility, as well as wholesalers.

And lastly, there was the peasant population, which, as in all ancient societies, provided the bulk of the country's inhabitants, and there were the bondmen. Zoroastrian literature attaches great significance to the conflict between rich and poor, between the *škōh* ('the poor') and the *xvadāy* ('the lord'), and the popular rebellions in the late fifth and early sixth centuries offer conclusive evidence that there were social tensions in the Sasanian empire, especially in times of crisis.

That a considerable part of the peasant population was not only burdened by the high taxes imposed on it and the way they were collected, but was also dependent on the landed aristocracy, is illustrated in the following episode handed down by Ibn Hauqal, an Arab geographer of the tenth century. King Kavad saw a woman beating a girl who was picking a pomegranate from a tree. When he took her to task, she explained that all the fruit of her garden had the king as an absent partner. She then pointed out that the ripe pomegranates could not be picked because the crop had not yet been assessed for the tax collection. Ibn Hauqal then continues:

And he [Kavad] did not rest until he had the whole of Fars divided into districts subject to land tax [*muqāṭa'āt wa-ḥarāǧat*], where at a set time what there was on the threshing-floors [*anādir*] was registered, and where the peasants [*akara*] and tenant farmers [*muzāra'ūn*] could freely dispose of [*tuṣarrafu*] the threshing-floors [*bayādir*].

This quotation mentions two groups of the rural population, free peasants and tenant farmers. The fact that the *akara* were assigned their own threshing-floors may imply that they had risen from dependent peasants to free ones on their own soil. Other testimonies, such as the seventh-century *kārnāmag* ('res gestae') of Khosrow I Anoshirvan, parts of which are contained in Ibn Miskawaih's *taǧārib al-umam* (tenth–eleventh century), also emphasize the king's solicitude for his *rā'īya* ('subjects'), i.e. the rural population. They maintain that unlike other rulers, who had discontinued levying taxes at certain times, he (Khosrow) had not only reorganized taxation, but also prevented injustice through accurate bookkeeping and close supervision. As a specific regulation, this *kārnāmag* mentions that each *qāḍī* ('judge') was ordered to summon the taxpayers (*ahlu l-ḥarāǧ*) without the knowledge of the tax collector ('*ummāl*) or landlord (*ulū l-amr*), to inquire about any injustice against them, and to report it in a document sealed by the *qāḍī* and the peasants. This document would then be read in the presence of the great men ('*uẓamā'*), the kings (*mulūk*) of the land, the judges and noblemen (*aḥrār*, *ašrāf*), i.e. the *vuzurgān*, *šahrdārān* and *dehkānān* of the Iranian sources. Tabari's accounts about the encroachments by the wealthy (and cavaliers) on the possessions of the weak under Khosrow's successor Hormizd, about the king's intercession for the poor and his overthrow by the nobility prove that these royal measures achieved no lasting success.

Zoroastrian and Arab sources emphasize that social mobility in the Sasanian empire was impeded by special assignments of activity, investigations before moving up in rank and even prescribed clothes. Of course, the ideal of class allegiance did not fully correspond with its practice.

On the subject of slaves in the Sasanian empire, other than the enslaved prisoners-of-war from Shapur's expeditions, our main source of information is the Middle Persian book of laws *Mādayān ī hazār dādestān*, conceived as a collection of legal cases under Khosrow II. Further data are contained in later Middle Persian works, as well as in the Christian–Syriac collection of laws by Isho'bukht. These legal books will be discussed in detail in a later section.

Aside from the terms *bandag* (cf. OP *bandaka*), designating both a free subject and a bondman, and *tan* ('body'), a word describing both a physically liable debtor and a person with limited legal capacity, the expression usually used for a slave was *anšahrīg* ('foreigner'). This at the same time points to the major source and cause of slavery, which was capture in war. Other known ways to serfdom were the sale of children by their fathers and descent from slaves. Here there occurred a change in the legal conception, so that at first the child's status was determined by that of its father and subsequently by that of its mother.

Although conceived as a 'thing' (*xvāstag*), the slave was also defined as a human being, a factor that distinguished him from other possessions and also protected him from cruel treatment. Slaves could be sold, leased or given away, furnished as security or 'owned' by several people. Any goods earned by slaves belonged to their owners. 'Slaves' also included individuals who might be described by the Latin expression *glebae adscripti*, that is, manpower bound to the soil. They were sold together with the land (*dastgird*) they cultivated. Slaves who adhered to the Zoroastrian faith could not be sold to 'infidels', and those who were owned by a non-Zoroastrian could leave him and obtain their freedom if they indemnified him for his loss. Slaves could appear at court as witnesses, and also as plaintiffs and defenders, they could be furnished with a 'special property' by their owners, and could be set free either completely or 'partially' (if they had more than one owner). Through a written confirmation (*āzād-hišt*), the liberated slave would become a free 'subject of the king of kings'. The Sasanian empire also had 'temple slaves', among whom the *anšahrīg ī ātaxš*, an unfree worker on the estates of a fire temple, is to be distinguished from the *ātaxš-bandag* or *ādurān-bandag*, a free man who could be engaged by the king to do service at a shrine. The most prominent example for such a *bandag* was our 'grand vizier' Mihr-Narseh, who performed service at shrines in the fifth century under Bahram V, then had to work as a 'temple slave' on a crown domain under Yazdgird II as punishment for an offence, and was later again engaged for 'holy service' under Peroz. The numbers of slaves cannot be ascertained, but they must have been quite substantial.

To go back to the law books, as our major sources for the 'household' and 'family' in the Sasanian period, they deserve presenting in greater detail.

The Sasanians never had anything like a generally valid code of laws, nor did they have a 'secular' catalogue of accepted conducts and norms, independent of Zoroastrian ethics. The 'Book of the Thousand Judgements' (*mādayān ī hazār dādestān*) must have been 'a kind of aid to orientation and rulings for jurists' (Macuch) because of its detailed and complicated casuistry, its precise legal terminology and its presentation of various expert opinions. It was composed in the period between Khosrow's accession and the Arab invasion of Iran (between 590 and 642 AD) by a man called Farrokhmard i Vahraman from Gor (Firuzabad) in the district of Ardakhshir-Khvarrah in Fars. The compiler not only used Middle Persian commentaries to the 'legal' *nasks* ('books') of the Avesta, but also drew upon collections of legal decisions and experts' memoranda, writings about the tasks of officials participating in legal proceedings and compilations of royal decrees. In addition, he must have had access to the state and private 'archives' of his homeland. In addition to the *Mādayān*, there exist other Middle Persian books concerning legal questions, but they are less important. A work that was considerably influenced by the Iranian–Zoroastrian law of the pre-Islamic Sasanian period is the *Corpus Iuris* by the Metropolitan of Persis, Mar Isho'bukht. Dating from the eighth century AD, and originally written in Middle Persian and addressed to the Christian community of Persis, it survives only in a Syriac translation made around the year 800. With its help, attempts are being made to read and interpret certain undefined legal expressions in the *Mādayān*. Further Christian legal books worth mentioning are a post-Sasanian text by the Metropolitan of Persis, Mar Simeon, which was also translated from Middle Persian into Syriac, and a specific Syriac text regarding questions of marriage law, which is said to have been written under the Catholicus Mar Aba in the reign of Khosrow I.

As for the Sasanian 'family', it would be more adequate to define it as a 'household', like that of ancient Greece and Rome, rather than as a 'family' in the modern sense. This does not say anything about the actual form of living together or the 'life cycle' of a 'family', nor can we expect more than limited answers to the question how many generations lived under one roof at any one time. After all, we owe our knowledge primarily to legally pre-scriptive, rather than historically descriptive testimonies.

Both the 'nuclear' and the 'extended' family are described in Middle Persian by the concepts *dūdag* (actually 'smoke') and *kadag* ('house'). The equivalent of the *pater familias* of the Roman tradition was the Iranian *kadag-xvāday* ('master of the house'), and his wife was called *kadag-bānūg*. The members of the house, who simultaneously formed a legal unit, a producing and consuming association and a worshipping community, were bound to one another by a plethora of regulations and obligations. There were members of the household 'in their own right' (the 'master of the house' and his adult sons and grandsons) and members 'in another's right' (women and minors). The 'family' formed part of greater agnatic units, similar to the Greek *genos* or the Latin *gens*, which were known by the words *nāf*, *tōm* and *gōhr* and could be of varying sizes. Just as the 'house' carried out ritual duties for the soul of its paternal ancestors, so the members of the *gens* cultivated the memory of their common ancestors, especially their original forebear, and organized common feasts and ceremonies. In this connection, the reader is reminded of the sacrificial obligations and commemorative fires encountered in Shapur's inscription. Although the 'family' possessed 'house and home' and had the right to use the communal pastures, mills, irrigation facilities and other establishments of the *gens*, it could only transfer possessions to members of its own unit. The latter, in their turn, could act as guardians, adoptive relations or heirs, depending on the closeness of their kinship.

The male members of a 'family' attained their majority at the age of fifteen, and were then received into the community in a festive ceremony (bestowal of belt and garment) as legally qualified adults (*tuvānīg*). An authoritative group of adult men of the *gens* headed by a 'Council of Seniors' was present whenever weddings were celebrated or legal cases negotiated within the *gens*. New members were usually accepted into the unit through *adrogatio* (adoption as one's child after consulting the *gens*). The closer agnatic relatives within these units (*hamnāfān*, *xvēšāvandān*, *āzādān*) for a long time formed a marriage unit, in other words marriages between blood-relations (Av. *xvaētvada θa*: 'marriage between agnates', MP *xvēdōdah*) were the normal practice. We should nevertheless be careful about postulating 'incestuous' unions (between 'full siblings' or between parents and their own children) as regards marriages within the royal house (see above). For all that, marriages between blood-relations were so common in Iran (and the adjacent regions, such as Mesopotamia and Osrhoene) that the Christian and (Eastern) Roman state authorities found it necessary to react by banning them to their subjects. For long periods, as we have seen, a person's descent largely determined his social rank and access to offices and titles. It is not surprising that the word *āzād* (which is close to the Latin *agnatus)* became used also to describe an aristocrat.

The usual form of marriage was the *pādixšayīh* union, which can be compared with the Roman *manus* marriage. When moving into her husband's 'house', the wife as mother of the children of the house, leader of the household and participant in the house cult, became subject to the power of the house father. As 'subject to power' (*framānburdārīh*) in the new 'household', she severed all legal connections with her previous family. The children from this marriage inherited their father's name, fortune and social rank as his legitimate descendants, but they also inherited his ritual and economic commitments. In the Sasanian period, it appears to have become a practice to draw up marriage contracts in which the bride's guardian and the bridegroom wrote down their mutual claims and commitments. A man could marry at the age of fifteen, but a woman could be married before she came of age, though not against her will. A man was also entitled to contract lawful marriages with several women. This, too, like marriages between blood-relations, has been fully confirmed for the royal house. For the rest of her life the wife was subject to power and unqualified to own property unless otherwise stated in the marriage contract. Her dowry remained her property during the marriage, with the husband merely acting as trustee; if the marriage was childless, it was returned to her paternal family after her death. Divorce could be sued for by either party, but the consent of the other party was necessary. The wife's agreement ceased to be required only if the marriage had remained childless or if there was proof of an offence on her part. A divorce, like a marriage, had to be made public and confirmed by a divorce document (*hilišn-nāmag*), which settled the return of the dowry and of a potential 'nuptial present' (MP *kābēn*, similar to Lat. *donatio propter nuptias*). In an intestate succession, the wife was considered *filii loco*, i.e. she inherited, like the son of the deceased, a full share of her husband's fortune. Her guardian then was her eldest adult son or, if she did not have one, the closest agnate of the deceased. If the marriage had been childless, the wife, after her husband's death, had to contract a marriage with his closest agnate (the so-called *čagar* marriage), like the levirate recorded in the Old Testament. At the same time, she remained the wife of the deceased 'with full rights' to his possessions, and the children of the new marriage became legitimate heirs and successors of the deceased, not of their real father. Levirate marriages, like marriages between blood-relations, were a subject of polemics among Christian jurists. Iranian legislation also included the 'inheriting daughter', a daughter who had no brothers, and who, for the preservation of her father's house, was married to an agnate of her father's, even if this involved the dissolution of an already existing marriage. Her children from the new union were recognized as the legitimate children and heirs of their maternal grandfather.

Apart from the *pādixšayīh* marriage, there were other forms of union between man and woman in Sasanian Iran. These include marriage through the woman's free choice of a partner without a formal 'change of family', and also a more ancient marriage in which, if there were good reasons or specific commitments, a husband would surrender his wife – with her fortune – to another man for a certain period. In such cases the woman remained the legitimate wife of her original husband, who now acted as her tutor, and the children from the new union counted as children of the first husband.

Another subject fully expounded in Sasanian law was the guardianship of minors and women, and of families without male members. This applies to 'legal' guardianship and the appointment of a guardian, and also to the description of his tasks and remuneration and the legal protection of the ward. In Iran there were different kinds of tutelage: 'natural' (*būdag*: within the family), 'appointed' (*gumārdag*: appointment by the members of the *gens* in the absence of male members of a family), and 'instituted' (*kardag*: appointment of a relative or outsider by the father of the family).

Due to their interest in the survival of a 'house' and in the fulfilment of ritual obligations, the legal authorities set great store by establishing clear regulations regarding inheritance and succession (*abarmānd*). They distinguished between succession of the heirs to the house (*a. ī pad xvēšīh*: the heirs are comparable to the *sui heredes* of the Roman law) and succession in the absence of a male heir to the house (*a. ī pad stūrīh*), in which case other people functioned as 'substitute heirs' (*stūr*); their task, whether they were 'natural' (inheriting daughter, widow in levirate), or substitute heirs appointed by the *gens* or by testament, was to 'provide' a 'son' (*stūrīh pus*) for the deceased, who could enter upon his entire succession.

There is more to be said about the Sasanian law of property, obligations and succession, but that would exceed the scope of the present book.

CHAPTER II

ERANSHAHR: THE EMPIRE, ITS INHABITANTS AND THEIR WAY OF LIFE

1. The empire and its administration, the court and tributes to the king

(Offerings shall be made for the benefit of the souls of those who live under the reign of Shapur, the king of kings:) For Ardashir, king of Adiabene; for Ardashir, king of Kirman; for Denag, queen of Meshan [Mesene], the property [*dastgird*] of Shapur; for Hamazasp, king of Iberia [Georgia]; for Valakhsh, the prince, son of Pabag; for Sasan, the prince who was brought up [?] with the Parikan; for Sasan, the prince who was brought up [?] with the Kadugan; for Narseh, the prince, son of Peroz; for Narseh, the prince, son of Dad-Spahr [?] [Parth./Greek son of Shapur]; for Shapur, the *bidaxš* ['viceroy']; for Pabag, the *hazāruft* ['chiliarch']; for Peroz, the *aspbed* ['master of the cavalry']; for Ardashir [from the house of] Varaz; for Ardashir [from the house of] Suren; for Narseh, lord of Undigan; for Ardashir [from the house of] Karin; for Vahnam, the *framadar* ['commander-in-chief']; for Friyog, satrap [*šahrab*] of Veh-Andiyok-Shabuhr; for Sridoy [the son of] Shahimust [?]; for Ardashir [with the surname] Ardashir-Shnom ['joy of Ardashir']; for Pakchihr [with the surname] Tahm-Shapur ['heroic Shapur']; for Ardashir, satrap of Goyman; for Chashmag [from] Nev-Shabuhr; for Vahnam [with the surname] Shapur-Shnom ['joy of Shapur']; for Tir-Mihr, commander-in-chief of the fortress of Shahrgird; for Zivak, the 'caller to the meal' [Greek *deipnoklētor*]; for Ardavan [from] Dumbavand; for Gundafarr, son of Avgan; for Razmayod and Pabag [with the surname] Peroz-Shapur ['victorious Shapur'], the sons of Shambid; for Varzin, satrap of Gay [Isfahan]; for Kardsrav, the *bidaxš* ['viceroy']; for Pabag, son of Vispur; for Valakhsh, son of Seluk [Seleucus]; for Yazdbad, the *handarzbed* ['adviser'] of the queens; for Pabag, the *šafšerdār* ['sword-bearer']; for Narseh, satrap of Rind; for Tiyanag, satrap of Hamadan; for Gulbed the *paristagbed* ['master of the servants']; for Goymard, son of Rastag; for Ardashir, son of Vifar; for Abursam, the son of Shapur, the *sālār ī darīgān* ['leader of the court domestics'/'head of the palace guards'?]; for Narseh, son of Barrag; for Shapur, son of Narseh; for Narseh, the 'master of supplies' [Greek *ho epi tēs annōnēs*]; for Hormizd, the *dibīrbed* ['master of scribes'], son of Hormizd, the *dibīrbed*; for

183

Naduk, the *zēndānīg* ['master of the state prison']; for Pabag, the *darbed* ['master of the gate']; for Pasfal, son of Pasfal; for Abdakhsh [?], son of the *dizbed* ['commander of the fortress']; for Kirdir, the *hērbed*; for Rastag, satrap of Veh-Ardakhshir; for Ardashir, son of the *bidaxš* ['viceroy']; for Mihrkhvast, the *ganzvar* ['treasurer']; for Shapur, the *framādār* ['commander']; for Ashtad [from the house of] Mihran, the *dibīr* ['scribe'] from Ray; for Sasan, the 'supervisor of the women's chambers' [*šabestān*: Greek *eunouchos*], son of Sasan; for Viroy, the *vāzārbed* ['who manages the trade']; for Ardashir, satrap of Niriz; for Baydad, son of Gulbed; for Kirdir-Ardavan; for Zurvandad, son of Bandag; for Vindar, son of Sasan; for Manzik, the eunuch; for Sasan, the *dādvar* ['judge']; for Valan, son of Nashpad and for Gulag the *varāzbed* ['master of the wild boars'].

In his *res gestae* (ŠKZ), Shapur enumerates the dignitaries, officials and aristocrats of his empire who are close to him and who are therefore entitled to have offerings made for the benefit of their souls. Lists of this kind have come down to us in other inscriptions too, among them one more in the *res gestae* of the second Sasanian king (in which he refers to the reigns of Pabag and Ardashir), and several in Narseh's Paikuli inscription. They are all similarly arranged, starting with the members of the royal house, followed by the most important noble clans and ending with other dignitaries and officials of the empire. Our aim here is to describe the early Sasanian state in its administrative aspects and to reconstruct the hierarchy of functions in the government of the empire and at court. Regarding 'imperial service', a key priority is to define territorial–administrative units ('parts of the empire', 'provinces'). For the early period, these are again found in the inscriptions of Shapur, Narseh and the Mobad Kirdir. Here is the beginning of the inscription ŠKZ:

And I [Shapur I] possess the lands [provinces; Greek *ethnē*]: Fars [Persis], Pahlav [Parthia], Huzestan [Khuzistan], Meshan [Maishan, Mesene], Asorestan [Mesopotamia], Nod-Ardakhshiragan [Adiabene], Arbayestan [Arabia], Adurbadagan [Atropatene], Armen [Armenia], Virozan [Iberia], Segan [Machelonia], Arran [Albania], Balasagan up to the Caucasus and to the 'gate of the Alans' and all of Padishkhvar[gar] [the entire Elburz chain = Tabaristan and Gelan (?)], Mad [Media], Gurgan [Hyrcania], Marv [Margiana], Harey [Aria], and all of Abarshahr [all the upper (= eastern, Parthian) provinces], Kerman [Kirman], Sakastan, Turgistan, Makuran, Pardan [Paradene], Hind [Sind] and Kushanshahr all the way to Pashkibur [Peshavar?] and to the borders of Kashgaria, Sogdia and Chach [Tashkent] and of that sea-coast Mazonshahr ['Oman'].

If we compare this enumeration with the list of dignitaries from the reign of Narseh in their territorial relations and with the – albeit incomplete

– classification of parts of the empire by Kirdir (from the reign of Bahram II), we notice that they have much in common, but that there are also certain differences, i.e. changes. For Shapur we find that certain regions were entrusted as 'kingdoms' to the sons of the 'king of kings' and other dynasts (MP *šāh*; Greek *basileus*). These regions lay at the borders of the empire and, in their geographical and political characteristics, must have been a heritage from the late Parthian period, where (in most cases?) Sasanian princes had now taken the places of the previous powerful 'petty kings'. Thus Shapur – again in connection with offerings and fires – mentions his following sons: Hormizd-Ardashir (the later Hormizd I) as 'great king of Armenia' and thereby crown prince, Shapur as 'King of Meshan', Narseh (the later 'king of kings') as 'king of Hind, Sakastan and Turgistan up to the seashore' or 'king of the Sakae', and Bahram (the later Bahram I) as 'king of Gelan'. In addition, there were Ardashir, king of Adiabene, Ardashir of Kerman and Hamazasp of Iberia. In its only partially preserved § 92, the Paikuli inscription also lists 'kings' (whose names are not specified) of Kushan(shahr), Choresmia, Pardan, Makran, Gurgan, Balasagan, Albania and Segan (see Map 4), as well as two royal individuals called Razgurd and Pand-Farrag (without specifying their kingdoms), and finally the Armenian Tirdad, the king of the Lakhmids, Amr, and his namesake from Edessa. Bear in mind, however, that the NPi does not describe all these kings as subjects of the Sasanian ruler. In § 93 of the same inscription, the enumeration of minor dynasts (? and/or local dignitaries?; MP *xvadāy*: 'lord') ends with a King Malukh, who does not seem to have ruled in Iran. The relationship of the local rulers with the 'king of kings' is usually referred to by scholars as 'vassalage'. This term, which applies to medieval Europe, incorporates the threefold condition of the oath of allegiance and military support on the one hand, and enfeoffment with usufruct of landed property on the other, conditions that, due to the lack of sources, cannot be confirmed for the period under discussion.

A second territorial unit after the 'kingdoms' is described by the word *šahr*, which in this case may perhaps be translated as 'province'. It was under the control of a *šahrab* (Greek *satrapēs*). Seven satraps with their administrative districts are known to us by name from the ŠKZ, but there are reasons to believe that their number (and hence the numbers of these provinces) was much greater in the third century. So the governors mentioned by Shapur in his inscription must have been only those who were particularly close to him. Whether the 'kingdoms' also had a *šahrab* as a kind of deputy of the *šāh* cannot be ascertained. It has been assumed that 'provinces' were established only where no other form of government existed, i.e. in all the regions directly subject to the 'king of kings', for instance in the former 'royal land' of the Parthian kings or in the newly conquered territories. Besides, the foundation of cities by the ruler was apparently possible only on 'royal land'. The proportionate sizes between a *šahr* of the Sasanians and the satrapies of the preceding empires cannot be determined. Our Map 4 shows the 'kingdoms' of the third century (according to ŠKZ and NPi) and – in the smaller sections – the late Sasanian administrative units of the most important regions of the empire.

We are far better informed about the empire's administration in the late Sasanian period (sixth/seventh century) than about its beginnings, since the seals and bullae for this later period and the legends on them contain extremely valuable material. This is true despite the fact that the sites where these testimonies were found (Qasr-i Abu Nasr near Shiraz; Takht-i Sulaiman; Susa/Turang Tepe; Tepe Kabudan [Gurgan]; Bishapur) are almost all situated in the west, so that the eastern parts of the empire yield comparatively scant evidence. For the late (and the preceding middle Sasanian) period, Syriac Acts of Martyrs and Nestorian synodal reports may provide additional information, but the evaluation of these sources is still in its initial stages. The Sasanian collection of laws *Mādayān ī Hazār Dādestān*, which has already been discussed, is probably right in attributing the introduction of 'administrative' seals to kings Kavad and Khosrow I. The recently undertaken analysis of glyptic material has not only contributed to clarifying some of the titles and functions, as well as the place-names (see Map 4), contained in the royal inscriptions, it has also yielded more detailed information about the names and functions of the provincial administrative 'élite'. The central administrative unit of the Sasanian empire was clearly the 'province' (*šahr*), which was itself divided into 'districts'. Almost all the officials referred to in the seals and bullae acted on a provincial level, only the *āmārgar* and the *framādār* could also function on a regional (i.e. supra-provincial) level, while '[the office of] the Magi' [*maguh*] remained on the 'district' level.

What were the tasks assigned to the individual officials and functionaries? The *šahrab* was the provincial governor who dealt with civil affairs and worked both with the *āmārgar* (in matters concerning taxes) and with the *ōstāndār* (in matters concerning the royal domains [?]). However – at least according to the bullae – he appears not to have shared any functions with members of the Zoroastrian clergy.

The *mogbed* (*mōbad*) of a province has been described as 'chef spirituel et ecclésiastique' in this sphere, and his tasks are believed to have included the administration of the domains of the clergy. The *mogbed* of Ardakhshir-Khvarrah, Veh-Shabuhr, is illustrated in Plate XXVIII. In the late Sasanian period there was, as already indicated, a 'Great Mobad' standing above the *mōbad*, and finally the *mōbadān mōbad* at the top of the Zoroastrian hierarchy. A relationship that cannot be defined with certainty is that between the *mogbed* and the *driyōšān ğādaggōv ud dādvar* ('protector of the poor and judge'), who also held a religious 'office'. This title presumably marks the survival of the function of *mogbed ud dādvar*, which has been attested for Kirdir (though with the addition of *hamšahr*, to make it embrace 'the whole empire'). The reason for its being changed (under Khosrow I?) in the administrative context was apparently to provide a more accurate description of the true mission of its holder, namely the legal representation of a 'poor man' at court, and also to differentiate its holder from the actual *mogbed*. Apart from these 'religious' legal experts, there were evidently judges (*dādvarān*) as well, who dispensed justice in 'civil' cases.

The *handarzbed* ('adviser') is known to have operated both at court and in a provincial context and must have been associated with pedagogic and advisory functions. Thus the Shapur inscription calls Yazdbad 'the adviser of the queens' and describes him as a eunuch. Apart from a provincial *handarzbed*, we also come across Magi (*mogān*) who served as *mogān-handarzbedān*.

The functions of the *āyēnbed*, attested both at court and in an administrative and religious context (Kirdir was an *āyēnbed* at the fire temple of Istakhr), remain obscure. Some associate this office with the 'financial' sphere (looking after the gifts received by the king), others with archival matters (keeping a list of customs and ceremonies, and also of dignitaries and their privileges) or with protocol (supervision of ceremonies). Similarly, little is known of the apparently significant tasks of a *framādār* ('commander-in-chief'). Two bearers of this title are mentioned in the Shapur inscription quoted above, without detailed geographical or functional specification. One of them was assigned to the great fire temple of Adur-i Gushnasp, another to a region consisting of several provinces. As for Mihr-Narseh, the powerful official under Yazdgird II (439–457), he even calls himself *vuzurg-framādār* ('great-framadar') in his Firuzabad inscription. The *vāspuhragān-framādār* may have been supervisor of the domains of the 'princes'. The *āmārgar*, known both on a provincial and on a regional level, handled important fiscal matters, possibly including tax revenues or a part of them.

'The office of the Magi' (*maguh*), which functioned exclusively on a 'district level', is only known from glyptics. It probably handled the local settlement of disputes and thus acted as a mediating authority to the *mogbed* or *driyōšān ğādaggōv ud dādvar*, who functioned on a provincial level. The 'judge', *mogbed* and *rad* (an important official in the Zoroastrian hierarchy whose tasks are not exactly known) were also the decisive authorities in the interrogation and conviction of Christians in times of persecution. They are mentioned together with the 'prison staff' (guardians, executioners etc.) in Syriac Acts of Martyrs.

Some of the officials acting on a provincial level had (at certain periods or starting from a certain period) a 'superior' on the imperial level, like the *hamšahr mogbed ud dādvar* or the *mōbadān mōbad* already referred to. In many cases, however, this kind of relationship cannot be pinned down (for instance with respect to *āmārgar* or *framādār*). Outstanding among offices of such empire-wide scope, whose holders appeared in the immediate entourage of the 'king of kings', were those of the *bidaxš* and the *argbed*. The *bidaxš*, probably always a member of the royal house, is etymologically interpreted as 'second king' and might hence be conceived as 'viceroy' or 'grand vizier'. The title of *argbed* is translated by some as 'commander of a fortress', by others as 'supreme tax collector'. His importance is underlined by his being named prior to the *bidaxš* and the princes in NPi, and also by the fact that an office-holder of this description appears several times as the authorized representative of the king. And lastly, the *zēndānīg* may have been the head of the 'state prison' called *gilkard* (MP 'made of earth/clay'), and known in the Western tradition as 'castle of oblivion', which is located in Susan on the Karun in Khuzistan. The military leadership of the empire will be the subject of a later section.

We come now to the 'court functions', some of which may already have existed in the Parthian period but eluded the record. Of particular importance here was the *hazāruft* ('chiliarch'), as pointed out by the Shapur inscription. He is not to be considered as a 'premier ministre', however, but as the head of the king's bodyguards, as he was in the Achaemenid period. At his side may have been the *sālār ī darīgān*, if he is rightly interpreted as the 'commander of the guards of the palace'. The *darbed* ('master of the gate') must have been the commander of the gate-keepers. Highly esteemed according to ŠKZ and NPi were also the (Greek) *deipnoklētor* ('caller to meals'; MP '*dnyk*), probably the 'chef de protocole', the *šafšērdār* as royal arms-bearer, the *paristagbed* ('master of the servants'; Greek *ho epi tēs hypēresias*) as the person in charge of all the services for the king, the head supply 'official' (Greek *ho epi tēs annōnēs*; MP *glstpty*) and the 'treasurer' (*ganzvar*). At Ardashir's court, there were in addition a 'marshal' (Parth. *'hwrpty*, Greek *ho epi tēs pathnēs*), a 'cupbearer' (MP *md'ly*, Greek *ho epi tou oinou*) and a 'master of the hunt' (MP *nhcyrpt*, Greek *ho epi tou kynhēgiou*), to be compared to the 'master of wild boars' (*varāzbed*) at the court of Shapur.

The *dibīrbed* as the head of the office of 'scribes' and other employees is also honourably mentioned by Shapur. The fact that the father of the holder of this title had also been 'head of scribes' indicates that this office required special abilities which could apparently be passed on within a family. Under the Sasanians, eunuchs served not only in the women's quarters but also in leading positions at court and in the empire. 'Singers' were also present at the Sasanian royal court to recite, replenish and transform the rich store of Iranian popular tradition. If, as assumed, the courts of the 'petty kings' and provincial governors were like miniature copies of the royal court, then the early Sasanian state, and the Parthian state on which it was based, can perhaps best be described as '*Personalverbandsstaat*' (a 'state based on personal relationships'), a phrase used in connection with medieval Europe.

Reference has already been made to the royal *dastgird*, that is, territories under the direct control of the king. There were, on the other hand, territories that belonged to the aristocracy and in which royal control could be exercised only indirectly. The imposition of taxes and levying of troops in these areas could therefore be done only through the agency of the land-owning magnates. Clearly it was only on 'royal land' that the kings could found cities (*šahrestān*), or resettle or rename them. No wonder, then, that the early rulers tried to raise tax revenues and strengthen their control over the country by increasing the number of cities (and of their inhabitants). Ardashir's elimination of the Parthian 'petty kings', his victory over Ardavan IV and his westward expansion gave him the opportunity to do so, while the absence of further territorial gains made it difficult for his successors to pursue his urbanization policy. This only changed again under Kavad and Khosrow I, who exploited the weakening of the aristocracy through the Mazdakite rebellions to convert land belonging to the aristocracy into royal land. Whether and to what extent the old Greek cities of Mesopotamia and Susiana were able to maintain their autonomy under the Sasanians is hard to ascertain. Susa, at any rate, definitely lost its political significance when Shapur II took ruthless measures against the city to enforce his policy of persecuting Christians. The reverse side of founding cities in the Sasanian period was the deportation of groups of people from their home towns, as is particularly well attested by the new settlement of parts of the population of Antiochia by Shapur I and Khosrow I (see below). The transplantation of rural people into the cities, as well as the admission of refugees or individuals immigrating of their own free will, played a relatively minor role in the urbanization process, since it was more useful to settle prisoners-of-war and deportees, thus increasing the number of workers, above all skilled labour, artists and artisans among the subjects.

Before the reign of Khosrow Anoshirvan the kings of Persia used to levy one-third of the revenue from their districts [Arab. *min ġallat kuwarihim*], and from some districts one-fourth, one-fifth or one-sixth depending on the irrigation and cultivation in the district [*'alā qadr širbihā wa-'imāratihā*], and a certain sum as poll-tax [*ǧizya*]. Now Kavad, the son of Peroz, had ordered towards the end of his reign that the land, whether plain or mountain, be surveyed, so that the land tax [*ḫarāǧ*] might be rightly determined ... But when his son Khosrow acceded to the throne, he had the survey completed and had the date palms and olive trees as well as the heads counted and thereupon the total amount established by his scribes ... When he [the scribe] read this out to him, Khosrow said to them ['the people' (*an-nās*)]: 'It is our intention to set fixed rates on the calculated sum of the now measured *ǧarīb* [*c.* 0.1 ha] of grainfields, as well as on the date palms, olive trees and heads, and to arrange that these be paid annually in three instalments: Thus money will be collected in our treasury so that, if news about a disorder or some evil should arrive from one of our frontier-posts or from a borderland, for the settlement or suppression of which we should need money, we would find it ready; for we do not wish to issue a new imposition for cases of that kind.' ... After careful deliberation they agreed to impose the land tax on the field-produce which feeds man and animal, namely wheat, barley, rice, grapes, alfalfa, date palms and olive trees. On each *ǧarīb* of land sown with wheat or barley they imposed 1 *dirham* of land tax, on the *ǧarīb* of vineyard 8, on the *ǧarīb* of alfalfa 7, on every 4 Persian date palms 1 *dirham*, on every 6 common date palms the same amount, and the same on every 6 olive trees ... All other crop yields ... they left tax-free, so that people might be well nourished. The poll-tax they imposed on everyone except noblemen, magnates, soldiers, priests, scribes and those [otherwise] occupied in the royal service. They arranged several classes at 12, 8, 6 and 4 *dirham*, depending on whether the man could achieve much or little. Those who were not yet 20 or more than 50 years old were exempt from poll-tax.

In this account about the fiscal reforms of Khosrow, Tabari compares the old taxation system with the new one of the Sasanians. While before, the harvest was assessed on the standing crop or on the threshing-floor, so that the state had to manage with revenues that changed from year to year, it now laid this risk at the owner's door and received calculable amounts for warfare and emergencies through a pre-set tax rate. But something else is also pointed out in this report: the differences in levies from the 'king's land' (a third) and from the districts which were not subject to the full royal taxing power (i.e. on which the landlords had their properties: a quarter to a sixth) were now eliminated. It is true that the owner of the land now bore the risk of fluctuating harvests, but for the ripe standing crop to be left to wither until the arrival of the tax assessor had been no less an evil previously. The dependence of the late Sasanian taxation system on late Roman–Byzantine models has been both postulated and argued against. Under Khosrow II the initially moderate but later enormously increased pressure of taxation caused endless complaints. Thus the alleged maxim of the reformer Khosrow I, which is handed down by Mas'udi, can be considered as timelessly valid, but was hardly observed in reality:

The kingdom relies on the army, and the army on money, and money on the ḫarāǧ and the ḫarāǧ on farming, and farming on justice, and justice on the integrity of officials, and the integrity of officials on the loyalty of the viziers, and at the top of it all is the watchfulness of the king regarding his own inclinations and his capacity to guide these so that he will control them and they will not control him.

In addition to the ḫarāǧ and the ǧizya as rural taxes, there were indirect taxes (e.g. customs) in urban areas, and presumably a poll-tax, too, for the urban population. There were times when extraordinary revenues such as plunder, protection and extortion monies from cities and territories in enemy country, as well as war reparations, would eke out the budgets of Sasanian kings, but likewise they may have burdened them in the event of foreign policy failures.

2. Agriculture, handicraft and trade – warfare and frontier defence: the economy and army in Sasanian Iran

As in almost all ancient states, agriculture was the leading form of economic activity in Sasanian Iran. The bulk of the population lived in the country and made their living by cultivating the soil as free or dependent farmers. It was in arable land that the 'élite' invested and reinvested their financial resources, and aside from noble descent, the keys to their social prestige and political ambitions were large landed estates and a great number of retainers. As for the king, his treasuries drew much more on rural than on urban taxes, and even recruits for his army came mainly from the country.

In his account of the taxation system, Tabari also informs us about the most important fruits of the earth: wheat, barley and rice as cereals; grape-vines, alfalfa, date palms and olive trees as special crops. Vegetables, sesame seed, cucumbers and cotton were not taxed, probably because they were mainly grown for the consumption of the owner himself and his household. Also untaxed were isolated date palms, since it was assumed that every passer-by would help himself to their fruit. Pasture-land is not mentioned by Tabari, but Mas'udi refers to a (high) tax of 7 *dirham* for a pasture in Iraq, pre-sumably to prevent the conversion of farmland into pasture.

Of all Iranian regions, Sasanian Khuzistan is the only one that has yet been examined in any detail from the point of view of demography, settle-ments and agrarian geography. While the major crops have been identified as cereals, rice, sugar-cane and dates, the most significant result of these investigations has been to show that in the Sasanian period, there was ap-parently a massive population migration into large urban centres, and a simultaneous decline of farm products. The blatant inconsistency between this phenomenon and the impressive investments in dams (see Plate XXVIa), canals and other irrigation systems, for which there is both archaeological and literary evidence, is not easy to explain.

Aside from farming, a great number of the king's subjects made their living by trade:

The excellent Pusai [a Christian martyr under Shapur II] descended from prisoners [-of-war] whom Shapur b. Hormizd had brought from Beth Rhomaye and settled in Veh-Shabuhr [Bishapur], a city in the province of Pars ... When this Shapur b. Hormizd, who had started the persecution of the eastern churches, built the city of Karka d-Ladan and settled prisoners of different regions in it, it pleased him also to settle among them about thirty families each of the ethnic groups of all the cities of the provinces of his empire, so that, as a result of intermarriage, the deported would be bound by the [ties of] family and affection and would not find it easy to gradually escape from their home. And among these they also settled the blessed Pusai, his wife, his children, his brothers and sisters and his entire household in Karka d-Ladan. Pusai was an excellent craftsman and a master at weaving and embroidering gold ornaments. Besides, he belonged to those craftsmen whom the king assembled from among the deportees and subjects of all nations and whom he formed into a 'union' ['synagogue'; *knūšyā*] with many subdivisions, and for whom he established a workshop next to his palace in Karka d-Ladan. And since the blessed Pusai was skilful in his trade, he was recommended to the king, who steadily extended to him great honour and presents and after a short time made him the 'chief craftsman' [*rēš ummānē*] because he distinguished himself more and more every day and met with approval ... A few days before the persecution against the churches arose ... the excellent Pusai was rendered a transient honour by King Shapur since he made him also the head of the craftsmen of the other provinces of the empire.

This account from the martyrology of Pusai illustrates two things: first of all, the already mentioned interest of the Sasanians in forcibly settling (captive) skilled workers in the empire (especially craftsmen), a fact for which there are numerous other testimonies, and second, the establishment of royal 'workshops' under special supervision. The bearer of the (Syriac) title *rēš ummānē*, who is elsewhere identified with the *qārōgbēð* (< MP **kirrōgbed*), had the members of various trades under his control, some of which were subdivided into further specializations. Pusai's *cursus honorum* implies that the Christian artisans at the royal workshops were limited in their freedom of movement (e.g. the choice of place), but that they had the *conubium* (right of contracting marriage) with non-Christian – probably Zoroastrian – Iranian girls. Depending on his sphere of activity, the *kirrōgbed* was commissioned by the king to supervise the work in the ateliers of the city or the empire, and the fact that this function for the whole empire was entrusted to a Christian appeared unusual to the Zoroastrians. Within the hierarchy of the urban population, the 'chief of the (royal) craftsmen' held pride of place among laymen, even taking precedence over the heads of the corporations, as witnessed by the signatures of the Nestorian Synod of 544. The outstanding position of the head of the artisans at the same time points to the great significance attributed to manufacture in urban life.

Workers or prisoners-of-war recruited by the state worked not only in the textile industry of Khuzistan, which owed its rise to deported Syrians, but also in the building trade (as stonemasons, brickmakers, builders) and as blacksmiths, locksmiths and dyers. The bridges, dams and other irrigation works constructed by Roman captives in Iran strike us even today as remarkable (see Plate XXVIa). As for those 'scientists' who either voluntarily or otherwise followed the summons of the Sasanian king, they will be discussed separately. The freedom of worship usually granted by the kings, the fact that population groups sharing the same origin, religion or language were settled at the same places, and the economic and social prestige they enjoyed, must have to a certain extent compensated the deported skilled workers for living away from home. There is hardly any evidence of resistance on the part of deported people or conscripts, although Tabari reports that builders of Khosrow II at the Mushaqqar fortress did threaten to run away unless they were supplied with women (prostitutes?).

The heads of the corporations of merchants, gold- and silversmiths and pewterers among the signatories of the synodal canons prove that apart from the royal workers and temporary conscripts in Veh-Andiyok-Shabuhr (Syr. Beth Lapat) – and probably at other places as well – there also lived free craftsmen who were organized into 'guilds'.

Sasanian merchants were known to be less interested in marketing their own goods than in transporting foreign products from west to east and from east to west in an active transit trade:

After these [the Indians] come the Persians, neighbours of the Romans. They are reported to be very skilled in all bad things and brave in wars. They are said to commit great crimes; and since they know of no natural dignity and are like animals without understanding, they sleep with their mothers and sisters. They also sin against that divinity that created them. But on the other hand, they are said to have plenty of everything. For since their neighbouring nations were granted the right to trade [*potestas negotii*], they seem to have everything in abundance ... Our country [the Imperium Romanum] borders on theirs ... There are ... Nisibis and Edessa, which in every respect have very good men; they are very skilful in trade and also good at hunting. Above all, they are rich and endowed with all goods; for the goods they receive from the Persians they themselves sell to the whole country of the Romans, and what they buy in Roman territory they again trade with the Persians, except ore and iron, for it is not allowed to supply the enemy with ore and iron.

Written by an anonymous author in 359/60 AD, this *Expositio totius mundi et gentium* presents the Sasanian Iranians in their role as middlemen, although in an as yet (until 363 AD) very unfavourable situation for Iranian merchants. The peace treaty between Diocletian and Narseh at the end of the third century provided that the Sasanians would accept Nisibis as the only centre for the exchange of goods between the two empires. This involved considerable additional expenditure and time for the Persians. The overland trade in luxury goods from China and India, as well as from eastern Iran and Armenia (e.g. raw silk and silk products, jewellery, spices, scents, hides, eunuch slaves and wild animals), had brought the Sasanians significant revenues until the end of the third century, and had made the Romans dependent on them, as they had been during the Parthian period. Roman – and later also Byzantine – efforts to circumvent the Sasanian empire by a northern route and to gain footholds on the Caspian Sea, in the Caucasus region and in Armenia, had met with only limited success. The form of trade established in the peace of 297/8 now guaranteed the Romans higher customs revenues, while for the Sasanians it not only entailed considerable financial losses, but also removed the possibility of collecting information about the *limes* of their western opponent while indulging in a little frontier-crossing traffic. Jovian's 'humiliating peace treaty' of 363, by which the Romans had to renounce important parts of eastern Mesopotamia (even Nisibis) – somewhat later they also lost almost all their influence in Armenia – temporarily restored to the Sasanians their old position in trade policy. But by 408/9, the Romans and Persians had reached a settlement which finally satisfied both sides. Trade was limited to Nisibis, Callinicum and the Armenian metropolis of Artaxata, two of which cities (Nisibis and Artaxata) were under Sasanian control. In the peace treaty between Khosrow I and Justinian (562 AD), three articles were devoted to questions of economic and commercial policy with no significant departure from the previous settlement. Articles 3 and 5 confirmed the customs places and added Dara to them (which was soon lost to the Byzantines, however), article 4 exempted goods accompanying diplomats of either country from customs and other trade restrictions, and article 5 placed Saracen (Arab) and other barbarian merchants on both sides under strict supervision. How much the Sasanians profited from transit trade is shown by contemporary Byzantine efforts to extend their own trading potentials and bypass Persian intervention by introducing sericulture, intensifying their contacts with Axum (Ethiopia) and southern Arabia, and establishing contact with the Turks (the successors of the Kushans and Hephthalites in the east).

Like the Parthians and the inhabitants of southern Mesopotamia, the Sasanians also kept up their contact with India by the sea route through the Persian Gulf:

[Mani reports that he went into the port of Pharat (Forat d-Meshan near present-day Basra)] ... There was someone ... in Pharat by the name of Og[gias(?)], a man who, because of his [influence] and his power over men, whose [leader he was, was famous. I saw how] the merchants who [prepared to sail in] ships to the Persians and Indians, sealed his [goods, but] did not [yet set sail] until he came on board ... Then [he (Oggias)] answered me: '[I] want to [board a] ship [and sail to] the Indians [so that] I receive ...' But I said [to him]: 'I ...' [here the text breaks off].

Another Manichaean text says about the return of the prophet:

When our father [Mani] returned from India and reached the city of Rev-Ardakhshir, he sent the presbyter Patticius with brother Hanni to India, to Deb.

What interests us in connection with Mani's voyage to India is not his motives for sailing east, but the fact that the trade with India (via Fars), which is so well attested for the Parthian period, continued under the Sasanians. India's geography and the customs, practices and religious convictions

of its inhabitants must have been well enough known in southern Mesopotamia for the prophet himself to venture on a mission to that country. As
for Deb, which was the goal of his voyage and that of his followers, it is
probably to be identified with Daibul (present-day Banbhore near Karachi in
Pakistan), so that he must have travelled no further than to the (extreme)
west of the sub-continent. From the fourth century on, there is a growing
number of references to relations between Iran and India, among which the
mission of the eastern Syrians (Nestorians) by sea and by land up to the
Malabar coast and as far as Sri Lanka is especially striking. The see of the
Metropolitan of Rev Ardakhshir was particularly concerned about these
Indian Christians and claimed certain rights to which it was not entitled.

Commercial activity in the Persian Gulf required control of at least the
north-eastern Arabian coastal regions. So it is not surprising that already
Ardashir I sought to bring the regions of Ahvaz and Meshan under his
control and founded cities there, even – according to Tabari – advancing as
far as Bahrain. After Arab incursions into Fars at the beginning of the reign
of Shapur II, the king took revenge by a brutal and extensive expedition into
Arabia, by building massive defence lines in southern Iraq, and by deporting
Arabs to Kerman and Ahvaz. Oman, which is geographically and geologically
more closely linked with south-western Iran than with north-eastern Arabia,
was under Sasanian control at least from the reign of Shapur I. On behalf
of the 'king of kings', the dynasty of the Lakhmids in Hira took charge of
protecting the Mesopotamian territories against the Byzantines, their (Arab)
Ghassanid allies and the Bedouins of the Najd. Al-Mundhir III of the *banū
Laḥm* dynasty (503–554) was even appointed by the Sasanians as ruler over
a major part of eastern Arabia, which included Bahrain, Oman, Yamama,
Najd and the Hejaz as far as Ta'if, and Sasanian influence intermittently
made itself felt as far as Yathrib (Medina). When Khosrow II thwarted the
attempt of the Lakhmid Nuʿman III to shake off Sasanian rule, this weakening of the Arabian 'buffer state' became one of the causes for the collapse of
the Arab front a few decades later (during the onslaught of the army of the
Prophet Muhammad).

Sasanian policy towards Arabia was not confined to the north of the
peninsula, however. Khosrow I sent an expeditionary force under Vahriz to
southern Arabia, which advanced as far as Sanʿaʾ, dislodged the Ethiopians,
who were allies of the Byzantines, from there and finally appointed a native
prince as a 'vassal' in Yemen. The Persian supremacy there did not end until
Muhammad's last years. The purpose of Sasanian control over South Arabia,

especially the Gulf of Aden, was of course severely to limit Byzantine trade through the Red Sea.

To the population of the eastern Roman empire, the Sasanians were significant as trade partners, but even more as military opponents. It happened often enough that the imperial army and the troops of the 'king of kings' collided, or that Persian units broke through the *limes*, plundering and pillaging. Contemporaries were greatly impressed even by the outward appearance of the Iranian soldiers:

... near daybreak a huge force of Persians appeared with Merena, general of their cavalry, two sons of the king, and many other magnates. Moreover, all the companies were clad in iron, and all parts of their bodies were covered with thick plates, so fitted that the stiff joints conformed with those of their limbs; and the forms of human faces were so skilfully fitted to their heads, that, since their entire bodies were plated with metal, arrows that fell upon them could lodge only where they could see a little through tiny openings fitted to the circle of the eye, or where through the tips of their noses they were able to get a little breath. Of these some, who were armed with pikes, stood so motionless that you would think them held fast by clamps of bronze. Hard by, the archers (for that nation has especially trusted in this art from the very cradle) were bending their flexible bows ... Behind them the gleaming elephants, with their awful figure and savage, gaping mouths, could scarcely be endured by the faint-hearted.

Ammianus Marcellinus's description of the Persian army at the time of the expedition of the emperor Julian in the year 363 AD shows that the backbone of the army (*spāh*) was – as with the Parthians – the heavily armed and armoured cavalry, although in the course of time the horses' plating had been steadily reduced. According to Tabari, a soldier serving as 'cavalier' under Khosrow I was required to be equipped with 'horse's armour, a coat of mail, a breast-plate, greaves, a sword, a lance, a shield, a cudgel ... an axe or a club, a quiver and two bows with strings on them and 30 arrows, and finally 2 turned strings'. According to Procopius, the Sasanian élite corps was also named the 'Immortals', like that of the Achaemenids. The light-armed cavalry was often recruited from allies, people from Sakastan, Gelan and Albania, as well as the Kushans, Hephthalites, Turks and Arabs.

The infantry consisted of bowmen, who protected themselves with elongated, curved shields made of wickerwork and untanned hides, and simple foot-soldiers. The latter were recruited from the rural population and received no pay, primarily serving as 'pages' for the armoured horsemen, guarding the baggage-train or taking part in siege and entrenchment works. Their weapons were spear and shield. The Persians had learnt siege techniques from the Romans, but had become as good as their opponents, if not better.

Until the sixth century, the leader of the Sasanian army was the *spāhbed*, who is already known from third-century inscriptions, and at his side – as commander of the cavalry – was the *aspbed*. The title *adrastadaran salanēs* (< MP *arteštārān sālār*: 'commander of the warriors') reported by Procopius must have distinguished a 'generalissimo' who was superior to the *spāhbed*. This appears to have been a creation of Mihr-Narseh at the beginning of the fifth century. Khosrow I replaced the thitherto single *spāhbed* with four officers of this title, each of whom was entrusted with the military command of a quarter of the empire. Prominent among other high military personnel were the *pāygōspānān* (military commanders of a province?) and *marzbānān* (commanders of the border-districts?). Khosrow's reforms also involved recruiting 'cavaliers' (Arab. *al-asāwira*) who, if they had no fortune, were provided with a horse, equipment and money. Detailed accounts were kept about the delivery of weapons, the salary, the nature of the horse and rider and the mustering of recruits. The border troops, who shared the king's special attention with the frontier fortifications, were allotted 'soldier's fiefs'.

Combats were mainly decided by a concentrated attack of the cavalry, supported by a hail of arrows from the bowmen. In the centre, near the imperial standard, stood the commander-in-chief, protected by the élite troops. This formation, together with the Persians' lack of stomach for close combat, as observed by Ammianus, were the grounds for many a defeat of the Sasanians. If the commander fell or fled, the soldiers gave up the battle as lost. Even the armoured horsemen, who had been so successful in battles against the Romans and Byzantines, were overpowered in the end: against the lightly armed and mobile horsemen of the Muslim army they fought a losing battle.

[In 421, in the battle against Byzantium, the Sasanian Blasses = Bahram V wrote a letter with the following proposal:] 'If your whole force has a man able to fight in single combat and to defeat a Persian selected by me, I shall immediately make a peace-treaty for 50 years with the customary provision of gifts.' When these terms had been agreed, the emperor of the Persians chose a Persian named Ardazanes from the division known as the Immortals, while the Romans selected Areobindus, a Gothic *comes foederatorum* … The Persian charged at him first with his lance, but Areobindus, bending down to his right, lassoed him, brought him down off his horse and killed him. Thereupon the Persian emperor made a peace treaty.

The chivalrous single combat, as described by Malalas, was a tradition in

Iran, but had even stricter regulations and higher ethical standards in the Sasanian period. It is not surprising that the Sasanians represented successful ventures in the form of single combats, as exemplified by the battle relief at Firuzabad (see Plate XX) and the famous cameo preserved in Paris (see Plate XXVIIb).

Soldierly virtues were always part of the Iranian ruler's proof of legitimacy. Thus the Sasanian kings would take the field at the head of their armies to acquire the charisma demanded of a sovereign through gallantry and military skill and to prove that they were favoured by the gods. On their reliefs and silver bowls, the kings had themselves represented as warriors, and this is also true of their special 'crown books', where each is shown with his individual garments and headgear. Like Caesar, Augustus and Xenophon, they also recorded their martial exploits and wrote military textbooks.

3. Zoroastrians, Manichaeans, Mazdakites, Christians and Jews: religious communities in the Sasanian empire

And afterwards, when Bahram [I], the king of kings, the son of Shapur, died, Bahram, the king of kings, the son of Bahram, the generous, the just, the friendly, the beneficent and pious in the empire, came to reign. And for love of Ohrmazd and the gods, and for the sake of his own soul, he raised my rank and my titles in the empire ... And in all the provinces, in every part of the empire, the acts of worshipping Ohrmazd and the gods were enhanced. And the Zoroastrian religion and the Magi were greatly honoured in the empire. And the gods, 'water', 'fire' and 'domestic animals' attained great satisfaction in the empire, but Ahriman and the idols suffered great blows and great damages. And the [false] doctrines of Ahriman and of the idols disappeared from the empire and lost credibility. And the Jews [yahūd], Buddhists [šaman], Hindus [brāman], Nazarenes [nāsrā], Christians [kristiyān], Baptists [makdag] and Manichaeans [zandīk] were smashed in the empire, their idols destroyed, and the habitations of the idols annihilated and turned into abodes and seats of the gods.

In his inscriptions, the 'priest' Kirdir states that thanks to his efforts under King Bahram II (276–293), Zoroastrianism was promoted in the empire and other religious communities were persecuted. For us this report is particularly revealing because first of all, it refers to the different religious persuasions in the empire by name, and secondly, it points to a specific phase in the political approach to religious minorities, a phase that must be examined in its historical context.

In the attempt to characterize Zoroastrianism in the Sasanian period, we are faced with a threefold dilemma: the problem of the lack of uniformity and synchronism in religious literature in Iran, the profusion of contradictory scholarly opinions in questions of detail, and finally the lack of conceptual accuracy and the lasting influence of stereotypes and static ideas bequeathed by earlier research. And yet certain fundamental points are incontestable: Sasanian Iran was Zoroastrianized to a greater extent than ever before in the country's previous history. The religious influence on legal culture, literature and pictorial symbolism, as well as funerary customs of the period (exposure of the body and burial of the bones) bear witness to this fact. Religious authorities were present at many places, from the village and its local centre of worship to the royal court, to watch over 'divine service', execution of rites and preservation of religious traditions. At the same time, a process of hierarchization can be observed with regard both to offices and functions (see above), and to sites of worship. The first written recording of the Avesta, undertaken to follow and compete with such models as the Torah, the Bible and Manichaean books, as well as the extensive literature concerning the holy texts, made the Zoroastrians into 'people of the book' and thus came to take on great significance for the further history of the community. The Sasanian kings acted as promoters of the Zoroastrian creed, founded holy fires and sanctuaries and boasted of their close and propitious relationship with the gods. As we have seen, they based much of their legitimacy on their 'divine right' to reign. Endowments for the benefit of the souls of the dead (and living) (MP *ruvānagān*) expressed the concern of the faithful for the fate of the soul after death. These endowments could turn out to be service to the community or assistance for the descendants of the deceased, depending on who was designated to receive their revenues.

Many questions remain unanswered. Were the kings 'orthodox' Zoroastrians or followers of the Zurvan 'heresy'? Did the early Sasanians really ban image-worship and replace it with fire-worship? Was the Avesta actually canonized under Ardashir I, as the *Dēnkard* will have us believe? And finally, is it true that at the incursion of Islam, Zoroastrianism had become so rigid a religion with its rituals and formalisms and its material and spiritual–moral demands that its followers found it rather burdensome, devoid of persuasive power and lacking in open-mindedness or readiness to reform? Or did merely external circumstances reduce it to a minority religion, and has the victory of Islam in its interpretation as salvation history even obstructed the view of many a modern observer?

The history of the Christians in the Sasanian empire poses less of a problem, even if it is often masked in European ecclesiastical history.

Christian communities had already started spreading in Mesopotamia and Iran in the second century, first under the Arsacids and later under the Sasanians, with Edessa apparently important as the centre of a Christian mission. However, the crucial role in the establishment of Christianity in the Sasanian empire was not played by this 'first evangelization', but by the deportation of several hundred thousand mostly Christian inhabitants of Roman Syria, Cilicia and Cappadocia by Shapur I. Both Shapur's great *res gestae* and the Christian–Arabic Chronicle of Se'ert confirm that those deported were settled in Mesopotamia, Persis and Parthia. There can be no doubt that economic and demographic reasons, rather than religious and political ones, induced Shapur to embark on a population transfer of such magnitude. This is confirmed by the colonization of the deported in newly built or renamed cities and settlements within fertile, but relatively sparsely populated regions such as Khuzistan or Meshan, by their employment in large construction projects, and by the comparatively high proportion of skilled workers and craftsmen among them.

By this policy, Shapur unintentionally promoted the spread of the Christian faith and Christian community. The process may have been accelerated by the king's steps to support the new settlers economically, the feeling of solidarity among the fellow-believers themselves, their sense of social advancement, and perhaps also by the idea of having thus escaped religious persecution (under Valerian). According to all our sources, the period of peace and prosperity for the Christian community lasted until the reign of Bahram II (276–293), under whom the first persecutions began. But even then, martyrdoms like the particularly well attested case of Bahram's concubine Candida remained exceptional until the fifth decade of the fourth century. At the beginning of this new century, the Sasanian empire became a refuge for many a Christian from the eastern Roman empire who sought protection from the persecutions of Galerius. The end of the third century already marked the first internal tensions among the Christians of the Sasanian empire, tensions brought about by a question of ecclesiastical organization, namely whether or not the bishop of Seleucia-Ctesiphon was entitled to the primacy among the bishops of the empire. In this conflict, it is true, personal ambitions and animosities appear to have played a much greater part than historical considerations or problems of administration and ecclesiastical law. For all that, the arguments resulted in only one bishop of the empire, presumably Yohannan bar Maryam of Arbela, being represented at the Council of Nicaea of 325.

For the Christians of the Persian empire, a new political situation emerged at the time. On the one hand, they had a new sovereign in Shapur II, who saw his main task as revising the dictated peace of Nisibis (297/8 AD) and was preparing with all his might for a war against Rome; on the other hand, the Roman emperor Constantine, who considered himself the sovereign of *all* Christians, had made them his protégés without their asking. Their possible role as vanguards of Rome was also perceived by Shapur. On 17 April 340 or 341, after the first failures of the Sasanians in their renewed fight against Rome, Shemʿon (Simeon) bar Sabbaʿe, the new metropolitan of Seleucia-Ctesiphon, was urged by the king to collect a special tax from the Christians to finance the costs of war. His refusal was the prelude to the first systematic persecution of the Christians in the Sasanian empire. In the martyrology of Simeon, Shapur accuses the bishop of having political motives for his attitude:

[The king] said: 'Simeon wants to make his followers and his people rebel against my Majesty and become slaves of the emperor who shares their faith. That is why he will not obey my command.'

That the Christians were not quite groundlessly exposed to the suspicion of being Rome's 'fifth column' is shown in an excerpt from the *Demonstrationes* of the 'Persian sage' Aphrahat, the most important intellectual representative of Christianity in the Sasanian empire at that period:

The good comes to the people of God, and well-being remains with him through whom the good comes [Constantius]. Evil was also roused because of the forces massed by the evil, the overbearing and proud [Shapur] ... That [Roman] empire will not be conquered, for the hero whose name is Jesus will come with his powers and his armour shall uphold the whole army of the empire.

In view of the barely controllable borders between the two empires in Mesopotamia and Armenia, another reproach levelled at the Christians also appears as not quite unfounded. The Chronicle of Arbela says among other things:

And they [the Jews and Manichaeans] explained to them [the Magi] that the Christians were all of them spies of the Romans. And that nothing happens in the kingdom that they do not write to their brothers who live there.

We have very little information about the Christians' own sense of identity in those days. We know hardly anything about their favourite activities, and even less about other details of their life and common interests. What we may reasonably assume is a special interest in freely practising their religion and organizing their churches, as well as spontaneously congregating in places where they could count on close contact with one another and a Christian way of life. About their own designation for themselves we learn from the martyrologies that they called themselves (Syr.) 'amma, which corresponds with the Greek *ethnos* or *laos*. In confessional situations or writings we also find, aside from hagiographical terms such as 'confessors', 'pure ones' or 'just ones', the phrase 'people of God' or the biblical description 'people arising from the heathens (and Jews)'. Terms referring to the ethnic, or rather geographical–cultural origin of the Christians are *nāṣrāye* (the native) and *krestyānē* (the erstwhile deported Christians and their descendants), corresponding with Kirdir's *nāsrā* and *kristiyān*, while in narratives about the Passion, the word *nāṣrāye* is almost exclusively put into the mouths of the persecutors. The Christians at this period referred to themselves as *mšīḥāyē*, i.e. 'those who believe in the Messiah = Christ', and later apparently as *krestyānē*.

It should be noted that their linguistic identity – like the Manichaeans, the majority spoke Syriac, and the deported people and their successors must also have continued speaking Greek for quite a long time – did not mark Christians as outsiders or a minority group. For one thing, Syriac was very widespread, and for another, Middle Persian, the language of the kings and priests, was not imposed as a state language in the multilingual Sasanian empire, indeed it was not even a lingua franca. In this respect, too, the Sasanians adhered to the successful Arsacid model. It is not to be ruled out that in everyday life the Christians also considered themselves as inhabitants of a city or region or even as people of Eranshahr, but in the martyrologies, the world was not divided between 'Romans' and 'Persians', but between the 'people of God' and the 'outsiders' or 'non-believers'. While under normal circumstances the Christians had no divided loyalties between the worldly and the divine lord, since the two forms of obedience did not exclude one another, this state of affairs changed when the policy of Shapur II demanded a decision between the two. An excerpt from the dialogue between the king and old Bishop Shem'on (Simeon), which might easily have stemmed from a Western martyrology, illustrates this conflict:

The king spoke: 'Where is your friendship for me?' Simeon said: 'I certainly love you and at all times I myself and my people pray for your Majesty, as our scriptures command us to do. But the love of my God is better than your friendship, oh king.'

Shapur's persecutions were followed, after a brief pause as a result of the peace treaty with Jovian (363 AD), by other, shorter ones until the mid-fifth century. At a synod in Seleucia-Ctesiphon in the year 410, the Sasanian Christians created their own ecclesiastical organization with its own hierarchy (under the Metropolitan of this city as the Katholikos) and its own ecclesiastical laws. The possibility of an intervention by the patriarch of Antiochia in differences between the bishops and head of the new Church of the East was forestalled in the year 424 by an eastern Syrian synod which refused to accept any authority above its own Katholikos. This made the Christian Church of the Persian empire completely independent and autocephalous, with its leader accordingly calling himself 'Katholikos-Patriarch'. While by accepting the Nicaean doctrine of 325, the synod of the year 410 had as yet conformed with the dogmatic developments of the Roman Church, the Sasanian Christians even tore down this bridge by officially embracing the Nestorian creed at the synod of Beth Lapat (Jundaisabur) in April 484. This break was not unpremeditated. First of all, Nestorius's doctrine of the two natures of Christ had found adherents precisely in the Persian border-districts, for instance in the 'Persian School' of Edessa, and secondly, it was a way to eliminate the slightest suspicion of a conspiracy with the Roman empire and thus prevent renewed persecutions.

It was ... not that the Church of the East withdrew from the union of 'orthodox' churches as a 'heretic sect' in consequence of its turning to Nestorianism. It was in the last analysis the Church of the Roman empire itself, which, by judging the Imperium and the Emperor as instruments of divine providence – unintentionally, though out of inner necessity – repelled that Church beyond the imperial borders, a Church which only *thereupon* joined a confession that was 'heretic' in the eyes of the Eastern Roman state Church. (Hage)

The Sasanian kings were well disposed towards this development. They used Christian bishops as envoys and counsellors, tolerated forcible conversions of other Christians by the Nestorians, and promoted – in their own interests as well – Nestorian culture and knowledge, for example at the 'Persian School', which had been transferred from Edessa to Nisibis, or in Jundaisabur in Khuzistan (see below). The most colourful Christian personality of the period was Barsauma, who fought for the success of the Nestorian confession, founded the new school in Nisibis and was also very active politically, but at the same time conjured up a schism because of his insubordination towards the Katholikos Babuwai. The altogether favourable situation of the Nestorians was only temporarily interrupted by Khosrow I's unconcealed antipathy for the Katholikos Mar Aba, by persecutions during the war against Byzantium (540–545) and by the victorious advance of Heraclius. But all this did not bring about a lasting estrangement between the kings and the Nestorians. What caused these Christians much more trouble were their conflicts with followers of other Christian confessions. With the arrival of the Arabs they nevertheless denied the Sasanians their support. A motive for their peaceful reception of the new masters may have been the Persian Christians' feeling of affinity with Christian Arab tribes.

Other Christian groups or groups under Christian influence had been in conflict with so-called 'orthodox Christianity', especially in Mesopotamia. These were, among others, the followers of Bardaisan, the Marcionites and the numerous Gnostic movements, such as the 'Baptist' community of the Elchasaites with its Judaizing Christian character. Mani, who was born in Babylonia on 14 April 216, belonged to the latter from the fourth year of his life until he received his divine revelations. When he appeared before the public, presumably in the year 240 AD, he started doing so outside the centres of the Sasanian empire, an exception being his immediate home. He taught in India and in the Sasanian–Roman borderland in Upper Mesopotamia. It was only after the accession of Shapur, whom he expected to be more liberal in religious affairs than Ardashir, that he also made his appearance at court, probably on the recommendation of Shapur's brother Peroz. Mani thereupon pursued his mission in the entourage of the king, and later with the support of royal safe-conducts. Although Manichaean reports, once purged of their hagiographical conventions, point to the fact 'that Mani's encounter with Shapur did not lead to the king's conversion [and] between the two per-sonalities ... a considerable distance existed' (Sundermann), it cannot be denied that the king was definitely interested in Mani's doctrine. Mani's dispatch of Patticius and Mar Adda to the Roman empire, which may be dated as early as the 240s AD, caused the Manichaean doctrine to take root above all in Egypt, and later in Palmyra as well. However, it must not be considered as a political mission to destabilize the Roman empire. The unim-peded development of Mani's syncretic doctrine within the Sasanian empire was ensured after the death of Shapur, to whom the prophet had dedicated his *Šābuhragān*, under his son Hormizd (270/72–273). It was only Shapur's elder son, Bahram (I), who broke with this policy of his predecessors. Shortly after the death of the king, Mani was ordered to the court at Beth Lapat (Jundaisabur) and died there in prison.

Whether it is true that the Zoroastrian priests at court were mainly responsible for Mani's death, as the Manichaeans maintained, cannot be ascertained. If the Manichaean sources are accurately interpreted, it was not immediately after Mani's death that the general persecution of minorities mentioned in Kirdir's inscriptions started, but after a reprieve of three years. However, as far as the Manichaeans were concerned, this reprieve continued until the last years of Bahram II. The 'leader of the community' (*archēgos*), Mar Sisin (Sisinnius), who had succeeded Mani, was executed, and many followers escaped into eastern Roman regions, to Arabia and especially further east, where Mani had founded a centre for the Manichaean mission. The situation temporarily eased when, according to Manichaean tradition, the next *archēgos*, Innaius, was able to cure the king of a grave illness and – together with the Arab regent of Hira – managed to persuade King Narseh to adopt a more tolerant attitude. But under Narseh's son Hormizd II the persecutions were resumed. The further history of the Manichaeans in Mesopotamia and Iran under the Sasanians has not been sufficiently investigated. The Christian martyrologies present them, along with the Jews and Zoroastrians, as informers against the Christians, but also as victims of the persecutions of Shapur II. For their part, the Christians of the fifth century were concerned lest the benevolent attitude of the kings towards themselves should be extended to the 'heretic' Manichaeans as well. Later on, Kavad and Khosrow I are said to have persecuted the followers of Mani, but with this kind of information we cannot be sure whether there was not often a confusion of the Manichaeans with the Mazdakites.

Already in Mani's lifetime his disciple Mar Ammo had carried out a successful mission in eastern Iran. These regions later became centres for the spread of Manichaeism – via the Silk Road – as far as Inner Asia and China. The contact of these missionaries with Buddhism, which flourished in the Tarim basin, is reflected in the terminology of the Manichaean–Parthian texts (see Plate XXXIb). Manichaeism even became a 'state religion' in the Uighur state (from 762 until its end in 840), and its communities and monasteries thrived for centuries, especially along the Silk Road (in the state of Qočo near Turfan, where the rich sources of Manichaean writings and archaeological finds originated) and – in native garb – in southern China.

From the founder of the religion himself, a description of his doctrine has come down to us:

The religion that I [Mani] have chosen is in ten things much better than the other, earlier religions. First: The earlier religions restricted themselves only to one country and one language. But my religion is known in all countries and in all languages and is taught in the most faraway countries. – Secondly: As long as there were pure leaders in the earlier religion, it was in order. But once the leaders had died, the religion became confused, and they became slack in words and deeds. And through ... [But my religion] will remain until the end [as a result of] vital [books], teachers, bishops, chosen people and hearers and through wisdom and works. – Thirdly: The previous souls that have not completed their work in their own religion come to my religion. Precisely for them it is a door towards salvation. – Fourthly: This revelation of mine of the two principles and my vital writings, my wisdom and my knowledge are much better than those of the earlier religions. – Fifthly: All writings, wisdom and parables of the earlier religions, because they [have been added to this religion of mine] ...

After reading this quotation, it is perhaps easier to understand why the new creed appeared as downright heresy to Christians and Zoroastrians alike and why they so resolutely fought against it. Here was someone who believed he could combine the great religions of the world (Christianity, Zoroastrianism, Buddhism) and at the same time supersede them, someone who – in another passage – referred to Zarathustra, Buddha, Jesus Christ and St Paul as his predecessors. He integrated his own ideas within the conceptual world of the people to be converted (thus facilitating their conversion to the new creed), promised them a better chance of salvation, and combined all this with harsh criticism against the officials of rival religions and the ossified structures of their communities. What must have particularly exasperated the Christians was that he modelled the construction of his 'Church' on theirs ([1 leader], 12 teachers, 72 bishops [360 presbyters], scribes, preachers, 'church musicians', monastery administrators). Mani had also planned ahead for the time after his death. To make sure his doctrine was passed on according to his wishes – unlike what had happened to the teachings of Zarathustra, Buddha and Jesus – he composed a written canon which he specially enjoined on his community.

But it was the creed itself, not only how it was transmitted, that exercised great fascination. The origin of evil in the world, as well as the possibilities to surmount it, were vividly explained (in word and image), people were offered a way to salvation through recognizing the mixture of good and evil, light and darkness, and through contributing towards changing this state of affairs by separating the particles of light from the world. Mani's followers did not seem to mind that he distinguished between – and even institutionally separated – two groups of men, the 'chosen' (Lat. *electi*) and the 'hearers' (*auditores*): while the 'chosen' completely followed Mani's prescriptions by living in a kind of monastic community where they could efficiently pursue the purification of light particles, the 'hearers' – though 'guilty' of damaging the light particles through their task of preparing food for the *electi* – were granted a remission of their sins and could hope to be transformed into 'chosen' through the transmigration of souls. It is not surprising that thanks to such mental and organizational advantages granted by its founder, Manichaeism could actually become a 'world religion' and survive for centuries despite the persecutions it suffered.

Entering into competition with Zoroastrianism, another 'heresy', Mazdakism, appeared in the fifth century AD:

And this about the opponents of the religion [and] the arch-heretics who have also been called Mazdakites [*mazdakīg-iz*], as [the religion] says about them: Look upon this my religion with spiritual force, look upon [it] well, oh Zarathustra, when many who are familiar with the heretics proclaim justice, activity and also priesthood [and] innocence, but few perform the manifest works. In the Mazdayasnic [Zoroastrian] religion this is [said]: Look upon the religion, and seek a means against them and those who in some way have been [even] more refractory than they in this earthly existence and the intangible one. Inborn justice [*āsnōmand ahlāyīh*] is the most excellent of existing things. And thus [proclaims] the Mazdayasnic religion: Among the families they distribute the allocations. Activity is for one's own [people] [*xvēšān*], they say. And they give a share to their own [people]. Food [*xvariśn*] they consider as an agreement [*paśn*], that is, they say: Food [shall be] in the proportion of hunger. And [of] descendants [*tōmag*] they say that kinship is through the mother. And [in the] manner of the wolf they give birth, that is, they do something in a wolfish way: Their procreating follows the course of lust. As the wolfcub [runs] behind its mother, so they determine kinship after mothers. They buy women [like] sheep, and the child is taken away by son [and] brother into [the community] [?]. [They say:] We have given them to you in community. Only then do you have full powers [over them] when [you have] stayed in the community. They do not even believe in the ordeal [divine verdict], not if someone carries it out to show his innocence. They also deceive children, that is, over them the contract-breaker must come, as to themselves.

In this admittedly difficult text, an excerpt from the 7th book of the Middle Persian Zoroastrian *Dēnkard*, a religious encyclopaedia of the ninth to tenth century, statements from the 'Mazdayasnic religion', in this case a commentary on a book of the Avesta, are quoted about the doctrine of the Mazdakites. We have already come across this religious community in connection with the social upheavals that shook Iran at the turn of the fifth–sixth centuries, after the bloody Hephthalite wars of King Peroz, and other misfortunes. At the time, a section of the peasant population had risen against the aristocracy and forcibly taken possession of their property and women.

They were manifestly encouraged by the social ethics proclaimed by Mazdak and temporarily even supported by King Kavad.

Mazdak's biography, his motives and the spiritual roots of his doctrine are a subject as contentious in ancient sources and modern scholarship as is the relationship between Mazdak, the religious community of the Mazdakites and the insurgents, and between the aims of Mazdak's doctrine and the effects of the Mazdakite popular risings. This is mainly because Mazdak's message has come down to us only from the mouth of his religious and political opponents, so that the creators of the tradition were Khosrow I and the Zoroastrian authorities, who emerged as victors from the conflicts of that period, rather than the Mazdakites or the rebellious peasants. Against this background, the passage quoted from the *Dēnkard* acquires special significance, for it enumerates – more clearly than the normally quoted Arabic and modern Persian sources – the original aims of the Mazdakite social doctrine, even if it repudiates them. Moreover, it does not connect the Mazdakites with the act of breaking open and plundering the granaries of the aristocracy and abducting their women. It thus at the same time confirms the views of those people who differentiate between the aims and motives of Mazdak and his followers and those of both the rebels and the advocates of the aristocracy, and also agrees with those who deny Mazdak's active participation in the popular rebellions.

What convictions and ways of life does our Zoroastrian polemicist actually attribute to the Mazdakites? For one thing, their concern for their 'own people', their 'family', probably in the sense that they were prepared to share women and properties within their local communities ('extended families'). To our commentator this must have appeared as 'unfair group egotism' (Sundermann). When eating is compared with an 'agreement', this can only mean that they consumed what was necessary for their survival and distributed the rest to their needy fellow-believers. What causes the critic a great deal of trouble is, however, the 'sharing of women', which turns up in all our sources, with its implications for family rights. To those who consider patrilineal descent and the preservation of the household in the male line as fundamental requirements and concerns of social life, the recognition of matrilineal descent with its result of uncertain paternity and the transfer of educational tasks to the community can only appear as monstrous. What remains obscure is the allusion to the purchase of women. Did the Mazdakites 'acquire' them in other communities of their fellow-believers or among people of a different faith? The rejection of the ordeal and the vow, both of which have deep roots in Zoroastrian law, point to resistance against insincere rituals. All the reproaches of the text refer to internal regulations of Mazdakite communities. The question whether Mazdak himself – or part of his following – aspired towards expanding their practices beyond the community in the interest of the poor and as a burden on the propertied, as some sources report, or whether this was the action of the rebellious peasants, Mazdak's ideals having rendering them independent, will have to be left unanswered.

Two more things are worth mentioning. For one thing, the Mazdakite doctrine did not content itself with regulating social behaviour, but based it on an elaborate theological theory which can be described as gnostic–syncretistic; and for another, the suppression of the popular rebellions and the persecution of the Mazdakites did not put an end to the creed. It survived the Sasanian empire, as well as further persecutions in the early Islamic period, although in a new garb and often underground.

What were the motives that guided kings and Zoroastrian priests in their dealings with Christians, Manichaeans and Mazdakites? And how are we to describe the relationships between all these groups? In many textbooks, the religious world of Sasanian Mesopotamia and Iran is presented as follows. In the face of a dominant Zoroastrian orientation newly invigorated and politically promoted by the Sasanian kings in close association with the clergy, followers of a different faith had a hard time. Supported by a hierarchically organized religious administration – in this context we often come across terms such as 'state religion' or 'state Church' – kings and Magi aimed at a general enforcement of the Zoroastrian cult throughout the empire. Deliberately departing from the policy of their Arsacid predecessors, they had no qualms about persecuting Christians, Jews, Manichaeans and other religious minorities. The reader is faced with the image of a strange state that was both extremely severe and single-minded in dealing with religious matters, and, with throne and altar going hand in hand, seemed to go through phases as early as the third century that were to be characteristic of the Imperium Romanum at a later period. This image also produces the impression that periods of persecuting minorities were the norm rather than the occasional result of specific circumstances.

If this conception is to be proven as unsatisfactory, we must first examine the ostensibly close association beween the (early) Sasanian state and the Zoroastrian cult in the empire. Both the Middle Persian Zoroastrian tradition and Perso-Arabic historiography contain the idea of a close union between

kingship or politics and religion. According to al-Mas'udi, the empire founder
is supposed to have given his successor Shapur the following advice:

Know then, my son, religion and kingship are inseparable and mutually dependent
brothers. For religion is the foundation of kingship and kingship is its protector.
Whatever lacks a solid foundation is doomed to failure, and what is not well protected
will vanish.

In the New Persian 'Letter of Tansar', which probably dates from the late
Sasanian period, but refers to Ardashir's reign, this idea is expressed as
follows:

For Church and State were born of the one womb, joined together and never to be
sundered. Virtue and corruption, health and sickness are of the same nature for both.

And finally, similar ideas are found in the 'Testament of Ardashir', which is
handed down in the tenth-century *Taǧārib al-umam* of Ibn Miskawaih. Here,
however, there is an additional reference to a possible rivalry between the two
powers, with the conclusion that religion takes precedence because it forms
the 'foundation' of the empire, while kingship is merely its 'pillar'.

These formulations have led certain scholars to conclude that a kind of
Zoroastrian 'state religion' prevailed as early as the third century. It was even
suggested that it had served as a model for the Roman empire, in which a
similar evolution was believed to have taken place during the following
century. However, not only the late sources but also the conflicts between
Sasanian kings and Zoroastrian priests reflected in the contemporary sources
should deter us from considering the picture of kingship and religion as
brothers as anything but a late Zoroastrian design of an ideal state, which
probably even emerged under Islamic influence.

Moreover, the differentiated religious–administrative hierarchy, which
Perso-Arabic sources already attribute to the third and fourth centuries, was
created in a lengthy process, as we have seen, and based on the model of
monarchic power. This being the case, the concept of 'state religion' and
'state Church' used by earlier scholars has to be discarded, and that not only
for semantic reasons – the concept of 'Church' suggesting false analogies
with Western evolution – but also on historical grounds.

Since even the terms applied have proved inappropriate, the rather static
and indiscriminate view of the Sasanian attitude towards their minorities
ought to give way to a more comprehensive analysis involving the critical
evaluation of sources and a closer examination of the period. Many factors

must be taken into account, including the policy of each individual king and his concept of his role, the interests of the Zoroastrian clergy and those of the religious minorities, as well as the prevailing situations in internal and external policy. Investigations into religious conditions in the Roman empire might serve as a guideline. Here research on ancient history has long tried to present the relationship between the Roman state and Christian and Manichaean religious minorities as a route whose separate stages depended on the combined effects of a great many different factors, such as: the basic religious convictions of the emperors and the religious–political reactions they deemed suitable or profitable under the prevailing conditions of the empire; the pagan society's lack of understanding for the forms of Christian worship and their different attitude towards life on earth; the assessment of Manichaeism as the 'Persian threat' or heresy by the state and Christian authorities; and the minorities' own appraisal of emperor and empire, as well as the development and theological and political evaluation of their organizations.

In our comments about the history of the Christians, Manichaeans and Mazdakites, we have already suggested that aside from religious rivalry among the various creeds represented in the Sasanian empire, factors of internal and external policy also considerably influenced the religious situation as well as the religious policy of the kings. If the latter emphasized their close relationship with the Zoroastrian gods and presented themselves as promoters of the Zoroastrian creed and cult, this did not mean that they granted the clergy an equal status or that they wanted to be seen as heads of a Zoroastrian state cult in the sense of a 'state Church'. Despite their more or less deep personal attachment to the Zoroastrian faith, none of them was a religious zealot like Kirdir, and their attitude in dealing with their subjects was determined by questions of loyalty or resistance, not by standard religious dictates. Shapur I deported the Christian inhabitants of Antiochia because he appreciated their professional diligence and craftsmanship, and he considered them as loyal subjects because he was aware of their intermittent persecution in the Roman empire. For the same reasons Narseh put an end to Kirdir's persecutions, because in view of Roman 'intolerance', Christian and Manichaean communities promised to be a reliable rather than a restless element of the population.

As far as we know, the influence of the clergy on politics was not always of equal impact, nor did it constantly grow. While nothing points to an independent role of the Zoroastrian clergy under Ardashir I, Shapur I and Hormizd I, and while it was apparently kept within limits under Bahram I and Narseh, the reigns of Bahram II, Hormizd II and Shapur II were phases in which the clergy was more powerful. Even if Kirdir owed his influence to his own capacities and the persuasiveness of his concepts, and even if the persecutions of the Manichaeans by Hormizd II are traditionally attributed to the insinuations of the Magi, the true reasons for the influence of the clergy lay in the specific factors of internal and external policy prevailing at each time. The reign of Bahram II was wracked by civil war within and by heavy setbacks in his conflict against Rome, forcing the king to cooperate more closely with the aristocracy and clergy. Hormizd II had tried – evidently without success – to repair the results of the dictated peace treaty of Nisibis on the battlefield, and must also have been under pressure regarding internal policy. Shapur II, who acceded to the throne after bitter quarrels, pursued the same foreign policy aims as his father, but instead of having to deal with the Romans as persecutors of Christians, now it was Christian supporters he confronted. Moreover, in carrying out his persecutions, he depended on the cooperation of the Zoroastrian priests who were now serving him as religious and legal authorities.

While Shapur's chief motives in dealing with the Christians were political, those of the Zoroastrian clergy were religious. In times of persecution, the two aims converged, and king and clergy joined hands in combined action. That the king was generally the key player is nevertheless quite obvious. He set the start or the systematization of persecutions and ended them – the rivalry of the Magi with the Christians was, of course, always taken for granted – he presented the required sacrifice as a proof of loyalty to crown and country, he personally intervened in the procedure, and he curbed the unbridled persecutions for reasons of state. To his successors from the end of the fifth century on, the Christians hardly presented any problems. Now that they had separated from their previous fellow-believers both from a christological and from an organizational point of view, it was even possible to turn their accomplishments to profit in many respects. The reaction of the kings to the doctrine of the Mazdakites was also decidedly pragmatic. Kavad supported them because he expected their social reforms to allay the misery of the people and lessen their dissatisfaction, and certainly also in the hope of strengthening his own position with respect to the aristocracy. Anoshirvan used the chaos to reform the state to his own benefit.

As for the Zoroastrian clergy, *vis-à-vis* Christians, Manichaeans and Mazdakites its members can be described on the one hand as religious and legal authorities, and on the other as religious rivals. The Zoroastrians,

Manichaeans and Mazdakites were in fact groups whose religions were closely related and who for that very reason clashed together in particularly fierce competition. Mani's claims to have perfected Zarathustra's doctrine, his conviction about the universality and special quality of his own message, as well as the rather mediocre success of the Zoroastrian mission outside of Iran, caused Kirdir and the Magi to regard the Manichaeans as their religious opponents *par excellence*. No wonder, then, that they used their stronger position under Bahram II to launch persecutions against the *electi* and *auditores*. However, Narseh's departure from the policy of his predecessors testifies to the modest or merely temporary success of this policy, and can also be regarded as an attempt to curtail the constantly growing power of Kirdir and the clergy. At the same time, the new tolerance towards the Manichaeans also made sense against the background of their persecution in the Roman empire. In comparison, Shapur I, who is otherwise also known as a monarch open to new ideas, had weighed the advantages of a syncretic and universal new doctrine to hold the empire together, but had, in the last analysis, found them too slight.

To sum up, on the subject of religious conditions in the Sasanian empire and on the sense of identity of the Christian and Manichaean subjects of the 'king of kings', many a fond misconception has to be discarded. Neither did there exist a generally close alliance between 'throne' and 'altar', nor is it appropriate to speak of a Sasanian 'state Church' or 'state religion'. Indeed, for the social identity of the parties concerned and for the relationships between them, similar factors came into play as those in the Roman empire. These were the personal religious convictions of individual rulers, and even more vitally the general situation in domestic and foreign politics and the political reaction of the kings to it, including their religious policy. Significant, too, was the conflict between the Zoroastrian clergy, for whom Iranism and Zoroastrianism coincided, and the religious orientations of Christians and Manichaeans, universal in theory, and now also in fact. Traditionally, this conflict was for a long time conceived as a struggle beween the 'people of the book' and the followers of Zarathustra's orally transmitted doctrine of salvation in its Sasanian garb, while those concerned saw it as a conflict between the 'people of god' or the *electi* and *auditores* on the one side and the *mogs*, *mōbads* and *hērbeds* on the other. In their dealings with minorities, state and religious authorities did not always act in unison. The reactions of the minorities to persecutions and the importance of martyrs for the further spread of their doctrines can be compared with similar situations in the West.

ERANSHAHR: THE EMPIRE, ITS INHABITANTS   215

Lastly, their common fate and common status as minorities – which was not temporary, as it was in the West – did not prevent the Christians and Manichaeans from looking on each other as rivals. To the Christians, Mani and his followers appeared just as much as 'arch-heretics' as they did to Kirdir and the Zoroastrian clergy, and so they did their utmost to prevent the success of the Manichaean mission. The Manichaeans, for their part, hoped to harm the Christians by helping the religious and legal authorities in tracking down Christian 'traitors'.

What remain to be discussed are the Jews of the Sasanian empire. With their centres in Mesopotamia, they were not as significant to the history of Iran as the Christians, Manichaeans or Mazdakites. Yet their history also tallies with the pattern described above. After a brief phase of uncertainty and repression under Ardashir, which can be fully explained by the change in dynasty and the good relations between the Jews and the Parthian authorities, Shapur I and the exiliarchs and rabbis came to an understanding by which the Jews were granted more freedom of movement and the Sasanians could count on their compliance with taxing and general legal prescriptions. Shapur's antagonism against Odaenthus of Palmyra, who had destroyed the Jewish centre of Nehardea when he invaded Babylonia, may have enhanced the favourable relationship between the king and his Jewish subjects. Despite Kirdir's assertion to the contrary, we hear nothing about persecutions in the Jewish records until the fifth century. In the wars between Rome and Shapur II, the Jews, unlike the Christians, were decidedly loyal in their attitude, with the exception of a few Messianic groups. The later massive repression by the state under Yazdgird II and Peroz was not a sign of religious intolerance, but was clearly a result of political actions by which the Jews expressed their attitude of imminent anticipation of the Messiah, whose appearance they connected with the 400th anniversary of the destruction of the temple in Jerusalem. On this occasion, Iranian sources mention attacks by the Jews of Isfahan on the city's Magi. Later persecutions were also politically motivated. Khosrow's general Mahbad killed the Jewish followers of the pretender to the throne, Bahram Chubin, and a further Messianic revolt in Babylonia was ruthlessly put down in 640. At the beginning of the seventh century, the Jews watched the Sasanian offensive against Byzantium with great expectancy and joyfully welcomed the conquest of Jerusalem.

When the Arab conquerors came to replace the Sasanian reign, they found an intact system of Jewish self-government, which was to become even more important under the caliphs. In the Sasanian period it was led by the exiliarch, a truly political official and rich landowner who, according to the sources, quite often fell out with sections of the religious authorities, the rabbis. These scholars had firmly entrenched the Palestinian rabbinical interpretation of the written and oral Torah in Babylonia, and were now trying to make it the foundation of popular education. On the whole they were successful, but there were always oppositional currents among the people against rabbinical religious 'tutelage' (as also against the political tutelage of the exiliarch). On the other hand, there were always rabbis to be found who did not represent the interests of their 'estate', but the claims and views of the exiliarch or those of the popular opposition. In the great rabbinical schools, like those of Sura (later Pumbedita) and Nehardea, the process of annotating and interpreting the Mishnah went on, and eventually led to the compilation of the Babylonian Talmud in the late sixth to early seventh century.

Little is known about the number of Jewish inhabitants in the Sasanian empire, but it must have been quite considerable, especially in Babylonia. By far the majority of the Jews made their living by farming, although handicraft and trade also played a part. They lived predominantly in villages, but also with many different ethnic, linguistic and religious groups in larger towns and cities, with no indication of closed Jewish districts. The Jews of Babylonia were not only separated in terms of education, activity or political responsibility, but also in social and economic respects. The wealthier landowners and notabilities set the tone in the rural communities.

Although the Jews were less irksome than the Manichaeans to the Zoroastrians, they antagonized the Christians all the more. Some of the martyrologies show an extremely anti-Jewish tendency, and the same is true of some writings of the Eastern Christian Church Fathers.

4. 'Wise king' and foreign knowledge – hunting and chess: culture in the late Sasanian period

People sing his [Khosrow's] praises and admire him more than he deserves – and not only Persians but some Romans too. They claim that he is devoted to literature and is very well versed in our philosophy, having had Greek works translated for him into the Persian language. It is said that he has drunk in more of the Stagirite [Aristotle] than the Paianian [Demosthenes] did of the son of Olorus [Thucydides], and that he is full of the doctrines of Plato the son of Ariston. The *Timaeus*, they say, is not beyond him, even though it is positively studded with geometrical theory, and inquires into the movements of nature, nor is the *Phaedo*, nor the *Gorgias* or any other of the more subtle and obscure dialogues – the *Parmenides*, for instance, I suppose.

With his excessive patriotism, the author of this passage, the Byzantine historian Agathias, challenges the admiration expressed for the enemy king in Syriac literature, where Khosrow Anoshirvan is described as a 'wise king' or as a king 'who has read all the books of the philosophers'. He also calls into question the claims and motives of Khosrow himself, as suggested in his res gestae (*kārnāmag*):

We have made inquiries about the rules of the inhabitants of the Roman empire and the Indian states [when preparing a book of laws?] ... We have never rejected anybody because of their different religion or origin. We have not jealously kept away from them what we affirm. And at the same time we have not disdained to learn what they stand for. For it is a fact that to have knowledge of the truth and of sciences and to study them is the highest thing with which a king can adorn himself. And the most disgraceful thing for kings is to disdain learning and be ashamed of exploring the sciences. He who does not learn is not wise.

Despite the unmistakable self-praise we notice here, the king's efforts for higher learning cannot be denied. Agathias himself reports that Anoshirvan had offered hospitality to the Neoplatonic philosophers, who had become homeless after their school in Athens was closed down, and when – disappointed by the country and its inhabitants – they wished to return home, he had granted them exemption from punishment in their own country during his peace negotiations with Byzantium. One of them, Priscianus Lydus, described Khosrow as anxious to learn and at the same time sceptical. Another visitor at the Sasanian court was the Greek-educated Syrian Uranius, whom Agathias with his chauvinistic bias could only conceive as a swindler. Khosrow had Uranius argue with the Magi about questions of cosmogony and the end of the world, about God, primary matter and the elements. In such discussions, which also included Christian authorities, the king himself is said to have participated and to have shown intelligence and willingness to learn in the arguments. Among his teachers the Nestorian chronicle of Se'ert mentions 'Mar Barsauma, Bishop of Qarda ... and ... Paulus, the Persian philosopher'. The latter, a former Nestorian bishop from Persis, even wrote an introduction to logic in Syriac for Anoshirvan, which has survived. The dedication to the king of this *Eisagoge* based on Aristotle and Porphyry is explained as follows: 'Philosophy, which is the true knowledge about all things, inhabits you. From this philosophy which is inherent in you I send you a gift.' It has often been pointed out that Syrian Christians played a significant part in communicating Greek knowledge to the Persians.

Khosrow's interest in the East is shown by his initiative in commissioning a translation of a version of the Indian book of fables the *Pañchatantra* ('Fivebook'), which the physician Burzoy had brought from India. This work is meant to teach political leadership, knowledge of human nature and shrewdness, and its maxims have been described as 'cleverness' (Mylius) or even Machiavellism. The Middle Persian version is lost, but there exists an eighth-century Arabic version by Ibn al-Muqaffa', which is based on the Middle Persian text. Partially modified to correspond with the Islamic sense of justice and published under the title *Kalīla wa-Dimna* (Kalila and Dimna are the names of two jackals who play the main part in the first chapter), it was not only extremely popular in the Near East, but was translated into various European languages in the Middle Ages, and later served as a source of inspiration to La Fontaine.

Besides philosophy, theology and statesmanship, Khosrow was also interested in foreign contributions to law and medicine. In his *res gestae* he refers to his interest in Eastern Roman and Indian law (see above), and in the 'Book of a Thousand Judgements' (*Mādayān ī hazār dādestān*) there are several references to the king and his legal advisers. Particularly worthy of note is a decree of the king regarding reforms in legal matters. Another proof of the open intellectual climate of the period is the Christian–Syriac book of laws (see above) dating from this period.

In the twentieth year of the reign of Khosrow [II] the physicians of Jundaisabur assembled for a scientific symposium by order of the king. Their debates were recorded. This memorable session took place under the presidency of Jibril Durustabad, the physician in ordinary to Khosrow, in the presence of Sufista'i and his colleagues, together with Yuhanna and a large number of other medical men. One has only to take a look at the questions and definitions discussed here to realize the extent of their knowledge and their experience. This high standard continued until the reign of the Caliph al-Mansur, who was taken ill after the building of the city of salvation [Baghdad] and summoned the physician Gurjis b. Jibril b. Bukhtishu' from this city [Jundaisabur].

As has long been known, Jundaisabur (Veh-Andiyok-Shabuhr) in Khuzistan was a centre of learning in the Sasanian and above all in the Islamic period. Particularly famous were the physicians of this centre, as shown by the above quotation from the 'History of Learned Men' by Ibn al-Qifti, a historian and biographer of the twelfth/thirteenth century. Qifti, and even earlier the polyhistor Maqdisi (tenth century), believed that people deported on the expeditions of Shapur I had established medicine in Khuzistan (and Fars). Barhebraeus (thirteenth century) claimed that the spread of 'Hippo-

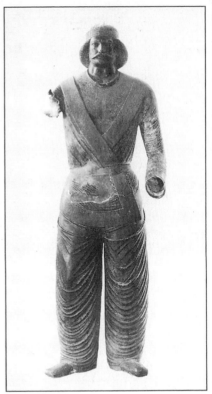

Plate XVIIc. ABOVE LEFT. Ivory rhytons or drinking vessels found in the Royal Treasury at Nisa, though Iranian in shape, depict Greek mythological scenes and figures. Parthian artifacts were much inspired by Hellenistic motifs.

Plate XVIIIa. ABOVE. The statue of a prince from Shami in south-western Iran wears the crossed-over and belted jacket and trousers originating from the pastoralist, horse-riding background of the Parthians. Parthian costumes and hairstyles were quite distinct from those of their Hellenistic and Achaemenid precursors.

Plate XVIIIb. LEFT. Coins of the Parthian period showed rulers with their distinctive hairstyles and costumes. *Top:* drachma of Arsaces I. *Obverse:* portrait of the king's head with soft hat. *Reverse:* the king with a bow seated on a *diphros* (throne). *Centre:* tetradrachma from the period of Orodes II. *Obverse:* portrait of the king. *Reverse:* Tyche hands the seated king a palm leaf.
Below: drachma from the period of Artabanus IV. *Obverse:* the king wearing tiara with diadem. *Reverse:* King Arsaces, founder of the Parthian dynasty, seated holding a bow.

Plate XIX. LEFT. The rock relief at Tang-i Sarvak (drawing shown here), made by the local rulers of Elymais in south-western Iran, depicts the 'vassal king' in full-scale armour. Lesser local kings, like their Parthian overlords, commemorated their victories in rock reliefs.

Plate XX. BELOW. A Sasanian rock relief in Firuzabad shows the Sasanian lord Ardashir I defeating the Parthian king Artabanus IV. Sasanians enthusiastically continued the Iranian tradition of rock carvings.

Plate XXI. ABOVE. The Sasanian rock relief at Naqsh-i Rustam depicts Ardashir I, founder of the dynasty, receiving the ring of power from Ahura Mazda, the Wise Lord of the Zoroastrian religion, which the Sasanians always fervently maintained. As heirs to their (Achaemenid) 'forefathers' the Sasanians sought legitimacy and continuity by carving their rock reliefs close to the Achaemenid tombs at Naqsh-i Rustam.

Plate XXII. BELOW. The rock relief at Naqsh-i Rustam, depicting two Sasanian victories in one image, shows the kneeling Roman emperor Philip the Arab paying homage to the victorious Shapur I on horseback, while Shapur at the same time grasps the hand of his captive, the Roman emperor Valerian. In the early period, victory over the Roman empire was the great military triumph of the Sasanian dynasty.

Plate XXIII. ABOVE. The rock relief at Taq-i Bustan near present-day Kermanshah in western Iran immortalizes the Sasanians' love of hunting. This scene was probably carved in the reign of Khosrow II.

Plate XXIV. BELOW. Between Shiraz and Firuzabad Ardashir I built the Qal'ah-i Dukhtar, a fortified palace on a rocky plateau over a ravine, which blocked access to Firuzabad.

te XXV. ABOVE. The Taq-i Kisra in
siphon included monumental
an arches in its residential palace
t for Shapur I (or Khosrow I?).
siphon, its site located in today's
, was one of the centres of the
anian empire.

te XXVIa. RIGHT. The dam at
shtar is one of several surviving
mples of Sasanian civil
ineering. Dams and bridges were
n built by Roman prisoners-of-

te XXVIb. RIGHT LOWER. Takht-i
aiman in Azerbaijan is a vast
nplex of sacred and secular
dings. It was the site of Adur
shnasp, one of the most important
ed fires of Sasanian Iran.

Plate XXVIIa. ABOVE TOP. Silver bowls depicting Sasanian
kings, such as this one showing Peroz hunting, may well have
had a political rather than a practical purpose, especially
since in the later period the kings controlled the production
of such bowls. They probably served as royal gifts with
designs which reinforced the symbols of royal power.

Plate XXVIIb. ABOVE. Cameos, such as this one perhaps
showing the victory of Shapur I over the Roman Emperor
Valerian in 260 AD and probably created by a Roman artist
by order of a later Sasanian king, were among a wide array
of arts and crafts which testify to the sophistication of
Sasanian royal art.

Plate XXVIII. RIGHT. Sasanian seals and bullae provide vital
information in identifying state and religious officials.
Top: seal depicting 'Veh-Shabuhr, Mogbed of Ardakhshir
Khvarrah'.
Centre: seal impression of 'Yazdan-Friy-Shabuhr, principal
envoy of Shabuhr [Shapur III], King of Kings, Son of
Shabuhr [Shapur II]'.
Lower: bull with five impressions including those of the
'Mogbed of Abarshahr [Nishapur]' *(left)* and 'Boy-shahrev-
(bay), the Magi, Son of ...' *(right)*

Plate XXIX. RIGHT. Sasanian coins,
their images, legends, style and
minting techniques, reveal the names
and chronology of Sasanian rulers.

Drachma of Ardashir I. *Obverse:* king
wearing crenellated crown of Ahura
Mazda. *Reverse:* fire altar.

Drachma of Shapur I.
Obverse: king with crenellated crown.
Reverse: fire altar with ceremonial
figures.

Drachma of Bahram II.
Obverse: king with queen and crown
prince. *Reverse:* fire altar with
ceremonial figures.

Drachma of Khosrow I.
Obverse: the king. *Reverse:* fire altar
with ceremonial figures.

Plate XXXa. BELOW. In Paikuli (today
in Iraqi Kurdistan) the tower of King
Narseh (a reconstruction illustrated
here) bore a bilingual inscription
describing his path to power. Such
monuments, with their often
multilingual descriptions of the feats
of kings, are primary albeit highly
biased source material on the
Sasanian empire.

Plate XXXb. BELOW RIGHT. Naqsh-i
Rajab rock relief shows a self-
testimonial of the mobad (priest)
Kerdir, one of the most influential
men in the Sasanian empire during
the third century.

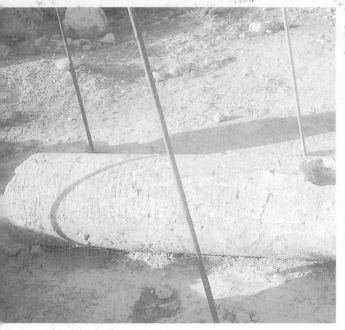

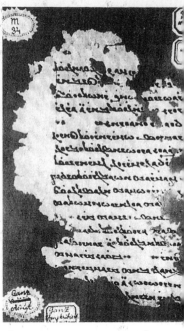

Plate XXXIa. ABOVE LEFT. The Bishapur commemorative bilingual inscription of the city's 'Governor' Shapur I, referring to 'a Sasanian er is an example of early Sasanian self-aggrandizement which also serves to date the rise of the dynasty and is thus one of the most significant inscriptive records of the period.

Plate XXXIb. ABOVE. This fragment of a Parthian-Manichean text from the Turfan oasis in Central Asia is a example of surviving documentary source material relating to the histo of the Manichean creed. It demonstrates the spread of Manichaeism from Mesopotamia an Iran to Central Asia and China alon the Silk Road.

Plate XXXII. LEFT. Firdausi's Shahnameh helped to perpetuate a knowledge of Iranian history along the lines set by the Sasanians. It is a useful source despite the epic poet' tendency to romanticize. In this miniature from a seventeenth-centu manuscript, the Sasanian king – wrongly attributed in the text as Shapur II – leads away the Roman Emperor Valerian. (In fact it was Shapur I who captured Valerian in 260 AD)

cratic medicine' could be traced back precisely to the physicians in ordinary to the daughter of the Roman emperor Aurelian and wife of Shapur, but these reports may be attributed to Christian pretences of an unbroken medical tradition at this centre. The first really reliable information is Qifti's report about the colloquium. Our sources about medicine in the Sasanian empire concur about the importance of Christian and especially Nestorian practicians, and also about the role of the kings as promoters of medical science. In our Qifti quotation these two facts are expressed on the one hand by the colloquium being held during the twentieth anniversary celebrations of the king's accession (610 AD), and on the other by the participants in the event, whose names (Gabriel, John) easily identify them as Christians. For the kings' interest in medicine, a further reason apart from utilitarian considerations may have been its affinity with philosophy (and astrology).

Aside from medical inspirations from the West, Iranian and Indian traditions were also assimilated. Burzoy, himself a physician from Nishapur (Nev-Shabuhr), reports about them in his introduction to the collection of fables. According to an Arabic source, Khosrow I is even said to have written a medical book himself, or rather to have compiled it from Greek and Indian works. It was through the Sasanian–Middle Persian intermediary that not only medical and pharmaceutical literature from East and West, but also Roman–Byzantine agricultural writings and the *Almagest* of Ptolemy, found their way into Arabic literature.

The late Sasanian period was altogether a time of literary flowering, even if the way had already been paved by major achievements in this field. The written recording of the Avesta had begun earlier through the introduction of a special script; there is evidence of bookkeeping and other documents from the early Sasanian period; the 'Iranian national history' had been in constant evolution and its compilation in written form must have started in the fifth century; and some of the didactic (*andarz*) literature already existed in the sixth century. Nevertheless, Khosrow I and his successors are credited with having especially contributed to promoting literature. Thus Veh-Shabuhr, the *mōbadān mōbad* under Anoshirvan, is said to have published the 21 *nasks* of the Avesta, and the *Xvadāy-nāmag* ('Book of Lords') apparently existed in an initial authoritative version in the reign of Khosrow I and was later repeatedly revised (and continued). And finally, numerous compilations of *andarz* texts, and even the publication of treatises of this nature of his own, are attributed to Anoshirvan and his entourage.

When Ardashir was 15 years old, news reached Ardavan [the last Parthian king] that Pabag had a son who was accomplished in the chivalrous arts ... [Ardavan asks Pabag to send him his son, and the latter does not dare disobey the command.] When he [Ardavan] saw Ardashir, he rejoiced, held him in esteem, and ordered that he should go hunting and to the ball game [polo] with his sons and cavaliers every day. Ardashir did so. With god's help he became more competent and more clever than all of them in the ball game, in riding, in chess and in backgammon.

The 'Ardashir romance', which was written in the late Sasanian period and subsequently revised, projects the social conditions of the time when it was composed into the period of the empire founder and is sometimes considered as a description of the lifestyle at the court of the last Sasanians. It is certainly true that after Khosrow's reforms and the creation of a service nobility, good breeding was now also practised in the company of the king. Obedience, elegant manners, culture, games and hunting were expected and practised. Exactly when polo (*čav[la]gān*), chess (*čatrang*) and backgammon (*nēv-ardaxšīr*) were introduced into Iran, whether in the late Sasanian or early Islamic period, can hardly be ascertained. Hunting had long been practised in Mesopotamia and Iran, both because of its affinity with warfare, and because of climatic and geographical conditions, as well as the profusion of game. It was the royal 'sport' *par excellence* and became an important theme in Sasanian figurative art (see Plates XXIII and XXVIIa) and literature. The text *Husrav rēdag* ('Khosrow and his page') even lists the animals that were hunted: the bull (*gāv*), the wild ass (*gōr*), the stag (*gavazn*) the wild boar (*varāz*), the young camel, the calf, buffalo, ass and gazelle, as well as hare and rabbit, partridge, pheasant, lark, crane, bustard, duck and peacock (*fraš(a)murv*). The references to birds show that hunting was practised not only as a test of strength, but also for entertainment and subsequent consumption. In general, this little book mentions the old courtly virtues and educational aims together with new 'ideals'.

Vaspur has learnt by heart Yasht and Hadokht, Yasn and Videvdat [Videvdad] like a Herbad [herbed] and studied the explanation [*zand*] for them. But at the same time he has busied himself with literature, history and learned speech. Of course, he also knows all the arts of military exercise and warfare, but apart from them playing the lyre, guitar and zither, singing and astrology, and every kind of board game. The king receives from his page satisfactory information about fine food and tasty fowl; about the preparation of jellied meat, ragout, preserves and stewed fruit; about fruit and wine. Then the boy wonder is questioned about music, the scent of flowers, about the best woman, the best animals to ride and other things. This page subdues lions and, which is a greater trial, resists the temptation of a beautiful woman ... (Altheim)

The king himself also set great store by ceremonial representation and the display of luxury. This is shown, to mention only three examples, by the royal titles quoted by Byzantine historians, by the enormous crown of Khosrow II, which impressed the Arabs, and by his huge carpet known as *vahār ī Husrav* ('Khosrow's spring') in his winter residence at Mada'in. That this sophisticated way of holding court did not rule out the inhuman treatment of conquered enemies, inferior rivals and even defenceless women and children cannot be concealed:

[When Shahrbaraz rose against Ardashir III, the gates of the city of Ctesiphon were opened to the usurper by treason.] He then entered, captured a number of the potentates, killed them, carried off their belongings and raped their women. By the order of Shahrbaraz, some people killed Ardashir ... in the second year [of his reign].

CONCLUSION

THE SURVIVAL AND
REDISCOVERY OF
ANCIENT IRAN

In the month of Spandarmad, in the second year of the reign of His Zoroastrian Majesty Shapur [II], the king of kings of Eran and Aneran, whose origin is from the gods. At that time when Shapur, the king of the Sakae, king of Hindustan, Sakistan and Turan down to the seashore ... travelled on this road, the road from Istakhr to Sakistan, and graciously came here to *sād-stūn* [100 columns = Persepolis], he ate bread in this building ... And he organized a great feast, and he had divine rituals performed, and he prayed for his father and his ancestors, and he prayed for Shapur, the king of kings, and he prayed for his own soul, and he also prayed for the one who had this building constructed.

When Shapur, the king of the Sakae, a son of Hormizd II, stopped at Persepolis in the year 311 AD and perpetuated his memory with this inscription in the ruins of Darius's palace (*tačara*), he knew neither the old name of this site nor anything about the men who had it built. It was merely its characteristic architecture that gave it its name. As already pointed out, any precise knowledge about the period of the Medes and Achaemenids must have been lost in south-western Iran under the Parthians, when myths and legends of the eastern Iranian tradition supplanted the local lore. However, the link between the Achaemenids and the Sasanians was not completely severed. The feeling for a specifically 'Persian', i.e. south-western Iranian, history and tradition was preserved through the existence of 'sacred sites' in Naqsh-i Rustam, Persepolis and elsewhere. The Sasanians worshipped their 'forefathers', from whose achievements and ownership titles they derived claims of their own, and – thanks to the Zoroastrian clergy – knew of Eranshahr's special place within the empire, of the disastrous reign of Alexander, and the particular qualities of kingship based on 'divine right'.

It was during the Sasanian period, too, that the official version of Iranian history was committed to writing (in the *Xvadāy-nāmag*). With stories from various legendary cycles, set in times long past or only just elapsed, placed in near or distant regions, put together in a chronological system and adapted to the religious, moral–ethical, but also literary 'ideals' of the day, the 'Book of Lords' became the most important heritage of Ancient Iran in Iran itself.

Since the inhabitants of Iran did not lose their self-consciousness in the early Islamic period, since the most significant historians were Iranian Muslims who wrote in Arabic, and since Iranian history was in many ways interwoven with that of the Arabs, the Iranians found an appreciative public in their attempt to integrate their pre-Islamic history from its mythical beginnings to the fall of the Sasanian empire into the salvation history presented by the Qur'ān. The dynastic change from the 'Arab' Umayyads to the 'Abbasids with their centre in Mesopotamia promoted this project. Ibn al-Muqaffa' (d. *c.* 756) and others contributed to it by translating Middle Persian works, including the *Xvadāy-nāmag*, into Arabic, and their successors Ibn Qutaiba (d. 889), al-Ya'qubi (d. 987), ad-Dinawari (d. end of ninth century), and above all at-Tabari (d. 923), each in his own way, secured ancient Iran its fitting place in historiography. Tabari's *Ta'rīḫ ar-rusul wa-l-mulūk* ('History of the Prophets and Kings') has been described as follows:

Like the prophetic function to the Israelites, kingship fell to the share of the Persians as a gift of god. The prophetic function and kingship converge in the caliphate appointed by god. The history of the Israelites and Persians is presented synchronously: at Adam's side stands the mythical original man and first king Gayumarth [Gayomard]; Solomon's story is followed by passages about the Persian kings until Ardashir; the description of the history of the Sasanians links up with that of Jesus and the Byzantines and leads directly to the life of Muhammad, the target of the history. The main part of the work consists of annals from the Hijra to the year 303/915, which are essentially limited to Islam and its realm, the new centre of the world. (Busse)

As might be expected, this work was soon translated into Persian. Tabari was followed by the Buyid historiographers, especially Hilal as-Sabi' (d. 1056) and Ibn Miskawaih (d. 1030). While the former tried to furnish proof for the Sasanian ancestry of the Buyids, who, being Iranians, wanted to establish their legitimacy by tracing themselves back to the old Iranian kings, Miskawaih pointed to the experiences (*taǧārib*) of previous nations, among them the ancient Iranians, which could be of use to a ruler in governing the state. It is in this context, too, that we come across his quotations from the '*res*

gestae of Khosrow I' and other (translated) Sasanian didactic writings. The
gap between the ancient Iranians and contemporary rulers was also bridged
by Abu Mansur al-Tha'alibi in the eleventh century: now even the Turkish
Ghaznavids, the opponents of the Buyids, emerged as heirs of ancient Iran.
Another genre that flourished in the early Islamic period were 'city chronicles' which could also link up with pre-Islamic tradition in Iran.

> My verse, a structure pointing to the skies,
> Whose solid strength destroying time defies ...
>
> Centuries may pass away, but still my page
> Will be the boast of each succeeding age.

It was from a New Persian prose translation of the 'Book of Lords',
collected by Zoroastrians in eastern Iran and compiled by Abu Mansur
Ma'mari, secretary of the municipal head of Tus (at the north-eastern border
of present-day Iran), that Abu l-Qasim Mansur Firdausi drew his material
when, between the years 975 and 1010, he decided to collect the stories about
pre-Islamic Iran into an epic poem. His *Shahnameh* ('Book of Kings'), 'an
initially disdained work of court art', soon became a piece of literature 'that
... an entire nation was to make its own and that, by its language and subject,
has ... to this day and despite all historical vicissitudes, made a major contribution to the unity of Iran and to the cultural community of the Middle
Eastern nations belonging to the Iranian linguistic family' (Sundermann). It
is the story of the world rulers and primeval kings, of the Kayanians who,
after the division of the world (into the empires of Rome, Turan and Iran),
ruled in Iran and were involved in wars against the Turanians in the east. It
is also the story of the fidelity of their 'vassals' (e.g. Rustam, the lord of
Sistan and Zabulistan), about the empire's enemy Alexander, through whom
Iran suffered a period of humiliation, and finally about the Sasanian kings,
their wars against Rome and the internal problems of their reign. Through
Firdausi these stories travelled far beyond the borders of Iran and became
famous all over the world. Heinrich Heine paid tribute to Firdausi's work in
the following poem:

> Unterdessen saß der Dichter
> An dem Webstuhl des Gedankens,
> Tag und Nacht, und webte emsig
> Seines Liedes Riesenteppich –
>
> Riesenteppich, wo der Dichter
> Wunderbar hineingewebt

Seiner Heimat Fabelchronik,
Farsistans uralte Kön'ge,

Lieblingshelden seines Volkes,
Rittertaten, Aventüren,
Zauberwesen und Dämonen,
Keck umrankt von Märchenblumen –

Alles blühend und lebendig,
Farbenglänzend, blühend, brennend,
Und wie himmlisch angestrahlt
Von dem heilgen Lichte Irans,

Von dem göttlich reinen Urlicht,
Dessen letzter Feuertempel,
Trotz dem Koran und dem Mufti,
In des Dichters Herzen flammte.

('Meanwhile the poet sat at the loom of inspiration day and night, busily weaving the giant carpet of his song. – Giant carpet into which the poet miraculously wove his country's legendary chronicles, the ancient kings of Farsistan, the heroes cherished by his people, chivalrous deeds and adventures, wizards and demonic creatures, boldly entwined with magic flowers – All blossoming and alive, sparkling with colours, blossoming, burning, and gloriously irradiated by the holy light of Iran, by the divine, pure, primeval light and the last fire temple which, despite the Koran and the mufti, flared up in the poet's heart.')

Plate XXXII is taken from one of the many richly illustrated manuscripts of the *Shahnameh*, the Berlin manuscript of 1605. The Sasanian Shapur, under the parasol, triumphantly leads the captive Roman emperor home. The event that actually happened under Shapur I (the capture of Valerian) is here wrongly attributed to Shapur II, who, though also successful in his wars against the Romans (peace of 363), captured neither Julian nor Jovian.

In Firdausi's *Shahnameh* the ruins of Persepolis are known by the name of *sad-sutūn* and *taxt-i Ğamšīd* ('throne [palace] of Ğ.'). The inscription of 311 AD clearly shows that *sad-sutūn* was a Sasanian name, and there is ample reason to believe that this is also true of *taxt-i Ğamšīd*. Since the *Xvadāy-nāmag* had connected Ardashir with the most famous of the ancient Iranian kings, it was quite natural that the imposing site near Istakhr, the Sasanian (and traditionally most ancient royal) residence, should be attributed to Jamshid. Later on, two similar names, *hazār sutūn* ('with 1,000 columns') and *čihil-minār* ('with 40 columns'), were sometimes used for *sad-sutūn*, and Jamshid was 'replaced' by the Kayanians Dara or Kai Husrav, or by Sulaiman

(Solomon), a familiar name through the Jewish–Muslim tradition. Other early Iranian sites were also associated with Solomon and members of his family. In Pasargadae, the tomb of Cyrus became known as *qabr-i mādar-i Sulaimān* ('tomb of Solomon's mother'), the tower building as *zindān-i Sulaimān* (Solomon's prison), and the citadel as *taxt-i Sulaimān* ('Solomon's throne'). The fire temple of Istakhr, which was converted into a mosque, is known as *masğid-i Sulaimān*. And finally, the Kayanian hero Rustam lent his name to the Sasanian reliefs on the rock face containing the tombs of the Achaemenid kings, and later to the entire place: *naqš-i Rustam* ('picture of Rustam').

The natives of Fars no longer had any genuine historical knowledge about ancient Iran when the first European travellers appeared in the country. Nor did these travellers know much more than what they had read in the Bible about the Persian kings and in the works of classical authors or the Alexander romance about the Achaemenids, Parthians and Sasanians. Here we must remember that part of the Western tradition was also being 're-discovered' by the humanists in Europe, and authors like Xenophon and Curtius who described Achaemenid Iran had a larger public than those who had written about the Parthian or Sasanian periods. To the modern reader, especially since the invention of printing, the most crucial factors in forming an image of Iran were the Old Testament descriptions, the biblical illustrations connected with it, and the 'world chronicles', which were partially based on the Bible. We should also bear in mind that in the Middle Ages, 'world history' at the same time meant 'salvation history', and that biblical nations, states, empires and personalities always had their specific place in the Christian story of salvation. From the Bible itself, which was considered as divinely revealed, the most familiar names were those of the Assyrian, Babylonian and Persian kings, officials and gods who were for the most part hostile towards the people of Israel (for example Sanherib/Sennacherib or Nebuchadnezzar/Nabuchodonosor), and in rare cases (e.g. Cyrus/Koresh) friendly. Even towns, places, rivers and regions of Mesopotamia or Iran meant something to anyone who read the Bible or had it read to him.

However, since lists of kings and chronicles for Mesopotamia and Iran were not enlarged upon in the biblical texts, the scant references to Assyrian, Babylonian and Iranian history and culture, or to the topography and geography of these places, yielded no real store of knowledge about these subjects. Nor had it been the intention of the authors of biblical texts to provide any kind of historical knowledge. It had been their aim to show God's hand in the history of his people, Israel, and it had been the aim of the prophets to exhort people to obey his Commandments, to threaten them with divine punishment if they failed to do so, and to lend the good and bad times of the people of Israel a 'theological' interpretation. In the same context, the historical characters had been provided with functions in the divine plan of redemption. Thus in Deutero-Isaiah Cyrus appears as the instrument of the deliverance of God's people from the Babylonian Captivity, and in Jeremiah Nebuchadnezzar is God's punishment personified.

To go back to the medieval conception of history, since 'historiographers' in late Christian antiquity focused on creation, revelation, the end of the world and the struggle between *civitas Dei* and *civitas Diaboli* (Augustine), and since they were fond of dividing history into periods, the vision of the 'four kingdoms of the world' in the Book of Daniel acquired special historical significance. As a result, the description of the history of the first kingdom of Babylonia and that of the second kingdom of Media/Persia enjoyed great popularity. As for the world chronicles, this genre of medieval 'historiography' with its 'redemptive' message and its usual beginning at a calculated date of creation was to present biblical or ecclesiastical history side-by-side with a parallel history of the heathen nations. Their models were the chronicles of Eusebius and Jerome. About 'ancient Iran' they contained what their authors had learnt from the Bible and other literary sources (certain classical authors, Church Fathers, et al.). In the illustrations, ancient Near Eastern rulers often appear in contemporary clothes, for instance as knights next to a 'snake' (cannon), as Cyrus appears at his conquest of Sardis in the Lübeck world chronicle of 1475. This telescoping of temporal horizons has been explained by reducing it to the following succinct formula:

Although chronologically this event has been recognized as belonging to the remote past, it is conceived in the context of the all-embracing continuum of divine creation, in which what is spatially or temporally remote is not relativized, but placed under the same conditions as local and present experience. (Metzler)

Although the exclusive assessment of ancient Iran from the outside was inevitable up to the nineteenth century, when cuneiform scripts were deciphered and the first excavations carried out (it actually continued for decades afterwards), and although even travellers were for a long time unable to interpret ruins and written records with any accuracy, their appearance in Persepolis and elsewhere nevertheless marked a break in the approach to ancient Iran. Not only did they (re-)acquaint Europe with the sites, monuments and written records of a highly developed ancient culture, but through their drawings, paintings and descriptions they also paved the way for the Iranian studies of later European scholarship.

When did travellers and diplomats first start looking for traces of the early kings of Iran? Probably the earliest information about Persepolis in European literature is a short passage in the account of the Franciscan friar Odoric of Pordenone, written around 1328. Here he describes a site in south-western Iran which he visited on his way to China, and which he called Comum: '... [this] was an huge and mightie city in olde time, and hath done in times past great damage unto the Romanes [!] ... In it there are stately palaces altogether destitute of inhabitants ...' More than 100 years later, Josaphat Barbaro, whom the Venetians had sent to the court of the Turkmenian prince Uzun Hasan in Tabriz to form an alliance against the Turks, wrote a detailed description of Persepolis, Naqsh-i Rustam and Cyrus's tomb in Pasargadae. However, he did not connect them with the Achaemenid kings, but with biblical personalities, and used the native names for the sites.

When after the discovery of the sea route to India, the European powers formed closer relations with Persia, their diplomats also visited the old Achaemenid and Sasanian sites in south-western Iran. Among them was the Spaniard Don Garcia Silva Figueroa, who first identified Chihil Minar with Persepolis. He made some accurate observations – he even carried with him a copy of the works of Diodorus, the most important ancient informant for Persepolis – but some of his remarks strike us as rather strange today. Unfortunately, the drawings he commissioned of buildings, reliefs and inscriptions are no longer extant. Another well prepared visitor to this site was the Italian Pietro Della Valle, whose comparisons between what he saw and what he read in the ancient sources have not lost their value. He is also credited with the first extant copies of Old Persian cuneiform characters (see below). In 1624, on his way back from India, the German Heinrich von Poser stopped in Shiraz and visited Persepolis, of which the natives told him that it had been built by King Jamshid. For a while, von Poser played with the idea of identifying Jamshid with Cyrus, but he finally rejected it. Among other visitors to Persepolis were the Englishman Thomas Herbert, Johann Albrecht von Mandelslo from Holstein and the Frenchman Jean François Tavernier. Although most of them correctly identified Chihil Minar or Takht-i Jamshid with Persepolis, we are struck by the lack of accuracy in their descriptions and even in their drawings, and also by their fanciful comments on what they had found. As has rightly been said, the only explanation for this phenomenon is that they found in Persepolis what they *wanted* to find there, whether illustrations of 'Olympic Games' on the reliefs, or Greek columns and representations of Greek phalanges, or temples or royal palaces.

Towards the end of the seventeenth century, nothing had changed as far as the accuracy in ascertaining functions and interpreting the site was concerned, yet the descriptions and drawings themselves had improved. This change is connected with the names of the Frenchmen Jean Thévenot and Jean Chardin, the Dutchman Cornelis de Bruijn and the Westphalian Engelbert Kaempfer. It is interesting that in Iranian affairs, Thévenot, Chardin and Kaempfer (as well as Tavernier) benefited from the advice, instruction and assistance of a man 'who never withheld from any traveller the experiences he had collected in Iran for decades: the Capuchin father Raphael du Mans, who had then been a resident of Isfahan for 38 years' (Hinz), a genius in mathematics, languages and politics.

Until well into the eighteenth century, improved knowledge about foreign cultures was mainly a by-product of the efforts of the great seafaring nations to open up new trade routes and contacts. This situation changed with the first exploring expedition properly speaking to that part of the world, the Danish expedition to Arabia in the years 1761–67. Financed by the Danish king, inspired and scientifically prepared by Professor Johann David Michaelis of Göttingen and organized by Johann Hartwig Ernst Bernstorff, the expedition was to fill in gaps in biblical science, history and philology, as well as in natural sciences and geography. On this journey the only surviving member, Carsten Niebuhr (from Meldorf in Dithmarschen), arrived in Persepolis in 1764 and stayed there for three weeks. His son, the famous historian of antiquity Barthold Georg Niebuhr, later described the impression this site had made on his father: 'The sight of these ruins remained indelibly with him throughout his life, to him they were the jewel of all he had seen.' In Persepolis Niebuhr took special pains with making careful copies of the many royal inscriptions in cuneiform characters. Several decades later, his copies formed the groundwork for deciphering all the cuneiform writing systems (see below). However, while carrying out this work, he overstrained his eyes so badly in the glaring sun reflected by the marble that he went blind in his old age.

Niebuhr's description of Persepolis led Johann Gottfried Herder to write a short treatise in 1787, in which he interpreted the entire site as the residence of the Achaemenid kings which Alexander had ordered to be set alight. He described the 'reliefs of tribute bringers' as 'a living chart of the provinces and peoples of the Persian empire with indications of their gifts, arts, natural products, costumes, etc. I hope to show it as a laudatory chart for the vast empire.' The nineteenth century produced the first pictorial reconstructions of the site, and later photographs as well. That was also when the first ancient Iranian art objects arrived in Europe.

Until the nineteenth century no one connected the ruins of Pasargadae with Cyrus II, and the Sasanian reliefs at Naqsh-i Rustam and elsewhere were still called 'Rustamic', for want of any other explanation. Susa, which was off the usual tracks and for a long time shunned because of its climate, did not become a focus of interest until the mid-nineteenth century. English 'excavators' went there in search of the palace of the biblical Esther. Scientific excavations began in Susa in 1884, and in Pasargadae, Persepolis, Naqsh-i Rustam and Istakhr in the 1920s or 1930s, and were continued until the Iranian Revolution (and partly after it). Explorers for a long time made overland trips and surveys to complement the work of the teams of Western European, North American, Japanese and Soviet archaeological institutes and groups of scholars established at many sites in Iran, Afghanistan and the Soviet Union: the French in Susa, Masjid-i Sulaiman, Bishapur and Ai Khanum, the Americans (and Italians) in Persepolis and surroundings, the British in Pasargadae and Shahr-i Qumis, the Italians in Sistan, the Japanese at Taq-i Bustan, the Germans in Bisutun and Takht-i Sulaiman, Soviet explorers in Nisa and elsewhere in today's Central Asian states of the CIS, and the Iranians in Bishapur and at many other places. Aerial photography and progressive excavation, conservation and dating techniques have meanwhile changed the methods and practices of Near Eastern archaeology, and so has the tendency to record and analyse all finds (not only the most spectacular) and to keep them in the country instead of transporting them to European or North American museums. In the course of time, many people have visited early Iranian sites or admired the objects found there in the exhibitions of their local museums, and hardly anyone has been able to resist the fascination of ancient Iranian cultures.

The year 1802 was a year of epoch-making significance for scholarship on ancient Iran. In July of that year Georg Friedrich Grotefend, a student at Göttingen, and his friend Wilhelm Johann Raphael Fiorillo were taking a walk in Hainburg. But we shall let Grotefend tell us the story himself:

In the month of July [1802], on a walk with my friend Fiorillo, the secretary of the Royal Library, we were arguing whether it was possible to discover the content of documents written in a totally unknown alphabet and language. I who am used from childhood to deciphering coded sentences in my mother tongue, expressed the opinion that it was quite possible. When he retorted that I could prove that best if I managed to interpret one of the cuneiform writings, I agreed to do so if he would help me by furnishing me with the entire special literature on the subject. When he had done so, I set about with the help of my friend tackling the easiest of all, the script that the highly renowned O. G. Tychsen had previously tried to read, and already a few weeks later, after applying all the tricks of decipherment, I was lucky enough to succeed in interpreting the major part of the inscriptions.

Before addressing the process of decipherment itself, we will have to go back a little. Who was Georg Friedrich Grotefend, who were his predecessors in trying his luck with the 'cuneiform scripts', and how did they go about it? Georg Friedrich Grotefend was born on 9 June 1775, the sixth child of Johann Christian Grotefend, master of the shoemakers guild in Hannoversch Münden. After attending the 'Lateinschule' (grammar school) there and the 'Pädagogium' at Ilfeld in the Harz (from 1792), he enrolled at the University of Göttingen to study theology and philology. His most famous teachers were the theologian Thomas Christian Tychsen (1758–1834), the classical scholar Gottlob Chr. Heyne (1729–1812) and the historian Arnold Ludwig Heeren (1760–1842). In his first (printed) work, a contribution to the Heyne Festschrift (*Commentatio de pasigraphia sive scriptura universali*), Grotefend discussed the problems of a universal script intelligible to all nations.

From Göttingen he was appointed head teacher of the gymnasium (secondary school) in Frankfurt on the Main. Here he became the co-founder of the Frankfurter Gelehrten-Verein für deutsche sprache, which brought him in touch with Goethe, Jacob Grimm, Alexander von Humboldt and Jean Paul. In 1819 he became a member of the Gesellschaft für Deutschlands ältere Geschichtskunde which was founded on the suggestion of the Reichs-freiherr Karl vom Stein and which published the *Monumenta Germaniae Historica*. From 1821 to 1849 Grotefend was the head of the Lyceum in Hanover. It was here that he died on 15 December 1853.

How much was known about cuneiform scripts in the year 1802? The mention of cuneiform inscriptions from here on will refer to those that were found in Persepolis and first became known in early modern Europe through a report from the Spanish and Portuguese ambassador at the Persian Safavid court, Antonio de Gouvea. In his *Relaçam en que se tratam das guerras* (Lisbon 1611), we come across the following sentence:

There is no one who can read this, since the characters are neither Persian nor

Arabic nor Armenian nor Hebrew ... All this leads to blotting out the memory of what the ambitious king so badly wanted to immortalize.

For all that, the ambassador was not in a position to identify the palace complex and hence the king he was referring to. This was done, as already mentioned, a few years later by his successor Garcia Silva Figueroa. It was he who first described cuneiform script, though he did not use this term:

There is a remarkable inscription carved in black jasper. Its characters are still un-damaged and beautiful [Lat. *integrae et venustae*] ... despite their great age. The characters of the script themselves are neither Chaldaic nor Hebrew, neither Greek nor Arabic, nor the characters of any other nation of whose previous existence we are aware today. They are triangular and shaped like a pyramid or small obelisk, as seen in the margin, and are all equal, except in their position and their sequence. But the combined characters thus formed are exceptionally distinct and varied.

On 13 and 14 October 1621, Pietro Della Valle visited Persepolis, a stay he described soon afterwards (21 October) in a letter to a friend. This letter, which was not published until 1658, contains the first copy of a cuneiform text, although only consisting of five characters:

$$\langle\! \mathrm{I} \quad \overline{\overline{\mathrm{III}}} \quad \mathrm{K} \quad \diagdown \quad \langle\!\langle \mathrm{II}$$

It was also Della Valle who first hit upon the correct assumption that the script ran from left to right. Further copies of inscriptions from Persepolis reached Europe in the drawings of the Englishman Thomas Herbert, the Frenchman Jean Chardin, the German Engelbert Kaempfer and the Dutch traveller Cornelis de Bruijn. Truly reliable copies of entire inscriptions were however first made by Carsten Niebuhr in the year 1765. In his report about the Arabia expedition, he printed copies of eleven cuneiform inscriptions in the second volume, which appeared in German in 1778 and in French in 1780.

Niebuhr not only confirmed Della Valle's assumption about the scripts running from left to right, he also observed that there were three different kinds of script (he called them 'alphabets') and that there was always one inscription written in each kind of script, i.e. the inscriptions were always arranged by threes. The one that was regularly placed on the top or left (i.e. at the beginning) appeared to Niebuhr to be the simplest, and according to his interpretation of the cuneiform characters it consisted only of 42 signs (there are in fact 36). No wonder, then, that the inscriptions of this particular kind were first to arouse the interest of the decipherers.

Since any attempt to decipher inscriptions in a totally unknown script
has to start with proper names, titles or the like, results in deciphering
cuneiform scripts could not be expected as long as there was no knowledge
of related languages or related inscription contents or formulae. Precisely
such progress in knowledge had been made meanwhile or shortly after
Niebuhr's publications. In 1762 Abraham Hyacinthe Anquetil-Duperron had
returned to Paris with Avesta manuscripts from India. His translation of the
'holy script' of the Zoroastrians lent the study of Iranian languages an
enormous impetus. In 1787 the French Orientalist Baron Antoine Sylvestre
de Sacy succeeded in deciphering other so far unknown scripts. During his
stay in Persepolis and surroundings, Niebuhr noticed, as Chardin and others
had done before him, that in addition to the cuneiform inscriptions in Naqsh-
i Rustam, there were others as well, some in Greek and some in two so far
unknown scripts, which he also published. De Sacy now succeeded in proving
that these were trilingual texts, i.e. that they were inscriptions with the same
content, the two uppermost versions of which were in the two western
Middle Iranian languages, Middle Persian and Parthian, written in a variant
of the Aramaic script (see below). By referring to the names, genealogies and
titles in the Greek text, he was in a position to translate the inscriptions and
to attribute them to the early Sasanian period (third century AD). At the same
time, his systematic procedure showed the way for future decipherers to
follow.

To go back to the cuneiform inscriptions, in 1798 Oluf Gerhard Tychsen,
an Orientalist from Rostock, wrote his *De cuneatis inscriptionibus Persepolitanis
lucubratio*, revealing that in the first and simplest kind of script, a single
slanting wedge served as a word-divider. He also correctly observed that the
three kinds of script must convey three different languages. The word-divider
was also identified by the Danish theologian Frederik Münter in his 'Versuch
über die keilförmigen Inschriften zu Persepolis' ('Essay about the cuneiform
inscriptions of Persepolis') (Copenhagen 1802). In addition, he maintained
that the inscriptions could stem only from the Achaemenid kings, so that
their language must be akin to that of the Avesta. Other assumptions of his
also proved correct. Thus he postulated the same content for all three
versions and rightly assumed that the frequently recurring groups of characters must denote the words 'king' or 'king of kings' (by connecting them
with the Sasanian inscriptions and with references to these titles in the
classical sources). However, he was not so lucky with some of his other
conclusions and hypotheses. The different kinds of script are not, as he

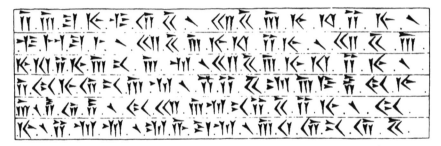

B

G

Figure 6 Inscriptions DPa and XPe from Persepolis
(drawings by C. Niebuhr)

assumed, an alphabetic, a syllabic and a logographic script, and he almost completely failed in his attempt to define the sign values. That was as far as deciphering had come on that memorable day in July 1802.

As already pointed out, the first and simplest script among the Achaemenid inscriptions formed the basis for deciphering cuneiform writing. This is the Old Persian cuneiform script created at the behest of Darius I to render the Old Persian language. It consists of vertical and horizontal wedges as well as angles (opening towards the right). It is 'a vague mixture of syllabic and alphabetic script' (Borger). This is illustrated in the table with the 36 phonic signs (see Figure 1, p. 9). These signs can be divided into four groups: A) 3 pure vowel-signs (*a*, *i*, *u*); B) 22 consonant-signs without (initial or final) vowel sound or with inherent /*a*/; C) 4 consonant-signs with inherent /*i*/ and D) 7 consonant-signs with inherent /*u*/. 'Already the inconsistent structure of the sign inventory – which for instance contains $d^{(a)}$, $d^{(u)}$, $t^{(a)}$, $t^{(u)}$ and $d^{(i)}$ but no $t^{(i)}$ – and the ambiguity of the 22 signs of group B, show that this script is neither phonemically nor phonetically consistent. The practical use of the 36 phonic signs was not possible without certain "orthographic rules", that is certain conventions that had to be observed for rendering particular phonemic sequences' (Schmitt). As a result of these conventions, there are several possibilities for interpreting each of the existing forms, and the correct philological and/or linguistic interpretation has to be ascertained. The fact that Grotefend and others managed despite these problems to lay the foundations for the decipherment of this script and for understanding the Old Persian language adds to our admiration for their achievement.

But to go back to the summer of 1802, how did Grotefend succeed in bettering previous attempts to decipher the Old Persian script, and what was his secret? The basic elements he used for deciphering the script were the inscriptions that Niebuhr called B and G [DPa and XPe] (see Figure 6).

In addition he knew – or rather agreed with the opinion – that the cuneiform script was to be read from left to right, that it probably dated from the Achaemenid period, and that the single slanting wedge was to be interpreted as a word-divider (so that the first line of inscription B consisted of two words). Like Münter he also considered the language of the inscriptions 'of the first kind' to be that of Anquetil-Duperron's 'Zend-Avesta'. Grotefend now noticed that among the words separated from one another by the word-divider, there was one that kept recurring. Read from left to right, it is the second word of line 1 in inscriptions B and G:

$$\text{.} \langle\!\langle \text{Y} \text{.} \overline{\langle\!\langle} \text{.} \overline{\text{YY}} \text{.} \text{Y}\langle\text{-.} \text{Y}\langle\text{Y} \text{.} \overline{\text{YY}} \text{.} \text{Y}\langle\text{-}$$

This word also occurs in line 2 of inscription B (as the fourth word altogether) and as the fifth word, running from the end of line 2 into line 3. Here, however, instead of consisting of 7 signs, as usual, it comprises 11, so it presumably has an ending of 4 signs. After the next word-divider (in line 3), it occurs again. What word could it be? Grotefend drew upon his knowledge of classical sources and also of Sasanian inscriptions (see above), in which he remembered that de Sacy had often read the word 'king', as well as the distinctly Iranian title 'king of kings'. If the word in question was indeed the king's title, then the first word in line 1 would have to be the king's name, as in the Sasanian inscriptions. Grotefend now noticed that the name occurring at the beginning of inscription B followed the title in inscription G. He therefore concluded that the inscriptions began with: 'X, king, powerful [?], king of kings, king of ... Y's son.'

The disclosure of the phonic values now followed by way of the name of the king (first word on line 1 of inscription B): Grotefend noticed that the name at the beginning of inscription B occurred again in the 3rd line of inscription G, but that there was an additional character near the end of the word. He concluded that it must be the genitive form of the name, so that the king in inscription G (first word, line 1) had to be the son of the king in inscription B. He thought of the names Darius and Xerxes, but did not know their Iranian forms. For Darius he finally tried DÂRHEÛSh (in accordance with the biblical form of this name, Dârjâvesh [*dryvš*]), and for Xerxes KhShHÊRShÊ.

𝍣𝍣. 𝍤𝍤𝍤. ᛝ𝅃. 𝐊ᛐ.-ᛉ𝐄. ᛘ𝍣𝍣.𝍦𝍦   𝍦𝍦𝍦𝐊.𝍦𝍦. 𝐊ᛐ. 𝍤𝍤𝍤.𝅃𝐊.𝍦𝍦𝍦. 𝍣𝍣𝍣

D   A   R   H   E   U   SH   KH SH H   E   R   SH   E

Grotefend must have been very pleased when he found that his characters for *sh* and *ê/â* (he considered *â* and *ê* as variants of the same sign) occurred precisely at the right place. Even if his *h*, as we know today, should have been read as *y*, he had found out the 1st, 2nd, 3rd, 6th and 7th characters of Darius's name (*d, a, r, u, š* [sh]), and the 1st, 2nd, 4th, 5th, 6th and 7th characters of Xerxes's name (*x* [*kh*], *š, a, r, š, a*). What he could not have known was that the Persian name of Darius was not Dârheûsh, but d-a-r-y-v-u-š (*dārayavauš*): *h* before *u* was not written, and as we have seen, the signs of this script are sometimes to be interpreted as characters (consonants without vowel sounds) and sometimes as syllables (consonants with inherent vowels).

Grotefend's next step was to tackle the word for 'king', of which he already knew 5 of the 7 signs:

𝍦𝍦 𝍣𝍣𝐊. 𝍤𝍤𝍤.𝐊ᛐ 𝐊𝍣.𝍣𝍣.𝐊ᛐ.

KH   SH   E   H   ?   ?   H

Since he had found *Khsheiô* as a royal title in Duperron's vocabulary of the 'Zend-Avesta', he read the title as KhShÊHIÔ, i.e. he supplied the two phonetic signs he was missing as *i* and *ô*; in fact, it should read x-š-a-y-θ-i-y (*xšāyaθiya*). The interpretation of further signs followed from the name of Darius's father, which was bound to occur in inscription B. Let us look again at the Niebuhr copies of inscriptions B and G. Having thought he had recognized the first word on line 4 of B as the genitive plural of 'Dahae', the name of a Scythian tribe – what it was in fact was the genitive plural of *dahyu*, 'land/people' (see above) – Grotefend rightly concluded that the following word (in the genitive singular) must be the name of Darius's father. That the name Hystaspes, which is known from Greek sources, was not accompanied by a royal title, corresponded with these sources and with the truth. As for the Old Persian form of the name Hystaspes, he assumed it to be (again by referring to Duperron's vocabulary):

$$\overrightarrow{\text{TT}}.\,\overrightarrow{\text{TT}}.\,\overline{\langle\langle}.\overline{\text{FTIT}}.\overline{\text{ITI}}.\overline{\text{TE}}.\overrightarrow{\text{TT}}$$
G   O   SH   T   A   S   P

Regarding *o* (in fact *i*), *sh* (*š*) and *a*, his previous attempts at reconstruction were confirmed. Among new characters Grotefend found *t*, *s* and *p*. The *g* is in fact to be interpreted as v^i, and the name as v^i-sh-t-a-s-p (*vištāspa*). In that same year of 1802 Grotefend also discovered the sign *f* as well as the logogram for 'king', and in 1815 the sign *k*, which later had to be changed to k^u. Further reading attempts misfired. Already his interpretation of the last line of inscription B (see below) shows how remote Grotefend was from a complete understanding of the Old Persian language (and script).

For the sake of clarity, we shall now present inscriptions B and G again in a) Grotefend's first reading, b) Grotefend's first translation, c) our contemporary linguistic transliteration and d) modern translation:

Inscription B = D(arius) P(ersepolis) a

a) *Dârheûsh Khshêhiôh/eghré Khshêhiôh Khshê/hiôhêchâo Khshêhiôh / Dâhûchâo Gôshtâspâh/ê bûn âkhêochôshôh Â/h ôoo Môro êzûchûsh.*

b) Darius, the strong king, king of kings, king of the Dahae, [son] of Hystaspes, descendant of the ruler of the world, under the male constellation Môro of the Ized.

c) *Dārayavauš xšāyaθiya vazṛka, xšāyaθiya xšāyaθiyānām, xšāyaθiya dahyūnām, Vištāspahyā puça, Haxāmanišiya, haya imam tačaram akunauš.*

d) Darius, the great king, king of kings, king of the countries/peoples, Hystaspes's son, the Achaemenid, who built this palace.

Inscription G = X(erxes) P(ersepolis) e

a) *Khshhêrshê Khshêhiôh eghr/é Khshêhiôh Khshêhiôh/êchâo Dârheâûsh Khshêhi/ôhâhê bûn âkhêochôshôh.*

b) Xerxes, the strong king, king of kings, [son] of King Darius, descendant of the ruler of the world.

c) *Xšayaršā xšāyaθiya vazṛka xšāyaθiya xšāyaθiyānām, Dārayavahauš xšāyaθiyahyā puça Haxāmanišiya.*

d) Xerxes, the great king, king of kings, King Darius's son, the Achaemenid.

There was a long way still to go before the definitive decipherment of Old Persian cuneiform script. Progress was made above all because a) there was a growing comprehension of Avestan and Old Indian (Sanskrit), languages that are related to Old Persian, and b) new texts were being discovered. In 1823 the Danish historian of literature Rasmus Christian Rask identified two signs that had been wrongly interpreted by Grotefend, namely *m* and *n*, and was therefore able to find out the correct reading of the dynastic name 'the Achaemenid' (*Haxāmanišiya*), as well as the genitive plural *ānām* (in 'king of kings') in the Darius inscription. The latter observation was particularly important because it proved the close relationship between Sanskrit and Old Persian (in Sanskrit the gen. pl. ending was also *ānām*). The application of the etymologizing method (the method which makes use of the kinship of languages) thus promised important results. This was the method successfully followed above all by the Norwegian scholar Christian Lassen, Professor of Sanskrit in Bonn, and the French Avesta scholar Eugène Burnouf, through whose investigations most of the signs of Old Persian were able to be read by means of a list of peoples in one of the inscriptions. Important, too, was Lassen's discovery that in the Old Persian script, as in the Indian alphabets, consonant signs do not reflect pure consonants but, with certain exceptions, also contain the vowel *a*, so that an *r* can be read both as the consonant *r* and as the syllabic sign *r^a*.

The second course, that of working with newly discovered texts, was followed above all by the English officer Henry Creswicke Rawlinson (1810–95), who can perhaps claim to be called 'the most successful decipherer of all' (Borger). Rawlinson was born in Chadlington Park, Oxforshire, in 1810, attended the Ealing School in London (but no university!) and in 1826 obtained a position as a cadet officer with the East India Company, which had the monopoly of trading with the East Indies. He did his military service in India until 1833, when he was assigned to reorganize the Iranian (Qajar) army. Between 1835 and 1839 he was military adviser to the Shah's brother in Kirmanshah, whence he was able to inspect both the inscriptions on the Elvend mountain south-west of Hamadan (DE, XE) and Darius's great *res gestae* on the Bisutun rock (DB). In a letter to his sister in 1835, he told her what he thought of himself and of his role in trying to decipher these inscriptions:

My antiquarian studies go on quietly and smoothly and despite the taunt which you may remember once expressing of the presumption of an ignoramus like myself attempting to decypher inscriptions which had baffled for centuries the most learned men in Europe, I have made very considerable progress in ascertaining the relative value of the characters ... I aspire to do for the cuneiform alphabet what Champollion has done for the hieroglyphics ... my character is one of restless, insatiable ambition – in whatever sphere I am thrown my whole spirit is absorbed in an eager struggle for the first place ...

How different his work was from Grotefend's is illustrated by the fact that Rawlinson himself copied the inscriptions he wanted to analyse on the spot. Here is how he describes what this actually meant in the case of the Bisutun inscription:

On reaching the recess which contains the Persian text of the record, ladders are indispensable in order to examine the upper portion of the tablet; and even with ladders there is considerable risk, for the foot-ledge is so narrow, about 18 inches, or at most 2 feet in breadth, that with a ladder long enough to reach the sculptures sufficient slope cannot be given to enable a person to ascend, and if the ladder be shortened in order to increase the slope, the upper inscriptions can only be copied by standing on the topmost step of the ladder, with no other support than steadying the body against the rock with the left arm, while the left hand holds the note-book and the right hand is employed with the pencil. In this position I copied all the upper inscriptions and the interest of the occupation entirely did away with any sense of danger.

To have a more tangible idea of this situation, the reader is referred to Plate I. Rawlinson copied a major part of the Old Persian version of DB between 1835 and 1837, and in 1844 and 1847, after the end of the Afghan war in which he participated, he was able to complete his copies. In 1846/ 47 he published the Old Persian, and in 1851 the Babylonian version of the Bisutun inscription.

Before approaching the problem of how Rawlinson achieved such progress in deciphering cuneiform script, we must briefly deal with the question of how much he knew about Grotefend's initial results. For this problem has led to an absurd and undignified dispute between two great Assyriologists. In his book *The Rise and Progress of Assyriology*, published in 1925, the Director of the Near-Eastern Department of the British Museum, Sir Ernest A. Wallis Budge, called Rawlinson the 'Father of the decipherment of Persian Cuneiform' (independently from Grotefend). This was contradicted in 1926 by the great German Assyriologist Bruno Meissner, who wrote in the journal *Literarische Wochenschrift*: 'The man who wrenched from the Sphinx her 2,000-year-old carefully kept secret of how to read cuneiform script [was] the German Grotefend ... Rawlinson as a great military man and politician knew well ... how to make a cat's paw of others.' Meissner even went so far as to urge people 'as far as possible to avoid the British Museum and any contact with its officials' in view of Budge's 'perfidious utterances'. Today we know that neither of these scholars had troubled to throw light upon the actual state of affairs. Before he began, Rawlinson apparently knew nothing about Grotefend's activities except for a few remarks in a book he had come across by Ker Porter (*Travels in Georgia, Persia, Armenia, Ancient Babylonia*, 2 vols, London 1821/22). It was only later that he came into contact with scholars like Lassen and found that he had indeed read almost all the signs on his own and independently, but that colleagues in Europe had in many respects stolen a march on him.

How had Rawlinson gone about it? In the Elvend inscriptions, which he recognized as almost identical, he had discovered words that differed from one another, which he assumed to be names of kings. Rawlinson's reasoning has been traced back as follows: 'One inscription contains two names, say A and towards the end B; the same is true of the other, which contains the name B and towards the end the name C. After A and B there is in each case a word that Rawlinson assumed to be "king"; it does not occur after C. This leads to the genealogy C – not-king, B – king, and A – king. The only series that comes into question is Hystaspes (C) – Darius (B) – Xerxes (A)' (Borger). As we have already observed, Grotefend had adopted a similar process. In the Bisutun inscription Rawlinson recognized the second word as the name Darius. He now hoped to find other ancestors of this king, whose names have been handed down by Herodotus (as ancestors of Darius's son Xerxes).

If I [Xerxes] fail to punish the Athenians, let me be no child of Darius, the son of Hystaspes, the son of Arsames, the son of Ariaramnes, the son of Teispes, the son of Cyrus, the son of Cambyses, the son of Teispes, the son of Achaemenes!

And indeed, on line 4/5 he found a name whose signs he could read as a-r-š-a-?; so the unknown sign had to be an *m*. In the middle of line 5 he found a-r-i-yᵃ-a-r-a-m-?, which had to be Ariaramnes; therefore, the last sign had to be an *n*. On the 6th line he found ?-x-a-m-n-i-š, hence Achaemenes; since *a* was already known and did not correspond with the first sign, Rawlinson read the first sign as hᵃ. And finally, on line 5/6 he found ?-i-š-p-a-i-š (Teispes); as the t-sign was already known, he replaced it with a t-sound as in English *nature* or Italian *città*, which is usually transcribed as č. The phonetic transcription of the names was thus: *Aršāma* (*Ṛšāma*), *Ariyāramna*, *Haxāmaniš*, *Čišpiš*.

With Rawlinson's publication of the Bisutun inscription and all the other Persian inscriptions, one important question had remained open; it concerned the consonants for which there were several signs. Two months before Rawlinson, who was once again late, but nevertheless provided further proof of his genius, the Irish country parson Hincks from Killyleagh near Belfast gave a lecture explaining that only some of the consonants could be combined with an *a*, other signs always contained a subsequent *i* or *u*. For example, in addition to the sign *m/m^a*, there was another sign for *m^i* and a third one for *m^u*, etc. (see Figure 1, p. 9).

Once the mystery of Old Persian cuneiform script was definitely solved, the way was shown for the decipherment of the other two scripts of the Achaemenid inscriptions. How this was done will no longer concern us here, since it can be read in many accounts about the history of decipherment.

The disclosure of the Avesta, the reading of the Middle Persian (and Parthian) versions of the Sasanian inscriptions and the decipherment of Old Persian cuneiform script marked the beginnings of the history of 'Iranian Studies' in Europe. These consist of research on the languages and literatures as well as the history and geography of the area inhabited by Iranians in the pre-Islamic and Islamic periods. Investigations about the Iranian Islamic period, and especially the New Iranian language and literature, are more closely related to Islamic studies, while the Old and Middle Iranian period and its languages and literatures are associated with Indo-European studies and research about the ancient Near East, ancient history and theology. It may be worth pointing out that what is called '*Iranistik*' (Iranian Studies) in Germany is primarily understood as a linguistic and philological discipline. The first milestones in this province were the *Altiranisches Wörterbuch* by Ch. Bartholomae, which appeared in 1904, and the *Grundriß der iranischen Philologie* by W. Geiger and E. Kuhn (2 vols, 1895–1904). Since the beginning of this century, the texts found in the Turfan oasis, the (further) inscriptions brought to light in Persepolis, Susa and elsewhere, the disclosure of newly found manuscripts of the Avesta, etc., have steadily given new impetus to Iranian studies and research about the written tradition of ancient Iran. The *Corpus Inscriptionum Iranicarum* (pts 1–3 and suppl., London 1955ff.), *Das Iranische Personennamenbuch* (ed. M. Mayrhofer, Vienna 1979ff.) and the *Compendium Linguarum Iranicarum* (ed. R. Schmitt, Wiesbaden 1989) are three of the most important fruits of Iranian studies.

POSTSCRIPT

We have reached the end of our account. It was not intended to provide exhaustive information about all the problems of ancient Iranian history and culture, nor was it meant as a chronological survey of historical events. But perhaps it has lived up to its promise of allowing ancient Persia its own voice and identity in revealing the specific character of its culture and in showing the traditions that influenced it and those that were of its own making. The dynasties of ancient Iran were not only those well-known great opponents of Greeks and Romans on the battlefield, but also their cherished trading partners. Under the Achaemenids, Greek philosophy flourished in Ionia, Greek mercenaries fought for Persian interests, and Greek statesmen served as counsellors to the great kings. The Parthians counted Greek citizens and settlers among their subjects and were impressed by Greek culture and learning. The Sasanians, though deporting Greeks and Romans from Syria, at the same time offered protection and refuge to persecuted minorities of the Roman empire, guaranteeing religious freedom and the chance of economic and social promotion to all those who proved loyal. As for the other side, Alexander and the Seleucids adopted political ideas and concepts from the Achaemenids.

As the empires of the Achaemenids, Parthians and Sasanians always embraced territories where non-Iranian groups of populations were at home, the problem of dealing with foreign languages, traditions and religious concepts, as well as with the political hopes and ambitions of previously independent nations, existed for all dynasties from the very beginning. On the whole, the long duration of their reign over 'Iran (and non-Iran)' speaks for a rather gentle, farsighted and altogether successful policy of the kings with respect to cultural, religious or political minorities. Their religious policy may stand as one of the many proofs for this theory. Religious conformity was never demanded as a means to safeguard the reign, and the ruling principle was always the advancement of reliable groups and communities and the punishment of disloyal ones. Thus the Jewish communities of Mesopotamia experienced a time of undreamt-of prosperity and cultural–religious creativity, while the Christians of the fourth century AD and the Mazdakites found themselves exposed to merciless persecutions.

Pre-Islamic Iran was also distinguished by the fact that it not only cultivated its own traditions and beliefs (such as the Zoroastrian view of cosmic and worldly events, the ideals of ancient Iranian kingship and the interest in entertaining and instructive accounts of Iranian history), but also eagerly assimilated those of other cultures, which it mixed, transformed and passed on. Achaemenid art and the role of the late Sasanians in transmitting Greek and Indian medical science to the Muslims may serve as examples.

Critical periods for the empire and throne were only partially a result of external pressure by Greeks, Macedonians and Romans from the West, people of the steppes from the East, and Arabs from the South; at least equally important were problems and conflicts within the empire. These consisted of tensions between the royal house and the landowning aristocracy, political ambitions of members of the royal family and the high aristocracy, as well as those of sections of the population suspected of being unreliable or disloyal, and occasional epidemics, famines and social conflicts. It could also happen that external and internal factors combined, as for instance during the great crisis of the Sasanian empire in the fifth century. While the reign of the Achaemenids ended rather surprisingly with Alexander's victories, and not as a result of insoluble problems within the empire, and while the replacement of the Parthians by the Sasanians was more due to Ardashir's political and military abilities than to the weakness of the Arsacid reign at that time, the end of the Sasanian empire in the seventh century was brought about by a combination of external and internal factors. The private interests of members of the high aristocracy, conflicts within the royal house, Khosrow's overtaxing of his forces in the war against Byzantium, and finally the elimination of the Lakhmid buffer-state, fostered the advances of the Prophet's powerful army against Mesopotamia and Iran.

Achaemenids, Arsacids and Sasanians determined the cultural traditions of Iran to very different extents. While the latter lived on as Iranian kings *par excellence* in the 'national history' they had compiled, the Parthians were reduced to 'petty kings' in it. Cyrus and his descendants were rediscovered only in our period and had to serve as questionable 'ancestors' of rulers in search of legitimacy. Even if Zoroastrianism was soon reduced to a minority religion in Iran itself and never attained the universal significance of Christianity, Judaism and Islam, Zarathustra's message has at all times found its admirers and followers.

In Europe, (early) modern travellers, decipherers and archaeologists revived the memory of the sites and monuments of ancient Iran, and Iranologists and historians have redefined and re-evaluated the characteristics of Iranian cultures. Anyone who wishes to form an idea of the wealth and variety of the subjects investigated, the questions asked and the methods employed in this and other types of research into ancient Iran may look up the numerous bibliographies, research reports, textbooks and articles mentioned in this book. But ancient Iran has not yielded all its secrets, and there is still many a surprise concealed in Iranian (or Afghan) soil, in museums and art collections, and much new ground to be broken by scholars. So the present account of ancient Persia can be no more than a preliminary history.

ABBREVIATIONS

A²Hc	(Inscription) c (of) A(rtaxerxes) II from H(amadan)
AAntHung	*Acta Antiqua Academiae Scientiarum Hungaricae*
AchHist	*Achaemenid History*, Leiden
AcIr	*Acta Iranica*, Leiden
AION	*Annali, Istituto Orientale di Napoli*
AIΩN	*Annali del Seminario di Studi del Mondo Classico.* Sezione linguistica. Istituto Universitario Orientale di Napoli, Pisa
AJA	*American Journal of Archaeology*
AMI	*Archäologische Mitteilungen aus Iran*
ANRm	(Relief) of A(rdakhshir I from) N(aqsh-i) R(usta)m
ANRW	*Aufstieg und Niedergang der Römischen Welt.* Festschrift J. Vogt, Berlin
AOAT	Alter Orient und Altes Testament
AoF	*Altorientalische Forschungen*
Arab.	Arabic
Aram.	Aramaic
ArOr	*Archiv Orientalni*
Av.	Avestan
Babyl.	Babylonian
BaM	*Baghdader Mitteilungen*
BCH	*Bulletin de Correspondance Hellénique*
BJbb	Bonner Jahrbücher
BSOAS	*Bulletin of the School of Oriental and African Studies*, London
CAH	*The Cambridge Ancient History*
CDAFI	*Cahiers de la Délégation Française en Iran*
CHI	*The Cambridge History of Iran*
CIG	Corpus Inscriptionum Graecarum
CMC	Codex Manichaicus Coloniensis/Cologne Mani Codex
CRAI	*Comptes Rendus de l'Académie des Inscriptions et Belles-Lettres*
D²Ha	(Inscription) a (of) D(arius) II (from) H(amadan)
DB	(Inscription of) D(arius I from) B(isutun)
DBa (sus.)	Elam. legend a (of the inscription of) D(arius I from) B(isutun)
DBb–j	Legends b–j (of the inscription of) D(arius I from) B(isutun)

DE	(Inscription of) D(arius I from) E(lvend)
DH	(Inscription of) D(arius I from) H(amadan)
DHA	*Dialogues d'Histoire Ancienne*
Dk	Denkard
DN	(Throne-bearer inscriptions of) D(arius I from) N(aqsh-i Rustam)
DNa	(Inscription) a (of) D(arius I from) N(aqsh-i Rustam)
DNb	(Inscription) b (of) D(arius I from) N(aqsh-i Rustam)
DPa	(Inscription) a (of) D(arius I from) P(ersepolis)
DPd	(Inscription) d (of) D(arius I from) P(ersepolis)
DPe	(Inscription) e (of) D(arius I from) P(ersepolis)
DPf	(Inscription) f (of)D(arius I from) P(ersepolis)
DPg	(Inscription) g (of) D(arius I from) P(ersepolis)
DPh	(Inscription) h (of) D(arius I from) P(ersepolis)
DSab	(Inscription) ab (of) D(arius I from) S(usa)
DSf	(Inscription) f (of) D(arius I from) S(usa)
DSm	(Inscription) m (of) D(arius I from) S(usa)
DSp	(Inscription) p (of) D(arius I from) S(usa)
DZc	(Inscription) c (of) D(arius I from) S(ue)z
Elam.	Elamite
EncIr	*Encyclopaedia Iranica*, London/Costa Mesa
FGrHist	*Die Fragmente der greichischien Historiker*, ed. F. Jacoby, Leiden 1923ff
Fort.	unpublished Persepolis tablet
GGA	*Göttingische Gelehrte Anzeigen*
Gr.	Greek
GRBS	*Greek, Roman and Byzantine Studies*
H.	unpublished Persepolis tablet
HdAW	*Handbuch der Altertumswissenschaft*, Munich
HZ	*Historische Zeitschrift*
IF	*Indogermanische Forschungen*
IIP	Inventaire des Inscriptions de Palmyre, Beirut/Damascus
IPNB	Iranisches Personennamenbuch, Vienna
IrAnt	*Iranica Antiqua*
JA	*Journal Asiatique*
JDAI	*Jahrbuch des Deutschen Archäologischen Instituts*
JHS	*Journal of Hellenic Studies*
JNES	*Journal of Near Eastern Studies*
JRAS	*Journal of the Royal Asiatic Society*

JS	*Journal des Savants*
JSAI	*Jerusalem Studies in Arabic and Islam*
JSOT	*Journal for the Study of the Old Testament*
KKZ	(Inscription of) K(irdir from the) K(a'ba-i) Z(ardusht)
KlP	Der Kleine Pauly
KNRm	(Inscription of) K(irdir from) N(aqsh-i) R(usta)m
KSM	(Inscription of) K(irdir from) S(ar) Mashhad
Lat.	Latin
LdM	*Lexikon des Mittelalters*, Zürich
MBAH	*Münstersche Beiträge zur antiken Handelsgeschichte*
MDAI	Mémoires de la Délégation Archéologique française en Iran
MP	Middle Persian
MS	Manuscript (version)
NABU	*Nouvelles Assyriologiques Brèves et Utilitaires*
NGWG	*Nachrichten von der Gesellschaft der Wissenschaften zu Göttingen. Philol.-hist. Kl.*
NPi	(Inscription of) N(arseh from) P(aikul)i
OGIS	Orientis Graeci Inscriptiones Selectae
OLP	Orientalia Lovaniensia Periodica
OLZ	*Orientalistische Literaturzeitung*
OP	Old Persian
Pa/Parth.	Parthian
PCPhS	*Proceedings of the Cambridge Philological Society*
PF	Persepolis Fortification (Tablet)
PFa	Persepolis Fortification (Tablet)
PFT	Persepolis Fortification Tablets
pl.	plural
PO	Patrologia Orientalis
PT	Persepolis Treasury (Tablet)
PTT	Persepolis Treasury Tablets
QdS	*Quaderni di Storia*
RE	*Pauly-Wissowas Realencyclopädie der classischen Altertumswissenschaft*
REA	*Revue des Études Anciennes*
Rend. Lincei	*Rendiconti della Classe di Scienze Morali, Storiche e Filologiche dell'Accademia dei Lincei*
RHE	*Revue d'Histoire Ecclésiastique*

SEG	Supplementum Epigraphicum Graecum
sg.	singular
StIr	*Studia Iranica*
Syr.	Syriac
ŠH	(Inscription of) Š(apur I from) H(ajjiabad)
ŠKZ	(Inscription of) Š(apur I from the) K(aʿba-i) Z(ardusht)
ŠNRb	(Inscription of) Š(apur I from) N(aqsh-i) R(aja)b
ŠNRm	(Inscription of) Š(apur I from) N(aqsh-i) R(usta)m
ŠPs	(Inscription of) Š(apur, king of the Sakae from) P(ersepolis)
ŠVŠ	(Inscription of) Š(apur I from) V(eh-)Š(abuhr)
T.	unpublished Persepolis Tablet
TAVO	*Tübinger Atlas des Vorderen Orients*
TRE	*Theologische Realenzyklopädie*, Berlin
TvG	*Tijdschrift voor Geschiedenis*
WO	*Welt des Orients*
XDNb	= XPl
XE	(Inscription of) X(erxes from) E(lvend)
XPb	(Inscription) b (of) X(erxes I from) P(ersepolis)
XPc	(Inscription) c (of) X(erxes I from) P(ersepolis)
XPe	(Inscription) e (of) X(erxes I from) P(ersepolis)
XPh	(Inscription) h (of) X(erxes I from) P(ersepolis)
XPl	(Inscription) l (of) X(erxes I from) P(ersepolis)
YCS	Yale Classical Studies
ZA	*Zeitschrift für Assyriologie*
ZDMG	*Zeitschrift der Deutschen Morgenländischen Gesellschaft*
ZfKG	*Zeitschrift für Kirchengeschichte*
ZKM	*Zeitschrift für die Kunde des Morgenlandes*
ZPE	*Zeitschrift für Papyrologie und Epigraphik*

For the ancient Greek authors and their works mentioned in the Bibliographical Essays, the abbreviations of Liddell/Scott, *A Greek–English Lexicon*, have been used.

BIBLIOGRAPHICAL ESSAYS

Introduction

The reader who is interested in the history and culture of Iran and seeks further information and literature is referred to several types of source material: handbooks, encyclopaedias and reference books, as well as bibliographies. The most important handbooks for the pre-Islamic history of Iran are vols II and III of the *Cambridge History of Iran*, Cambridge 1983–85 (of which vol. III, 1–2, on the Parthian–Sasanian period is by far the better one); also useful, on the political history, is the work of R. N. Frye, *The History of Ancient Iran*, Munich 1984.

For reference works/encyclopaedias, we recommend the excellent *Encyclopaedia Iranica* (EncIr), London/Costa Mesa 1986ff, of which six volumes have so far appeared (letters A–Da), as well as *Pauly-Wissowas Real-Encyclopädie der classischen Altertumswissenschaft* (RE), ed. G. Wissowa et al., Stuttgart 1893ff (in more than 80 volumes, including articles about the history of Iran), and *Der kleine Pauly* (KlP), ed. K. Ziegler et al., 5 vols, Stuttgart 1964–75 (the most reasonably priced encyclopaedia – also available in a pocket edition – for any questions regarding classical antiquity, including articles on the history of Iran). The third edition of *The Oxford Classical Dictionary* (OCD) will soon be available. In addition there are special encyclopaedias on cultures with which the Iranians were in touch, e.g. *Lexikon der Ägyptologie*, ed. W. Helck/E. Otto, Wiesbaden 1972ff, *Reallexikon der Assyriologie*, ed. E. Ebeling et al., Berlin 1928ff (so far published up to the letter M), as well as *The Oxford Dictionary of Byzantium*, ed. A. Kazhdan, 3 vols, Oxford 1991. We should also recommend the just published four-volume work *Civilizations of the Ancient Near East*, ed. J. Sasson, New York 1995, which contains excellent essays on all subjects of ancient Near Eastern history and culture. For the Old Testament one may consult *The Anchor Bible Dictionary*, 6 vols, New York 1992.

The following are the (thematic) bibliographies. On the subject of Iranian history and culture, the reader is referred to the annual volumes of the *Abstracta Iranica*, supplement to 'Studia Iranica', Louvain 1977ff; special bibliographies on archaeological research in Iran: P. Calmeyer, 'Archäologische Bibliographie' in each issue of *AMI* N. F., Berlin 1973ff, and L. Vanden Berghe, *Bibliographie analytique de l'archéologie de l'Iran antique*, Leiden 1979; Suppl. I–II, Leiden 1981–87; on (Old Iranian) languages: 'Indogermanische Chronik', in each issue of *Die Sprache*, Vienna, as well as in the annual *Bibliographie Linguistique*, ed. M. Janse/H. Borkent, Dordrecht et al. More recent literature about (cuneiform) cultures of the ancient East is to be found in the 'Keilschriftbibliographie', in each issue of *Orientalia* N. S. 9ff, Rome 1940ff, as well as in the *Oriental Institute Research Archives Acquisitions List(s)*, Chicago 1991ff. On all questions about the Old Testament environment consult: *Elenchus Bibliographicus Biblicus* or *Elenchus of Biblical Bibliography*, Rome 1920ff; *Internationale Zeitschriftenschau für Bibelwissenschaft und Grenzgebiete*, Düsseldorf 1951/52ff. The (only important) bibliography on all questions of Graeco-Roman antiquity is the annual *L'Année Philologique*, ed. J. Marouzeau/J. Ernst, Paris 1928ff.

On the beginnings of Iranian supremacy in the Near East the most recent work is that of P. Högemann (*Das alte Vorderasien und die Achämeniden* [Beih. TAVO, series B, 98], Wiesbaden 1992); however, the chief emphasis of his investigation falls not so much on the history of events as on the influences of preceding empires on the early Persian empire.

On the (historical) geography of Iran see *The Cambridge History of Iran*, vol. 1, ed. W. R. Fisher, Cambridge 1968; E. Ehlers, *Iran. Grundzüge einer geographischen Landeskunde*, Darmstadt 1980, as well as the corresponding articles in the *EncIr*; on Afghanistan see E. Grötzbach, *Afghanistan*, Darmstadt 1990. On the political idea of Iran see Gh. Gnoli, *The Idea of Iran*, Rome 1989, and B. G. Fragner, 'Historische Wurzeln neuzeitlicher iranischer Identität: Zur Geschichte des politischen Begriffs "Iran" im späten Mittelalter und in der Neuzeit', *Studia Semitica Necnon Iranica. R. Macuch Septuagenario*, ed. M. Macuch et al., Wiesbaden 1989, 79–100. On the political uses of ancient Iranian history see H. Sancisi-Weerdenburg, 'Cyrus en de Sjah', *Groniek* 62, 1979, 3–9.

PART ONE

Iran from Cyrus to Alexander the Great

1. The Testimonies: 1–4

Bibliography: U. Weber/J. Wiesehöfer, *Das Reich der Achaimeniden*, Berlin 1996. Maps of the empire have been published by G. Gropp and P. Högemann for the *Tübinger Atlas des Vorderen Orients* (TAVO). On the history of the Achaemenid empire there are numerous handbooks available (see above). Some of them tend to view the empire from the West (Greece), without due consideration for the contexts of Eastern traditions and the results of more recent investigations. On the political history of the empire, which is only marginally discussed here, see especially M. A. Dandamaev, *A Political History of the Achaemenid Empire*, transl. by W. Vogelsang, Leiden 1989, and E. M. Yamauchi, *Persia and the Bible*, Grand Rapids 1990. Although the latter work, which seeks to convey the latest state of research, may be criticized for its assessment of Old Testament traditions, it contains important information about the sources, social and religious conditions in the empire, etc. Also useful is M. A. Dandamaev/V. G. Lukonin, *The Culture and Social Institutions of Ancient Iran*, Cambridge 1989. The comprehensive work by P. Briant, *De Cyrus à Alexandre. Une histoire de l'Empire achéménide*, to be published in Leiden in 1996, is bound to become a 'standard work' on the history of the Achaemenid empire. Although they are collections of individual articles, the volumes of *Achaemenid History I–VIII*, Leiden 1987ff, specifically represent the results of a 'new view' of the Achaemenid empire. For initial information, the article 'Achaemenid Dynasty' by R. Schmitt (*EncIr* I, 1986, 414–26) and the richly illustrated little book by P. Briant (*Darius, les Perses et l'Empire* [Découvertes Gallimard], Paris 1992) are also useful.

1. (pp. 7–13) Information on linguistic conditions in Iran is provided by A. V. Rossi in his two articles 'La varietà linguistica nell'Iran achemenide', *AIΩN* 3, 1981, 141–211, and 'Glottonimia ed etnonimia nell'Iran achemenide', *AIΩN* 6, 1984, 39–65. On the Old Persian language see W. Brandenstein/M. Mayrhofer, *Handbuch des Altpersischen*,Wiesbaden 1964, and R. Schmitt, 'Altpersisch', *Compendium Linguarum Iranicarum*, ed. R. Schmitt, Wiesbaden 1989, 56–85. Iranian onomastics (including the parallel tradition) is competently dealt with in *Das Iranische Personennamenbuch*, ed. M. Mayrhofer, Vienna (although only a few fascicles of it have hitherto appeared). A survey of (written) sources can be found in W. Hinz, 'Die Quellen', *Beiträge zur Achämenidengeschichte*, ed. G. Walser, Wiesbaden 1972, 5–14, and now also in L. Cagni/A. V. Rossi/R. Contini, in *Rivista Biblica* 34, 1–2, 1986, 11–109. A more recent edition of Achaemenid royal inscriptions (in all versions) to replace the old one by F. H. Weissbach (*Die Keilschriften der Achämeniden*, Leipzig 1911) is long overdue. Some of the material from Susa is now presented by M.-J. Steve, in *Nouveaux mélanges épigraphiques*, Nice 1987. On Old Persian script see the works mentioned on the Old Persian language. For Old Persian inscriptions, R. G. Kent, *Old Persian. Grammar, Texts, Lexicon*, New Haven 2nd edn (revised) 1953, is still the standard edition; a more recent survey of the available material (with commentary) is provided by M. Mayrhofer, *Supplement zur Sammlung der altpersischen Inschriften*, Vienna 1978. On the Elamite language, see the grammar by F. Grillot-Susini (*Eléments de grammaire élamite*, Paris 1987), the syllabary by M.-J. Steve (*Syllabaire élamite*, Neuchâtel/Paris 1992) and the dictionary by W. Hinz/H. Koch (*Elamisches Wörterbuch*, 2 vols, Berlin 1987). PFT and PTT: The standard editions are those by R. T. Hallock (*Persepolis Fortification Tablets*, Chicago 1969; id., 'Selected Fortification Texts', *CDAFI* 8, 1978, 109–36) and G. G. Cameron (*Persepolis Treasury Tablets*, Chicago 1948). These also contain detailed historico-philological commentaries. About the abbreviations for the tablets: PF = Hallock 1969; PFa = Hallock 1978; PT = Cameron 1948; Fort./H./T. = unpublished material. Aside from the Elamite texts, the Persepolis archives contained one Akkadian Treasury text (PT 85) and one Akkadian Fortification text (W. M. Stolper, 'The Neo-Babylonian Text from the

Persepolis Fortification', *JNES* 43, 1984, 299–310), together with 700 (as yet un-published) Aramaic Fortification tablets, and one Greek (Hallock, PFT, 2) and one Phrygian tablet. As already pointed out, the discontinuance of the tradition after 458 is to be explained by the administration's switch to the Aramaic script and language and the corresponding (transient and non-preserved) writing materials. Comprehensive historical analyses of the texts have also been made by W. Hinz ('Achämenidische Hofverwaltung', *ZA* 61, 1971, 260–311; *Darius und die Perser*, 2 vols, Baden-Baden 1976–79), H. Koch (*Verwaltung und Wirtschaft im persischen Kernland zur Zeit der Achämeniden*, Wiesbaden 1990; *Es kündet Dareios der König. Vom Leben im persischen Großreich*, Mainz 1992) and D. M. Lewis ('The Persepolis Fortification Texts', *AchHist* IV, Leiden 1990, 1–6). In addition, there are plenty of special studies and contributions which will be mentioned where relevant. On the Babylonian sources see A. Kuhrt, 'Achaemenid Babylonia: Sources and Problems', *AchHist* IV, Leiden 1990, 177–94; historical analysis of the material has been carried out by id., 'The Achaemenid Empire: A Babylonian Perspective', *PCPhS* 214, 1988, 60–76, and especially M. W. Stolper, *Entrepreneurs and Empire*, Leiden 1985. On the Aramaic language and script, see S. Segert, *Altaramäische Grammatik*, Leipzig 4th edn 1990, on sources in this language see E. Lipinski's report ('Araméen d'Empire', *La langue dans l'antiquité*, ed. P. Swiggers/A. Wouters, Louvain 1990, 94–133). The Stele of Xanthus: H. Metzger/E. Laroche/A. Dupont-Sommer/M. Mayrhofer, *Fouilles de Xanthos VI: La stèle trilingue du Letôon*, Paris 1979. On the Greek authors there is often a lack of historico-philological commentaries on the 'Iranian' sections of their work, an exception being D. Asheri's commentary on Herodotus's Book III (*Erodoto. Le Storie, Libro III: La Persia*, Milan 1990). On Xenophon's *Anabasis* and *Cyropaedia* see Ch. Tuplin, 'Modern and Ancient Travellers in the Achaemenid Empire: Byron's *Road to Oxiana* and Xenophon's *Anabasis*', *AchHist* VII, Leiden 1991, 37–57, and H. Sancisi-Weerdenburg, 'The Death of Cyrus: Xenophon's *Cyropaedia* as a Source for Iranian History', *AcIr* 25, 1985, 459–71. There is a particularly regrettable lack of commentaries on Plutarch ('The Life of Artaxerxes'), Strabo and Xenophon. On the Hellenocentrism of the sources (and research) see H. Sancisi-Weerdenburg, in *Bibliotheca Orientalis* 44, 1987, 489–95. On the fourth-century authors, see below. The latest edition of the text of Darius's letter to Gadatas, by F. Lochner-Hüttenbach, is in Brandenstein/Mayrhofer (see above), 91–98. On the Sardis inscription see F. Gschnitzer, 'Eine persische Kultstiftung in Sardeis und die "Sippengötter" Vorderasiens', *Im Bannkreis des Alten Orients* (Festschrift K. Oberhuber), Innsbruck 1986, 45–54. The alleged inscription on Cyrus's tomb is competently discussed by R. Schmitt, 'Achaimenideninschriften in griechischer literarischer Überlieferung', *AcIr* 28, 1988, 17–38; see also Heinrichs, '"Asiens König". Die Inschriften des Kyrosgrabs und das achämenidische Reichsverständnis', *Zu Alexander d. Gr. Festschrift G. Wirth*, vol. 1, Amsterdam 1987, 487–540. On further Greek sources and Greek knowledge about cuneiform script see R. Schmitt, 'Assyria

Grammata und ähnliche. Was wußten die Griechen von Keilschrift und Keil-inschriften?', *Zum Umgang mit fremden Sprachen in der griechisch-römischen Antike*, ed. C. W. Müller et al., Stuttgart 1992, 21–35.

On the books of the Old Testament, see the introduction by W. H. Schmidt, Berlin 5th edn 1995, and on their historical context see H. Donner, *Geschichte des Volkes Israel und seiner Nachbarn in Grundzügen*, vol. 2, 2nd edn Göttingen 1995.

On the Avesta the most important data may be found in the article of that title by J. Kellens in *EncIr* III, 1989, 35–44.

2. (pp. 13–21)   The Bisutun Inscription (DB) is published with commentaries in the *Corpus Inscriptionum Iranicarum* (Babyl. version by E. v. Voigtlander, London 1978; Aram. version by J. C. Greenfield/B. Porten, London 1982; OP version by R. Schmitt, London 1991). A German translation (of all versions) by R. Borger/W. Hinz can be found in *Texte aus der Umwelt des Alten Testaments*, vol. 1, Gütersloh 1982–85, 419–50. The most important data on relief and inscription (as well as the historical context) are to be found in the article 'Bīsotūn' in *EncIr* IV, 1990, 289–305 (authors: H. Luschey/R. Schmitt). The new reading of the crucial passages of § 70 of the OP version, in which Darius talks about the 'invention of the script', is the work of R. Schmitt (*Epigraphisch-exegetische Noten zu Dareios' Bisutun-Inschriften*, Vienna 1990, 56–60), who rightly reads *dipiçira* ('script form'). Darius first speaks about the Old Persian cuneiform script and then ('besides, in Aryan') about the 'inner form', about the possibility 'to write' a text 'in Aryan [Persian]' as well. Persian sacrifices: Hdt. III 131f; sacrifices to the mountains: PF 1955. 1960. Comparison with *res gestae*: F. Hampl, '"Denkwürdigkeiten" und "Tatenberichte" aus der Alten Welt als histor-ische Dokumente', *Geschichte als kritische Wissenschaft*, vol. 3, ed. I. Weiler, Darmstadt 1979, 167–220. Translation of §§ 60–61 based on Schmitt (see above); this edition is also used in the subsequent text. Replica from Babylon: U. Seidl, 'Ein Relief Dareios' I. in Babylon, *AMI* N. F. 9, 1976, 125–30. About the relief composition and its prototypes see M. C. Root, *The King and Kingship in Achaemenid Art*, Leiden 1979, *passim*. Winged man: X^{v}arənah: P. Calmeyer, 'Fortuna – Tyche – Khvarnah', *JDAI* 94, 1979, 347–65; most recent interpretation as Ahura Mazda by W. Nagel/B. Jacobs, 'Königsgräber und Sonnengottheit bei altiranischen Dynastien', *IrAnt* 24, 1989, 337–89. Scythian campaign: this campaign is not to be mistaken (or equated) with the campaign against the 'European Scythians' reported by Herodotus. On the special character of the Aramaic script: quotation from Borger, *Chronologie*, 28. DNb quota-tion in the Aramaic copy: N. Sims-Williams, 'The Final Paragraph of the Tomb-Inscription of Darius I (DNb, 50–60)', *BSOAS* 44, 1981, 1–7. My observations about (the ahistorical character of) the relief composition are based on P. Calmeyer, 'Dareios in Bagastana und Xerxes in Persepolis. Zur parataktischen Komposition achaimeni-discher Herrscherdarstellungen', *Visible Religion* 4/5 1985/86, 76–95.

3. (pp. 21–6) Persepolis. A short but pertinent characterization of Achaemenid art by P. Calmeyer can be found in the excellent (and richly illustrated) work *Der Alte Orient*, ed. B. Hrouda, Gütersloh 1990, 418–42. An 'archaeological guide' to P. by P. Calmeyer/W. Kleiss is forthcoming. I have also derived great benefit from the works of M. C. Root, especially from her exhibition catalogue *Crowning Glories. Persian Kingship and the Power of Creative Continuity*, Ann Arbor 1990. The results of excavations in Persepolis were published by E. F. Schmidt, *Persepolis I–III*, Chicago 1953–70, and A. B. Tilia, *Studies and Restorations at Persepolis and other Sites of Fars*, vols I–II, Rome 1972–78. An impression of the grandeur of the site is conveyed in *Persepolis-Rekonstruktionen* by F. Krefter (Berlin 1971). The attractive catalogue of the exhibition *Persepolis*, Mainz 1988, was produced by L. Trümpelmann (although with certain rather unconventional interpretations). On the history of Persepolis see Calmeyer, 'Das Persepolis der Spätzeit', *AchHist* IV, Leiden 1990, 7–36. Ancient account of Persepolis: D.S. XVII 70f (Engl. transl. C. Bradford Welles). On the reliefs of the 'tribute bearers' and the 'enthroned king' see G. Walser, *Die Völkerschaften auf den Reliefs von Persepolis,* Berlin 1966. DNa 38–47: transl. after R. G. Kent. On the message of the reliefs and the function of Persepolis, see the opinions of Calmeyer, *Dareios in Bagastana* (see above) and Sancisi-Weerdenburg, 'Nowruz in Persepolis', *AchHist* VII, Leiden 1991, 173–201. Greeks in Persepolis: graffiti by Pytharchus and others (G. Pugliese Caratelli, 'Greek Inscriptions in the Middle East', *East and West* 16, 1966, 31–6); Greek male and female workers: PF 1798 et al., PT 15; PF 1224. Persepolis and Athens: Root, 'The Parthenon Frieze and the Apadana Reliefs at Persepolis: Reassessing a Programmatic Relationship', *AJA* 89, 1985, 103–20. On the destiny of Persepolis: see below; on the result of the fire: Sancisi-Weerdenburg, 'Alexander and Persepolis', *Alexander the Great: Reality and Myth*, Rome 1993, 177–88.

4. (pp. 26–8) On Pasargadae see the excavation report by D. Stronach, *Pasargadae*, Oxford 1978; on the *paradeisos*, id., 'The Royal Garden at Pasargadai', *Archaeologia Iranica et Orientalis* (Festschrift L. Vanden Berghe), vol. 1, Ghent 1989, 475–502. Site of the battle against the Medes: Str. XV 3, 8. Function of the *Zindān*: see Sancisi-Weerdenburg, 'The Zendan and the Ka'bah', *Kunst, Kultur und Geschichte der Achämenidenzeit und ihr Fortleben*, ed. H. Koch/D. N. MacKenzie, Berlin 1983, 145–51 (buildings for royal investiture), and G. Ahn, *Religiöse Herrscherlegitimation im achämenidischen Iran* (*AcIr* 31), Leiden 1992, 203ff (building for preserving the royal fire). Royal investiture: P. Briant, 'Le roi est mort: vive le roi', *La religion iranienne à l'époque achéménide*, ed. J. Kellens, Ghent 1991, 1–11.

   On Susa in the Achaemenid period, see the comprehensive summary by R. Boucharlat, 'Suse et la Susiane à l'époque achéménide', *AchHist* IV, Leiden 1990, 149–75. This city is presented in a broader historical and cultural context by the exhibition catalogue *The Royal City of Susa*, ed. P. O. Harper et al., New York 1992.

DSf 22–55: transl. after R. G. Kent. On the Darius statue see J. Perrot et al., in *CDAFI* 4, 1974; on the composition and historical background Ch. Tuplin and P. Calmeyer, in *AchHist* VI, Leiden 1991, 237–83 and 285–303, respectively.

On Naqsh-i Rustam see the literature quoted for Persepolis. The coins are discussed by I. Carradice, 'The "Regal" Coinage of the Persian Empire', *Coinage and Administration in the Athenian and Persian Empires*, ed. I. C., Oxford 1987, 73–107, L. Mildenberg, über das Münzwesen im Reich der Achämeniden', *AMI* N.F. 26, 1993, 55–79, as well as in numerous contributions to the omnibus volume *L'or perse et l'histoire grecque* (REA 91, 1–2), Bordeaux 1989 (1990). On seals, essential data are found in Root, *Crowning Glories,* 32–45. A corpus of the seals of the Persepolis tablets is forthcoming. Other art objects are presented by P. R. S. Moorey, 'The Persian Empire', *CAH.* Plates to Vol. IV², ed. J. Boardman et al., Cambridge 1988, 45–94. Prototypes for parts of the 'Achaemenid style': Apadana: Hasanlu, Media; gate-guarding genii: Assyria, Elam; brick reliefs: Babylonia, Elam; coins with the motif of a lion killing a bull: Lydia; rock tombs, towers, changing colours in stone architecture: Urartu; own creations: column capitals with foreparts of bulls, pavilion-shaped palace architecture (details after Calmeyer, in *Der Alte Orient* [see above], 439f).

On regional-local art we might refer to the steles from Dascylium (M. Nollé, *Denkmäler vom Satrapensitz Daskyleion*, Berlin 1992) or the funerary art of Lycia (*Götter, Heroen, Herrscher in Lykien*, Vienna/Munich 1990), on the Graeco-Roman 'images' to the 'Alexander mosaic' (B. Andreae, *Das Alexandermosaik aus Pompeji*, Recklinghausen 1977) or the 'Darius vase' from Naples; on the 'Persian fashion' in Athens and elsewhere, see M. Miller, *Perserie. The Arts of the East in Fifth Century Athens*, Ph.D. Cambridge/Mass. 1985, and M. C. Root, 'From the Heart. Powerful Persianisms in the Art of the Western Empire', *AchHist* VI, Leiden 1991, 1–29.

2. The King and his Subjects: 1–4

1. (pp. 29–33)   On the kingship of the Achaemenid rulers and on their legitimacy to the throne see the summary in R. Schmitt, 'Achaemenid Dynasty', in the *EncIr* (see above), and especially G. Ahn, *Religiöse Herrscherlegitimation im achämenidischen Iran (AcIr* 31), Leiden 1992. On the iconographical representation of the 'royal ideology' see the pioneering work by M. C. Root, *The King and Kingship in Achaemenid Art*, Leiden 1979. Royal titulature: R. Schmitt, 'Königtum im Alten Iran', *Saeculum* 28, 1977, 384–95; B. Kienast, 'Zur Herkunft der achämenidischen Königstitulatur', *Festschrift für H. R. Roemer*, Beirut 1979, 351–64. Xerxes's reduction of the formula 'king of the countries containing all races' to 'king of the countries containing many races' is considered to be connected with his acknowledgement of his defeat by the Greeks. The reader is reminded that in those parts of the empire that had their specific monarchic traditions (e.g. Babylonia and Egypt) the kings

sought to emphasize their legitimacy as rulers by adopting the native titles. Thus Cyrus proclaims in the 'Cyrus Cylinder' (see below): 'I am Cyrus, king of the world, great king, mighty king, king of Babylon, king of Sumer and Akkad, king of the four quarters [of the world]', and Darius calls himself, in the Egyptian inscription on his statue from Heliopolis/Susa, 'the king of Upper and Lower Egypt, ... the living image of Re'. Achaemenes: (mythical?) forefather of Darius and eponymous ancestor of the family; Cyrus does not mention him in his genealogy on the Cyrus Cylinder; if it is true that the alleged inscriptions of Cyrus from Pasargadae, in which he calls himself an Achaemenid, only go back to Darius, then we may have doubts about Cyrus's belonging to the Achaemenid clan (J. Wiesehöfer, *Der Aufstand Gaumātas und die Anfänge Dareios'* I, Bonn 1978, 186ff); a different opinion: C. Herrenschmidt, 'Notes sur la parenté chez les Perses au début de l'empire achéménide', *AchHist* II, Leiden 1987, 66–67. *Alexander and the Achaemenids*: P. Briant, *Alexandre le Grand*, Paris 4th edn 1994, 89ff. Succession to the throne: ancient quotation: Plu. Art. 2; Xerxes and Demaratus: Hdt. VII 3. Throne-names: R. Schmitt, 'Thronnamen bei den Achaimeniden', *Beiträge zur Namenforschung*, N. F. 12, 1977, 422–25; id., 'Achaemenid Throne-Names', *AION* 42, 1982, 83–95. Synarchy: P. Calmeyer, 'Zur Genese altiranischer Motive', V: Synarchie', *AMI* N. F. 9, 1976, 63–95. King and Gods: Calmeyer, 'Zur bedingten Göttlichkeit des Großkönigs', *AMI* N. F., 14, 1981, 55–60; see also H. Humbach, 'Herrscher, Gott und Gottessohn in Iran und in angrenzenden Ländern', *Menschwerdung Gottes – Vergöttlichung von Menschen*, ed. D. Zeller, Freiburg/Göttingen 1988, 89–114; Ahn, *Herrscherlegitimation*, 18off. Death of a king and accession of his successor to the throne: see P. Briant, 'Le roi est mort: vive le roi!', *La religion iranienne à l'époque achéménide*, ed. J. Kellens, Ghent 1991, 1–11, an article to which we are indebted for the following passage. Funeral procession of Artaxerxes I: Ctesias (*FGrHist* 688 F 15). Royal initiation: Plu. Art. 3, 1–2 (Eng. transl. Bernadotte Perrin, Loeb Classics); function of the Zindān: see above. Ceremonies and 'Divine Right' in the inscriptions: C. Herrenschmidt, 'Les créations d'Ahuramazda', *StIr* 6, 1977, 24. Royal qualities: quotation: DNb 5–45; *hainā, dušiyāra, drauga*: DPd 15–20 (with parallels in the Avesta); on all this see Ahn, *Herrscherlegitimation*, 246ff.

2. (pp. 34–8) For this section we are much indebted to the highly stimulating article of P. Briant, 'Hérodote et la société perse', *Hérodote et les peuples non grecs* (Entretiens sur l'Antiquité Classique, t. 35), Vandoeuvres/Geneva 1990, 69–113; see also P. Calmeyer, 'Zur Darstellung von Standesunterschieden in Persepolis', *AMI* N. F., 24, 1991, 35–51. A 'Prosopography of the Persian empire from 550 to 450 BC' by J. M. Balcer was published in Lewiston 1993. Ps.-Arist., Mu. 398 a. Interpretation of DPd: Briant, *Rois, tributs et paysans*, Paris 1982, 435–56. Darius as a 'gardener': W. Fauth, 'Der königliche Gärtner und Jäger im Paradeisos', *Persica* 8, 1979, 1–53. In this connection we might point to a passage in the king's letter to Gadatas: 'That

you cultivate my land by planting fruit from beyond the Euphrates in the coastal regions of Asia Minor, this decision of yours I praise, and therefore great favour will be reserved for you in the house of the king.' Herodotus about Persian tribes and clans: I 125; on the differentiation between nomadic and farming tribes see Briant, 'Hérodote' (see above), 78–81. Ancient Iranian concepts: Briant, 'La Perse avant l'Empire', *IrAnt* 19, 1984, 105–10. On the 'revalorization' of Persis by Darius: F. Gschnitzer, 'Zur Stellung des persischen Stammlandes im Achaimenidenreich', *Ad bene et fideliter seminandum. Festgabe K. Deller z. 21. Februar 1987* (AOAT, 220), Neukirchen 1988, 87–122. *Skauθi-/tunuvant-*: DNb 8–11; the Babylonian version shows that this is not a contrast between 'free' or 'unfree' people. Greek sources: Hdt. VII 40–41 (contrast between the 'best and noblest of the Persians' – [horsemen] 'selected among all Persians'); I 133 (contrast between 'rich' [*eudaimones*] and 'poor' [*penētes*]); Str. XV 3, 19 ('leaders' [*hēgemones*] – 'the masses' [*hoi polloi*]); Strabo quotation: XV 3, 20; see Hdt. I 134; Aelianus: V.H. I 31. Hierarchy of nobility: cf. Hdt. I 96 et al. (*dokimoi*) with III 155 (*dokimōtatos*) or III 74 (*en ainē – en ainē megistē*), I 206 et al. (*prōtoi*) – D.S. XIX 22, 2 (*tōn Persōn hoi malista timōmenoi*); XIX 48, 5 (*henos de tōn epiphanestatōn*) et al. '*Pater familias*': Hdt. I 137; IV 84; VII 38–39; see also Ael. V.H. I 34; Intaphernes: Hdt. III 119; succession: Hdt. VIII 130; Arr. An. II 1, 3. Polygamy and the large number of children: Hdt. I 135s; quotation: Str. XV 3, 17. But I am not sure whether we can really speak of a 'politique nataliste' of the great king (see Briant, *Hérodote*, 85). Privileges of the fellow conspirators: Hdt. III 84. 118; Otanes: III 83–84; D.S. XXXI 19; Plb. V 43. Darius's marriages: Hdt. VII 2. 97; III 68–69; VII 224. See C. Herrenschmidt, 'Notes sur la parenté chez les Perses', *AchHist* II, Leiden 1987, 58–61; Darius II and Parysatis: Ctes. (*FGrHist* 688 F 15). Endogamous policy of the kings: on marriage between siblings see below; *syngeneis*: they are probably to be considered as true 'relatives' of the king, not as bearers of an honorary title; see J.-D. Gauger, 'Zu einem offenen Problem des hellenistischen Hoftitelsystems', *Bonner Festgabe J. Straub*, Bonn 1977, 137–58. On *polydōria* see below; on 'friends' and 'benefactors' of the great king see Wiesehöfer's 'Zu den "Freunden" und "Wohltätern" des Großkönigs' in *StIr* 9, 1980, 7–21. *kurtaš*: see below.

3. (pp. 38–41) On the 'king on tour' see the informative essay by P. Briant, 'Le nomadisme du Grand Roi', *IrAnt* 23, 1988, 253–73. Subjects bearing gifts: quotations: Ael. V.H. I 31; I 33. On the significance of water (as a gift, etc.) to the king, see Briant, 'L'eau du Grand Roi', *Drinking in Ancient Societies*, ed. L. Milano, Padova 1994, 45–65. Sojourn in the residences: quotation: X. Cyr. VIII 6, 22. Further evidence: Str. XVI 1, 16; Ath. XII 513–14; Ael. N.A. III, 13; X 16; climatic conditions: Str. XV 3, 10; D.S. XIX 19, 2; 21, 2–3; 28, 1–2; 39, 1; change of residence and 'effeminacy': X. Ages. 9. A quite different interpretation of the Achaemenid 'king on tour', though clearly with a contemporary bias, is provided by Aelius

Aristides: 'Because of their mistrust and their fear of residing at the same place, they in truth kept their own country on a tight rein and thus controlled now Babylon, now Susa and finally Ecbatana, without being able to maintain their country constantly as a whole, and without caring for it like good shepherds' (Aristid. Rom. 18). Gifts: Ael. V.H. (see above); Plu. Art. 4, 5; spectators: Curt. IV 16, 15; see D.S. XVIII 28, 1; reception in the cities and residences: most of our texts describe the reception of Alexander (e.g. in Babylon: Curt. V 1, 17–23) or of Hellenistic kings, but we cannot go wrong in assuming that this corresponds with Achaemenid customs. Preparation of journeys: Hdt. VII 32; Ael. NA. XV 26; ceremonials: e.g. Curt. V 1, 17–23; Arr. An. III 16, 3. Sinaites and Artaxerxes: Ael. V.H. I 32; see Plu. Art. 4, 5; 5, 1; popularity of Artaxerxes and his wife Statira: Plu. Art. 5, 6. Entertaining the king: Theopomp. Hist. (Ath. IV 145 a); Uruk: M. A. Dandamayev, 'Royal *paradeisoi* in Babylonia', *AcIr* 23, 1984, 113–17; urban expenditures: Hdt. VII 118–20. Banquet: quotation: Heraclid. (Ath. IV 145 a–f); see P. Briant, 'Table du roi, tribut et re-distribution chez les Achéménides', *Le tribut dans l'Empire perse*, ed. P. Briant/ C. Herrenschmidt, Paris 1989, 35–44 and H. Sancisi-Weerdenburg, 'Persian Food: Stereotypes and Political Identity', *Food in Antiquity*, ed. J. Wilkins et al., Exeter 1995, 286–302. Royal baggage-train and suite in Cilicia: Curt. III 3, 14–25; 13, 10–11; booty in Damascus: Ath. XIII 608 a. Table luxury and 'effeminacy': Polyaen. IV 3, 32. The combination of table requisites handed down by this author is commented upon by D. M. Lewis, 'The King's Dinner (Polyaen. IV 3, 32)', *AchHist* II, Leiden 1987, 79–87. Royal tent: Curt. III 3, 8 et al.; cf. H. v. Gall, 'Das persische Königszelt und die Hallenarchitektur in Iran und Griechenland', *Festschrift für F. Brommer*, ed. U. Höckmann/A. Krug, Mainz 1977, 119–32; Alexander and the royal insignia: Arr. An. II 11, 5; Curt. III 11, 12; D.S. XVII 34, 3–6. Cf. Arr. An. II 11, 6; Plu. Alex. 21, 2; Curt. III 12, 5 ff; D.S. XVII 37, 3 (on Alexander's definite assumption of the insignia).

4. (pp. 42–55) Preliminary reflections of the author on this section are already contained in his article 'Kyros und die unterworfenen Völker', *QdS* 13. 26, 1987, 107–26. On Xerxes see also the article by H. Sancisi-Weerdenburg, 'The Personality of Xerxes, King of Kings', *Archaeologia Iranica et Orientalis*, Miscellanea in honorem L. Vanden Berghe, ed. L. de Meyer/E. Haerinck, vol. 1, Ghent 1989, 549–61. Encyclopaedia article: *Meyers Enzyklopädisches Lexikon in 25 Bänden*, 9th edn, Mann-heim, Vienna/Zurich: vol. 14, 1975, 525 (Cyrus), and vol. 25, 1979, 554 (Xerxes). Cyrus in the Iranian tradition: alleged inscriptions from Pasargadae (which were in fact those of Darius): J. Wiesehöfer, *Der Aufstand Gaumātas und die Anfänge Dareios' I.*, Bonn 1978, 15 with note 4; 186–98; 226–9; Pasargadae and Cyrus's tomb: archaeo-logy: see above; the ancient tradition is found in Aristobul. *FGrHist* 139 F 51 b (=Str. XV 3, 7); cf. Arr. An. VI 29, 4–11; Cyrus in 'popular tradition': P. Briant, *Rois, tributs et paysans*, Paris 1982, 491–506, and H. Sancisi-Weerdenburg, 'The Death

of Cyrus', *AcIr* 25, 1985, esp. 461–3. Herodotus and Cyrus: military and political skill: see I 77; 79; 126; 191; mildness and kindness: I 86–90 (Croesus); see I 130; III 159; Cyrus as 'father': III 89. Xenophon, *Cyr.*: quotation I 1, 6; VIII 8, 1–2 (Eng. transl. Walter Miller, Loeb Classics). Cyrus in the 'Old Testament': 2 Chr. 36, 22–23; Ezra I, 1–8; 3, 7; 4, 3–5; 5, 13–17; 6, 13–14; Isaiah 44, 24–28; 45, 1–9; Dan. 1, 21; 6, 29; 10, 1; quotation: Isaiah 44, 24. 28; 45, 1 (transl. King James version) Cyrus in Babylonian sources: A. Kuhrt, 'Babylonia from Cyrus to Xerxes', *CAH* IV, Cambridge 2nd edn 1988, 112–38; Cyrus Cylinder: P.-R. Berger, 'Der Kyros-Zylinder mit dem Zusatzfragment BIN II Nr. 32 und die akkadischen Personennamen im Danielbuch', *ZA* 64, 1975, 193–203; on the character and content: Kuhrt, 'The Cyrus Cylinder and Achaemenid Imperial Policy', *JSOT* 25, 1983, 83–94; quotation: Vv. 7–8. 11–12. 20–22. 24–26. 30–32 (Eng. transl. A.L. Oppenheim). Life of Xerxes: parents: Hdt. VII 2; education (quotation): Pl. Lg. 695 d–e (Eng. transl. T. J. Saunders); successors of Darius: Hdt. VII 3–4; rebellions: Hdt. VII 4–5 (Egypt); on the rebellions in Babylonia 481 and 479 see Briant, 'La date des révoltes babyloniennes contre Xerxès', *StIr* 21, 1992, 7–20; quotation (conduct in Egypt): Hdt. VII 7 (Eng. transl. A. de Sélincourt); Xerxes and Esagila: quotations: Hdt. I 183 and Str. XVI 1, 5; episodes on the Greek expedition: punishing the Hellespont: Hdt. VII 36; the son of Pythius: VII 38–39; Leonidas's body insulted: VII 235; the Acropolis burnt: VIII 53; Xerxes and the women of his court: IX 108–113; death: Ctes. *FGrHist* 688 F 13; Xerxes reliefs: the geometrical and thematic centre of the two Apadana façades in Persepolis must originally have contained the 'Treasury reliefs', but these were later removed and replaced by images of Persian and Median guards (A. B. Tilia, *Studies and Restorations at Persepolis and Other Sites of Fars*, I, Rome 1972, 173ff); A. Sh. Shahbazi has plausibly explained the 'storage' of the Treasury reliefs ('The Persepolis "Treasury Reliefs" Once More', *AMI* N. F. 9, 1976, 151–56): for the successor of Xerxes, Artaxerxes I, the portraits of his father and brother (Darius is portrayed on them as crown prince behind his father Xerxes) were sacrosanct, and those of the murderers and conspirators (who were presumably also portrayed) intolerable. The reliefs were therefore taken into the Treasury and replaced by those of the guards who had beaten back the usurper. Aeschylus: *Pers.* 754ff. XPh: see R. G. Kent, *Old Persian*, New Haven 2nd edn, 1953, 112; on the new copy from Pasargadae, the most recent account is by D. Stronach, *Pasargadae*, Oxford 1978, 152 and pls 123, 161b; quotation XPh 28–41. XPl: W. Hinz, *Altiranische Funde und Forschungen*, Berlin 1969, 45ff; on justifying the abbreviation XPl (instead of XDNb) see K. Hoffmann, in *Die Sprache* 20, 1974, 16 n. 4. Xerxes's 'lack of spiritual independence': quotation: Hinz, *Darius und die Perser*, vol. 2, Baden-Baden 1979, 11. Cyrus in Herodotus: negative aspects: I 114–15. 141. 153. 189; see J. G. Gammie 'Herodotus on Kings and Tyrants', *JNES* 45, 1986, 178–9; death: I 204–14; see Sancisi-Weerdenburg, 'Death' (see above), 464–6; Herodotus and Iranian oral tradition: see I 214; on the background of the 'legend' about the exposure of Cyrus see

G. Binder, *Die Aussetzung des Königskindes Kyros und Romulus*, Meisenheim 1964, 17–28, 175–82, and R. Drews, 'Sargon, Cyrus and Mesopotamian Folk History', *JNES* 33, 1974, 387–93. Xenophon, *Cyr.*: character: see Sancisi-Weerdenburg, 'Death' (see above), 459: 'Is it a didactic pamphlet, a romantic history, a fictitious biography, a philosophical treatise or a combination of some or all these elements?'; 'Greek character': H. R. Breitenbach, 'Xenophon von Athen', RE IX A 2, 2nd edn 1983, passim; Iranian influence: among others W. Knauth/S. Nadjmabadi, *Das altiranische Fürstenideal von Xenophon bis Ferdousi*, Wiesbaden 1975, and Sancisi-Weerdenburg, *Yaunā en Persai*, Groningen 1981, 185ff (with earlier literature). Cyrus in the 'Old Testament': quotations: E. Zenger, 'Israels Suche nach einem neuen Selbstverständnis zu Beginn der Perserzeit', *Bibel und Kirche*, 1984 3, 123; Historicity of Cyrus's actions: ib., 123–4. 'Cyrus Cylinder': see Kuhrt, *Cyrus Cylinder* (see above). Cyrus and Astyages: Nabonidus Chronicle II 3–4 (A. K. Grayson, *Assyrian and Babylonian Chronicles*, Locust Valley/New York 1975, 106); fate of Astyages: Hdt. I 130; Ctes. *FGrHist* 688 F 9; Sippar Cylinder (transl. H. Tadmor, 'The Inscriptions of Nabunaid', *Studies in Honor of B. Landsberger*, Chicago 1965, 351). Cyrus in Babylonia: A. Kuhrt, 'Nabonidus and the Babylonian Priesthood', *Pagan Priests*, ed. M. Beard/J. North, Ithaca 1990, 117–55; criticism of Cyrus: 'Dynastic Prophecy' II 22–24 (Grayson, *Babylonian Historical Literary Texts*, Toronto 1975, 25); Nabonidus's fate: 'Dynastic Prophecy' II 20–21 (Grayson 33); Berossus *FGrHist* 680 F 9 (indulgence); otherwise: X. *Cyr.* VII 5, 29–33. Cyrus and Croesus: Nabonidus Chronicle II 15–17 (Grayson, *Chronicles*, 107): in general, the missing name of the country west of the Tigris is supplied as *Lu-u(d)-du;* on the argument see Wiesehöfer, *Kyros*, 124–5; Eus. Chron. (Armen.) p. 33, 8–9 Kaerst: 'Croesus was killed by Cyrus, who eliminated the Lydian sovereignty'; vase painting of Myson: G 197 (J. Beazley, *Attic Red Figure Vase Painters*, Oxford 2nd edn 1963, 238, 1); Hdt. I 86ff; Bacchyl. 3, 23ff Maehler. On all this see W. Burkert, 'Das Ende des Kroisos', *Catalepton*. Festschrift B. Wyss, ed. Ch. Schäublin, Basel 1985, 4–15 (quotation: p. 14). After the Pactyas revolt, Cyrus apparently had followers of this rebel deported to Mesopotamia, where they are mentioned in the texts of the Murašû archives (I. Eph'al, 'The Western Minorities in Babylonia in the 6th–5th Centuries B.C.E.', *Orientalia* N. S. 47, 1978, 80, 83). Cyrus and Ionia: Ionian troops on Croesus's side: Hdt. I 75; Cyrus's reaction: Hdt. I 141; Priene and Magnesia: Hdt. I 161; Harpagus campaign: Hdt. I 162ff; Phocaea and Teos: Hdt. I 162. 168; Smyrna: E. Akurgal, *Alt-Smyrna I*, Ankara 1983, 50–56, 74–75, 123 (and ills); Phocaeans clearing their temples: Hdt. I 164; tribute imposed on Ionians: Hdt. I 171; see II 1; III 1. 31; burden of taxation: V. La Bua, 'La prima conquista persiana della Ionia', *Studi E. Manni*, vol. 4, Rome 1980, 1291. Herodotus's portrait of Xerxes: Sancisi-Weerdenburg personality (see above), 552–57; decision to fight against Greece: Hdt. VII 5. 7.18; 'divine intervention': in this connection, we are particularly reminded of Xerxes's dreams in Hdt. (H. A. Gärtner, 'Les rêves de Xerxès et d'Artabane chez Hérodote', *Ktema* 8, 1983, 11–18;

H. Schwabl, 'Zu den Träumen bei Homer und Herodot', *Arētēs Mnēmē*, Athens 1983, 17–27); the king at Salamis: Hdt. VIII 67 reports that before the battle, Xerxes paid a visit to the fleet and took the first seat (*proizeto*); see also VIII 69: 'Nevertheless his orders were that the advice of the majority should be followed, for he believed that in the battles off Euboea his men had shirked their duty because he was not himself present – whereas this time he had made arrangements to watch the fight with his own eyes' (transl. A. de Sélincourt). 'Deeper meaning' of the Masistes-story: Sancisi-Weerdenburg, *Yaunā* (see above), 48ff, 122ff; Hdt. quotation: IX 110–11; yet another cruelty of Amestris (Hdt. VII 114) may be explained as a 'religious-ritual' rather than a 'personal' act (Sancisi-Weerdenburg, *Yaunā*, 65). Similar motives may also be assumed for Xerxes's punishment of the Hellespont. Xerxes in Babylonia: quotation: Hinz, *Darius und die Perser*, vol. 2, 17; Xerxes's policies in Babylonia: A. Kuhrt/S. Sherwin-White, 'Xerxes's Destruction of Babylonian Temples', *AchHist* II, Leiden 1987, 69–78. '*Daivā* inscription': Sancisi-Weerdenburg, *Yaunā*, 1ff; the 'timeless' interpretation of the inscription is also suggested by the presumable late dating (Sancisi-Weerdenburg, ib.). However, Ahn in *Herrscherlegitimation*, 111ff, considers XPh as proof that concrete steps were being taken towards the 'Iranization' of Fars. Imitations of inscriptions and reliefs: XE and XV are also to be explained in this sense. Sacrifice in Athens: Hdt. VIII 54. Cyrus and his 'models': J. Harmatta, 'The Literary Patterns of the Babylonian Edict of Cyrus', *AAntHung* 19, 1971, 217–31; Kuhrt, *Cyrus Cylinder* (see above), esp. 88; R. J. van der Spek, 'Cyrus de Pers in Assyrisch perspectief', *TvG* 96, 1983, 1–27. Methods of Cyrus and Xerxes: quotation: G. Walser, *Hellas und Iran*, Darmstadt 1984, 14.

3. The Empire, the Peoples and the Tributes: 1–3

1. (p. 56–9) Quotation: DB I 11–12; *xšaçam manā frābara* and the like: DB I 12.24–25. 60–61; DPd 3–4; DPh 8; DSf 10–11; DSm 3; DSp 2; DZc 3–4; DH 6–7; D²Ha 23; A²Hc 18–19. 19–20. *Xšaça*: on its meaning 'kingdom', 'empire', rather than 'reign', see R. Schmitt, 'Königtum im Alten Iran', *Saeculum* 28, 1977, 391–92. *Xšaçapāvan-*/Satrap: Schmitt, 'Der Titel "Satrap"', *Studies in Greek, Italic and Indo-European Linguistics*. Offered to L. R. Palmer, Innsbruck 1976, 373–90. 'Land held by the kings': F. Gschnitzer, 'Zur Stellung des persischen Stammlandes im Achaimenidenreich', *Ad bene et fideliter seminandum*. Festgabe f. K. Deller, Neukirchen 1988, 94f; quotation: Th. VIII 18, 1. 'World empires': D. Metzler, 'Reichsbildung und Geschichtsbild bei den Achämeniden', Seminar: *Die Entstehung der antiken Klassengesellschaft*, ed. H. G. Kippenberg, Frankfurt 1977, 285–9, quotation: p. 285; idea of world empires at later periods: F. Vittinghoff, 'Zum geschichtlichen Selbstverständnis der Spätantike', *HZ* 198, 1964, 543ff. 'Romanization': W. Dahlheim, *Geschichte der römischen Kaiserzeit*, Munich 2nd edn 1989, 112–15. 241–7 (with

discussion on research); Tacitus quotation: Agr. 21. Persians and local élites: P. Briant, 'Pouvoir central et polycentrisme culturel dans l'Empire achéménide', *AchHist* I, Leiden 1987, 1–32 (Briant uses the term *ethno-classe dominante* for the Persian élite of the empire); he examines the policy of the great kings with respect to the local élites by using Egypt as an example: 'Ethno-classe dominante et populations soumises dans l'Empire achéménide: le cas de l'Egypte', *AchHist* III, Leiden 1988, 137–74; Mausolus: S. Hornblower, *Mausolus*, Oxford 1982; *Bēlšunu/Belesys*: M. W. Stolper, 'Bēlšunu the Satrap', *Language, Literature and History*. Philological and Historical Studies Presented to E. Reiner, New Haven 1987, 389–402; Memnon/Mentor: Briant, 'Les Iraniens d'Asie Mineure après la chute de l'Empire achéménide', *DHA* 11, 1985, 181–5 (the rise of these two was a result of their being connected with the family of the satrap of Phrygia-on-the-Hellespont). Persian 'exclusiveness': we should bear in mind that – especially since Darius I – the significance of Persia/Persis was emphasized in the empire as a whole (Gschnitzer, *Stellung*, 87–102; see [on Xerxes] F. Joannès, 'La titulature de Xerxès, *NABU* 25, 1989), and that Darius expressly referred to himself as *Pārsa, Pārsahya puça* ('a Persian, son of a Persian'). Positive view of the Achaemenids by the local élites: for a long time, Alexander's conquest of Babylon(ia) was believed to have been regarded by the local élite as an act of 'liberation' (see the accounts of the Alexander historians); nowadays this view is being challenged (see A. Kuhrt, 'The Achaemenid Empire. A Babylonian Perspective', *PCPhS* 214, 1988, 68–71). Alexander as an 'Achaemenid': Briant, *Rois, tributs et paysans*, Paris 1982, 318–30. 'Decentralization' and central control: Briant, 'Pouvoir central' (see above). 'Colossus on feet of clay': H. Bengtson, *Griechische Geschichte*, Munich 5th edn 1977, 387 (after W. Kolbe [1931]); this is rightly contradicted: H. Sancisi-Weerdenburg, 'Decadence in the Empire or Decadence in the Sources?', *AchHist* I, Leiden 1987, 33–46; Briant, 'Histoire et Idéologie: les Grecs et la "décadence perse"', *Mélanges P. Levêque*, vol. 2, Paris 1989, 33–47.

2. (pp. 59–62) This section owes its major observations to the works of P. Calmeyer and Ch. Tuplin. On the administration of satrapies in the late Persian empire, an appendix volume to *TAVO* by B. Jacobs has just been (1995) published. Th. Petit has presented *Satrapes et satrapies dans l'empire achéménide de Cyrus le Grand à Xerxès Ier* (Paris 1990). Calmeyer has made several contributions to the study of Achaemenid administrative or imperial units ('Zur Rechtfertigung einiger großköniglicher Inschriften und Darstellungen: Die Yaunā', *Kunst, Kultur und Geschichte der Achämenidenzeit und ihr Fortleben*, ed. H. Koch/D. N. MacKenzie, Berlin 1983, 153–67; 'Zur Genese altiranischer Motive, VIII: Die "statistische Landcharte" des Perserreiches', *AMI* N. F. 15, 1982, 105–87; 16, 1983, 141–222; 20, 1987, 129–46; 'Die sogenannte fünfte Satrapie und die achaimenidischen Documente', *Transeuphratène* 3, 1990, 109–29); to Tuplin we are indebted for the most comprehensive work on the Achaemenid system of administration and taxation ('The Administration of the

Achaemenid Empire', *Coinage and Administration in the Athenian and Persian Empires*, ed. I. Carradice, Oxford 1987, 109–66). *Dahyu-*: 'country': used in this sense in the editions of inscriptions by Weissbach and Kent (see above); oscillating between 'country' and 'people': C. Herrenschmidt, 'Désignation de l'Empire et concepts politiques de Darius Ier d'après ses inscriptions en vieux-perse', *StIr* 5, 1976, 49–50, 51–52, 62–63; Calmeyer, *Fünfte Satrapie* (see above, quotation: p. 110); 'people', 'population': most recent work P. Lecoq, 'Observations sur le sens du mot *dahyu* dans les inscriptions achéménides', *Transeuphratène* 3, 1990, 131–40. Classifying principle of inscriptional and iconographic 'lists': Calmeyer (see above); quotations: *AMI* N. F. 16, 1983, 218; 'Daivā inscription': XPh 13–28. Lists of army detachments: Hdt. VII 61ff 89; see Arr. An. III 8, 3–4. 11, 3; Curt. IV 12, 6–7; D.S. XVII 59 (Gaugamela); Curt. III 2, 1–2 (before Issus); Nep. Dat. 8 (on the army of Autophradates). Herodotus's 'fiscal units': III 89ff; see Calmeyer (see above). A quite different interpretation of the sources is provided by P. Högemann (*Das alte Vorderasien und die Achämeniden*, Wiesbaden 1992): he believes Herodotus's *nomoi* to be the provinces newly created by Darius (subdivisions of Cyrus's satrapies), which were modelled on Assyrian–Babylonian prototypes. Plato's Parts of the Empire: Lg. 695c–d; Ep. VII 332b; see Calmeyer, *AMI* N. F. 20, 1987, 133–40. Further lists: Calmeyer, *AMI* N. F. 15, 1982, 173ff. Lists of satrapies: D.S. XVIII 5–6. 39; Curt. X 10, 1–4; Just. XIII 4, 10–24; see Calmeyer (see above). Satraps: Different terms: Tuplin (see above) 114 n. 22. Högemann identifies the following (Western) 'names of countries' from DB with (Cyrus's) satrapies: Elam, Media, Aθurā, Egypt, Armenia, Katpatuka and Lydia. He maintains that in order to prevent secession by powerful satraps and for other reasons, Darius had undertaken territorial changes in the old Median empire and in Anatolia, and had divided the whole empire into provinces. In his opinion, military and civil authorities had been separated (between *strategoi/* satraps and provincial governors). Later there had been a 'feudalization of provinces and offices'. *Šakin māti*: Nabū-aḫḫē-bulliṭ (eighth year of the reign of Nabonidus until third year of Cyrus); Högemann considers this official as the model 'provincial governor' of Darius's reform. *Bēl pāḫati bābili ú ebir nāri*: Gubaru et al. (from the fourth year of Cyrus); on conditions in Babylonia see A. Kuhrt, 'Babylonia from Cyrus to Xerxes', *CAH* IV, Cambridge 2nd edn 1988, 112–38; F. Joannès, 'Pouvoirs locaux et organisations du territoire en Babylonie achéménide', *Transeuphratène* 3, 1990, 173–89. *Karanos*: Plu. Art. 2, 3; X. HG I 4, 3–4; < OP **kārana-* (R. Schmitt, 'Rez. G. Widengren, Feudalismus', *GGA* 223, 1971, 216–25); on functions: N. Sekunda, 'Achaemenid Military Terminology', *AMI* N. F. 21, 1988, 74. Dynasts and city kings: Tuplin (see above), 114–15. The formula 'dynasts, kings, cities, peoples', which is known from the Seleucid period, is assumed to be based on the Achaemenid model (see Briant, *Rois, tributs et paysans*, Paris 1982, 48 n. 3). Independent 'populations': e.g. in the uplands of Mysia, Pisidia/Lycaonia (see Tuplin, 114–15 n. 26). Achaemenid kings and 'peoples of the mountains': Briant, *État et pasteurs*, Paris/Cambridge

1982, 57–112; see Arr. An. III 17, 1ff: 'Leaving Susa and crossing the river Pasitigris [Karun], Alexander invaded the land of the Uxians. The Uxians who inhabited the plains had obeyed the Persian satrap, and now surrendered to Alexander; but the Uxian hillmen, as they were called, were not subject to Persia, and now sent a message to Alexander that they would only permit him to take the route towards Persia with his army if they received what they used to receive from the Persian king on his passage.' Alexander, however, broke their resistance with brutal violence, which points to the fact that he had a much more 'inflexible' concept of sovereignty. The hillmen, on their part, had supplied the Achaemenids with soldiers. 'Officials' on the satrapal level: on the honorary titles *philoi*, *homotrapezoi* and *skēptuchoi* see the evidence in Tuplin, 117 n. 32; cavalry commanders: X. HG III 4, 13; An. VI 4, 24–5; 'Men under the governor' etc. Neh. 4, 2. 23; 5, 10. 14–18; *syngeneis* of Spithridates: D.S. XVII 20, 2; 21, 2; *phoinikistēs*: X. An. I 2, 20; *grammateus*: Hdt. III 128; on further evidence for satrapal 'scribes' see Tuplin, 118; *dātabara* et al.: Tuplin, 118–20 (the Aramaic sources from Egypt distinguish between 'judges', 'provincial judges' and 'royal judges'); 'overseers': see OP **frasaka* in Ezra 5, 6; 6, 6 etc.; 'eyes and ears' of the king': a regular spying system has been assumed, mainly on the basis of X. Cyr. VIII 2, 10–12, the 'eyes and ears' (*ophthalmoi kai ōta*) of the king. In fact, however, there was only *one* 'eye' of the king (see Hdt. I 114; A. Pers. 980; Ar. Ach. 92–93; Plu. Art. 12), and Xenophon wanted to emphasize that apart from the well known 'eye', many of his subjects served the king as 'eyes' and 'ears'. There existed no 'ears' of the king as an institution, and OP **gaušaka* ('listener') (attested in Egypt) does not mean 'spy'. Officials on the provincial level: hyparchs et al.: see Tuplin, 120–21 (with evidence); N. Sekunda has postulated 'dukedoms' for Lydia and Phrygia-on-the-Hellespont (in *AchHist* III, Leiden 1988, 175–96; *REA* 87, 1985, 7–29); on the *pāḫatu* see Kuhrt and Joannès (see above) on the *pḥw'* etc. and their officials: Lemaire (see above); on the administration of (southern) Egypt: J. Wiese-höfer, in *AchHist* VI, Leiden 1991, 305–309. Local level: *Kōmarchēs*: X. An. IV 5, 10. 24. 27–30. 32. 34–35; 6, 1–3; Achaemenids and subject cities: Tuplin, 'Adminis-tration', 127–8; 'Treasuries', food depots etc. (and their officials): Tuplin, 128–31; garrisons: above all Tuplin, 'Xenophon and the Garrisons of the Achaemenid Empire', *AMI* N. F. 20, 1987, 167–245; there were garrisons in urban citadels (with special 'connections' with the royal centre) and garrisons in the country under a chiliarch. Landed estates and 'fiefs': Tuplin, 133–7. Apart from landed estates, there were also 'royal' villages, paradeisoi, herds of horses, etc. Certain villages supplied the women of the royal house with textiles etc. (see above); landed estates were often run (or farmed out) by royal agents. The *oikoi* and *chōrai* bestowed on aristocrats and 'benefactors' (together with *oiketai*) are to be distinguished from the cities and landed estates whose revenues and taxes were 'conferred' by the king (e.g. to Themistocles) (see Briant, 'Dons de terres et de villes', *REA* 87, 1985, 53–72). In the latter case, the question arises whether the revenues were freely put at the disposal of the recipients, or whether they were meant to 'redistribute' them locally (Sancisi-Weerdenburg, quoted by Kuhrt, in *Le tribut*, 220f). On 'military fiefs' in Babylonia, which were granted by the king in exchange for military service, see M. W. Stolper, *Entrepreneurs and Empire*, Leiden 1985 (these 'fiefs' will be discussed in more detail in the following chapter); other military settlements: Tuplin, 'Administration', 137 n. 107–8; settlements for the deported: see Tuplin 116 n. 28.

3. (pp. 63–5) Authoritative on all questions regarding the Achaemenid taxation system are Ch. Tuplin's article 'The Administration of the Achaemenid Empire', *Coinage and Administration in the Athenian and Persian Empires*, ed. I. Carradice, Oxford 1987, esp. 137–58, and the articles in the omnibus volume *Le Tribut dans l'Empire perse*, ed. P. Briant/C. Herrenschmidt, Paris 1989. 'Gifts' (*dōra*) under Cyrus and Cambyses: we must bear in mind that in the Assyrian empire, there was a great range of 'gifts': particularly spectacular ones, irregularly given on certain occasions, e.g. after the conquest of a region (as a kind of reparation payment); obligatory ones that were regularly delivered on special occasions (as proof of courtesy or loyalty); gifts handed to the king by embassies or at audiences; 'ceremonial' gifts as signs of friendly relations between equals (see A. Kuhrt, 'Conclusions', *Le Tribut*, 221); Högemann (*Vorderasien*, 274) mentions 'imposition of tributes, requisitions of natural produce and confiscations'. A. Pers. 582ff; Hdt. quotation: III 89. The original Greek term for tribute (e.g. in the Persian empire) was *dasmos*. In contradistinction, the Delian Confederacy called their contributions *phoroi*. After the change of the confederacy into a sovereignty (*archē*) of Athens, *phoros* was also used as a term for the tribute of subject people. On partly autonomous groups and groups exempt from tribute/taxes see Hdt. III 91. 97 (quotation) and J. Wiesehöfer, in *Le Tribut*, 183–91. The historical reasons for the 'tribute exemption' and other privileges of Persis are discussed by F. Gschnitzer, 'Zur Stellung des persischen Stammlandes im Achaimenidenreich', *Ad bene et fideliter seminandum*. Festgabe f. K. Deller (AOAT, 220), Neukirchen 1988, 87–122: he conjectures a connection between the Intaphernes crisis, the reform of the empire and the privileges of Persis. There is reason to believe that Cambyses already had 'tax reform' plans in order to build up a fleet and to finance his Egyptian venture (see H. T. Wallinga, 'The Ionian Revolt', *Mnemosyne* 37, 1984, 407–9). In the author's opinion, the difference between *phoros* and *dōra* is not material (gold, metals – natural produce), but conceptual; on imposts in natural produce and precious metals see Högemann, 282f. On transport and hoarding of tribute see Polyclitus (*FGrHist* 128 F 3), the Alexander historians (Arr. An. III 16, 7; D.S. XVII 66. 70; Curt. III 2, 11; 17, 70; Plu. Alex. 36f; Str. XV 3, 9) as well as Nepos (Dat. 4, 2). On Achaemenid care for the land see Tuplin (see above), 143–5. That the Achaemenids invested their resources in precious metals for political purposes, e.g. to support their foreign friends and ward off their enemies, is all too familiar in its Greek variant (see D. M. Lewis, 'Persian Gold in Greek International Relations',

REA 91, 1989, 227–34). On the 'treasures' of the Achaemenids, whose partial utilization by Alexander is said to have given the economy of the empire an enormous impetus, see F. de Callatay, 'Les trésors achéménides et les monnayages d'Alexandre', *REA* 91, 1989, 259–77. The establishment of tribute acting as an example: Wallinga, 'Persian Tribute and Delian Tribute', *Le Tribut* (see above), 173–81.

4. Everyday Life in Achaemenid Persis: 1–6

An excellent example for the possibility of a comparison between Greek and Iranian source material is M. Brosius's dissertation *Royal and Non-Royal Women in Achaemenid Persia (559–331 B.C.)* (MS), Oxford 1991 (to appear in 1996), which I read in manuscript, and for which I express my cordial thanks to the author. Number of workers mentioned: M. A. Dandamaev, 'Forced Labour in the Palace Economy in Achaemenid Iran', *AoF* 2, 1975, 71–78 (surely accurate in its general trend). Walks of life and activities: Quotation: Koch, *Verwaltung*, 3.

1. (pp. 68–71) Prosopography of the high aristocracy according to classical sources and the tablets: Lewis, *Sparta and Persia*, Leiden 1977, esp. 1–26; id., 'Postscript 1984' in: A. R. Burn, *Persia and the Greeks*, London 2nd edn 1984; id., 'Persians in Herodotus', *The Greek Historians. Literature and History. Papers Presented to A. E. Raubitschek*, Stanford 1985, 101–17. I am also indebted to these works for my examples. Artystone in Herodotus: III 88; VII 69. 72. 78. Text quotations: PF 1795; Fort. 6764. References to Artystone's activities: PF 718. 1836–39. 733–34. 2035. Gobryas in Herodotus: III 70. 73. 78; IV 132. 134; Gobryas and Mardonius: VII 2. 5. 97. Gobryas as fellow conspirator and in Elam: DB IV 84; V 7ff. Gobryas on Darius's tomb relief: illustration in Hinz, *Darius und die Perser*, vol. 1, Baden-Baden 1976, 165. Gobryas *en route*: PF 688; H-2533 (Brosius, 94 n. 18); Radushnamuya: PF 684; Radushdukka: Fort. 1017 (identification: Brosius, 154); Artazostra (quotation): PFa 5. Artaphernes (quotation): PF1404. Farnaka: Koch, *Es kündet Dareios der König*, Mainz 1992, 36–41; although I disagree with her identification of F. on the Treasury reliefs; Farnaka and his *entourage* (quotation): PFa 4. 'Salary scale': Koch, 'Zu den Lohnverhältnissen der Dareioszeit in Persien', *Kunst, Kultur und Geschichte der Achämenidenzeit und ihr Fortleben*, ed. H. Koch/D. N. MacKenzie, Berlin 1983, 19–50; table in text: Ib., 46–47. On unminted silver see Hdt. III 96: 'The tribute [*phoros*] is stored by the king in this fashion: he melts it down and pours it into earthen vessels; when the vessel is full he breaks the earthenware away and when he needs money [*chrēmata*] coins [cuts up] [*katakoptei*] as much as will serve his purpose.' *Kurtaš*: discussion in M. W. Stolper, *Entrepreneurs and Empire*, Leiden 1985, 56–59.

2. (pp. 71–75) Farnaka and Chiçavahush: details after Koch, *Verwaltung*, 224ff; *Es kündet*, 43f. Known successors to F. are: Artavardya (from 496 BC), Aspachanah

(from 494), Artatakhma (from 482), Artathura (from 466 BC), and those to Ch. are: Vratayanta (no date), Baratkama (in 490), Dargayush (484–482), again Chiçavahush (471–468 BC). Gṛdapatiš and subordinates: Koch, *Verwaltung*, 237ff. *Ganzabara*: Koch, ib., 235ff. Treasuries: Koch, passim; example: PF 864. Taxes and tributes: Koch, 'Steuern in der achämenidischen Persis?', *ZA* 70, 1980, 105–37; id., 'Tribut und Abgaben in Persis und Elymais', *Le Tribut*, 121–8; disagreements between scholars: see the articles of Koch and C. Herrenschmidt, in *Le tribut* (e.g. their different definitions of the tasks of the official called *bāṢkara*). Domains of the kings/aristocracy: example: PF 1837; further evidence in the tablets: royal domain (PF 1987); estates of Artystone (PF 1836–37), of Arsames (T-958; unpubl.), of Artabama (PF 27a); on examples of estates outside Persis: Tuplin, 'Achaemenid Administration', 133ff. *Paradeisoi* and royal interest in farming: Tuplin, 143ff; Xenophon quotation: Oec. IV 13 (Eng. transl. E. C. Marchant); *partetaš* on the tablets: examples in Hinz/Koch, *Elamisches Wörterbuch*, vol. 1, 160; royal control: X. Oec. IV 8. Irrigation system: king as owner (Hdt. III 117; Tuplin, 144); *qanāts*: Briant, *Rois*, 405ff; H. Goblot, *Les qanats*, Paris 1979; Cofferdams: F. Hartung/Gh. R. Kuros, 'Historische Talsperren in Iran', G. Garbrecht, *Historische Talsperren*, 1987, 221–74; articles by W. Kleiss, in *AMI* N. F. 15, 1982; 20, 1987; 21, 1988. Food: Koch, *Es kündet*, 271ff; Strabo quotation: XV 3, 18; 'Persian fruit': Thphr. 4, 4 (*mēlon mēdikon*); Plin. n. h. XII 15 (*malus Medica*): lemon (tree); Apic. 4, 2, 34 (*[malum] Persicum*) > 'peach'; cardamum: H. Sancisi-Weerdenburg, 'Persian food: Stereotypes and Political Identity', *Foods in Antiquity*, ed. J. Wilkins, Exeter 1995, 286–302.

3. (pp. 75–9) Infrastructure and communications: fundamental work has been done by Briant ('De Sardes à Suse'), *AchHist* VI, Leiden 1991, 67–82; D. F. Graf ('The Persian Royal Road System', *AchHist* VIII: *Continuity and Change*, ed. H. Sancisi-Weerdenburg/A. Kuhrt/M.C. Root, Leiden 1994, 167–89) and J. Wiesehöfer ('Beobachtungen zum Handel des Achämenidenreiches', *MBAH* 1, 1982, 5–16). 'Road controllers' (Elam. *datimara*): PFa 30; 'travelling companions' (Elam. *barriš-dama*): see PF 1363. 1409. 1572; 'caravan leaders' (Elam. *karabattiš*): PF 1340. 1341. 1375; 'express messengers' (Elam. *pirradaziš*): example: PF 1285; see 1315. 1320. 1329 et al. 'Guards along the road': Hdt. VII 239; relay riders: Hdt. VIII 98; X. Cyr. VIII 6, 17f; express messengers: Esther 3, 12f.; 8, 10; Nic. Dam. (*FGrHist* 90 F4); fire signals: Hdt. IX 3; Ps.-Arist., Mu. 398a et al; calling posts: D.S. XIX 17, 6 (though hardly possible over long distances); 'mirror signals': Hdt. VI 115 (flashing with a shield). See for all forms of communication W. Leiner, *Die Signaltechnik der Antike*, Stuttgart 1982, esp. 69ff; *astandēs*: Plu. Alex. 18, 2. Ancient Near Eastern prototypes, royal roads, purpose of roads: see the above-mentioned works by Briant, Graf, Wiesehöfer. Persepolis–Susa road: W. Kleiss, 'Ein Abschnitt der achaemenidischen Königsstraße von Pasargadae und Persepolis nach Susa, bei Naqsh-i Rustam', *AMI* N. F. 14, 1981, 45–54; W. M. Sumner, 'Achaemenid Settlement in the Persepolis

Plain', *AJA* 90, 1982, 1–31; Koch, 'Die achämenidische Poststraße von Persepolis nach Susa', *AMI* N. F. 19, 1986, 133–47. Hdt. about the 'royal road': V 52; on the *stathmoi* see also Ctes. (*FGrHist* 688 F 33). Messengers of the king: Hdt. VIII 98; see A. A. 282; X. Cyr. VIII 6, 17f; *angaros*: see R. Schmitt, 'Zur Méconnaissance altiranischen Sprachgutes im Griechischen', *Glotta* 49, 1971, 97ff. Road section near Pasargadae: Stronach, *Pasargadae*, Oxford 1978, 166f. Mesopotamia–Bactria: Ctes. (*FGrHist* 688 F 33); Wiesehöfer, 10 (with earlier literature). Travellers to Media: PFa 31; Egypt: PF 1544; see also the Arshama letters (e.g. P. Grelot, *Documents araméens d'Egypte*, Paris 1972, Nr. 67; B. Porten/A. Yardeni, *Textbook of Aramaic Documents from Ancient Egypt*, vol. 1: *Letters*, Jerusalem 1986, 144); Bactria: PF 1287. 1555; Kirman; PF1289. 1330. 1332. 1348. 1377. 1398 f. 1436. 1439. 1466; PFa 35; Aria: PF 1361. 1438. 1540. 2056; Sagartia: PF 1501; PFa 31; Babylonia: PF 1512. 1541 (?); Maka: PF 2050; Arachosia: PF 1351. 1385. 1443. 1477. 1484. 1510. 2049; Qandahar: PF 1340. 1358. 1550; Hindush: PF 1318. 1383. 1399. 1524. 1552. 1556. 1572; on travellers to and from the East see W. Vogelsang, *The Rise and Organisation of the Achaemenid Empire. The Eastern Iranian Evidence*, Leiden 1992, 165ff. Carriages and condition of roads: Ar. Ach. 68–71; see Hdt. VII 83; X. Cyr. VI 2, 36; D.S. XVIII 26ff; Curt. X 10, 20. Surveys: Hdt. V 52ff; Ctes. (*FGrHist* 688 F 33); Xen. An. I 2, 5f; Megasthenes: in Str. XV 1, 50; etymology of 'Parasang': J. Marquart, *Das erste Kapitel der Gaθa uštavatī* (Yasna 43), Rome 1930, 4; see R. Schmitt, 'Medisches und persisches Sprachgut bei Herodot', *ZDMG* 117, 1967, 138; milestone from Pasargadae: D. M. Lewis, 'The Seleucid Inscription', Stronach, *Pasargadae*, 159–61. Elam as a 'littoral province': P. Högemann, in *Stuttgarter Kolloquium zur historischen Geographie des Altertums 2, 1984, und 3, 1987*, ed. E. Olshausen/H. Sonnabend, Bonn 1991, 133–47. On canal and river navigation (in Babylonia, Asia Minor and Egypt) as well as maritime traffic see Briant, 75 ff. Characterization of Persis: quotation: Curt. V 4, 5–9; see Arr. Ind. 39, 2–4; Str. XV 3, 1; archaeological surveys: see Sumner (see above); workers in Tauka: example PF 1557; see PF 1363. 2055 (150 Thracian workers); PF 1368 (304 workers); PFa 30 (303 Lycian workers); PFa 30 (980 Cappadocian workers) etc.; *Taokē:* Ptol. Geog. VI 4, 2. 7. Iranians as 'city-dwellers': Eratosth. in Str. I 4, 9; on 'urbanization' under the Achaemenids see D. Metzler, *Ziele und Formen königlicher Innenpolitik im vorislamischen Iran*, postdoctoral thesis (MS), Münster 1977, 42ff; locating the places mentioned on the tablets remains a great problem; some of the attempts by recent research seem rather hypothetical.

4. (pp. 79–89) 'Persian Decadence': see P. Briant, 'Historie et idéologie. Les Grecs et la "décadence perse"', *Mélanges P. Lévêque*, Besançon 1989, 33–47. Quotation: Pla. Lg. 695 a–b (Eng. transl. T. J. Saunders); see K. Schöpsdau, 'Persien und Athen in Platons Nomoi', *Pratum Saraviense. Festgabe f. P. Steinmetz*, ed. W. Görler/ S. Koster, Stuttgart 1990, 25–39; X. Cyr. VIII 1ff; Isocrates: see especially Paneg. 41; the great king as a tyrant: A. Pers. 242 et al.; cf. K. Raaflaub, *Die Entdeckung der*

Freiheit (Vestigia, 37), Munich 1985. Herodotus: IX 122. Greeks, barbarians and their residences: Hdt. passim; Isoc. or. 5, 121–3; cf. J. Heinrichs, *Ionien nach Salamis* (Antiquitas, I, 39), Bonn 1989, 129ff. Persian educational aims: Hdt. I 136; X. An. I 9, 3; Cyr. I 2, 2ff; DNb 5–45 (Eng. transl. based on R. G. Kent); Arbinas: SEG XXVIII 1245, 14 f. Marriage policy and 'women's/men's quarters': a crucial reference for my account on this subject was the already mentioned diss. by M. Brosius (Oxford). Cambyses and his sisters: Hdt. III 31; on the identification of the sisters and on Cambyses's motives see Brosius, ib.; Artaxerxes and Atossa: Plu. Art. 23, 3; on the *gynē tou basileōs*: see Brosius, ib.; on the privileged position of the 'king's mother': see Brosius, ib. Artabama: her estate: PFa 27; *kurtaš Irdabamana*: documents compiled by Brosius, ib.; seal of Artabama: ill. in Koch, *Es kündet Dareios*, fig. 170; allowances for A.: PF 735–40; PFa 27. Women in the king's entourage: see above, ch. II, 3. Women in seclusion: Plu. Them. 26; 'Harem': it is not by chance that part of the terrace complex in Persepolis has been given this name. 'Persian decadence' (as a concept of scholars): quotation: H. Bengtson, *Griechische Geschichte* (*HdAW* III 4), Munich 5th edn 1977, 102; see: J. Wiesehöfer, '"Denn es sind welthistorische Siege" ... Nineteenth and Twentieth-Century German Views of the Persian Wars', *Culture and History* 12, 1992, 61–83; id., 'Das Bild der Achaimeniden in der Zeit des Nationalsozialismus', *AchHist* III, Leiden 1988, 1–14; id., 'Zur Geschichte der Begriffe "Arier" und "arisch" in der deutschen Sprachwissenschaft und Althistorie des 19. und der ersten Hälfte des 20. Jahrhunderts', *AchHist* V, Leiden 1990, 147–63; quotation: W. Wüst, *Indogermanisches Bekenntnis*, Berlin 1942, 29. *Arašsap/pašap/harrinup*: Brosius, ib. (with earlier literature). 'Special rations' for nursing mothers: quotations: PF 1221; 1232; promoting the number of births: Hdt. I 136; see Str. XV 3, 17; DB IV 54–56.

5. (pp. 89–94) On the Persian army see the summary by A. Sh. Shahbazi, 'Army, I', *EncIr* II, 1987, esp. 491–4; N. Sekunda, 'Achaemenid Military Terminology', *AMI* N. F. 21, 1988, 69–77, and now P. Högemann, *Das alte Vorderasien und die Achämeniden*, Wiesbaden 1992, 297–319. Sources: A. Bovon, 'La représentation des guerriers perses et la notion du barbare dans la Ire moitié du Ve siècle', *BCH* 87, 1963, 579–602; V. v. Graeve, *Der Alexandersarkophag und seine Werkstatt*, Berlin 1970, 95ff; representations and reconstructions: N. Sekunda, *The Persian Army 560–330 BC*, London 1992. Cyrus's army: Hdt. I 125. *Kāra*: J. Wiesehöfer, *Der Aufstand Gaumātas und die Anfänge Dareios' I.*, Bonn 1978, 93ff; types of armies: Högemann, ib. (with reference to possible prototypes). Commanders-in chief: among them were Mazares, Harpagus, Takhmaspada, Datis and other Medes. On clothing and arms of the ethnically classified units: Hdt. VII 61ff; see S. Bittner, *Tracht und Bewaffnung des persischen Heeres zur Zeit der Achaemeniden*, Munich 2nd edn 1987. Darius as model: DNb 41–45. Formation at Cunaxa: X. An. I 8, 9 (Eng. transl. Rex Warner, Penguin Classics). Greek mercenaries: see already Hdt. I 171; III 1, 25; see H. W. Parke,

Greek Mercenary Soldiers, Oxford 1933; G. F. Seibt, *Griechische Söldner im Achai-menidenreich*, Bonn 1977; Remuneration: X. An. I 3, 21. Great Satraps' Revolt: M. Weiskopf, *The So-Called 'Great Satraps' Revolt'*, *366–360 B.C.*, Stuttgart 1989; opposite approach by R. A. Moysey, 'Diodorus, the Satraps and the Decline of the Persian Empire', *Ancient History Bulletin* 5. 4, 1991, 111–20. Numbers of soldiers: Hdt. VII 228. 185f; X. An. I 7, 12; Arr. An. II 8, 8; III 8, 6. Fallen commanders: Hdt. VII 89 (Ariabignes); III 12 (Achaemenes); A. Pers. 36f (Arsames); Hdt. VII 224 (Abrocomas, Hyperanthes) et al. Elite units: quotation: Hdt. VII 41. 83. According to Heraclid. Cym. (*FGrHist* 689 F 1) they were a detachment of the 10,000 Im-mortals. *Hazārapatiš*: E. Benveniste, *Titres et noms propres en Iranien ancien*, Paris 1966, 67–71; Tithraustes: Nep. Con. 3, 2–3. Darius as 'lance-bearer': Hdt. III 139. Plataea: Hdt. IX 63. *Anušiya/anaoša*: A. Pagliaro, 'Riflesse di etimologie iraniche nella tradizione storiografica greca', *Rend. Lincei*, ser. VIII. 9, 1954, 146–51; but see: Gh. Gnoli, 'Antico-persiano *anušya* e gli immortali di Erodoto', *AcIr* 21, 1981, 266–80, and Sekunda, 70. Weapons: quotation: Str. XV 3, 19 (Eng. transl. H. L. Jones); see Hdt. VII 61; clothing: P. Calmeyer, 'Zur Genese altiranischer Motive, X: Die elamisch-persische Tracht', *AMI* N. F. 21, 1988, 27–51; A. Sh. Shahbazi, 'Clothing II', *EncIr* V, 1992, 723–37; armour-platings, tips of lances and arrow-heads were among objects found in the Persepolis Treasury; on coats-of-mail see also Hdt. VII 61; IX 22–4; adopted from Egypt: Hdt. I 135. Clothing and arms of the cavalry: quotation: X. An. I 8, 3ff; armoured cavalry from Babylonia: E. Ebeling, 'Die Rüstung eines babylonischen Panzerreiters nach einem Vertrage aus der Zeit Darius' II.', *ZA* N. F. 16, 1952, 204–13, esp. p. 210. Elephants at Gaugamela: Arr. An. III 8. Stand-ards: Hdt. IX 59; royal standard: X. An. I 10, 13; Curt. III 3, 10; on the standard on the Alexander mosaic see T. Hölscher, 'Zur Deutung des Alexandermosaiks', *Anadolu* 22, 1981/83, 297–307 (with earlier literature). Garrisons: see above. Fleet: see the sometimes differing opinions of Högemann, 311–19, and H. T. Wallinga, *Ships and Sea-Power before the Great Persian War* (Mnemosyne, Suppl. 121), Leiden 1993. Tactics: Shahbazi, *Army*, 493f.

6. (pp. 94–101)   The Religion of the Achaemenids: see the comprehensive account of investigations and discussions in G. Ahn, *Religiöse Herrscherlegitimation im achämenidischen Iran* (*AcIr* 31), Leiden/Louvain 1992, 93ff. Avesta and Zarathustra: J. Kellens, 'Avesta', *EncIr* III, 1989, 35–44; id., *Zoroastre et l'Avesta ancien*, Paris 1991; H. Humbach, *A Western Approach to Zarathushtra*, Bombay 1984; id., *The Gāthās of Zarathushtra and the Other Old Avestan Texts*, p.1, Heidelberg 1991; Gh. Gnoli, *Zoroaster's Time and Homeland*, Naples 1980; id., *De Zoroastre à Mani*, Paris 1985; M. Boyce, *A History of Zoroastrianism*, vols 1–2, Leiden 1975–82. Avesta alphabet, commitment to writing and manuscripts: K. Hoffmann/J. Narten, *Der sasanidische Archetypus*, Wiesbaden 1989. Alexander and the Avesta: J. Wiesehöfer, 'Zum Nachleben von Achaimeniden und Alexander in Iran', *AchHist* VIII, Leiden

1994, pp. 389–97. Anquetil-Duperron: J. Duchesne-Guillemin, in *EncIr* II, 1987, 100–101. Time and place of origin of the Avesta: see Gnoli, *Zoroaster's Time*, 159ff; Kellens, 'Avestique', *Compendium Linguarum Iranicarum*, ed. R. Schmitt, Wiesbaden 1989, 32ff. An extremely early dating is maintained by M. Boyce (see above); on criticism against it see Duchesne-Guillemin, 'Johanna Narten, Mary Boyce, George Dumézil', *Proceedings of the First European Conference of Iranian Studies, Turin 1987*, ed. Gh. Gnoli/A. Panaino, Rome 1990, 86ff. Spread of Zoroastrianism: outlined here are the approaches of Hoffmann ('Das Avesta in der Persis', *Prolegomena to the Sources on the History of Pre-Islamic Central Asia*, ed. J. Harmatta, Budapest 1979, 89–93), Gnoli and Boyce. Late dating of Zarathustra: this theory, which the author used to support, is today represented by very few scholars; to my mind Shahbazi, Gnoli, Humbach et al. have clearly demonstrated the Sasanian 'construction' of the date. Achaemenids and Zoroastrianism: see Ahn, 93ff (with the earlier literature). Characteristics of the doctrine of Zarathustra and the Younger Avesta: see Humbach, *Gāthās*, and Kellens, *Zoroastre*; the author has deliberately steered clear of the arguments about the figure of Zarathustra and the character and 'place in life' of the Gathas. Characterization of original Mazdaism: quotation: Kellens, 'Characters of Ancient Mazdaism', *History and Anthropology* 3, 1987, 257; eschatology: classical quotation: Plu. Is. and Osir. 46–47 (Eng. transl. F. C. Babbit, Loeb Classics); the controversy about cosmogony in the Gathas mainly hinges on the translation and interpretation of Yasna 30, 3–6; see Gnoli's ('Zoroastrianism', *Religions of Antiquity*, ed. R. M. Seltzer, New York/London 1989, 132f) and Humbach's translations (*Gāthās*, pp. 1, 123f). We have also avoided dealing with the question of 'Zurvanism', i.e. the belief in a divinity ('time') considered to be the 'father' of the twins Ahura Mazda and Angra Mainyu (see Gnoli, 'Zurvanism', *The Encyclopaedia of Religion*, ed. M. Eliade). Ahura Mazda and the other gods: see Ahn, 102ff. 'Truth' and 'Falsehood': Hdt. I 136. 138.; *aša-drug*: Boyce, *History II*, 181. Burial customs: Vd. 5, 1–4. 6, 26–9, 44–51; for a discussion: Ahn, 122ff. Religious conditions in Persis: quotation: PF 1956; in detail: H. Koch, *Die religiösen Verhältnisse der Dareioszeit*, Wiesbaden 1977; summarizing: id., 'Zu Religion und Kulten im achämenidischen Kernland', *La religion iranienne à l'époque achéménide*, ed. J. Kellens, Ghent 1991, 87–109. The Iranian personal names on the tablets are misleading if used as evidence of the religious convictions of their bearers (see R. Schmitt, 'Name und Religion', ib., 111–28). Magi and their tasks: dream interpretation: Hdt. I 107f. 120. 128; VII 19; Cic. De Div. I 23, 46; functions of priests: Hdt. I 132; Str. XV 3, 13f et al.; guarding tombs: Aristobul. (*FGrHist* 129 F 51 a); Ctes. (*FGrHist* 688 F 13); education of princes: Pla. Alc. I 121 d; Plu. Art. 3 et al.; administration: see the role of Gaumāta; on Magi in Babylonia see M. A. Dandamayev/V. Livshits, 'Zattumēšu, a Magus in Babylonia', *AcIr* 28, 1988, 457–9; royal investiture: Plu. Art. 3; upholders of tradition: see below.

PART TWO

Interlude

5. Macedonian Domination over Iran

Alexander and Iran: J. Wiesehöfer, *Die 'dunklen Jahrhunderte' der Persis*. Untersuchungen zu Geschichte und Kultur von Fārs in frühhellenistischer Zeit (330–140 v. Chr.) (Zetemata, 90), Munich 1994. Seleucids and Iran: S. Sherwin-White/ A. Kuhrt, *From Samarkhand to Sardis*, London 1993 (an excellent handbook on the Seleucid empire); Wiesehöfer, 'Discordia et Defectio – Dynamis kai Pithanourgia: 'Die frühen Seleukiden und Iran', *Akkulturation im Hellenismus*, ed. B. Funck, Tübingen (in press). The 'Achaemenid' Alexander: P. Briant, *Alexandre le Grand*, Paris 4th edn 1994; Wiesehöfer, *Jahrhunderte; Kleinasien*: see Curt. IV 10, 11. 14, 2; Polyaen. IV 3, 18; Correspondence after Issus: Arr. An. II 14, 1–9; see Briant, *Rois, tributs et paysans*, Paris 1982, 357–403, esp. 360–71 or 371–84; and M. Zahrnt, 'Die Frage der Grenze bei den Verhandlungen zwischen Dareios und Alexander', *Stuttgarter Kolloquium zur historischen Geographie des Altertums* 4, 1990, Amsterdam 1994, 67–82. Alexander in Persis: Arr. An. III 18, 2–12; Curt. V 3, 1–7, 10; Plu. Alex. 37, 1–38, 7; D.S. XVII 68, 1–72, 4; Str. XV 3, 6–8; Wiesehöfer, *Jahrhunderte; Brand von Persepolis*: Arr. An. III 18, 11–12; Curt. V 7, 3–7; lit. arch./ (*FGrHist* 137 F 11); Plu. Alex. 38, 1–7; D.S. XVII 72, 1–7; Ps. Callisth. II 17, 11; Str. XV 3, 6; on the interpretation of this and, above all, on the archaeological data (burning down only the rooms known [through inscriptions] to have been those of Xerxes and/or those that contained precious objects which served as 'royal gifts' or paraphernalia) see H. Sancisi-Weerdenburg, 'Alexander and Persepolis', *Alexander the Great: Reality and Myth*, Rome 1993, 177–88. Alexander and Darius III: Arr. An. III 22, 1. 6; Curt. VI 2, 9; D.S. XVII 73, 3. 77, 4; Plu. Alex. 43, 5–7; Just. XI 15, 15 Plin. n.h. XXXVI 132. Bessus: Arr. An. IV 7, 3–4. Curt. VII 5, 40; 10, 10; D.S. XVII 83, 9; on the time of his taking over the Persian court ceremonials et al., see A. B. Bosworth, 'Alexander and the Iranians', *JHS* 100, 1980, 6. Eastern Iran: F. L. Holt, *Alexander the Great and Bactria*, Leiden 1988, 52ff. The plundering of Cyrus's tomb and resistance in Persis: Arr. An. VI 30, 1–2; Curt. X 1, 37; Wiesehöfer, *Jahrhunderte*; Alexander tradition in Iran: J. Wiesehöfer, 'Zum Nachleben von Achaimeniden und Alexander in Iran', *AchHist* VIII, Leiden, 1994, 389–97. Peucestas: W. Heckel, *The Marshals of Alexander's Empire*, London/New York 1992, 263ff; assessment of his policy: Wiesehöfer, *Jahrhunderte*. Settlers' rebellion in Bactria: D.S. XVII 99, 5–6; XVIII 7, 1–9; Holt, *Alexander*, 70ff. Chandragupta: Sherwin-White/Kuhrt, 92ff. Media Atropatene: M. Schottky, *Media Atropatene und Groß-Armenien in hellenistischer Zeit*, Bonn 1989. Satraps of the 'Upper Satrapies': L. Schober, *Untersuchungen zur Geschichte Babyloniens und der Oberen Satrapien von 323–303 v. Chr.*, Frankfurt 1981; feast at Persepolis: quotation: D.S. XIX 22, 1–3; see Wiesehöfer, *Jahrhunderte*; dismissal of Peucestas:

D.S. XIX 48, 1ff. Founding of the empire by Seleucus I: Sherwin-White/Kuhrt, 8ff; Seleucus and Chandragupta: App. Syr. 55; Str. XV 2, 9; Choresmia: Curt. VIII 1, 8; Arr. An. IV 15, 4–5; H.-P. Francfort, 'Central Asia and Eastern Iran', *CAH* IV 2nd edn, London 1988, 186–89; Bactria/Sogdia: see below; founding of cities: Sherwin-White/Kuhrt, 20f. Seleucid policy: Re-assessment by Sherwin-White/Kuhrt and Wiesehöfer, *Discordia*; see also Briant, 'The Seleucid Kingdom, the Achaemenid Empire and the History of the Near East in the First Millennium B.C.', *Religion and Religious Practices in the Seleucid Kingdom*, ed. P. Bilde et al., Aarhus 1990, 40–65. Media: Plb. X 27; Ptol. VI 2, 17; Isid Char.; inscription of Nihāvand: L. Robert, 'Inscriptions séleucides de Phrygie et d'Iran', *Hellenica* 7, 1949, 5–22; see inscription of Kirmanshah: Robert, 'Encore une inscription grecque de l'Iran', *CRAI* 1967, 281–96; Karaftū: P. Bernard, 'Heraclès, les grottes de Karafto et le sanctuaire du mont Sambulos en Iran', *StIr* 9, 1980, 301–24; the mint of Ecbatana: O. Mørkholm, *Early Hellenistic Coinage*, Cambridge 1991. Persis: Wiesehöfer, *Jahrhunderte*; Molon rebellion: Plb. V 40ff; Seleucids and the Persian Gulf: J.-F. Salles, 'The Arab-Persian Gulf under the Seleucids', *Hellenism in the East*, ed. A. Kuhrt/S. Sherwin-White, London 1987, 75–109. Susa/Susiana: Greek colony: OGIS 233; inscriptions: SEG VII 2–6. 15. 17–26; archaeology: R. Boucharlat, 'Suse marché agricole ou relais du grand commerce. Suse et la Susiane à l'époque des grands empires', *Paléorient* 11, 1985, 71–81. Aria/Drangiana: Sherwin-White/Kuhrt 79–81. Hyrcania: App. Syr. 57; inscription: L. Robert, 'Inscription hellénistique d'Iran', *Hellenica* 11/12, 1960, 85–91; Plb. X 31, 5. 48; Sherwin-White/Kuhrt, 81f. Margiana: Str. XI 10, 2; Gyaur-Kale: V. M. Masson, *Das Land der tausend Städte*, Munich 1982, 141ff. Parthia: Sherwin-White/Kuhrt, 84–90. (Western) Arachosia: P. Daffinà, *L'immigrazione dei Sakā nella Drangiana*, Rome 1967; P. Bernard, in *Fouilles d'Aï Khanoum* IV, Paris 1985, 85–95; Aśoka edicts: U. Schneider, *Die großen Felsen-Edikte Aśokas*, Wiesbaden 1978; Iranian influence on the Aramaic version from Qandahar: H. Donner/W. Röllig, *Kanaanäische und aramäische Inschriften*, vol. 2, Wiesbaden 3rd edn 1973–79, 335–7; the Greek influence: R. Schmitt, 'Ex Occidente Lux. Griechen und griechische Sprache im hellenistischen Fernen Osten', *Beiträge zur hellenistischen Literatur und ihrer Rezeption in Rom*, ed. P. Steinmetz, Stuttgart 1990, 41–58, esp. 41–51. Bactria: Masson, *Land*; Francfort, *Central Asia*; Bernard, *Fouilles d'Aï Khanoum*; id., 'Alexandre et l'Asie Centrale', *StIr* 19, 1990, 21–38; Alexandria Eschatē: F. Schwarz, *Alexanders des Großen Feldzüge in Turkestan*, Munich 1893, 47–51; Bernard, in *Abstracta Iranica* 10, 1987, No. 176. 203; Aï Khanum: *Fouilles de Aï Khanoum* Iff, Paris 1973 ff; Bernard, in *Scientific American* 1982. Greeks in A. Kh. and Greek inscriptions from eastern Iran: Schmitt, *Ex Occidente*, 54ff (with translations); Takht-i Sangin: I. R. Pitschikjan, *Oxos-Schatz und Oxos-Tempel*, Berlin 1992 (with contestable theories); Bernard, 'Le Marsyas d'Apamée, l'Oxus et la colonisation séleucide en Bactriane', *StIr* 16, 1987, 103–15; Qandahar: see above. Sogdia: Masson, *Land*, 95ff; Bernard, *Alexandre*. North-eastern Iran at a later period: *Histoire et cultes de l'Asie*

Centrale préislamique, ed. P. Bernard/F. Grenet, Paris 1991; see also *History of Civiliza-tions of Central Asia*, vol. 2, Paris 1994 (for the time from 700 BC to AD 250).

PART THREE
Iran from Arsaces I to Artabanus IV

For bibliographies, reference books and handbooks on the history of Iran, the reader is referred to the literature mentioned under Part I; on basic literature about the Parthian period, see: *The Cambridge History of Iran*, vols III 1–2, Cambridge 1983; N. C. Debevoise, *A Political History of Parthia*, Chicago 1938; M. A. R. Colledge, *The Parthians*, London 1967, and especially K. Schippmann, *Grundzüge der parthischen Geschichte*, Darmstadt 1980. Also useful are the *Prosopographische Studien zur Geschichte des Partherreiches auf der Grundlage antiker literarischer Überlieferung* (Bonn 1988) by M. Karras-Klapproth. On relations between the Parthians and Rome see also K. H. Ziegler, *Die Beziehungen zwischen Rom und dem Partherreich*, Wiesbaden 1964, and E. Dąbrowa, *La politique de l'état parthe à l'égard de Rome*, Cracow 1983. J. Wolski, *L'Empire des Arsacides (AcIr, 32)*, Louvain 1993, will probably become a standard work.

6. The Testimonies: 1–2

1. (pp. 117–25) History and characteristics of the Iranian languages: *Compendium Linguarum Iranicarum*, ed. R. Schmitt, Wiesbaden 1989 (with articles by R. Schmitt on the Middle Iranian, W. Sundermann on the Western Middle Iranian languages, Parthian and Middle Persian, N. Sims-Williams on the Eastern Middle Iranian languages, Sogdian and Bactrian, and H. Humbach on Choresmian); quotations: Schmitt, 96, and Sundermann, 107. Languages of the Parthian West: Schmitt, 'Die Ostgrenze von Armenien über Mesopotamien, Syrien bis Arabien', *Die Sprachen im Römischen Reich der Kaiserzeit* (BJbb, Beih. 40), Bonn 1980, 187–214; K. Beyer, *Die aramäischen Texte vom Toten Meer*, Göttingen 1984; J. Oelsner, *Materialien zur babylonischen Gesellschaft und Kultur in hellenistischer Zeit*, Budapest 1986, 137ff; on the 'survival' of the Babylonian language: Iambl. Babyl. 2, 7ff Habrich. Documents from Nisa: I. M. D'jakonov/V. A. Livšic, *Dokumenty iz Nisy I v. do n.è.*, Moscow 1960; id., *Parthian Economic Documents from Nisa*, ed. D. N. MacKenzie, London 1976–79; V. A. Livshits, 'New Parthian Documents from South Turkmenistan', *AAntHung* 25, 1977, 157–85. Avroman documents: E. H. Minns, 'Parchments of the Parthian Period from Avroman in Kurdistan', *JHS* 35, 1915, 22–65 (see MacKenzie, *EncIr* III, 1989, 111). Parchments and papyri from Dura: *Excavations at Dura-Europos. Final Reports*, vol. 5, pt 1: The Excavations, Parchments and Papyri, ed. C. B. Welles, New Haven 1959; see also R. N. Frye, *The Parthian and Middle Persian Inscriptions of Dura-Europos*, London 1968, and J. Harmatta, 'Die parthischen Ostraka

aus Dura-Europos', *AAntHung* 6, 1958, 87–175. Ostraca from Shahr-i Qumis: A. D. H. Bivar, in *JRAS* 1970, 63–6, and *Iran* 19, 1981, 81–84. Inscription from Khung-i Nauruzi: Harmatta, 'Parthia and Elymais in the 2nd Century B.C.', *AAntHung* 29, 1984, 189–217; inscr. from Sar Pul-i Zuhab: G. Gropp, 'Die parthische Inschrift von Sar-Pol-e Zohāb', *ZDMG* 118, 1968, 315–19; inscr. from Susa: W. B. Henning, 'The Monuments and Inscriptions of Tang-i Sarvāk', *Asia Major* n. s. 2, 1951, 176. Aramaic–Elymaic inscriptions: Henning, 151–78; Harmatta, in R. Ghirshman, *Terrasses sacrées de Bard-e Néchandeh et Masjid-i Solaiman* (MDAI, XLV), vol. 1, Paris 1976. Inscriptions from Assur: literature in Beyer, *Texte*, 47 n. 2; *Hatra*: ib. Greek inscriptions from Bisutun: OGIS 431; but see T. S. Kawami, *Monumental Art of the Parthian Period in Iran* (*AcIr*, 26), Leiden 1987, 155–7; CIG III 4674, Kawami, 157–9. Letter from Artabanus to the archontes in Susa: C. B. Welles, *Royal Correspondence in the Hellenistic Period*, New Haven 1934, No. 75. Bilingual inscription on the Heracles statue: F. A. Pennacchietti, 'L'iscrizione bilingue greco-partica dell' Eracle di Seleucia', *Mesopotamia* 22, 1987, 169–85; D. S. Potter, 'The Inscription of the Bronze Herakles from Mesene: Vologeses IV's War with Rome and the Date of Tacitus' *Annales*', *ZPE* 88, 1991, 277–90, and P. Bernard, 'Vicissitudes au gré de l'histoire: d'une statue en bronze d'Héraclès entre Séleucie du Tigre et la Mésène', *JS* 1990, 3–68. Akkadian texts from Babylonia: Oelsner, *Materialien*; Babylonia between 141 and 126: Sherwin-White/Kuhrt, *From Samarkhand to Sardis*, London 1993, 124f; text from Uruk: K. Kessler, 'Eine arsakidenzeitliche Urkunde aus Warka', *BaM* 15, 1984, 273–81; 'Graeco-Babyloniaca': Oelsner, 239ff; Sherwin-White/Kuhrt, 160f; S. Maul, 'Neues zu den "Graeco-Babyloniaca"', *ZA* 81, 1991, 87–107. Chinese historiography: F. Hirth, *China and the Roman Orient*, Shanghai 1885; J. J. M. de Groot, *Chinesische Urkunden zur Geschichte Asiens*, 2 vols, Berlin 1921. Iranian tradition: M. Boyce, 'Parthian Writings and Literature', *CHI* III 2, Cambridge 1983, 1151–65; E. Yarshater, 'Iranian National History', *CHI* III 1, Cambridge 1983, 359–477.

2. (pp. 125–9) For the archaeology of the Parthian empire, K. Schippmann's article 'Archaeology III' in *EncIr* II, 1987, 298–301, can serve as an introduction. Sculpture and relief art is discussed in T. S. Kawami's monograph *Monumental Art of the Parthian Period in Iran* (*AcIr*, 26), Leiden 1987. Nisa (and surroundings): V. M. Masson, *Das Land der tausend Städte*, Munich 1982, 113ff; Mihrdātkirt: 'Fortress of Mithridates' (built there by M. I or II); Rhytons: M. E. Masson/G. A. Pugačenkova, *The Parthian Rhytons of Nisa*, Florence 1982; use of rhytons: Masson/Pugačenkova: religious-Zoroastrian context (libation); P. Bernard, in *Histoire et cultes de l'Asie Centrale préislamique*, Paris 1991, 31–8: banquets in the council of a Greek settlement in the East; origin: Bernard: war-booty from such a town in Syria or Bactria; friezes: Bernard, 'Les rhytons de Nisa, I', *JS* 1985, 25–118; Chuvin, in *Histoire et cultes*, 23–29. Hecatompylus/Shahr-i Qumis: Plin. n. h. VI 62; Plb. X 28,

7; J. Hansman, 'The Problems of Qumis', *JRAS* 1968, 111–39; J. Hansman/
D. Stronach, 'Excavations at Shahr-i Qumis, 1967', *JRAS* 1970, 29–62: '... 1971', ib.
1974, 8–22. Bisutun: Ctesias (*FGrHist* 688 F 1 = D.S. II 13, 1–2); see D.S. XVII 110,
5; Isid. Char. § 5; St. Byz. p. 155 ed. A. Meineke; inscription: L. Robert, *Gnomon* 35,
1963, 76; ill.: Sherwin-White/Kuhrt, *From Samarkhand* pl. 28; Parthian reliefs:
Kawami, 155–62, pls 1–5; other places in Media: Schippmann, *EncIr* II, 1987, 300.
Khuzistan: rock reliefs: L. Vanden Berghe/K. Schippmann, *Les reliefs rupestres
d'Elymaide (Iran) de l'époque parthe*, Ghent 1985. Parthian art: M. I. Rostovtzeff,
'Dura and the problem of Parthian Art', *YCS* 5, 1935, 155–304; M. A. R. Colledge,
Parthian Art, Ithaca 1977; S. B. Downey, 'Art in Iran IV', *EncIr* II, 1987, 580–85.
Hatra: Downey, *Mesopotamian Religious Architecture*, Princeton 1988, 159ff (with
earlier literature). Statue of Shami: H. Seyrig, 'La grande statue parthe de Shami et
la sculpture palmyrienne', *Syria* 20, 1939, 177–82. 'Colourful barbarians': R. M.
Schneider, *Bunte Barbaren*, Worms 1986. Arsacid coinage: M. Alram, 'Arsacid Coin-
age', *EncIr* III, 1989, 536–40; D. G. Sellwood, *An Introduction to the Coinage of
Parthia*, London 2nd edn 1980; 'Vassal coinages': Alram, 'Die Vorbildwirkung der
arsakidischen Münzprägung', *Litterae Numismaticae Vindobonenses* 3, 1987, 117–46.
Other archaeological art forms: Ceramics: E. Haerinck, *La céramique en Iran pendant
la période parthe*, Ghent 1983; Jewellery: B. Musche, *Vorderasiatischer Schmuck zur
Zeit der Arsakiden und der Sasaniden*, Leiden 1988.

7. The King and his Subjects: 1–2

1. (pp. 130–6) Ancient sources on the beginnings of the Parthian reign: Str. XI 9,
2; Just. XLI, 9–12. 4, 5, 6; Arr. Parth. (*FGrHist* 156 F1 = Phot. 17 a 34ff; Sync. 539,
7 Dindorf); another version names Andragoras as the ancestor of the Parthian kings
(Just. XII 4, 12), the Iranian 'national history' traces Arsaces's line of ancestors back
to Kai Qubad, his son Kai Arash, Dara, the son of Humai or the legendary bowman
Arash (A. Sh. Shahbazi, 'Arsacids I', *EncIr* II, 1987, 525). Chronology: most recent
Wiesehöfer, *Discordia*. Tiridates: while some scholars deny the historicity of this
brother of Arsaces because he is not mentioned in Strabo and Justin (see most
recently Wolski, 'L'origine de la relation d'Arrien sur la paire des frères Arsacides,
Arsace et Téridate', *AAntHung* 24, 1976/77, 63–70), others see in him a non-ruling
brother of the founder of the empire (see G. A. Košelenko, 'La genealogia dei primi
Arsacidi', *Mesopotamia* 17, 1982, 133–46). Geography: Ch. Brunner, 'Geographical
and Administrative Divisions', *CHI* III 2, Cambridge 1983, 769; first acquisitions:
Sherwin-White/Kuhrt, *From Samarkhand*, 84–90. 'Royal legends': Cyrus: esp. Hdt.
I 107–22 (see above); Sasan: Kārnāmag-i Ardaxšīr-i Pābagān I-III (Germ. transl. Th.
Nöldeke, in *Bezzenbergers Beiträge* 1878, 22ff); on the widespread influence of this
story see M. Frenschkowski, 'Iranische Königslegenden in der Adiabene', *ZDMG*
140, 1990, 213–33. Kingship: An article by the author is in press. Arsaces and

Artaxerxes (II): Ctes. (*FGrHist* 688 F 15: Arsacas/Arsaces; F 15a: Arsicas), Dinon (*FGrHist* 690 F14: Oarses); see Schmitt, 'Achaemenid Throne-Names', *AION* 42, 1982, 83–95. 'The 7 conspirators': Calmeyer, 'Die "statistische Landcharte" des Perserreiches. Nachträge und Korrekturen', *AMI* N. F. 20, 1989, 133–40, esp. 138–40. Artaxšahrakān: I. M. D'jakonov/V. A. Livšic, *Dokumenty iz Nisy I v. do n.è.*, Moscow 1960, 20. Biruni: ātār 112f Sachau (transl., 116). Royal titulature: Harmatta, 'Parthia and Elymais in the 2nd Century BC', *AAntHung* 29, 1981, 189–217, esp. 202; J. Wolski, 'Le titre de "Roi des Rois" dans l'idéologie monarchique des Arsacides', *From Alexander to Kül Tegin*, ed. J. Harmatta, Budapest 1990, 11–18. This dates it distinctly earlier than was assumed by J. Neusner ('Parthian Political Ideology', *IrAnt* 3, 1963, 40–59). Claims of Artabanus: Tac. Ann. VI 31; J. Wiesehöfer, 'Iranische Ansprüche an Rom auf ehemals achaimenidische Territorien', *AMI* N. F. 19, 1986, 177–85. Parthians as 'petty kings': Evidence: ib., 177f n. 6. Philhellenism: Wolski, 'Sur le "Philhellénisme" des Arsacides', *Gerion* 1, 1983, 145–56; Euripides's *The Bacchae*: Plu. Crass. 33 (Eng. transl. Dryden). This text somewhat further on also testifies to the royal distribution of gifts to deserving subjects. 'Iranism' of the Arsacids: Valakhsh: DkM 412, 5–11; see Gh. Gnoli, *The Idea of Iran*, Rome 1989, 116–19. 'Iranian National History': E. Yarshater, 'Iranian National History', *CHI* III 1, Cambridge 1983, 429ff; Sasanian and Achaemenid 'ancestry': ŠKZ pa. 16; Greek 34–36 (*ahēnagān–progonoi*); see Gnoli, 'L'inscription de Šābuhr à la Kaʿbe-ye Zardošt et la propagande sassanide', *Histoire et cultes de l'Asie préislamique*, Paris 1991, 57–59; *gōsān*: M. Boyce, 'The Parthian *gōsān* and the Iranian Minstrel Tradition', *JRAS* 1957, 10–45, quotation p. 10f; 'Vis and Ramin': V. Minorsky, 'Vis o Ramin, a Parthian Romance', id., *Iranica*, Tehran 1964, 151ff; Eng. transl. of Persian text: G. Morrison, New York 1972.

2. (pp. 136–43)   References to Parthia by ancient authors: quotation: Just. XLI 1, 12; see Str. XI 9, 1, who calls it *aporos* (here: without provisions). Parthia (*Parθava*) under the Achaemenids: DB II 92–III 10; the Babylonian version of the Bisutun inscription mentions the following number of enemies killed and captured, respectively, in the two battles fought there: 1st battle: 6,346/4,346; 2nd battle: 6,570/4,192; despite our general scepticism with regard to figures, this may not be far from the truth (great rebellion, merciless suppression, 'densely populated' Parthia). Dara: Plin. n. h. VI 46. Parthian 'history' of the late Bronze and (early) Iron Age: W. Vogelsang, *The Rise and Organisation of the Achaemenid Empire*, Leiden 1992, 267ff. Social structure of Parthia: quotations: Just. XLI 2, 1–6. 3, 4 (*probulorum* after Seel; other proposals: *populorum*, *praepositorum*); Plu. Crass. 30; on the *servi*: Wolski, 'Les relations de Justin et de Plutarque sur les esclaves et la population dépendante dans l'empire parthe', *IrAnt* 18, 1983, 145–57; G. A. Košelenko, 'Les cavaliers parthes', *DHA* 6, 1980, 177–99; numbers of Surena's forces: 1,000 cataphracts, unnamed number of mounted bowmen, as well as men in the baggage-train, etc., altogether

10,000 men (Košelenko); 1,000 cataphracts and 9,000 light cavalry (Wolski); 1,000 cataphracts, 10,000 lightly armed mounted bondmen (H. v. Gall, *Das Reiterkampfbild in der iranischen und iranisch beeinflußten Kunst parthischer und sasanidischer Zeit*, Berlin 1990, 76 n. 157). Slaves: Plin. ep. X 74; D.S. XXXIV/XXXV 21. 'Aristocracy' and 'common people': Amm. Marc. XXIII 6, 1; Tac. Ann. XII 10. *Megistanes*: Sen. ep. 21, 4; on Surena and Monaeses see Karras-Klapproth, *Prosopographie*, 165–71, or 90–92. Sasanian 'classes of nobility': see below. Manesus: P. Dura X (C. B. Welles, *The Parchments and Papyri*, 116). *Āzād*: M. L. Chaumont, 'Azad', *EncIr* III, 1989, 169f. Ranks of nobility in the Parthian empire: Wolski, 'L'aristocratie parthe et les commencements du féodalisme en Iran', *IrAnt* 7, 1967, 133–44; Court titles: OGIS 430. King and aristocracy: Wolski, 'Remarques critiques sur les institutions des Arsacides', *Eos* 46, 1952/53, 59–82; id., 'L'état parthe des Arsacides', *Palaeologia* 7, 3–4, 1959, 325–32 (with justified criticism of the theory of 'elected kingship'); crowning right of the Suren clan: Plu. Crass. 21; Tac. Ann. VI 42; quotations: Just. XLI 5, 8ff; Tac. Ann. VI 42, 4 (Phraates and Hiero) (Eng. transl. J. Jackson); Just. XLII 4, 1 (Mithridates II); king and mercenaries: Wolski, 'Le rôle et l'importance des mercenaires dans l'État parthe', *IrAnt* 5, 1965, 103–15: mercenaries as troops exclusively at the king's disposal; see Hdn. III 1, 2, where the king can call upon no troops of his own and has to rely on the units of the aristocracy. 'Feudal system': criticism by C. Herrenschmidt, 'Banda II', *EncIr* III, 1989, 684. Parthians and Greeks: inscription: SEG VII 39; theatre, agora, gymnasion: D.S. XXXIV/XXXV 21. Posidon. (*FGrHist* 87 F 13); Just. XLII 1, 3; Apamea-Silhu (and Susa): OGIS 233; location of A.-S.: G. Le Rider, *Suse sous les Séleucides et les Parthes*, Paris 1965, 260 n. 2; Archedemus: Plu. Mor. 605 B; Xenon: G. J. P. McEwan, 'Arsacid Temple Records', *Iraq* 43, 1981, 132–4; Syrinx: Plb. X 27–31; similar evidence was found in the excavations of Shahr-i Qumis (Hecatompylus): J. Hansman/D. Stronach, *JRAS* 1970, 29–62; Phraates II: Just. XLII 1; D.S. XXXIV/XXXV 21; Susa: Le Rider; R. Boucharlat, 'Suse, marché agricole ou relais du grand commerce', *Paléorient* 11/12, 1985, 76f; inscriptions: SEG VII 13; RC 75 (see Le Rider, 275f); Seleucia-on-the-Tigris: quotation Tac. Ann. VI 42; *'degeneratio'* idea: quotation: *neque in barbarum corrupta*; see H. Sonnabend, *Fremdenbild und Politik*, Frankfurt 1986, 216ff. Population: Plin. n. h. VI 122; here he maintains that Ctesiphon was deliberately founded 'against' S., but the Seleucia–Babylon equivalent should warn us off such interpretations (see Sherwin-White, 'Seleucid Babylonia', *Hellenism in the East*, London 1987, 20); interpretation of the episode: 'aristocracy' of the Greeks vs. 'democracy' of the natives (U. Kahrstedt, *Artabanos III. und seine Erben*, Bern 1950, 49); class struggle between poor and rich (N. Pigulevskaja, *Les villes de l'état iranien aux époques parthes et sassanides*, Paris/The Hague 1963, 62f, 85); Parthian kings and Seleucia in minting: Le Rider, passim; 'Orientalization' after 42: Kahrstedt, 48; Artabanus guided by his own interests: Tac.: *ex suo uso*. Parthians and Jews: J. Neusner, *A History of the Jews in Babylonia*, vol. 1, Leiden 1965; A. Oppenheimer, *Babylonia Judaica*, Wiesbaden, 1983.

8. Satraps, Traders, Soldiers and Priests

Administration: quotation: Plin. n.h. VI 112 (Eng. transl. H. Rackham); history of the 'vassal kingdoms': Persis: it is provided almost exclusively by the coinage (see M. Alram, 'Die Vorbildwirkung der arsakidischen Münzprägung', *Litterae Numismaticae Vindobonenses* 3, 1987, 127–30); Elymais: see Le Rider, *Suse sous les Séleucides et les Parthes*, Paris 1965; Vanden Berghe/Schippmann, *Les reliefs rupestres d'Elymaide*, Ghent 1985, 13–30; E. Dąbrowa, 'Die Politik der Arsakiden auf dem Gebiet des südlichen Mesopotamiens und im Becken des Persischen Meerbusens in der Zweiten Hälfte des 1. Jahrhunderts n. Chr.', *Mesopotamia* 26, 1991, 141–53; Mesene: J. Hansman, 'Characene, Charax', *EncIr* V, 1992, 363–5; Hatra: H. J. W. Drijvers, 'Hatra, Palmyra und Edessa', *ANRW* II 8, 1978, 799–906; Osrhoene: Drijvers, ib.; Adiabene: D. Sellwood, 'Adiabene', *EncIr* I, 1987, 456–9; Media Atropatene: K. Schippmann, 'Azerbaijan III', *EncIr* III, 1989, 222–4; M. Schottky, 'Gibt es Münzen atropatenischer Könige?', *AMI* N.F. 23, 1990, 211–27; Hyrcania: Dąbrowa, 'Vologèse Ier et l'Hyrcanie', *IrAnt* 19, 1984, 141–47; 'kingdoms' in ŠKZ: R. Gyselen, *La géographie administrative de l'Empire sassanide*, Paris 1989, 88f and passim. Parthian confirmation of regional autonomy: Persis: J. Wiesehöfer, *Die 'dunklen Jahrhunderte' der Persis*, Munich 1994, 112f; Elymais et al.: Alram, ib. Izates: J. A.J. XX 54f; see U. Kahrstedt, *Artabanos III. und seine Erben*, Bern 1950; Izates is rewarded by wearing 'an upright tiara [*tiara orthē*: a symbol of a great king] and resting on a golden bed', and in addition he is territorially 'compensated'. Mithridates of Mesene: D. T. Potts, 'Arabia and the Kingdom of Characene', *Araby the Blest*, ed. D. T. Potts, Copenhagen 1988, 143ff. 'Vassal kings' from the Arsacid family: see Tac. Ann. XII 14; XV 2: Vologeses I here calls Media the second and Armenia the third degree of power (*tertius potentiae gradus*); in the Achaemenid period there were similar rules for Bactria, and in the Sasanian period the crown-prince often governed Armenia. Satraps/*stratēgoi*: see Kahrstedt, *Artabanos*, 70ff; the Graeco-Roman terms are in fact often ambiguous (see Le Rider, *Suse*, 274–6); in a Graeco-Palmyrean inscription of 131 AD, a Palmyrean is mentioned as the satrap of King Meredates of Mesene in the Thilouana (H. Seyrig, 'Inscriptions grecques de l'agora de Palmyre', *Syria* 22, 1941, 253ff; IIP Fasc. X, No. 38); the inscription dates from the time when Mesene was independent from the Parthian empire. *Praefecturae*: Tac. Ann. VI 42, 4; XI 8; evidence of the title of satrap in Nisa: *ḫštrp* (Ph. Gignoux, *Glossaire des Inscriptions Pehlevies et Parthes*, London 1972, 53); Bisutun: *Satrapēs tōn Satrapōn*; Nisa: Gignoux, see above; Dura: P. Dura X. Agriculture in Susiana: R. J. Wenke, 'Imperial Investments and Agricultural Developments in Parthian and Sasanian Khuzestan', *Mesopotamia* 10/11, 1976, 31–121; Boucharlat, 'Suse, marché agricole', *Paléorient* 11/12, 1985, 79f. Trade: on the Roman India trade see *Rome and India. The Ancient Sea Trade*, ed. V. Begley/R. D. De Puma, Madison/London 1991; on Roman trade with the East (via Palmyra): R. Drexhage, *Untersuchungen zum römischen Osthandel*,

Bonn 1988; Caracallas' offer: Hdn. IV 10, 4; temple in Vologesias: R. Mouterde/
A. Poidebard, 'La voie antique des caravanes entre Palmyre et Hit au IIe siècle ap.
J.-C.', *Syria* 12, 1931, 101–15; SEG VII 135; bilingual inscription from Palmyra:
H. Seyrig, *Inscriptions*, 256ff; IIP Fasc. X, No. 114; Palmyreans on Bahrain et al.:
D. T. Potts, 'Northeastern Arabia: From the Seleucids to the Earliest Caliphs',
Expedition 26. 3, 1984, 27; J. Starcky, *Palmyre*, Paris 1952, 70–76; merchandise:
Periplus Maris Erythraei 41. 49 (and commentary in the edition by L. Casson,
Princeton 1989); see S. E. Sidebotham, *Roman Economic Policy in the Erythra
Thalassa*, Leiden 1986, 13–36; Parthian goods: Schippmann, *Grundzüge der parthischen
Geschichte*, Darmstadt 1980, 92; 'heavenly horses': A. Waley, 'The Heavenly Horses
of Ferghana: A New View', *History Today* 5, 1955, 95–103; Isidorus of Charax:
M.-L. Chaumont, 'La route royale des Parthes de Zeugma à Séleucie du Tigre
d'après l'itinéraire d'Isidore de Charax', *Syria* 61, 1984, 63–107; M. Gawlikowski,
'La route de l'Euphrate d'Isidore à Julien', *Géographie historique au Proche-Orient*,
Paris 1988, 77–97; G. Walser, 'Die Route des Isidorus von Charax durch Iran', *AMI*
N.F. 18, 1985, 145–156; Silk Road: H.-J. Klimkeit, *Die Seidenstraße*, Cologne 2nd edn
1990; H. W. Haussig, *Die Geschichte Zentralasiens und der Seidenstraße in vorislamischer
Zeit*, Darmstadt 2nd edn 1992. Army: A. Sh. Shahbazi, 'Army I', *EncIr* II, 1987,
494–96; P. Wilcox, *Rome's Enemies. Parthians and Sasanid Persians*, London 1986
(with attempts at colour reconstructions); H. v. Gall, *Das Reiterkampfbild in der
iranischen und iranisch beeinflußten Kunst parthischer und sasanidischer Zeit*, Berlin 1990;
Chronicle of Arbela: 8 Kawerau (transl. 27); mercenaries: see above; lances: quotation:
Plu. Crass. 27, 2; tactics and procedure of battle at Carrhae: Plu. Crass. 24f; 'Parthian
shot': Just. XLI 2, 7; M. Rostovtzeff, 'The Parthian Shot', *AJA* 47, 1943, 174ff;
horses: quotation: Just. XLI 43, 4. Religion of the Arsacids: M. Boyce, 'Arsacid
Religion', *EncIr* II, 1987, 540f; priests in Nisa: Gignoux, *Glossaire*, see above;
calendar: Boyce, ib.; exposure of the dead: Just. XLI 3, 5; according to Isid. Char.
12, the kings were buried in mausoleums (*taphai*) in Nisa; *Valaxš*: see above; royal
fire: Isid. Char. 11; 'marriage between relatives': E. H. Minns, 'Parchment of the
Parthian Period from Avroman in Kurdistan', *JHS* 35, 1915, 28; 'Arsacid era':
Shahbazi, 'The Arsacid Era', *EncIr* II, 1987, 541f.

PART FOUR

Iran from Ardashir I to Yazdgird III

For bibliographies and reference works on the history of the Sasanian empire, see the
literature mentioned under Introduction. Useful handbooks on this period are as
follows: A. Christensen, *L'Iran sous les Sassanides*, Copenhagen 2nd edn 1944 (for a
long time a standard book, this is still a useful, systematic work, although now
somewhat out of date, and although it does not differentiate the sources according
to their time and place of origin and their relevance to certain parts of Sasanian

history); K. Schippmann, *Grundzüge der Geschichte des sasanidischen Reiches*, Darmstadt 1990. Again we recommend vol. III 1 and 2 of the *Cambridge History of Iran*, Cambridge 1983, and R. N. Frye, *The History of Iran*, Munich 1984. Excellent maps have been provided by E. Kettenhofen for the *Tübinger Atlas des Vorderen Orients* (TAVO): see maps B VII ('Römer und Sāsāniden in der Zeit der Reichskrise [224–284 AD]'), B VI 1 ('Östlicher Mittelmeerraum und Mesopotamien [284–337 AD]') and B VI 3 ('Das Sāsānidenreich'). A reassessment of sources is advocated by Ph. Gignoux, 'Pour une nouvelle histoire de l'Iran sasanide', *Middle Iranian Studies*, ed. W. Skalmowski/A. von Tangerloo, Louvain 1984, 253–62. On the languages and writing systems of this period, the reader is referred to the literature mentioned under Part III. On names (and prosopography) of the Sasanian period, see Gignoux, *Noms propres sassanides en Moyen-Perse épigraphique* (IPNB II 2), Vienna 1986. A collection of sources (in translation) on Roman–Sasanian relations of the 3rd and 4th centuries has been published: M. H. Dodgeon/S. N. C. Lieu (ed.), *The Roman Eastern Frontier and the Persian Wars AD 226–363*, London 1991).

9. The Testimonies: 1–2

1. (pp. 153–9) The epigraphic sources for the Sasanian empire are quite easily accessible today (incl. German translations): M. Back, *Die sassanidischen Staatsinschriften* (*AcIr* 18), Leiden/Tehran/Lüttich 1978 (reviewed by Gignoux, *StIr* 13, 1984, 268–73, and D. N. MacKenzie, *IF* 87, 1982, 280–97); quotation: ŠKZ MP 1./Pa. 1/Gr. 1f; MP 20ff/Pa. 15ff/Gr. 34ff; H. Humbach/P. O. Skjærvø, *The Sassanian Inscription of Paikuli*, 3 pts, Wiesbaden 1978–83; P. O. Skjærvø, 'L'inscription d'Abnūn et l'imparfait en moyen-perse', *StIr.* 21, 1992, 153–60; Ph. Gignoux, *Les quatre inscriptions du mage Kirdīr*, Paris 1991; id., 'D'Abnūn à Māhān. Étude de deux inscriptions sassanides', *StIr* 20, 1991, 9–22. Aside from the Roman-Byzantine authors presented here, we might mention the Chronicon Paschale ('Easter chronicle'), the 4th-century epitomizers, Eusebius, Hieronymus, the Historia Augusta, Lactance, Libanius, Malalas, Orosius, the Latin panegyrists, Petrus Patricius, the 13th book of the Oracula Sibyllina, the 'Church historians' Socrates and Sozomen, the Suda, Zonaras, Zosimus et al. Almost all of them are also available in translation (sometimes with commentaries). On the Christian literature of the East the most informative works are still A. Baumstark, *Geschichte der syrischen Literatur mit Ausschluß der christlich-palästinensischen Texte*, Bonn 1922 (repr. Berlin 1968), and G. Graf, *Geschichte der christlichen arabischen Literatur*, 5 vols, Vatican City 1944–53 (repr. 1964–66); thoroughly useful is *Kleines Wörterbuch des christlichen Orients*, ed. J. Aßfalg/P. Krüger, Wiesbaden 1975; martyrologies are collected in editions by S. E. Assemani, *Acta Sanctorum Martyrum Orientalium et Occidentalium in duas partes distributa*, Rome 1748 (repr. Farigliano 1970), and P. Bedjan, *Acta martyrum et sanctorum*, vols I–VII, Paris/Leipzig 1890–97 (repr. Hildesheim 1968); excerpts from

these have been translated by O. Braun, *Ausgewählte Akten persischer Märtyrer*, Kempten/Munich 1915 (quotation: p. 116); G. Hoffmann, *Auszüge aus syrischen Akten persischer Märtyrer*, Leipzig 1880, and in *Holy Women of the Syrian Orient*, transl. S. P. Brock/S. A. Harvey, Berkeley 1987. The most important chronicles are (for our subject) the (Arabic) Nestorian chronicle of Seʿert (*Histoire nestorienne*, ed. A. Scher, 2 parts in 4 vols, Paris 1908–18), and *Die Chronik von Arbela*, ed. and transl. P. Kawerau, 2 vols, Louvain 1985, the authenticity and reliability of which has been disputed (see the argument between J. M. Fiey and P. Kawerau, in *RHE* 81, 1986, 544–8, and 82, 1987, 338–40); however, internal evidence and the rendering of Iranian names in the chronicle appear to speak for its authenticity. The major editions of Manichaean writings are: C. Schmidt/H. J. Polotsky, *Ein Mani-Fund in Ägypten. Originalschriften des Mani und seiner Schüler*, Berlin 1933, 4–90; *Manichäische Hand-schriften der Sammlung A. Chester Beatty*, vol. 1: Manichäische Homilien, ed. H. J. Polotsky, Stuttgart 1934; *Manichaean Manuscripts in the Chester Beatty Collection*, vol. II: A Manichaean Psalm-Book, pt 2, ed. C. R. C. Allberry, Stuttgart 1938; *Manichäische Handschriften der Staatlichen Museen Berlin*, vol. 1: Kephalaia, 1. Hälfte (Lfg. 1–10), ed. H. J. Polotsky/A. Böhlig, Stuttgart 1940; 2. Hälfte (Lfg. 11/12), ed. A. Böhlig, Stuttgart 1966; *The Manichaean Coptic Papyri in the Chester Beatty Library: Facsimile Edition*, vol. 1–2, Geneva 1986. F. C. Andreas/W. Henning, *Mitteliranische Manichaica aus Chinesisch-Turkestan I–III*, Berlin 1932–34; W. Sundermann, *Mittel-persische und parthische kosmogonische und Parabeltexte der Manichäer*, Berlin 1973; M. Boyce, *A Reader in Manichaean Middle Persian and Parthian*, Tehran/Liège 1975; Sundermann, *Mitteliranische manichäische Texte kirchengeschichtlichen Inhalts*, Berlin 1981. An excellent compendium of selected documents in translation (with a compre-hensive introduction) is *Die Gnosis*, Bd. 3: Der Manichäismus, with the cooperation of J. P. Asmussen, and with introduction, translation and commentary by A. Böhlig, Zürich/Munich 2nd edn 1995; on the 'Cologne Mani Codex' see *Der Kölner Mani-Kodex. Über das Werden seines Leibes. Kritische Edition, aufgrund der von A. Heinrichs und L. Koenen besorgten Erstedition* (the latter is still significant because of its detailed historical commentary), ed. and transl. L. Koenen/C. Römer, Opladen 1988; *Der Kölner Mani-Kodex. Abbildungen und diplomatischer Text*, ed. L. Koenen/C. Römer, Bonn 1985 (further readings and corrections by the editors in the *ZPE*). Important articles on the CMC are found in: *Codex Manichaicus Coloniensis: Atti del simposio intern. (Rende Amantea*, 3–7 September 1984), ed. L. Cirillo/A. Roselli, Cosenza 1986. The major editions of Armenian texts are: Agathangelos, *History of the Armeni-ans*, transl. and comm. R. W. Thomson, Albany 1976; Moses Khorenatsʻi, *History of the Armenians*, transl. and comm. R. W. Thomson, Cambridge/London 1978; Eḷišē, *History of Vardan and the Armenian War*, transl. and comm. R. W. Thomson, Cambridge/London 1982; *The Epic Histories Attributed to Pʻawstos Buzand* [Faustos Buzandatsʻi], transl. and comm. N. G. Garsoian, Cambridge 1989; V. Langlois, *Collec-tion des historiens anciens et modernes de l'Arménie*, 2 vols, Paris 1867–69; a critical evaluation of this literature as source material is provided by Gignoux, 'Pour une évaluation de la contribution des sources arméniennes à l'histoire sassanide', *AAntHung* 31, 1985–88, 53–65; and now also by E. Kettenhofen in his postdoctoral thesis *Tirdād und die Inschrift von Paikuli*, Wiesbaden 1995. On Middle Persian literature, see M. Boyce, 'Middle Persian Literature', *Handbuch der Orientalistik*, I. Abt., Bd. 4, 2. Abschn., Lfg. 1, Leiden/Cologne 1968, 31–66; J. P. de Menasce, 'Zoroastrian Pahlavi Writings', *CHI* III 2, 1983, 1166–95, and E. Yarshater, 'Iranian National History', *CHI* III 1, 1983, 359–477. On the Arab authors, ample information is provided in the histories of literature by C. Brockelmann (*Geschichte der arabischen Literatur*, vols 1–2, Leiden 2nd edn 1943–49; suppl. 1–3, Leiden 1937–42), F. Sezgin (*Geschichte des arabischen Schrifttums*, vol. 1, Leiden 1967) and H. Busse (in *Grundriß der arabischen Philologie*, ed. H. Gätje, vol. 2, Wiesbaden 1987, 264–97). I shall therefore only refer to a few translated works: al-Bīrūnī, *The Chronology of Ancient Nations*, transl. E. Sachau, London 1879; Ibn an-Nadīm, *al-Fihrist*, transl. B. Dodge, 2 vols, New York 1970; al-Mas'ūdī, *murūǧ aǧ-ǧahab*, ed. and transl. M. de Meynard/ P. de Curteille, 9 vols, Paris 1861–77; new revised edition by Ch. Pellat, Paris 1962ff. Excerpts from this work have been translated and annotated by G. Rotter (Al-Mas'ūdī, *Bis zu den Grenzen der Erde*, Tübingen 1978); aṭ Ṭabarī, *Geschichte der Perser und Araber zur Zeit der Sasaniden. Aus der arabischen Chronik des Tabari*, transl. Th. Nöldeke, Leiden 1879. Other authors to be mentioned are: Ibn Qutaiba, ad-Dinawari, al-Yaqubi, Hamza al-Isfahani, ath-Tha'alibi, Ibn Miskawaih et al. These works will be further discussed in the Conclusion. As for the intellectual background of Arabic historiography, see M. Springberg-Hinsen, *Die Zeit vor dem Islam in arabischen Universalgeschichten des 9. bis 12. Jahrhunderts*, Würzburg/Altenberge 1989. The New Persian adaptation of the *Xvadāynāmag* in Firdausi's *Šāhnāme* (J. Mohl edition: *Le livre des Rois I-VII*, Paris 1838–55) is impressively discussed by W. Sundermann, in *Schāhnāme. Das persische Königsbuch. Miniaturen und Texte der Berliner Handschrift von 1605*, ed. V. Enderlein/W. Sundermann, Leipzig/Weimar 1988, 5–29. We shall refer to this again.

2. (p. 160–4) The best introductions to the archaeology and art of the Sasanian period are: R. Ghirshman, *Iran. Parthes et Sassanides*, Paris 1962 (with some 'idiosyncratic' interpretations); G. Herrmann, *The Iranian Revival*, London 1977, and her article 'The Art of the Sasanians', in *The Arts of Persia*, ed. R. W. Ferrier, New Haven 1989, 61–79; D. Shepherd, 'Sasanian Art', *CHI* III 2, 1983, 1113–29. 1366–75, and P. O. Harper, 'Art, Sasanian', *EncIr* II, 1987, 585–94. On the reliefs much interesting information appears in L. Vanden Berghe, *Reliefs rupestres de l'Iran ancien*, Brussels 1984, as well as in the series *Iranische Denkmäler* published by the German Archaeological Institute in Berlin (so far there are monographs on the following reliefs: Bishapur I–VI, Naqsh-i Rustam 5.6.8.; Darab; Sarab-i Bahram; Sarab-i Qandil; Sar Mashhad); on the reliefs of Ardashir and Shapur see also W. Hinz,

Altiranische Funde und Forschungen, Berlin 1969, and M. Meyer, 'Die Felsbilder Shapurs I.', *JDAI* 105, 1990, 237–302; on ANRm I see Hinz, on ŠNRm 6 the volume by G. Herrmann in the above-mentioned series *Iranische Denkmäler*; quotation: ŠKZ Pa. 3f/Gr. 6ff; Pa. 9ff/Gr. 19ff; Taq-i Bustan: K. Tanabe, 'Iconography of the Royal-Hunt Bas-Reliefs at Taq-i Bustan', *Orient* (Tokyo) 19, 1983, 103–16; S. Fukai et al., *Taq-i Bustan I–IV*, Tokyo 1968–84; some of the sculptures are differently dated by H. v. Gall, *Das Reiterkampfbild in der iranischen und iranisch beeinflußten Kunst*, Berlin 1990. Architecture: an excellent general introduction is provided by D. Huff, 'Architecture III', *EncIr* II, 1987, 329–34. Urban planning: id., 'Sasanian Cities', *A General Study of Urbanization and Urban Planning in Iran*, ed. M. Y. Kiani, Tehran 1986, 176–204; Firuzabad: L. Trümpelmann, *Zwischen Persepolis und Firuzabad*, Mainz 1991, 63–71; Bishapur: R. Ghirshman, *Bichapour I–II*, Paris 1956–71; Jundaisabur: D. T. Potts, 'Gundeshapur and the Gondeisos', *IrAnt* 24, 1989, 323–35. Palaces: L. Bier, 'Sasanian Palaces in Perspective', *Archaeology* 35. 1, 1982, 29–36; W. Kleiss, *Die Entwicklung von Palästen und palastartigen Wohnbauten in Iran*, Vienna 1989; Ardashir's palaces: G. Gerster/D. Huff, 'Die Paläste des Königs Ardaschir', *Bild der Wissenschaft* 11, 1977, 48–60; Bishapur: see above; Ctesiphon: E. J. Keall, 'Ayvān (or Tāq)-e Kesrā', *EncIr* III, 1989, 155–9; Qasr-i Shirin: J. Schmidt, 'Qasr-i Šīrīn. Feuertempel oder Palast?', *BaM* 9, 1978, 39–47; on war damage in Iran see M. Charlesworth, 'Preliminary Report on War-Damaged Cities and Sites in South-Western and Western Iran', *Iran* 25, 1987, XV–XVI. Bridges: L. Bier, 'Notes on Mihr Narseh's Bridge Near Firuzabad', *AMI* N.F. 19, 1986, 263–8. Fortifications: R. N. Frye, 'The Sasanian System of Walls of Defense', *Studies in Memory of G. Wiet*, ed. M. Rosen-Ayalon, Jerusalem 1977, 7–15; R. Boucharlat, 'La forteresse sassanide du Tūrāng-Tepe', *Le Plateau iranien et l'Asie Centrale des origines à la conquête islamique*, Paris 1977, 329–42. Fire temples: a standard work is K. Schippmann, *Die iranischen Feuerheiligtümer*, Berlin 1971; see Boucharlat, 'Chahar Taq et temple du feu sassanide', *De l'Indus aux Balkans*. Recueil à la mémoire de J. Deshayes, Paris 1985, 461–78; Takht-i Sulaiman: R. Naumann, *Die Ruinen von Tacht-e Suleiman und Zendan-e Suleiman*, Berlin 1977; Huff, 'Recherches archéologiques à Takht-i Suleiman', *CRAI* 1978, 774–89. Metalwork: P. O. Harper, *Silver Vessels of the Sasanian Period*, vol. 1: Royal Imagery, New York 1981. Textiles: S. M. Bier, in *The Royal Hunter*, ed. P. O. Harper, New York 1978, 119ff; on clothing see E. H. Peck, 'Clothing IV', *EncIr* V, 1992, 739–52. Glass: S. Fukai, *Persian Glass*, New York 1977. Shapur cameo: v. Gall, *Reiterkampfbild*, 56–59 (but he relates it to Shapur II and Jovian). Stuccowork: J. Kröger, *Sasanidischer Stuckdekor*, Mainz 1982. Seals and bullae: major publications: A. D. H. Bivar, *Catalogue of the Western Asiatic Seals in the British Museum. Stamp Seals, II: The Sasanian Dynasty*, London 1969; *Sasanian Remains from Qasr-i Abu Nasr: Seals,* ed. R. N. Frye, Cambridge/Mass. 1973; R. Göbl, *Der sāsānidische Siegelkanon*, Braunschweig 1973; id., *Die Tonbullen vom Taht-e Suleiman*, Berlin 1976; Gignoux, *Catalogue des sceaux, camées et bulles sasanides de la Bibliothèque*

Nationale et du Musée du Louvre, II: Les sceaux et bulles inscrits, Paris 1978; Ph. Gignoux/R. Gyselen, *Sceaux sasanides de diverses collections privées*, Louvain 1982; idem, *Bulles et sceaux sassanides de diverses collections*, Paris 1987 (both authors regularly publish pieces newly found in the art market and others from collections). An onomastic study of these pieces – mainly dating from a later period – (as well as inscriptions and coins) is published in Gignoux, *Noms propres sassanides en Moyen-Perse épigraphique* (IPNB II, 2), Vienna 1986. Coins: major comprehensive descriptions: R. Göbl, *Sasanian Numismatics*, Braunschweig 1971; D. Sellwood et al., *An Introduction to Sasanian Coins*, London 1985; M. Alram, *Nomina Propria in Nummis* (IPNB, IV), Vienna 1986, 186–216; pls 22–6; Kushano-Sasanian coins: see Alram, as well as J. Cribb, 'Numismatic Evidence for Kushano-Sasanian Chronology', *StIr* 19, 1990, 151–93.

10. The King and his Subjects: 1–2

1. (pp. 165–71) Quotation: ŠNRb. Eranshahr: Gh. Gnoli, *The Idea of Iran*, Rome 1989; Aneran: literally 'Non-Iran'; this is an ethno-linguistic concept describing the political and religious enemies of Iran (and Zoroastrianism). In ŠKZ Shapur uses it to denote all the regions he (temporarily) conquered (Syria, Cappadocia, Cilicia), while he counts Armenia and the Caucasus region as part of Eran, although they were primarily inhabited by non-Iranian people. Kirdir lists Armenia, Georgia, Albania, Balasagan, as well as Syria and Asia Minor, as regions of Aneran (see Ph. Gignoux, 'Anērān', *EncIr* II, 1987, 30f.). King and gods: W. Sundermann, '*Kē čihr az yazdān*. Zur Titulatur der Sasanidenkönige', *ArOr* 56, 1988, 338–40; H. Humbach, 'Herrscher, Gott und Gottessohn in Iran und in angrenzenden Ländern', *Menschwerdung Gottes – Vergöttlichung von Herrschern*, ed. D. Zeller, Fribourg/Göttingen 1988, 89–114. Quotation: Humbach, 104. The 'vagueness' of the Greek translation (and even of the MP *čihr*, which may signify 'seed', 'descent', but also 'visible form, appearance, face' as well as 'essence', 'nature') points to the fact that the Sasanian royal title could be – and probably was – interpreted in different ways. Thus the Christian–Syriac literature contains both formulations that might be translated as 'from the seed of the Gods' and correspond with *ek genous theōn* in their construction, and phrases that can be interpreted as a translation of *kē čihr az yazdān* ('whose nature is from the Gods'). 'With the Zoroastrian conception, it [the interpretation of *čihr* as 'nature, character'] was indeed more compatible than the king's claim to divine ancestry and divine procreation, which is not confirmed by the extant Zoroastrian literature. On the other hand, the idea of the king as the image of deity was quite familiar to it, and this could also be understood in the sense of the king's divine nature, since the term *čihr* combines the inner, corporeal nature of man and its perceptible appearance. Although there is also evidence of the idea of the king as descending from the gods, this must be a reflex of old Iranian or Iranicized notions

that were unable to stand their ground against the orthodox views of the Zoroastrian priests' (Sundermann, 340).

Sasanians as promoters of Zoroastrianism: quotation ŠKZ Pa.17/Gr. 37ff; see K. Mosig-Walburg, *Die frühen sasanidischen Könige als Vertreter und Förderer der zarathustrischen Religion*, Frankfurt 1982. Royal fire and 'era': quotation: ŠVŠ; R. Altheim-Stiehl, 'Das früheste Datum der sasanidischen Geschichte, vermittelt durch die Zeitangabe der mittelpersisch-parthischen Inschrift aus Bīšāpūr', *AMI* N.F. 11, 1978, 113–16; see however Sundermann, 'Shapur's Coronation', *Bulletin of the Asia Institute* N. S. 4, 1990, 295–99, as well as L. Richter-Bernburg, 'Mani's Dodecads and Sasanian Chronology', *ZPE* 95, 1993, 71–80. See now the date given in the inscription of Abnun (see above), which confirms Ardashir's death and the beginning of Shapur's single reign in the spring of 242 AD and Shapur's first year of reign as 239/40 AD. Coins: see Mosig-Walburg; *xvarrah*: Gnoli, *Idea*, 148–51 (with earlier literature); Ardashir romance: quotation: Kārnāmag ī Ardaxšīr Pābagān, ch. 3 (transl. based on G. Widengren); see Th. Nöldeke, 'Geschichte des Artachšīr-î Pâpakân aus dem Pahlevi übersetzt', *Bezzenbergers Beiträge* 1878, 22–69. On the Sasanians' claim to Achaemenid patrimony see J. Wiesehöfer, 'Iranische Ansprüche an Rom auf ehemals achaimenidische Territorien', *AMI* N.F. 19, 1986, 177–85, and Gh. Gnoli, 'L'inscription de Šābuhr à la Kaʿbe-ye Zardošt et la propagande sassanide', *Histoire et cultes de l'Asie Centrale préislamique*, ed. P. Bernard/F. Grenet, Paris 1991, 57–63 (diff. view: E. Kettenhofen, 'Einige Überlegungen zur sasanidischen Politik gegenüber Rom im 3. Jh. n. Chr.', *The Roman and Byzantine Army in the East*, ed. E. Dąbrowa, Cracow 1994, 99–108). Sasan: quotation: Karnāmag, ch. 1. Genealogy in Tabari: quotation: I, 813, 12–814, 4 de Goeje; transl. 2f Nöldeke. Succession provisions: Paikuli: see the notes of P. O. Skjærvø in *The Sasanian Inscription of Paikuli*, pt 3. 2, Wiesbaden 1983, 13, and Sundermann, 'Rez. *The Sasanian Inscription of Paikuli*', *Kratylos* 28, 1983, 84f. Khosrow II: quotation: Theophyl. Sim. IV 8 (transl. based on P. Schreiner). 'King's Council': quotation: NPi § 68; transl. based on Humbach/ Skjærvø; cf. §§ 73 and 75, where this 'sham consultation' is called *ʾplʾsy/ʾprʾs*. The order of the people to be consulted follows from §§ 4–5 (for the succession after the death of Bahram II): 1. Narseh himself, as the person with the greatest right to the succession; 2. the 'princes'; 3. the 'magnates', 'nobles', Persians and Parthians (see Sundermann, 84). Investiture and coronation: M.-L. Chaumont, 'Où les rois sassanides étaient-ils couronnés?', *JA* 252, 1964, 58–75; quotation: Letter of Tansar 39f Minovi (Eng. transl. M. Boyce). The 'Letter of Tansar' is a New Persian translation of an Arabic translation of a Sasanian 'original', probably from the late Sasanian period. It purports to be a letter from a religious adviser of Ardashir I known from the Zoroastrian tradition and called Tansar (other reading: Tosar), who is describing the advantages of the reign of the first Sasanian king and thus trying to make the king of Tabaristan take Ardashir's side. Crown: compare the formula 'in the year in which ... King Shapur ... put on the great diadem [*diadēma megiston*] [i.e. became king]' in *CMC* 18, 4–8; on the 'crown' see Chaumont, 'A propos de la chute de Hatra et du couronnement de Shapur Ier', *AAntHung* 27, 1979, 217–22, and Skjærvø, in *The Sasanian Inscription*, pt 3. 1, 28f; 51f; 93 and pt 3. 2, 26f. A 'coronation book' used by the Arab author Hamza of Isfahan, presumably an official Sasanian 'album', informs us about the crown, robe and trousers of each king, the colours of which serve to identify him as an individual. Synarchy: see Sundermann, *Shapur's Coronation*. Idealization of Ardashir: NPi § 65.

2. (pp. 171–82) Quotation: ŠH 1–6. This inscription describes an archery contest between the king and his suite, in which Shapur 'broke a record'. Ranks of nobility: NPi 2–3 (85); ŠKZ 22/17/39ff. King and aristocracy: P. O. Skjærvø, 'The Interpretation of the Paikuli Inscription', *Akten d. VII. Intern. Kongr.f. Iran. Kunst und Archäologie 1976* (AMI, Suppl. vol. 6), Berlin 1979, 329–31; 'Persians and Parthians': NPi 3 (§ 5) et al. Bestowal of marks of distinction: quotation: Amm. XVIII 5, 6; cf. KKZ 4/KNRm 9f/KSM 5 ('The King of Kings Hormizd bestowed on me the tiara [*kulāf*] and the belt [*kamar*], and he raised my position [*gāh*; throne, i.e. the place near the king] and my rank'); place of honour according to lineage: quotation: Procop. Pers. I 6, 13; cf. I 13, 16 (Mihran is in fact the name of a noble clan); marks of distinction: tiaras: H. v. Gall, *Das Reiterkampfbild in der iranischen und iranisch beeinflußten Kunst parthischer und sasanidischer Zeit*, Berlin 1990, 23–26; tiara, belt, earrings: E. H. Peck, 'Clothing IV', *EncIr* V, 1992, 739–52; changes in the late period: Theophyl. Sim. I 9 ('... since it is a familiar habit of Persians to bear names according to distinguished positions, as if they disdained to be called by their birth names'); see Procop. Pers. I 17, 26–8 (a Mihran is punished by being deprived of a golden hairband: 'For in that country no one is allowed to wear a ring or a belt, a clasp or any other object of gold without royal bestowal'). For other examples see Tabari I, 990, 16f de Goeje; Theophyl. Sim. III 8 and Dinawari 85, 6f Guirg. On the Mazdakite movement, see below; weakening of the aristocracy: O. Klima, *Mazdak*, Prague 1957, passim: noblemen affected: see W. Sundermann, 'Mazdak und die mazdakitischen Volksaufstände', *Altertum* 23. 4, 1977, 245–9. Reforms of Kavad I and Khosrow I: quotation: Tabari I, 897, 1ff de Goeje, transl. based on Nöldeke, 163–5; on 'cavaliers' and *dehkānān* see F. Altheim/R. Stiehl, *Ein asiatischer Staat*, Wiesbaden 1954, 129ff; id., *Finanzgeschichte der Spätantike*, Frankfurt 1957, 57ff. Whether this new order can rightly be called a 'feudal order' is a matter of definition. King and aristocracy during the late phase of the empire: Altheim/Stiehl, *Finanzgeschichte*, 75ff; Bahram Chubin: A. Sh. Shahbazi, 'Bahrām VI Čōbīn', *EncIr* III, 1989, 519–22; romance: see Altheim, *Geschichte der Hunnen*, vol. 4, Berlin 1962, 234ff; reproaches against Khosrow II: Tabari I, 1046, 14ff de Goeje. Women of the royal household: Adur Anahid: ŠKZ 23/18/39; 25/20/47; see Ph. Gignoux, *EncIr* I, 1985, 472; Khoranzem: ŠKZ 25/20/46f; there exists a seal of hers (Gignoux, *Catalogue des sceaux, camées et bulles sasanides*, Paris 1978, 4. 77); Denag (sister of

Ardashir I): ŠKZ 29/23/56; her seal: A. Ja. Borisov/V. G. Lukonin, *Sasanidskie Gemmy*, Leningrad 1963, 48, No. 2. It bears the legend 'Denag, Queen of Queens, head of the Eunuch section'; alleged father–daughter and sister–brother marriage: see W. Hinz, *Altiranische Funde und Forschungen*, Berlin 1969, 124; 126; against this theory: A. Maricq, 'Res Gestae Divi Saporis', *Syria* 35, 1958, 334f; J. Harmatta, 'Sino-Iranica', *AAntHung* 19, 1971, 127–31; Bahram II and his family on coins: R. Göbl, *Sasanian Numismatics*, Braunschweig 1971, 43–45; pls 4f, Nos 54–71; women on seals: Ph. Gignoux/R. Gyselen, 'Sceaux de femmes à l'époque sassanide', *Archaeologia Iranica et Orientalis*. Miscellanea in honorem L. Vanden Berghe, vol. 2, Ghent 1989, 877–96; ruling queens: Puran; see Tabari I, 1064, 1ff de Goeje et al.; Azarmigdukht: Gignoux, *EncIr III*, 1989, 190. Religious dignitaries: Gignoux, 'Éléments de prosopographie de quelques mobads sasanides', *JA* 1982, 257–69; id., 'Die religiöse Administration in sasanidischer Zeit: Ein Überblick', *Kunst, Kultur und Geschichte der Achämenidenzeit und ihr Fortleben*, ed. H. Koch/D. N. MacKenzie (*AMI*, suppl. vol. 10), Berlin 1983, 253–66; id., 'Pour une esquisse des fonctions religieuses sous les Sasanides', *JSAI* 7, 1986, 93–108. Kirdir: quotation: KNRb 22ff; interpretation of his title under Bahram II: Ph. Huyse/P. O. Skjærvø (personal communication by Ph. H.); see the different reading 'Kirdir, the Mobad of the blessed Bahram and of Ohrmazd' by F. Grenet, 'Observations sur les titres de Kirdīr', *StIr* 19, 1990, 87–94; *mōbad* and *dādvar*: KKZ 8/KSM 12/KNRm 24f.; Kirdīr as *āyēnbed*: Gignoux, *Esquisse*, 96–102; Kirdīr as the most powerful religious dignitary: Gignoux, 'Church–State Relations in the Sasanian Period', *Bulletin of the Middle Eastern Culture Center in Japan* 1, 1984, 78. Hierarchization of offices and jurisdictions: Gignoux, *Administration*, 257. Mihr-Narseh: Tabari 1, 869, 6ff de Goeje; Avestan 'classes': M. Shaki, 'Class System III', *EncIr* V, 1992, 654. 'Middle classes': (deported) Christians as skilled workers, artisans, physicians etc.: W. Schwaigert, *Das Christentum in Ḥūzistān im Rahmen der frühen Kirchengeschichte Persiens bis zur Synode von Seleukeia-Ktesiphon im Jahre 410*, Diss. Marburg 1989, 19f; 24–38, as well as S. N. C. Lieu, 'Captives, Refugees and Exiles', *The Defence of the Roman and Byzantine East*, ed. Ph. Freeman/D. Kennedy, vol. 2, Oxford 1986, 476–83; the martyr Pusai as 'head of the artisans': see below; on the 'academy' in Jundaisabur (Veh-Andiyok-Shabuhr), see below; on wholesale trade, see below. Peasant population: *škōh/xvadāy*: Shaki, 656f; in general: Altheim/Stiehl, 'Die Lage der Bauern unter den späten Sāsāniden', *Die Rolle der Volksmassen in der Geschichte der vorkapitalistischen Gesellschaftsformationen*, ed. J. Herrmann/I. Sellnow, Berlin 1975, 79–86; Kavad and the girl: Ibn Hauqal 303, 19ff Kramers; quotation: 304, 8ff; transl. based on R. Altheim-Stiehl; peasants in the Kārnāmag of Khosrow I: M. Grignaschi, 'Quelques spécimens de la littérature sassanide', *JA* 254, 1966, 6ff, 16–45; Altheim/Stiehl, *Lage*, 83ff. The text emphasizes the mutual dependence between army and peasants (protection vs. provision). Earlier tax suspensions: Grignaschi, 18; cf. Tabari 1, 866, 3ff de Goeje (Bahram V) and 1, 873, 20ff de Goeje (Peroz). Reports about irregularities: Grignaschi, 22 with note. Encroachments of the wealthy: Tabari 1, 988, 15ff de Goeje. Social mobility: D. Metzler, *Ziele und Formen königlicher Innenpolitik im vorislamischen Iran*, Münster 1977, 245f. Slavery in the Sasanian empire: M. Macuch, 'Barda and Bardadārī II', *EncIr* III, 1989, 763–6. Law books: *Mādayān ī hazār dādestān* (actually: *Hazār dādestān*): editions: *Mâdigân-î Hazâr Dâdistân*, ed. J. J. Modi, Poona 1901; T. D. Anklesaria, *The Social Code of the Parsis in Sassanian Times or Mâdigân i Hazâr Dâdistân*, pt II, Bombay 1913; whole or part editions: S. J. Bulsara, *The Laws of the Ancient Persians as Found in the 'Matîkdân ê hazâr Dâtastân' or 'The Digest of a Thousand Points of Law'*, Bombay 1937; M. Macuch, *Das sasanidische Rechtsbuch 'Mātakdān ī Hazār Dātistān' (Teil II)*, Wiesbaden 1981; A. Perikhanian, *Sasanidskij Sudebnik*, Erivan 1973. See now the excellent study of M. Macuch, *Rechtskasuistik und Gerichtspraxis zu Beginn des siebenten Jahrhunderts in Iran (Iranica*, 1), Wiesbaden 1993; I was, however, not able to revise this chapter in the light of her arguments. Quotation: Macuch, 'Ein mittelpersischer *terminus technicus* im syrischen Rechtskodex des Īshōbōht und im sasanidischen Rechtsbuch', *Studia Semitica necnon Iranica*. R. Macuch Septuagenario ab amicis et discipulis dedicata, ed. M. Macuch et al., Wiesbaden 1989, 150 n. 7. On the content of the *Mādayān* see also Perikhanian, 'Iranian Society and Law', *CHI* III 2, 1983, 627–80. Other Middle Persian works dealing with legal questions are mentioned, together with editions and translations, in Macuch, *Rechtskasuistik*, 1ff. Legal book of Isho'bukht: edition: *Syrische Rechtsbücher*, ed. E. Sachau, vol. 3, Berlin 1914; see Macuch, *Terminus* (with earlier literature). Legal writings of Mar Simeon: edition: Sachau, ib. Legal writings on marital questions: edition: ib. Iranian family laws: my arguments are based on Perikhanian's account in 'Society', but see now also Macuch, *Rechtskasuistik*. Marriage between blood relations: Polemics of Isho'bukht: Sachau, 30–43; see also *Synodicon Orientale*, ed. J. B. Chabot, Paris 1902, 82, 29–83, 2; 118, 15–17; 149, 29–150, 2 (synodal letter of Mar Aba from the year 544 about the prohibition of such unions, 'which the Magi [Zoroastrians] contract'; decisions of the synods of 576 and 585). Reaction of Byzantines: A. D. Lee, 'Close-Kin Marriage in Late Antique Mesopotamia', *GRBS* 29, 1988, 403–13; curiously enough, Kirdir in one of his inscriptions prides himself on having brought about many marriages of the kind (KKZ 14). Polemic against the levirate: Isho'bukht (Sachau, 42–5). Law of things and obligations: see Perikhanian's article as well as Macuch, *Rechtskasuistik*.

11. Eranshahr: The Empire, its Inhabitants: 1–4

1. (pp. 183–91) A standard book on the administration of the Sasanian empire is R. Gyselen, *La géographie administrative de l'Empire sassanide*, Paris 1989, which primarily deals with the analysis of sigillographic material, but also provides information on other testimonies. Further important contributions, especially on the Sasanian administrative system, are V. G. Lukonin, 'Political, Social and Administrative

Institutions, Taxes and Trade', *CHI* III 2, 1983, 681–746, as well as numerous articles by Ph. Gignoux (see below). The map of the Sasanian empire by E. Kettenhofen (TAVO B VI 3) is very helpful. On the Sasanian taxation system, standard works are still: F. Altheim/R. Stiehl, *Ein asiatischer Staat*, Wiesbaden 1954, and id., *Finanzgeschichte der Spätantike*, Frankfurt 1957. The court of Shapur I (quotation): ŠKZ MP. 30ff/Pa. 24ff/Gr. 59ff; transl. based on M. Back with modifications by the author; other lists: ŠKZ 28ff/22ff/54ff (reigns of Pabag and Ardashir); NPi MP. 6f/ Pa. 6f (§ 16); 15ff/13ff (§ 32); 47ff, 141ff (§§ 92f.). The empire and its provinces: ŠKZ 1ff/1ff/2ff (quotation); KNRm 34f./KSM 16f; NPi 44ff/41ff (§§ 92f) with comm. by P. O. Skjærvø (*Paikuli* 3. 2, 120ff); see also P. Calmeyer, 'Die "statistische Landcharte des Perserreiches" – II', *AMI* N.F. 16, 1983, 160–67. 'Kingdoms': see map 4; 'kings': ŠKZ 23ff/18ff/40ff; 25f/20f./47f; 30f/24f./59f; NPi 44ff/41ff (§§ 92f). *Šahrab*: see initial quotation (ŠKZ); total number under Shapur: Gyselen, 89f. Sources on administration in the late Sasanian period: seals/bullae: see literature in Gyselen; martyrologies: see above; synodal accounts: J. B. Chabot, *Synodicon Orientale ou recueil des Synodes Nestoriens*, Paris 1902. Introduction of 'administrative' seals: *Mādayān Hazār Dādestān* 93, 4–9 Perikhanian. 'Provinces' and 'Districts': see Gyselen's geographical definitions, 41ff. Tasks of the officials: see Gyselen (with earlier literature); *šahrab*: Gyselen, 28f; *mogbed*: ib., 28–31; *driyōšān ğādaggōv ud dādvar:* ib., 31–33; *dādvar*: ib., 34; *handarzbed*: ib., 33f; ŠKZ see initial quotation; *mogān-handarzbed*: Gyselen, 33f; *āyēnbed:* ib., 34; Kirdir as *a*.: KKZ 8; *framādār*: Gyselen, 37f.; *āmārgar: ib.*, 35–37; *maguh*: reading based on W. Sundermann; Gyselen, 38–40; 'religious' officials in trials of Christians and 'prison staff': Ph. Gignoux, 'Die religiöse Administration in sasanidischer Zeit: Ein Überblick', *Kunst, Kultur und Geschichte der Achämenidenzeit und ihr Fortleben*, ed. H. Koch/D. N. MacKenzie, Berlin 1983, 253–66. *Bidaxš*: Sundermann, *EncIr* IV, 1990, 242–4. *Argbed*: M.-L. Chaumont, *EncIr* II, 1987, 400f. (*zēndānīg* and) state prison: E. Kettenhofen, 'Das Staatsgefängnis der Sāsāniden', *WO* 19, 1988, 96–101. Court appointments: Lukonin, 709–13; *hazāruft, sālār ī darīgān* and *darbed*: Chaumont, 'Chiliarque et curopalate à la cour des Sassanides', *IrAnt* 10, 1973, 139–65. *Dastgird* and urbanization policy: Altheim/Stiehl, *Asiatischer Staat*, 12ff; D. Metzler, *Ziele und Formen königlicher Innenpolitik im vorislamischen Iran*, Münster 1977, 177ff; Susa: Altheim/Stiehl, ib., 28f; R. Boucharlat, 'Suse à l'époque sasanide', *Mesopotamia* 22, 1987, 357–66; deportations: Metzler, ib.; Veh-Andiyok-Shabuhr: see below; Veh-Andiyok-Husrav: Tabari 1, 898, 6ff. de Goeje ('Then Khosrow had a plan of Antiochia made, with precise details of the dimensions of the city, the number of houses in it, its streets and all other things in it. Then he had a city built in faithful imitation of it near Mada'in [Ctesiphon and neighbouring cities]; so the city which is called the "Roman" one was carefully designed after the plan of Antiochia. Then he had the inhabitants of Antiochia brought to the new city and settled there. When they entered it through the city gate, each of them went into a dwelling which so closely resembled his own in Antiochia that it seemed he had never left that city' (transl. based on Altheim/Stiehl); see Ya'qubi, *ta'rīḫ* 1, 186, 15ff Houtsma. On all this, see Altheim/Stiehl, *Asiatischer Staat*, 44f; refugees et al.: see below. Sasanian taxation system: quotation: Tabari 1, 960, 7ff de Goeje (transl. based on Nöldeke with modifications by Altheim/Stiehl); other ancient records and their analysis in Altheim/Stiehl, *Finanzgeschichte*, 7ff; on further taxes and imposts see M. Grignaschi, 'La riforma tributaria di Ḫosrō I e il feudalismo Sassanide', *La Persia nel Medioevo*, Rome 1971, 87–131; late Roman–Byzantine model: E. Stein, 'Ein Kapitel vom persischen und vom byzantinischen Staate', *Byzantinisch-neugriechische Jahrbücher* 1, 1920, 50–87; Altheim/Stiehl, ib., 31ff; N. V. Pigulevskaja, *Les villes de l'état iranien aux époques parthe et sassanide*, Paris 1963, 229; other point of view: G. Garsoian, 'Byzantium and the Sasanians', *CHI* III 1, 1983, 587f (not an imperial, but a regional model from Syria). Khosrow's maxims: *murūǧ* 1, 311, 18ff. Pellat (transl. Altheim/Stiehl). Urban taxes: Altheim/Stiehl, *Finanzgeschichte*, 45ff. Exceptional revenues: ib., 49ff.

2. (pp. 191–9) Agriculture in Sasanian Iran: Tabari 1, 960, 7ff de Goeje; untaxed agricultural crops: Baladhuri 271 de Goeje; see Th. Nöldeke, *Geschichte der Perser und Araber zur Zeit der Sasaniden*, Leiden 1879, 245 n. 4–5; date palms: ib.; pastures: Mas'udi, *murūǧ* 1, 309, 19 Pellat. Farming in Khuzistan: R. J. Wenke, 'Imperial Investments and Agricultural Developments in Parthian and Sasanian Khuzestan, 150 BC to AD 640', *Mesopotamia* 10–11, 1975–76, 31–221 (partly against R. McAdams, 'Agriculture and Urban Life in Early South-Western Iran', *Science* 136, 1962, 109–22; see Wenke, 133). Handicrafts in Iran: quotation (Pusai's career): P. Bedjan, *Acta martyrum et sanctorum*, vol. II, 208ff; settlement of artisans and skilled workers: see D. Metzler, *Ziele und Formen königlicher Innenpolitik im vorislamischen Iran*, Münster 1977, 213ff; *rēš ummānē = qārōḡbēḏ*: Bedjan II 204, 17f (Simon A-Martyrium) (see also S. E. Assemani, *Acta Sanctorum Martyrum Orientalium et Occidentalium in duas partes distributa*, Rome 1748 (repr. Farigliano 1970), 1, 34, 33–5, 1, and M. Kmosko, 'S. Simeon Bar Sabba'e', *Patrologia Syriaca* I 2, Paris 1907, 744, 25–775, 1: in the so-called Simon A-Martyrium, *qārōḡbēḏ* is interpreted as: *aḥīd ummānē ∂-malkā*); on Pusai and the martyrs in Khuzistan see W. Schwaigert, *Das Christentum in Ḫūzistān im Rahmen der frühen Kirchengeschichte Persiens bis zur Synode von Seleukeia-Ktesiphon im Jahre 410*, Diss. Marburg 1989; Synod of 544: *Synod. Orientale*, ed. Chabot 78f/331f. Khuzistan's textile industry: Schwaigert, 157f; dyers: Chron. Se'ert PO IV 3, 296, 3 Scher; builders, smiths, locksmiths: Metzler, 229ff. Resistance: Tabari I, 986 de Goeje; Nöldeke, 26of. Corporations (and crafts in general): N. Pigulevskaja, *Les villes de l'état iranien aux époques parthe et sassanide*, Paris 1963, 116ff; 159ff; A. Tafazzoli, 'A List of Trades and Crafts in the Sassanian Period', *AMI* N. F. 7, 1974, 191–6, containing a list of 26 different 'trades' in the Sasanian period. Trade in the Sasanian empire: quotation: Expositio XIX; XXII; on this work, see J. Rougé, *Expositio totius mundi et gentium*, Paris 1966, and H.-J. Drexhage, 'Die "Expositio

totius mundi et gentium"', *MBAH* 2.1, 1983, 3–41. On trade and economy in Sasanian–(Eastern) Roman treaties and agreements see E. Winter, in *MBAH* 6. 2, 1987, 46–74; 297: Petrus Patricius fr. 14 (FHG IV 189); 408/09: Cod. Iust. IV 63, 4; 562: Men. Prot. fr. 6, 1 p. 71f Blockley; espionage: A. D. Lee, *Information and Frontiers*, Cambridge 1993; sericulture: Procop. Got. IV 17, 1ff; Byzantine contacts with Axum and South Arabia: Procop. Pers. I 19, 1; 20, 9ff; Byzantium and the Turks: Men. Prot. fr. 19ff. pp. 171ff. Blockley; on Byzantine trade with the East see Pigulevskaja, *Byzanz auf den Wegen nach Indien*, Berlin/Amsterdam 1969. Iran and India: see especially D. Whitehouse/ A. Williamson, 'Sasanian Maritime Trade', *Iran* 11, 1973, 35–49; quotation: CMC 144, 3ff; transl. L. Koenen/C. Römer; Mani's return: W. Sundermann, *Mitteliranische manichäische Texte kirchengeschichtlichen Inhalts*, Berlin 1981, No. 4 a. 1 (pp. 56f); on Mani's voyage see Sundermann, 'Mani, India and the Manichaean Religion', *South Asian Studies* 2, 1986, 11–19; and now C. Römer, *Manis frühe Missionsreisen nach der Kölner Manibiographie*, Opladen 1994; Nestorians and India: C. D. G. Müller, *Geschichte der orientalischen Nationalkirchen*, Göttingen 1981, D 311ff; see also Whitehouse, 'Epilogue: Roman Trade in Perspective', *Rome and India*, ed. V. Begley/R. D. De Puma, Madison/London 1991, 217, and G. Gropp, 'Christian Maritime Trade of the Sasanian Age in the Persian Gulf', *Golf-Archäologie*, ed. K. Schippmann et al., Buch am Erlbach 1991, 83–8. Sasanians and Arabia: C. E. Bosworth, 'Iran and the Arabs before Islam', *CHI* III 1, 1983, 593–612; North-eastern Arabia: D. T. Potts, *The Arabian Gulf in Antiquity*, vol. 2, Oxford 1990, 197ff; Southern Arabia: Potts, 296ff. The army in Sasanian Iran: A. Sh. Shahbazi, 'Army II', *EncIr* II, 1987, esp. 496–9; quotation: Amm. XXV 1, 11–14 (Eng. transl. John C. Rolfe); cf. XXIV 6, 8; 'cavaliers' of Khosrow I: Tabari 1, 964, 9 f de Goeje; transl. Nöldeke 248f; and Dinawari 74, 15f Guirg.; 'Immortals': Procop. Pers. I 14, 44; bowmen and infantry: Amm. XXIV 6, 8; and XXIII 6, 83; Procop. Pers. I 14, 24. 52; siege technique: Amm. XIX 5f; XX 6f. 11. *Spāhbed*: ŠKZ 29; NPi 17; *aspbed*: ŠKZ 31; *adrastadaran salanēs*: Procop. Pers. I 16, 18; Sundermann, *EncIr* II, 1987, 662; Khosrow's reforms: Mas'ūdī, murūǧī, 311, 23f Pellat; Tabari 1, 894, 5f de Goeje; transl. Nöldeke 155; 4 *spāhbed*: Gh. Gnoli, 'The Quadripartition of the Sasanian Empire', *East & West* N. S. 35, 1985, 265–70, as well as (based on the reading of a bulla legend) Ph. Gignoux, 'A propos de quelques inscriptions et bulles sassanides', *Histoire et cultes de l'Asie Centrale préislamique*, Paris 1991, 67–69; *paygōspān* and *marzbān*: Gignoux, 'L'organisation administrative sasanide: Le cas du *marzbān*', *JSAI* 4, 1984, 1–29; recruiting, accounting and soldiers' fiefs: F. Altheim/ R. Stiehl, *Finanzgeschichte der Spätantike*, Frankfurt 1957, 62ff. Weaknesses of the Persians: Amm. XXV 1, 18. Single combat: quotation: Malalas XIV 23 (transl. E. Jeffreys et al.) Royal legitimacy: see Hamza Isf. 50ff Gottw. Kings as authors: Shahbazi, 498f.

3. (pp. 199–216) Religious conditions in the Sasanian empire: see the articles in the

CHI III 2, 1983, and for the 3rd and 4th centuries J. Wiesehöfer, 'Geteilte Loyalitäten. Religiöse Minderheiten des 3. und 4. Jahrhunderts n. Chr. im Spannungsfeld zwischen Rom und dem sāsānidischen Iran', *Klio* 75, 1993 (with earlier literature); quotation: KKZ 7ff/KNRm 20ff/KSM 10ff. Zoroastrianism under the Sasanians: see esp. H. W. Bailey, *Zoroastrian Problems in the Ninth-century Books*, Oxford 1943, 2nd edn 1971; M. Boyce, *Zoroastrians. Their Religious Beliefs and Practices*, London 2nd edn 1984; *Textual Sources for the Study of Zoroastrianism*, ed. and transl. by M. Boyce, Manchester 1984 (source book in translation); J. Duchesne-Guillemin, 'Zoroastrian Religion', *CHI* III 2, 1983, 866–908; Gh. Gnoli, 'Politica religiosa e concezione della regalità sotto i Sassanidi', *La Persia nel Medioevo*, Rome 1971, 225–51; R. C. Zaehner, *The Teachings of the Magi*, London 1956 (source vol.), and id., *The Dawn and Twilight of Zoroastrianism*, Oxford 1961. See also the literature referred to in Part I, ch. 4, vi. Burials: D. Huff, 'Zum Problem zoroastrischer Grabanlagen in Fars, I: Gräber', *AMI* N.F. 21, 1988, 145–76. Hierarchization of places of worship: Boyce, *Zoroastrians*, 123ff, as well as the articles 'Ādur Buzēn-Mihr', 'Ādur Farnbāg' and 'Ādur Gušnasp', in *EncIr* I, 1985, 472–6. Foundations for the benefit of the souls: M. Macuch, 'Charitable Foundations, I', *EncIr* V, 1992, 380–82 (with earlier literature). The theories of the Zurvanism of the kings (see Part I, ch. 4, vi) and of 'iconoclasm' are supported among others by M. Boyce, but are not beyond controversy. Canonization of the Avesta: *Dēnkard* (Dk 316, 21–317, 5; 321, 9–12 ed. Dresden). Christians in the Sasanian empire: summaries: A. S. Atiya, *A History of Eastern Christianity*, Millwood 2nd edn 1991; C. D. G. Müller, *Geschichte der orientalischen Nationalkirchen*, Göttingen 1981; on the beginnings see M.-L. Chaumont, *La christianisation de l'Empire iranien*, Louvain 1988, 1–53, and W. Schwaigert, *Das Christentum in Ḫūzistān im Rahmen der frühen Kirchengeschichte Persiens*, Diss. Marburg 1989, 1–11. Settlement of the deported: ŠKZ Pa. 15f/Gr. 34–6; Chron. Seʿert PO IV 3, 220–23 Scher; Schwaigert, 19–38, Chaumont, 74–9, and S. N. C. Lieu, 'Captives, Refugees and Exiles', *The Defence of the Roman and Byzantine East*, ed. Ph. Freeman/D. Kennedy, vol. 2, Oxford 1986, 476–83; positive effect on the spread of Christianity: Chron. Seʿert PO IV 3, 222, 5. 7–9; 223, 1–2 Scher; see Mari b. Sulaiman (H. Gismondi, *Maris Amri et Slibae de patriarchis Nestorianorum commentaria*, pt. 1, Rome 1899) 8, 19–20. Martyrdom of Candida and persecutions under Bahram II: it is difficult to find evidence for the persecution of Christians under Bahram and Kirdir; see Chron. Seʿert PO IV 3, 238 Scher, where there is nominal evidence for only two martyrs (Qariba, Qandida); for Qandida there exists a martyrology (S. P. Brock, *Syriac Perspectives on Late Antiquity*, London 1984, IX, 167–81). Christianity under Bahram III, Narseh and Hormizd II: Chron. Seʿert PO IV 3, 254, 8–9. 12; 255, 2 Scher. Ecclesiastical organization: Schwaigert, 50–102; Chaumont, 140–47. Council of Nicaea: Chaumont, 147–54. On Constantine and Shapur II see the differing points of view of T. D. Barnes, 'Constantine and the Christians of Persia', *JRS* 75, 1985, 126–36, and M. R. Vivian, *A Letter to Shapur*,

Ph. D. Univ. of California, Santa Barbara 1987 (including the ancient tradition). Cause of persecutions: futile siege of Nisibis (Chronicle of Arbela 52, 9–11 Kawerau); persecutions: Schwaigert, 103–75. Quotation: P. Bedjan (*Acta martyrum et sanctorum*, vol. I–VII, Paris 1890–97) II 136, 10–14; transl. O. Braun, *Ausgewählte Akten persischer Märtyrer*, Kempten/Munich 1915, 9; see Chron. Se'ert PO IV 3, 299, 10 Scher; Christians' refusal to serve in the army: Bedjan II 351 (martyrology of 'Aqqebshma'); Chronicle of Arbela 54, 2–3 Kawerau; tax edict and reasons for Christian refusal: Bedjan II 136, 5–16; 137, 17; 138, 3; 140, 15–17. Aphrahat: quotation: Dem. V 1. 24 Parisot; on A. see Blum, *TRE* I, 1977, 625ff. Espionage: quotation: Chronicle of Arbela 53, 22–24 Kawerau; see also Bedjan II 143, 9–17; 334; see Lieu, *Captives*, 491–5 and Lee, *Information*. The Christians' definition of themselves: Brock, *Perspectives*, IV, 93f; VI, 12f; *nāṣrāyē/kresṭyānē*: Brock, IV, 91–95 (with other interpretations). 'Ecclesiastical languages' of the East: W. Hage, 'Einheimische Volkssprachen und syrische Kirchensprache in der nestorianischen Asienmission', *Erkenntnisse und Meinungen II*, ed. G. Wiessner, Wiesbaden 1978, 131–60, and Brock VI, 17f. Shapur and Simeon: quotation: Bedjan II 189, 1–5. Further persecutions: Schwaigert, 103–75. History of the Christians in the fourth and fifth centuries: see above-mentioned literature and esp. Hage, 'Die oströmische Staatskirche und die Christenheit des Perserreiches', *ZfKG* 84, 1973, 174–87. Synod of 410: *Synodicon Orientale*, ed. J. B. Chabot, 17–36/253–75; see C. D. G. Müller, 'Stellung und Bedeutung des Katholikos-Patriarchen von Seleukeia-Ktesiphon im Altertum', *Oriens Christianus* 53, 1969, esp. 229–31; id., *Geschichte*, D 295f. Synod of 424: *Synodicon*, 43–54/285–98; Müller, *Stellung*, 233. Synod of 484: Müller, *Geschichte*, D 298; this synod was later replaced by that of 486, so that only the latter appears in the Synodal Acts (*Synodicon*, 53–60/299–307). Significance of the 'break': Hage, *Staatskirche*, 182ff; quotation: p. 184. See the words Barsauma is said to have addressed to King Peroz: 'Only if the confession of the Christians in your lands differs from the confession of the Christians in the lands of the Greeks will their heart and their mind turn towards you.' (Barhebraeus, chron. eccl. 3, 65, 16f; transl. Altheim/Stiehl). Christians as envoys: L. Sako, *Le rôle de la hiérarchie syriaque orientale dans les rapports diplomatiques entre la Perse et Byzance aux Ve-VIIe siècles*, Paris 1986. Barsauma: S. Gero, *Barsauma of Nisibis and Persian Christianity in the Fifth Century*, Louvain 1981. School of Nisibis: A. Vööbus, *History of the School of Nisibis*, Louvain 1965. Khosrow and Mar Aba: Barhebraeus, chron. eccl. 3, 91, 7ff. In 562 a special agreement about the Christians was concluded in connection with the peace treaty between Khosrow and Justinian (see K. Güterbock, *Byzanz und Persien in ihren diplomatisch-völkerrechtlichen Beziehungen im Zeitalter Justinians*, Berlin 1906, 93–9). Concerning the close relations between the kings and Nestorian Christians, the Chronicle of Se'ert reports that the Nestorians were 'in the service' of the king (PO VII 2, 147, 5 Scher). Khosrow II and the Christians: W. S. McCullough, *A Short History of Syriac Christianity to the Rise of Islam*, Chicago 1982, 157ff. Mani and the Elchasaites: see several articles in the conference volume *Codex Manichaicus Coloniensis*, ed. L. Cirillo/A. Roselli, Cosenza 1986, as well as *Der Kölner Mani-Codex. Über das Werden seines Leibes.* Kritische Edition, ed. and transl. L. Koenen/C. Römer, Bonn 1985, XVIII n. 12. Life of Mani: S. N. C. Lieu, *Manichaeism in the Later Roman Empire and Medieval China*, Tübingen 2nd edn 1992, 1ff., and W. Sundermann, 'Studien zur kirchengeschichtlichen Literatur der iranischen Manichäer I-III', *AoF* 13, 1986, 40–92. 239–317; 14, 1987, 41–107. The rise of Mani: CMC 18, 1ff; Fihrist 1, 328, 17–20 Flügel; see Sundermann, *Studien III*, 75f. Mani in India: M 4575 (= Sundermann, *Mitteliranische manichäische Texte kirchengeschichtlichen Inhalts*, Berlin 1981, 4a.1/R, pp. 56f); see Sundermann, 'Mani, India and the Manichaean Religion', *South Asian Studies* 2, 1986, 11–19 and Römer, *Missionsreisen*. Mani in the region bordering on Upper Mesopotamia: Ceph. I, 16, 1–2; see Sundermann, *Studien III*, 63f. Mani at court: Ceph. I, 15, 27–33; Peroz: Fihrist I, 328, 26f Flügel; see Sundermann, *Studien III*, 56–60; meeting with Shapur (I): Ceph. I, 15, 31–16, 2; see M. Hutter, *Mani und die Sasaniden*, Innsbruck 1988, 21. Mission: Hutter, 21–24. Shapur and Manichaeism: quotation: Sundermann, *Studien III*, 80. Western mission: see Lieu, *Manichaeism*, 90ff. *Šābuhragān*: Biruni, aṯār 207, 13–19 Sachau; see D. N. MacKenzie, 'Mani's *Šābuhragān*', *BSOAS* 42, 1979, 500–34; 43, 1980, 288–310. Mani and Hormizd I: N. Sims-Williams, 'The Sogdian Fragments of Leningrad II: Mani at the Court of the Shahanshah', *Bulletin of the Asia Institute* 4, 1990, 281–88. Mani's end: Sundermann, *Studien II*, 253–268; III, 76–78. 87. 89–91; see Hutter, 27–31. Magis and Mani's death: see Psalm-Book II, 16, 19–23; see 15, 5–12 (Magis as responsible for it); traditional accounts of his death, however, show that the king alone was responsible for it. Persecutions: Hom. 76–78; end: 83, 21–85. On the further history of the Manichaeans in the Sasanian empire see Lieu, *Manichaeism*, 109ff. On the Eastern mission (and the Manichaean communities in Inner Asia and China): Lieu, 219ff. Mani's description of his religion: quotation: M 5794 I = M. Boyce, *A Reader in Manichaean Middle Persian and Parthian*, Leiden 1975, 29f; on Mani's doctrine and 'church' see A. Böhlig, 'Manichäismus', *TRE* 22, 1991, 25–45 (with a detailed bibliography); an excellent brief characterization is provided by C. Römer, in *Mani. Auf der Spur einer verschollenen Religion*, Freiburg 1993, 21ff. Mazdakism: quotation: Dk 318, 11ff Dresden; 653, 10–654, 8 Madan; transl. W. Sundermann ('Neue Erkenntnisse über die mazdakitische Soziallehre', *Das Altertum* 34. 3, 1988, 17). Mazdak and his doctrine: the most important (older) literature is to be found in M. Shaki, 'The Social Doctrine of Mazdak in the Light of Middle Persian Evidence', *ArOr* 46, 1978, 289–306; Sundermann, 'Mazdak und die mazdakitischen Volksaufstände', *Das Altertum* 23. 4, 1977, 245–9, and especially E. Yarshater, 'Mazdakism', *CHI* III 2, 1983, 991–1024; for the theory about the different parts of the 'Mazdakite movement' I am indebted to Sundermann, *Mazdak*, and for the interpretation of the *Dēnkard* passage to Sundermann, *Erkenntnisse*; the revolt as a consequence of Kavad's cadastral survey and tax reform is postulated by

P. Crone ('Kavād's Heresy and Mazdak's Revolt', *Iran* 29, 1991, 21–42). Religious policy of the Sasanians: see Wiesehöfer, 'Loyalitäten'. 'Throne' and 'altar': quotations: Mas'udi, murūğ 1, 289, 14ff Pellat; Letter of Tansar 8 Minovi (transl. Boyce, 33f); for these and other documents see Ph. Gignoux, 'Church–State Relations in the Sasanian Period', *Bulletin of the Middle Eastern Culture Center in Japan* 1, 1984, 72–80; Sh. Shaked ('Administrative Functions of Priests in the Sasanian Period', *Proceedings of the First European Conference of Iranian Studies*, pt 1, ed. Gh. Gnoli/A. Panaino, Rome 1990, 262–4) considers the image of the 'twins' as still Sasanian. Narseh and the clergy: in NPi 16/14, Kirdir is (again only) called '*mōbad* of Ohrmazd' and is the only mentioned religious dignitary. Hormizd II and the Magi: C. Schmidt/H. J. Polotsky, *Ein Mani-Fund aus Ägypten*, Berlin 1933, 29. Reign of Bahram II: E. Winter, *Die sāsānidisch-römischen Friedensverträge des 3. Jahrhunderts n. Chr.*, Frankfurt 1988, 128–51; cf. Chronicle of Arbela 37, 20–40, 3 Kawerau, about the rising of a *mōbad* against Bahram III (= Bahram II). Hormizd II: Wiesehöfer, 'Hormizd II. und Rom', *Migratio et Commutatio* (FS Th. Pekáry), ed. H.-J. Drexhage/J. Sünskes, St. Katharinen 1989, 68–71; the Manichaean persecutions may have been a result of Hormizd's weakened position after his unsuccessful campaign. The Christians remained unmolested because, due to the persecutions of Christians in the West, they were considered as 'loyal'. Shapur II: accession to the throne: see M. Azarnoush, 'Šâpûr II, Ardašîr II, and Šâpûr III. Another Perspective', *AMI* N.F. 19, 1986, 219–47; motives: Schwaigert, 237–39; role in the persecutions: ib., 132–5. It is probably no accident that precisely for his reign, the Zoroastrian tradition mentions a particularly remarkable Zoroastrian priest (Adurbad i Mahrspandan) (A. Tafazzoli, *EncIr* I, 1985, 477). Zoroastrian clergy and Manichaeans: Hutter (with the remarks of Sundermann, *OLZ* 85, 1990, 203–5); Sundermann, *Studien III*, 56 n. 109 (*zandīk*); Gnoli, *De Zoroastre à Mani*, Paris 1985, 83 (conflict between Manichaean 'universalism' and Zoroastrian 'nationalism'). Jews in the Sasanian empire: J. Neusner, *A History of the Jews in Babylonia*, vols 2–5, Leiden 1960–70; see id., *Israel and Iran in Talmudic Times*, Lanham et al. 1986, and *Israel's Politics in Sasanian Iran*, Lanham et al. 1986; on the communities see A. Oppenheimer, *Babylonia Judaica*, Wiesbaden 1984; Christian hostility against Jews: Schwaigert 124–8. The Buddhists (and Hindus), whose persecution was advocated in Kirdir's inscription, have been left out in this chapter: see R. E. Emmerick, 'Buddhism among Iranian Peoples', *CHI* III 2, 1983, 956ff.

4. (pp. 216–21)   On late Sasanian culture it is still rewarding – despite all the more recent progress made on questions of detail – to read F. Altheim/R. Stiehl, *Geschichte der Hunnen*, vol. 3, Berlin 1961, 85ff and vol. 5, Berlin 1962, 195ff. Khosrow the 'wise king': quotation: Agathias II 28 (Eng. transl. Averil Cameron); on Agathias's prejudices see A. Cameron, 'Agathias on the Sassanians', *Dumbarton Oaks Papers* 23/24, 1969/70, 172–4, and J.-F. Duneau, 'Quelques aspects de la pénétration de

l'hellénisme dans l'empire perse sassanide', *Mélanges R. Crozet*, vol. 1, Poitiers 1966, 16–20; 'wise king': quotations: Barhebraeus, chron. eccl. 3, 91, 8f Abbeloos-Lamy; Michael Syr. 366 v. 11f Syr.; 2, 339 transl. Chabot. Khosrow's *kārnāmag*: attested in the Kitāb al-Fihrist of an-Nadim, an Arabic 'bio-bibliography' of the tenth century (I, 305, 10 Flügel), and in excerpts (in Arabic translation) handed down by Ibn Miskawaih; quotation: 206, 4ff Caetani (transl. Altheim/Stiehl). Neoplatonists in the Persian empire: Agathias II 30f. Priscianus Lydus: *Solutiones eorum de quibus dubitavit Chosroes, Persarum rex* (ed. I. Bywater, suppl. Arist. I, 2, 39f). Uranius: Agathias II 29f. Arguments: Barhebraeus, chron. eccl. 3, 89, 5ff; Michael Syr. ib. Teachers: Chron. Se'ert PO VII 2, 147, 1ff Scher. 'Paulus the Persian': person: Barhebraeus, chron. eccl. 3, 97, 17ff; see W. Wolska, *La topographie chrétienne de Cosmas Indico-pleustes*, Paris 1962, 67 n. 3, and L. van Rompay, *Graeco-Syriaca*, Leiden 1978, 28 n. 66; work: J. P. N. Land, *Anecdota Syriaca IV*, Leiden 1895, 1–32 (text) = 1–30 (transl.); here based on the transl. of Altheim/Stiehl. Syrian Christians and Greek science: see the articles of S. P. Brock in his collection *Syriac Perspectives on Late Antiquity*, London 1984. *Kalīla wa-Dimna: Pañchatantra*: see K. Mylius, *Geschichte der Literatur im alten Indien*, Leipzig 1983, 200ff; Arabic version of Ibn al-Muqaffa': ed. L. Cheikho, Beirut 1905; transl. A. Miquel, *Le livre de Kalila et Dimna*, Paris 1957; on the Syriac version, dating somewhat earlier than the Middle Persian one, and on other Near Eastern and European versions, see the corresponding articles in handbooks on the history of the respective literatures. Khosrow and law: *Mādayān*: A. Perikhanian, 'Iranian Society and Law', *CHI* III 2, 1983, 629f and Macuch, *Rechtskasuistik*, 14f. Medicine: quotation: Qifti, ta'rīḫ al-ḥukamā 133, 13ff Lippert; alleged beginnings of medicine in Jundaisabur: Maqdisī III 157, 1ff Huart; Qifti 133, 2ff Lippert; Barhebraeus, chron. Syr. 57, 11ff. Bedjan (transl. E. A. W. Budge I 56f); id., ta'rīḫ 76, 16ff Ṣālḥānī; 'Hippocratic medicine': Barhebraeus, chron. Syr. 57, 15 Bedjan; ta'rīḫ 76, 18 Ṣālḥānī. On Greek influence on Persian anthropological ideas see H. W. Bailey, *Zoroastrian Problems in the Ninth-Century Books*, Oxford 2nd edn 1971, 78–119. On the first Christian 'hospitals' in Nisibis, Jundaisabur and other Nestorian centres see L. Richter-Bernburg, 'Boktīšū°', *EncIr* IV, 1990, 333f; on Ǧibrīl see ib., 334 (the assembly cannot be dated within the reign of Khosrow I, as was done by H. H. Schöffler, *Die Akademie von Gondischapur*, Stuttgart 1979, 40, et al.); *durustābād* < MP *drustabed* ('chief physician'). In the entourage of both Khosrows, there were physicians who had been trained in Nisibis (Richter-Bernburg, ib.). About Khosrow I, Zacharias Rhet. (II 217, 20ff Brooks) reports that he himself had founded and equipped a hospital. On Burzoy see D. Khaleghi-Motlagh, 'Borzūya', *EncIr* IV, 1990, 381f, and now especially F. de Blois, *Burzōy's Voyage to India and the Origin of the Book of Kalilah wa Dimna*, London 1990. According to Ibn Qutaiba, ma'ārif 658, 17ff Okacha and Tabari I, 845, 14ff de Goeje, Indian medicine had already reached Khuzistan under Shapur II. On the tradition of medicine in Iran see C. Elgood, *A Medical History of Persia and the Eastern Caliphate*, Cambridge 1951, and

D. Brandenburg, *Priesterärzte und Heilkunst im alten Persien*, Stuttgart 1969. Khosrow
I as a medical 'author': see F. Sezgin, *Geschichte des arabischen Schrifttums*, vol. 3,
Wiesbaden 1970, 186. On the transmission of Greek and Indian knowledge of
pharmacology, medicine, agronomy and astronomy, see M. Ullmann, *Islamic Medicine*,
Edinburgh 1978, 16ff. Literature in the (late) Sasanian empire: see the articles by
M. Boyce, 'Middle Persian Literature', *HdO* I 4, 2, 1, Leiden 1968, 31–66; J. C.
Tavadia, *Die mittelpersische Sprache und Literatur der Zarathustrier*, Leipzig 1956, and
J. de Menasce, 'Zoroastrian Pahlavi Writings', *CHI* III 2, 1983, 1166–95. Publication
of the Avesta: see H. W. Bailey, *Zoroastrian Problems in the Ninth-Century Books*,
Oxford 2nd edn 1971, 173. *Xvadāy-nāmag*: Th. Nöldeke, *Das iranische Nationalepos*,
Leipzig 1920, 12ff; A. Sh. Shahbazi, 'On the Xʷadāy-nāmag', *AcIr* 30, 1990, 208–29.
Andarz literature: S. Shaked, *EncIr* II, 1987, 11–16, esp. p. 15. Court culture: quota-
tion: Kārnāmag-ī Ardaxšīr ī Pābagān, ch. 1, transl. based on Nöldeke, 39; in general:
F. Altheim, *Geschichte der Hunnen*, vol. 5, Berlin 1962, 195ff. Chess: B. Utas, 'Chess',
EncIr V, 1992, 393–6, esp. p. 394. Hunting: see Ph. Gignoux, 'La chasse dans l'Iran
sāsānide', *Iranian Studies*, ed. Gh. Gnoli, Rome 1983, 101–18; game preserves were
already known in the Achaemenid period (see above) and are also attested under the
Sasanians. Courtly culture and lifestyle: *Husrav ud rēdag*: J. M. Unvala, *Der Pahlavi-
Text 'Der König Husrav und sein Knabe'*, Diss. Heidelberg 1917; quotation: Altheim,
Hunnen 5, 202f. Royal titulature: see Menander Prot. fr. 6, 1 p. 62 Blockley: '*Theios,
agathos, eirēnopatrios, archaios Chosroēs, basileus basileōn, eutychēs, eusebēs, agathopoios,
hotini hoi theoi megalēn tychēn kai megalēn basileian dedōkasi, gigas gigantōn, hos ek
theōn charaktērizetai*' ('the divine, the good father of peace, the time-honoured
Khosrow, the king of kings, blessed, pious and beneficent, on whom the Gods have
bestowed much fortune and a great empire, giant of giants, created after the image
of gods'). Crown of Khosrow II: Tabari 1, 2446, 11ff de Goeje. Carpet of Khosrow
II: 'Sixty times sixty yards as a single carpet by the dimension of its surface, on which
the paths formed figures, the separating parts rivers, the intervals between them hills.
On its border earth sown with spring growth out of silk against branches of gold,
and its blossoms of gold, silver and the like' (Tabari I, 2452, 7ff; transl. by Altheim/
Stiehl); see M. G. Morony, 'Bahār-e Kesrā', *EncIr* III, 1989, 479. On other examples
of late Sasanian splendour see Altheim, *Hunnen* 5, 195ff (especially for the literary
sources), as well as D. Shepherd and P. Harper, in *CHI* III 2, 1983, 1055ff (for the
works of art). Brutality of warfare: Tabari 1, 1062, 14ff; Ya'qubi 1, 197, 4ff Houtsma;
Dinawari 116, 7ff Guirg. (Revolt of Shahrbaraz; quotation: Tabari 1, 1062, 14ff;
transl. Nöldeke, 388); see Tabari 1, 2023, 16ff; 2254, 17ff (Sasanian troops in Sawad).

Conclusion

Survival and Rediscovery of Ancient Iran: important literature: A. Gabriel, *Die
Erforschung Persiens*, Vienna 1952; *Achaemenid History VII:* Through Travellers' Eyes,

ed. H. Sancisi-Weerdenburg/J. W. Drijvers, Leiden 1991; Gh. Homayoun, *Iran in europäischen Bildzeugnissen vom Ausgang des Mittelalters bis ins achtzehnte Jahrhundert*, Diss. Cologne 1967; *Persepolis en Pasargadae in wisselend perspectief*, ed. Sancisi-Weerdenburg, Groningen/Leiden 1989; A. Sh. Shahbazi, 'From Parsa to Taxt-e Jamsid', *AMI* N.F. 10, 1977, 197–207; J. Wiesehöfer, *Ausbau des Schriftbezugs als Fortschritt der Wissenschaft. Die Entzifferung der Keilschrift*, Hagen 1987. Quotation: ŠPs-I; transl. based on M. Back. On early Islamic historiography (and its picture of ancient Iran) see H. Busse, 'Arabische Historiographie und Geographie', *Grundriß der Arabischen Philologie*, vol. 2, ed. H. Gätje, Wiesbaden 1987, 264–97; M. Springberg-Hinsen, *Die Zeit vor dem Islam in arabischen Universalgeschichten des 9. bis 12. Jahrhunderts*, Würzburg/Altenberge 1989; quotation: Busse, 271; urban history: the ninth-century work *Šahristānīhā ī Ērān* describes the major cities of Iran with their 'history', using old oral traditions (J. Marquart, *A Catalogue of the Provincial Capitals of Ērānšahr*, ed. G. Messina, Rome 1931). Firdausi: on himself and his *Šāhnāme* see A. Sh. Shahbazi, *Ferdowsī*, Costa Mesa 1991, and W. Sundermann, in *Schāhnāme. Das persische Königsbuch. Miniaturen und Texte der Berliner Handschrift von 1605*, ed. V. Enderlein/W. Sundermann, Leipzig/Weimar 1988, 5–29 (with literature); introductory quotation from Firdausi (Eng. transl. Sir William Jones); characterization of his work: quotation: Sundermann, 8. Alexander's image in Iran: Wiesehöfer, 'Zum Nachleben von Achaimeniden und Alexander in Iran', *AchHist* VIII, 1994, 389–97; to simplify matters, we can distinguish between two Alexander images: one image goes back to the Zoroastrian tradition and to the 'offence' committed by Alexander through his campaign, so that he is viewed as evil (*gizistag*) personified, and as having more than any other man brought ruin and destruction on Eranshahr; the other image is that of a Persian prince and a powerful king, who is later described as a Muslim, a sage or even a prophet. Both images already existed simultaneously in the late Sasanian period. H. Heine: from: 'Der Dichter Firdusi' (1851). 'Survival' of Persepolis: W. Ouseley, *Travels in Various Countries of the East*, vol. 2, London 1821, 241–411; Shahbazi, *Parsa*; H. Arndt, *Persepolis*, Stuttgart 1984 (with texts). Pasargadae: G. N. Curzon, *Persia and the Persian Question*, vol. II, London 1892, 71–90; D. Stronach, *Pasargadae*, Oxford 1978, 3; Sancisi-Weerdenburg, in *AchHist* VII, 25–7. Naqsh-i Rustam: Curzon II, 117ff. On the interpretations of ruined Iranian sites based on Jewish–Islamic traditions, see A. S. Melikian-Chirvani, in *Le monde iranien et l'Islam*, ed. J. Aubin, Geneva/Paris 1971, 6ff. On the evocation or rediscovery of the ancient authors in the age of humanism see R. Pfeiffer, *Die klassische Philologie von Petrarca bis Mommsen*, Munich 1982. Alexander romance: J. Gruber et al., 'Alexander d. Gr., B: Alexanderdichtung', *LdM* I, 1980, 355–66. Bible illustration: J. M. Plotzek, in *LdM* II, 1983, 83–8; there is a lack of publications regarding the image of Iran in biblical research. Daniel: K. Koch, *Das Buch Daniel*, Darmstadt 1980, 182–213. Medieval world chronicles: G. Wirth et al., 'Chronik', *LdM* II, 1983, 1954–2028; the full title of the Lübeck World Chronicle is:

Chronicarum et historiarum epitome, rudimentum novitiorum nuncupate; quotation: D. Metzler, 'Die Achämeniden im Geschichtsbewußtsein des 15. und 16. Jahrhunderts', *Kunst, Kultur und Geschichte der Achämenidenzeit und ihr Fortleben*, ed. H. Koch/D. N. MacKenzie, Berlin 1983, 290. On medieval historical thinking, see. F.-J. Schmale, *Funktion und Formen mittelalterlicher Geschichtsschreibung*, Darmstadt 1985. Travellers in Iran: see the literature at the beginning of these essays; on the genre of travelogues and on their approach to foreign cultures (in the early modern period) see M. Harbsmeier, 'Reisebeschreibungen als mentalitätsgeschichtliche Quellen', *Reiseberichte als Quellen europäischer Kulturgeschichte*, ed. A. Maçzak/H. J. Teuteberg, Wolfenbüttel 1982, 1–31; Osterhammel, 'Distanzerfahrung. Darstellungsweisen des Fremden im 18. Jahrhundert', *Der europäische Beobachter außereuropäischer Kulturen*, ed. H.-J. König et al., Berlin 1989, 9–42, and 'Reisen an die Grenzen der Welt. Asien im Reisebericht des 17. und 18. Jahrhunderts', *Der Reisebericht*, ed. P. J. Brenner, Frankfurt 1989, 224–60. Odoric of Pordenone: H. Cordier, *Les voyages en Asie du bienheureux frère Odorico de Pordenone*, Paris 1891; quotation: Eng. transl. Richard Hakluyt, 410 (Comum is a corruption of *Kūh-i Mihr* ['Mithra's mountain']; see Shahbazi, 206). Barbaro: J. Barbaro/A. Contarini, *Travels to Tana and Persia*, London 1873. Silva y Figueroa: *L'Ambassade de D. Garcia de Silva Figueroa en Perse*, Paris 1667. Della Valle: *Viaggi di Pietro della Valle*, Bologna 1672; see P. Bietenholz, *Pietro Della Valle (1586–1652)*, Basel/Stuttgart 1962. Von Poser: *Der beeden Königl. Erb Fürstenthümer Schweidnitz und Janer in Schlesien Hochverordneten Landes Bestellter Des Hoch Edelgebornen Herrn Heinrich von Poser und Groß Nedlitz Lebens und Todes Geschichte*, Jena 1675; extracts publ. by F. H. Kochwasser, in *Festgabe deutscher Iranisten zur 2500-Jahrfeier Irans*, Stuttgart 1971, 80–93. Herbert: Th. Herbert, *Some Yeares Travels into Divers Parts of Asia and Afrique*, London 1677. Mandelslo: J. A. v. Mandelslo, *Morgenlaendische Reyse-Beschreibung*, ed. A. Olearius, Hamburg 1658; *Journal und Observation (1637–1640)*, ed. M. Refslund-Klemann, Copenhagen 1942 (diary); Olearius transformed Mandelslo's diary, making it into a description of his own. Compare an article of the author to be printed in the 'Gedenkschrift' for the late D. M. Lewis. Tavernier: J. B. Tavernier, *Les six voyages de Jean Baptiste Tavernier*, Paris 1679. Thévenot: J. de Thévenot, *Suite du voyage de Mr. de Thévenot au Levant. Seconde partie*, Paris 1689. Chardin: J. Chardin, *Voyages du Chevalier Chardin en Perse et autres lieux de l'Orient*, new edn, Amsterdam 1735. De Bruijn: C. de Bruijn, *Reizen over Moskovie, door Persie en Indie*, Amsterdam 1711; cf. J. W. Drijvers, in *Engelbert Kaempfer. Werk und Wirkung*, ed. D. Haberland, Stuttgart 1993, 85–104. Kaempfer: E. Kaempfer, *Amoenitates exoticae*, Lemgo 1712 (and many manuscript records in the British Library that have hardly been studied); see Wiesehöfer, in *Engelbert Kaempfer*, 105–32. Du Mans: S. Schuster-Walser, *Das Ṣafawidische Persien im Spiegel europäischer Reiseberichte*, Baden-Baden/Hamburg 1970. Niebuhr and the Arabian expedition: C. Niebuhr, *Reisebeschreibung nach Arabien und anderen umliegenden Ländern*, 3 vols, Copenhagen 1774–1837 (see esp. vol. 2); personality and expedition: *Carsten Niebuhr und die Arabische Reise 1761–1767*, ed. D. Lohmeier, Heide 1986 (catalogue of exhibition); Niebuhr, Herder and the inscriptions: Harbsmeier, 'Before Decipherment. Persepolitan Hypotheses in Late Eighteenth Century', *Culture and History* 11, 1992, 23–59; quotation: B. G. Niebuhr, *Carsten Niebuhr's Leben*, Kiel 1817, 32. Herder: J. G. Herder, *Persepolis. Eine Mutmaßung*, Gotha 1787 (2nd ed. 1798) (= *Herders Sämmtliche Werke*, ed. B. Suphan, vol. 15, Berlin 1888, 571ff); 'tribute bearers': ib. (*Sämmtliche Werke*, vol. 15, 592); quotation: *Persepolitanische Briefe (1798–1803)* (= *Sämmtliche Werke*, vol. 24, Berlin 1886, 503); see P. Calmeyer, 'Achaimeniden und Persepolis bei J. G. Herder', *AchHist* VII, 135–45. Nineteenth-century drawings and reconstructions: Sancisi-Weerdenburg, in *AchHist* VII, 27ff (NB especially the names of R. Ker Porter [*Travels in Georgia, Persia, Armenia, Ancient Babylonia*, London 1821], Ch. Texier [*Description de l'Arménie, la Perse et la Mésopotamie*, vols 1–2, Paris 1839] and E. Flandin/P. Coste [*Voyage en Perse*, vols 1–2, Paris 1851]). Earliest photographs: F. Stolze /F. C. Andreas, *Persepolis*, 2 vols, Berlin 1882. Antiques: Sancisi-Weerdenburg, ib., 27f. On the archaeological excavations see for each site the literature mentioned in the 'source chapters' (and the relevant archaeological bibliographies by Vanden Berghe and Calmeyer [Bibliographical essay on Introduction]). Among 'modern' travellers, the most important are Sir Aurel Stein, Ernst Herzfeld and L. Vanden Berghe; the latter two were also active as excavators, in Persepolis and Luristan, respectively.

On the decipherment of cuneiform script see the corresponding chapters in E. A. Wallis Budge, *The Rise and Progress of Assyriology*, London 1925; J. Friedrich, *Entzifferung verschollener Schriften und Sprachen*, Berlin 1954; M. Pope, *The Story of Decipherment from Egyptian Hieroglyphic to Linear B*, London 1975; Ch. Bermant/ E. Weitzman, *Ebla*, Frankfurt 1979 (Engl. London 1979), and now esp. E. Doblhofer, *Die Entzifferung alter Schriften und Sprachen*, Stuttgart 1993. The term 'cuneiform script': the expression *cuneiformis* ('wedge-shaped') was first used – though as a second alternative to *pyramidalis* – by Thomas Hyde in his *Historia religionis veterum Persarum* (Oxford 1700, 525). It overshadowed Kaempfer's more expressive term *litterae cuneatae* (which was also used by Grotefend), and is called *cuneiform* (writing) in English, (*écriture*) *cunéiforme* in French, *klinopis'* as the loan translation in Russian, (*ḫaṭṭ*) *mismārī* and *ḫaṭṭe mīxī* ('nail-shaped script') in Arabic and Persian, respectively, *çivi yazisi* ('nail script') in Turkish or even *kusabi-gata-moji* ('wedge-shaped sign') in Japanese. Grotefend's '*Praevia*': Grotefend summarized the results of his investigations in a report written in Latin (*Praevia de cuneatis, quas vocant, inscriptionibus Persepolitanis legendis et explicandis relatio*). This was presented to the 'Royal Society of Sciences' (i.e. the present-day 'Academy') of Göttingen by the theologian Th. Ch. Tychsen on 4 September, 2 October and 13 November 1802 and on 20 May 1803. Reviews by Tychsen appeared in the *GGA* 1802, pp. 1481–87; 1769–1722; 1803, pp. 593–5; 1161–64. However, the *Praevia relatio* was not printed until 90 years later (W. Meyer, 'G. Fr. Grotefend's erste Nachricht von seiner Entzifferung der Keilschrift',

NGWG 14, 1893, 573–616 [separate reprint Darmstadt 1972]). A. J. Silvestre de Sacy (see below) meanwhile reviewed and evaluated Grotefend's major results in his 'Lettre à M. Millin sur les inscriptions des monuments persépolitains' (in *Magasin encyclopédique* VIII. 5, 1803, 438–67), and Grotefend himself summarized his results in the article 'Über die Erklärung der Keilschriften und besonders der Inschriften von Persepolis', published as an appendix to a new edition of the work of his teacher, A. L. Heeren, *Ideen über die Politik, den Verkehr und den Handel der vornehmsten Völker der alten Welt*, vol. 1, Göttingen 1805. Grotefend's original manuscript of the first *Praevia* was discovered by the Assyriologist R. Borger in December 1974 in Grotefend's literary bequest at the Göttingen University library. His version of the text and his commentary remain the standard work on the subject: R. Borger, 'Grotefends erste "Praevia". Einführung-Faksimile-Übersetzung-Kommentar', *Welt des Alten Orients*. Keilschrift – Grabungen – Gelehrte, Göttingen 2nd edn 1975, 155–84. Had he not died in 1820, Carl Bellino, the Swabian secretary of Claudius James Rich, an English resident in Baghdad, would have earned great fame. By that time, Bellino (together with Rich) had already copied all the cuneiform inscriptions within his reach (mainly Babylonian–Assyrian texts) and sent his copies to Grotefend. In 1820 he started copying DE and XE; in addition, he had firmly resolved to copy the Bisutun inscription and a long inscription on a rock tomb near Persepolis. His premature death prevented him from doing so. The correspondence between Grotefend and Bellino was published by W. Schramm, 'Carl Bellino an G. Fr. Grotefend. Briefe und Inschriften', *ZA* 64, 1974, 250–90. On Bellino see R. D. Barnett, 'Charles Bellino and the Beginnings of Assyriology', *Iraq* 36, 1974, 5–28. Grotefend's step-by-step method of decipherment is described in Borger, *Praevia*, and by W. Hinz in the same catalogue ('Grotefends genialer Entzifferungsversuch'), pp. 15–18. Grotefend's biography: K. Brethauer/W. R. Röhrbein, in *Welt des Alten Orients*, 9–14; G. Steiner, 'Eine zeitgenössische Würdigung der Entzifferungsarbeit von Georg Friedrich Grotefend', *AchHist* VII, Leiden 1991, 109–21. De Gouvea: quotation: *Relaçam*, Lisbon 1611, 32. Garcia Silva Figueroa: quotation: *De rebus Persarum epistola*, Antwerp 1620, 6. In Figueroa's book, however, there is only an isosceles triangle (a large Greek delta) illustrated in the margin. Della Valle: Cuneiform signs: *Viaggi di Pietro della Valle*, pt 2, Bologna 1672, 340. Niebuhr: copies: *Reisebeschreibung*, vol. 2, Copenhagen 1778, pls XXIV, XXXI (inscriptions A-L: A = XPb; B-D = DPa; E-G = XPe; H = DPd; I = DPe; K = DPf; L = DPg); Commentary: pp. 138f. Duperron: especially important among the works of Abraham Hyacinthe Anquetil-Duperron is his *Zend-Avesta. Ouvrage de Zoroastre*, Paris 1771. On his person see R. Schwab, *Vie d'Anquetil-Duperron*, Paris 1934. See also: D. Metzler, 'A. H. Anquetil-Duperron (1731–1805) und das Konzept der Achsenzeit', *AchHist* VII, 123–33. De Sacy: *Mémoires sur diverses antiquités de la Perse*, Paris 1793, 1–124 (based partially on the manuscript of a lecture given in the Académie des Inscriptions in 1787); Niebuhr's copies: *Reisebeschreibung*, vol. 2, Pl. XXVII (inscriptions F-I). Tychsen and

Münter: R. Schmitt, 'Dänische Forscher bei der Erschließung der Achaimeniden-Inschriften', *Acta Orientalia* 47, 1989, 13–26. Characteristics of Old Persian cuneiform writing: Schmitt, in *Compendium Linguarum Iranicarum*, Wiesbaden, 1989, 56–85; quotation: p. 64. Father and son as kings: the chronologically also possible father-and-son combination of Cyrus (II the Gr., 559–530) and Cambyses (II, 530–522) was ruled out by Grotefend because in inscriptions B and G the two names bore different initial letters. Khsheiô: in Anquetil-Duperron's *Zend-Avesta*, vol. 2, Paris 1771, there is a 'vocabulaire zend, pehlevi et françois', pp. 432–75, and a 'vocabulaire pehlevi, persan et françois', pp. 476–526. The word *Khsheiô* is on p. 442. Dahae: Hdt. I 125: *Daoi*; in his second *Praevia* Grotefend corrected this reading, following a 'doctissimus censor' among his acquaintances (Th. Ch. Tychsen), and replaced it with 'peoples'. Grotefend's first reading of the inscriptions: it corresponds with the version in the original manuscript of the *Praevia* found by Borger in 1974 and its printed copy published by W. Meyer in 1893 respectively. Further history of the decipherment of cuneiform writing: Old Persian script: comprehensive descriptions in Pope, *Decipherment*, 102–10; Bermant/Weitzman, *Ebla* (Germ.), 183–9, and esp. R. Borger, 'Die Entzifferungsgeschichte der altpersischen Keilschrift nach Grotefends ersten Erfolgen', in *Persica* 7, 1975–78, 7–19, and Doblhofer, *Entzifferung*, 125–43; other cuneiform script systems: Pope, 111–23; Bermant/Weitzman, 189–226; Doblhofer, 144–83. Rask: *Über das Alter und die Echtheit der Zend-Sprache und des Zend-Avesta*, Berlin 1826 (Dan., Copenhagen 1826); on Rask and his achievement see Schmitt, *Forscher*, 21–23. Lassen: *Die altpersischen Keil-Inschriften von Persepolis*, Bonn 1836. Other, later, works: 'Die neuesten Fortschritte in der Entzifferung der einfachen Persepolitanischen Keilschrift', *ZKM* 2, 1839, 165–76; 'Die Altpersischen Keilinschriften nach HRn. N. L. Westergaard's Mitteilungen', *ZKM* 6, 1845, 1–188; 467–580. Burnouf: *Mémoire sur deux inscriptions cunéiformes trouvées près d'Hamadan et qui font maintenant partie des papiers du Dr Schulz*, Paris 1836. Rawlinson: a biography of Rawlinson was written by his brother George Rawlinson, *A Memoir of Major-General Sir Henry Creswicke Rawlinson*, London 1898. R. Borger ('Dokumente zur Entzifferung der altpersischen Keilschrift durch H. C. Rawlinson', *Persica* 7, 1975–78, 1–5) has mainly compiled correspondence on this subject. The quotation about Rawlinson's method of working is from Budge, *Rise*; Rawlinson himself described his method in the journal *Archaeologia* 34, 1852, 71; Elvend inscriptions: DE = inscription of Darius I on the Elvend mountain; XE = inscription of Xerxes I on the Elvend mountain. Budge/Meissner controversy: Budge, 51; Meissner, in *Literarische Wochenschrift* 1926, 923–5. Rawlinson on Grotefend: 'Professor Grotefend has certainly the credit of being the first who opened a gallery into this rich treasure house of antiquity. In deciphering the names of Cyrus, Darius, Xerxes, and Hystaspes, he obtained the true determination of nearly a third of the entire alphabet, and thus at once supplied a sure and ample basis for further research' (*JRAS* 10, 1846/47, 3–4). Grotefend did not always display such generosity with respect to his competitors (such as Lassen etc.) (examples in Borger, *Entzifferungsgeschichte*, 14). 'Iranian Studies' and 'Iranistik': see the articles in *Iranian Studies* 20. 2–4, 1987 (*Iranian Studies in Europe and Japan*, ed. R. Matthee/N. Keddie), and *Guide to Iranian Studies in Europe*, pt 1: Institutions and Teaching Programmes in Twelve Countries of Western Europe, Leiden 1988.

BIBLIOGRAPHIC POSTSCRIPT TO THE PAPERBACK EDITION

Since the first edition of the book was published only in 1996, there was no need to revise it as regards content. What we thought would be a good idea, however, was to give, in the light of new evidence and literature, a kind of supplement to the bibliographical essays of the book (confining ourselves almost exclusively to books).

Introduction

For reference works/encyclopaedias, we now also recommend the following items: *The Oxford Encyclopedia of Archaeology in the Near East*, ed. E. M. Meyers, 5 vols, New York/Oxford 1997 (with an overview of archaeological periods and sites); *Der Neue Pauly (DNP)*, ed. H. Cancik/H. Schneider, Stuttgart/Weimar 1996ff (a totally revised edition of the RE/KlP including articles on the history and culture of Ancient Iran). The *Oxford Classical Dictionary*, 3rd edn, ed. S. Hornblower/A. Spawforth, appeared in 1996.

As far as textbooks and general literature are concerned, we refer you to: J. Curtis, *Ancient Persia*, London 2000 (a small but useful overview); J. Wiesehöfer, *Das frühe Persien*, Munich 1999 (a kind of short version of this book, which includes, however, chapters on the history of events of the respective Iranian dynasties); A. Kuhrt, *The Ancient Near East c. 3000–330 BC*, 2 vols, London 1995 (exemplary history of the Ancient Near East, including the history and culture of the Achaemenids); cf. also H. J. Nissen, *Geschichte Alt-Vorderasiens*, Munich 1999. Apart from that the reader is referred to some new books on special topics, which cover the whole period of pre-Islamic Iran: G. Gnoli, *Iran als religiöser Begriff im Mazdaismus*, Opladen 1993 (on the term 'Iran'); *History of Civilizations of Central Asia*, vols 2–3, Paris 1994–96; *La Persia e l'Asia Centrale da Alessandro al X secolo*, Rome 1996; *Coins, Art and Archaeology*, ed. M. Alram/D. E. Klimburg-Salter, Vienna 1999 (on Eastern Iranian and Kushan history and culture); *Die Seidenstraße*, ed. U. Hübner e.a., Hamburg (in press); D. T. Potts, *The Archaeology of Elam*, Cambridge 1999 (on Elam and Elymais); *The Indian Ocean in Antiquity*, ed. J. Reade, London 1996; R.

Schmitt, *Die iranischen Sprachen in Geschichte und Gegenwart*, Wiesbaden 2000 (excellent introduction into the history of Iranian languages); *Proceedings of the Third European Conference of Iranian Studies*, pt. 1, ed. N. Sims-Williams, Wiesbaden 1998 (Old and Middle Iranian Studies); Gh. Gnoli, *Zoroaster in History*, New York 2000. There are two new brilliantly commented and illustrated exhibition catalogues: *Weihrauch und Seide. Alte Kulturen an der Seidenstraße*, ed. W. Seipel, Vienna 1996 (Silk Road art and history); *7000 Jahre persische Kunst. Meisterwerke aus dem Iranischen Nationalmuseum in Teheran*, ed. W. Seipel, Vienna 2000. As far as maps are concerned, we recommend B. Hourcade/M. Taleghani/M.-H. Papoli-Yazdi, *Atlas d'Iran*, Paris 1997 and especially *The Barrington Atlas of the Greek and Roman World*, ed. R. J. A. Talbert, Princeton/Oxford 2000 (including maps on Mesopotamia and Iran).

Part One: Iran from Cyrus to Alexander the Great

Supplementary (commented) bibliographies (to that of Weber/Wiesehöfer) were published by P. Briant: 'Bulletin d'histoire achéménide, I', *Topoi Suppl. 1*, 1997, 5–127 (it is now also available on the very useful homepage: www.achemenet.com, where one can also find a collection of sources, essays, etc. on Achaemenid affairs); *Bulletin d'histoire achéménide, II*, Paris 2001. The outstanding handbook by the same author: P. Briant, *Histoire de l'empire perse de Cyrus à Alexandre*, Paris 1996 will appear in a revised English translation with Eisenbrauns in 2001 (cf. the comments on this book in: 'Actes du séminaire international (Lyon, 31 mars – 1er avril 1997 autour de l'ouvrage de P. Briant, Histoire de l'Empire perse, Paris 1996', *Topoi Suppl. 1*, 1997, 129–434).

There are some new editions of testimonies of Achaemenid times: P. Lecoq, *Les inscriptions de la Perse achéménide*, Paris 1997 (a commented French translation of the royal inscriptions); R. Schmitt, *The Old Persian Inscriptions of Naqsh-i Rustam and Persepolis*, London 2000 (exemplary edition of royal inscriptions with an English translation; see also R. Schmitt, *Beiträge zu altpersischen Inschriften*, Wiesbaden 1999); B. Porten, *The Elephantine Papyri in English*, Leiden, 1996; I. Eph'al/J. Naveh, *Aramaic Ostraca of the Fourth Century BC from Idumaea*, Jerusalem 1996; A. Cohen, *The Alexander Mosaic*, Cambridge 1997. We should also mention some other very useful monographs on special topics: M. Brosius, *Women in Ancient Persia*, Oxford 1996; M. C. Miller, *Athens and Persia in the Fifth Century B.C.: A Study in Cultural Receptivity*, Cambridge 1997; A. de Jong, *Traditions of the Magi. Zoroastrianism in Greek and Latin Literature*, Leiden 1997; B. Hutzfeld, *Das Bild der Perser in der griechischen Dichtung des 5. vorchristlichen Jahrhunderts*, Wiesbaden 1999 (the Greek view of the Persians).

Part Two: Macedonian Domination over Iran

As far as the testimonies of this period are concerned, the tablets from Babylonia also give some insights into the Iranian Policy of Alexander the Great and his successors; cf. therefore the following editions: A. J. Sachs/H. Hunger, *Astronomical Diaries and Related Texts from Babylonia*, 3 vols, Vienna 1988–1996; G. F. Del Monte, *Testi della Babilonia Ellenistica, vol. 1: Testi Cronografici*, Rome 1997. Seleucid concern for Iran was examined by: J. Wiesehöfer, '*Discordia et Defectio – Dynamis kai Pithanourgia. Die frühen Seleukiden und Iran*', *Hellenismus*, ed. B. Funck, Tübingen 1996, 29–56. There were also published some other new monographs on Hellenistic Iran: H. Klinkott, *Die Satrapienregister der Alexander- und Diadochenzeit*, Stuttgart 2000 (on the early hellenistic lists of satrapies); F. L. Holt, *Thundering Zeus. The Making of Hellenistic Bactria*, Berkeley e.a. 1998; W. Posch, *Baktrien zwischen Griechen und Kuschan*, Wiesbaden 1995 (on the history of Bactria (and Ai Khanum) in the time of the nomads' raids; with a special focus on Chinese sources); B. A. Litvinsky/I. R. Pichikian, *The Hellenistic Temple of the Oxus in Bactria*, vol. 1, Moscow 2000 (on Takht-i Sangin; in Russian with engl. summary); N. Sims-Williams, *New Light on Ancient Afghanistan: The Decipherment of Bactrian*, London 1997.

Part Three: Iran from Arsaces I to Artabanus IV

The Aramaic inscriptions of Parthian times from Eastern Mesopotamia have been edited and translated (into German) by: K. Beyer, *Die aramäischen Inschriften aus Assur, Hatra und dem übrigen Ostmesopotamien*, Göttingen 1998. The reader may find an overview of the testimonies (together with that of scholarly arguments and desiderata) in: *Das Partherreich und seine Zeugnisse – The Arsacid Empire: Sources and Documentation*, ed. J. Wiesehöfer, Stuttgart 1998. The Chinese sources are collected and commented on in: D. D. Leslie/K. H. J. Gardiner, *The Roman Empire in Chinese Sources*, Roma 1996. Other important literature: *Mesopotamia and Iran in the Parthian and Sasanian Periods*, ed. J. Curtis, London 2000 (a collection of articles on different topics); M. Olbrycht, *Parthia et ulteriores gentes. Die politischen Beziehungen zwischen dem arsakidischen Iran und den Nomaden der eurasischen Steppen*, Munich 1998 (on Arsacid relations with the peoples of the steppe); M. Schuol, *Die Charakene. Ein mesopotamisches Königreich in hellenistisch-parthischer Zeit*, Stuttgart 2000 (a first regional history (i.e. of southern Babylonia) and an attempt to describe the relations between the centre and a 'vassal kingdom'; it includes a collection of the respective sources). Cf. a new journal (not only dealing with Parthian affairs): *Parthica. Incontri di culture nel mondo antico*, 1, 1999ff.

Part Four: Iran from Ardashir to Yazdgird III

An exemplary new commented edition of the most famous Sasanian inscription may be found in: Ph. Huyse, *Die dreisprachige Inschrift Šābuhrs I. an der Ka'ba-i Zardušt (ŠKZ)*, 2 vols, London 1999; the same compliment applies to the edition of the late Sasanian papyri, parchments and ostraca: D. Weber, *Ostraca, Papyri und Pergamente*, London 1992. A commented English translation of the respective parts of Tabari's historiographical work was published by C. E. Bosworth: *The History of al-Ṭabarī, vol. V: The Sāsānids, the Byzantines, the Lakmids, and Yemen*, Albany 1999. An overview of the sources has been provided by: C. G. Cereti, 'Primary Sources for the History of Inner and Outer Iran in the Sasanian Period', *Archivum Eurasiae Medii Aevi* 9, 1997, 17–71.

Other reference works and textbooks: C. G. Cereti, *Letteratura Pahlavi*, Milano 2000 (a literary history); M. Abka'i-Khavari, *Das Bild des Königs in der Sasanidenzeit*, Hildesheim 2000 (royal ideology, representation and imagery); *Ērān du Anērān. Studien zu ost-westlichen Kulturkontakten in sasanidischer Zeit*, ed. J. Wiesehöfer, Stuttgart (in press); E. Kettenhofen, *Tirdād und die Inschrift von Paikuli*, Wiesbaden 1995 (on Armeno-Iranian relations in the 3rd/4th centuries); G. Greatrex, *Rome and Persia at War, 502–532*, Leeds 1998; *The Byzantine and Early Islamic Near East, III: States, Resources and Armies*, ed. A. Cameron, Princeton 1995 (cf. J. Howard-Johnston's comparison of Byzantine-Sasanian institutions and Z. Rubin on Khosrow's reforms); A. Panaino, *La novella degli scacchi e della tavola reale*, Milano 1999 (a commented edition of a middle-Persian treatise on chess, together with an introduction into late Sasanian culture); M. Macuch, *Rechtskasuistik und Gerichtspraxis zu Beginn des siebenten Jahrhunderts in Iran*, Wiesbaden 1993 (an excellent treatise on late Sasanian law); G. B. Mikkelsen, *Bibliographia Manichaica*, Turnhout 1997.

Conclusion

The view of New Persian as a means of 'Iranian nationalism' is rightly tackled by: B. G. Fragner, *Die "Persephonie": Regionalität, Identität und Sprachkontakt in der Geschichte Asiens*, Berlin 1999. The importance of Early Modern travelogues for a study of both European mentalities and the history of Oriental studies is underlined in: J. Osterhammel, *Die Entzauberung Asiens. Europa und die asiatischen Reiche im 18. Jahrhundert*, Munich 1998 (an excellent book, which deserves an English translation); *Carsten Niebuhr und seine Zeit*, ed. J. Wiesehöfer /S. Conermann, Stuttgart (in press; with an overview of former 'orientalistic' endeavours).

CHRONOLOGICAL TABLE

Iran under the Achaemenids

550/49	The Persian *Cyrus (II?)* defeats his overlord, the Median 'king' *Astyages*, and captures *Ecbatana*.
547/46	The Persians conquer the Lydian kingdom. The Lydian King *Croesus* is killed at the capture of *Sardis*.
539	Cyrus's troops under Ugbaru capture *Babylon*.
530	Cyrus is killed in the battle against the Massagetae on the Jaxartes and is buried in Pasargadae.
530–522	He is succeeded by his son *Cambyses* (II). C. has his brother *Bardiya* disposed of as a potential rival for the throne.
525	Persian troops under Cambyses conquer Egypt.
522/21	The Median Magus *Gaumata* rises in Iran and gains a following by granting temporary exemption from taxes and military service. After ruling for seven months, G. is murdered by seven aristocratic conspirators. One of them, the Achaemenid *Darius*, is chosen as king. He succeeds in putting down a number of rebellions against his regime. For his *res gestae* on the Bisutun cliff, the newly created Old Persian cuneiform script is used for the first time.
519	Darius subdues the Scythian 'king' *Skunkha*.
c. 510	Despite an unsuccessful campaign against the 'European' Scythians, *Thracia* is conquered. The Macedonian king acknowledges Persian suzerainty. – In the east, the empire is extended as far as the Indus valley.
507/06	Athenian envoys formally subject themselves to the great king.
500–494	Ionian *poleis* on the coast of Asia Minor rise against Persian sovereignty, but are defeated despite Athenian and Eretrian assistance ('*Ionian rebellion*'). Miletus is conquered and its leading class deported.
492	*Mardonius* recaptures the Macedonian–Thracian area for the Persians.
490	A seaborne Persian expedition under *Datis* and *Artaphernes* against Athens and Eretria is defeated near *Marathon*.
486	Darius dies. His son Xerxes succeeds him (486–465). At the beginning

of his reign, rebellions in Egypt (485) and Babylonia (481) are put down.

480/79   The great *campaign against Greece* fails despite initial successes at *Salamis* by sea and *Plataea* (479) on land. A further revolt in Babylonia is put down (479).

465   Xerxes and Darius, his heir to the throne, are both murdered. He is succeeded by his younger son, Artaxerxes (I).

465–424   The reign of *Artaxerxes I* is marked by his defeat at the *Eurymedon* against the members of the 'Delian League' but also by his successes in *Egypt* (against Inarus and Athens) and on Cyprus.

423   After the king's death, the heir to the throne *Xerxes II* is assassinated. The successor is *Darius II*.

423–404   By diplomatic methods and military pressure, D. succeeds in recapturing the coastal cities of Asia Minor (through the support of Sparta in the *Peloponnesian War*).

404–359   *Artaxerxes II*, the son of Darius, is challenged by his brother *Cyrus the Younger*, but the latter is killed in the battle of *Cunaxa* (401) near Babylon. The Persian empire loses *Egypt*. In the '*King's peace*' (387/86), western Asia Minor is definitely yielded to the king by the Greeks. *Revolts by satraps* in the west are unsuccessful.

359–338   In the reign of *Artaxerxes III*, the son of A. II, further rebellions in *Asia Minor* and *Phoenicia* are suppressed. In 343/42, *Egypt* is reconquered.

336   Following the assassination of the king (338) and shortly afterwards that of his son and successor *Arses*, *Darius III*, another great-grandson of Darius II, ascends the throne.

334–330   *Alexander (III)* of Macedonia attacks the Persian empire and, after victories at *Granicus*, *Issus* and *Gaugamela*, seizes the entire west, Mesopotamia and the Iranian residences. The fleeing Darius is assassinated by the satrap Bessus (330).

The Macedonian dominion over Iran

330–323   *Alexander* conquers *eastern Iran* and the *Indus valley*. He acts as successor to the Achaemenids. Iranians serve in his entourage and in the army.

312–306   Under *Seleucus I* Iran becomes part of the Seleucid empire.

305   In the treaty with *Chandragupta* the *upper Indus region*, *Gandhara*, *Paropamisadae* and *eastern Arachosia* are yielded to the expanding Maurya kingdom.

c. 250   In *Bactria*, *Diodotus I* and *II* found the '*Graeco-Bactrian kingdom*'; somewhat later, the Parthian satrap *Andragoras* also tries to break away from the Seleucid empire, but he is killed in battle against the Parnians under *Arsaces* (see Arsacids).

206   *Antiochus III* is temporarily able to enforce recognition of Seleucid sovereignty in eastern Iran again.

1st half of 2nd century   The fall of the Maurya dynasty contributes to the expansion of the Bactrian Greeks as far as the Indus valley.

Mid-2nd century   *Elymais* and *Persis* break away from the Seleucid empire.

141–126   The Parthians conquer western Iran and Mesopotamia.

c. 130   The Graeco-Bactrian kingdom succumbs to the onset of the *Yueh-chih*. The last remnants of the *Indo-Bactrian kingdoms* hold out for another half century.

Iran under the Arsacids

Until 239   The Parnians led by *Arsaces* occupy the Parthian territories north of the *Kopet Dagh*. The new masters, who are soon to be called *Parthians*, also conquer Hyrcania.

230–228   Arsaces is able to stand his ground against *Seleucus II*.

210–208   After the successful eastern campaign of *Antiochus III*, the Parthians are forced to acknowledge Seleucid sovereignty and perhaps even to evacuate territories south of the Kopet Dagh.

After 188   After the defeat of Antiochus III against Rome, the Parthians again secede and spread their reign further south and west.

171–139/38   *Mithridates I* conquers *western Iran* and *Mesopotamia*. In the east, parts of the Graeco-Bactrian kingdom are annexed. A Seleucid counterblow under *Demetrius II* (139) miscarries. The Parthian king assumes the Achaemenid title of 'king of kings'.

139/38–124/23   *Phraates II* and *Artabanus I* secure western Iran and Mesopotamia against the Seleucids (victory over the initially successful *Antiochus VII* in 129) and *Characene*, but are killed in their fight against the people of the north-eastern steppes.

124/23–88/87   *Mithridates II* restores Parthia's position as a great power. First Parthian intervention in *Armenia*. The Parthian envoy Orobazus meets *Sulla* (the Roman propraetor of Cilicia) (96).

69/66   In their treaties with *Lucullus* and *Pompey*, the Parthians recognize the *Euphrates* as their *border*.

53   The treaties are broken by *Crassus*. His invasion of the Parthian empire is stopped by the Parthian general *Surenas* at the battle of *Carrhae*. Death of Crassus.

44   *Caesar* is planning an expedition against the Parthians when he is assassinated.

41–38   The Parthians under *Pacorus* and *Q. Labienus* temporarily conquer *Syria* and parts of *Asia Minor*, but are repulsed by *C. Ventidius Bassus*.

36   Despite a dynastic crisis in the Arsacid empire, *Antony's* campaign in *Armenia* and *Media Atropatene* miscarries.

20   Peace treaty between *Phraates IV* and Rome. Diplomatic success of *Augustus*: the Parthians give back the standards won in 53 and later and acknowledge Roman sovereignty in Armenia. Sons of Phraates are resident in Rome.

12 AD   Against *Vonones I*, who was brought up in Rome, the Parthian aristocracy raises *Artabanus II* to the throne. His policy soon meets with resistance, fomented by Rome through the dispatch of pretenders to the throne.

38–45   After the death of Artabanus, power struggles between *Vardanes* and *Gotarzes II*.

51–63   Conflicts about *Armenia* between Rome and Parthia under *Vologeses I*.

63   Treaty of Rhandeia: the Armenian kingdom becomes an Arsacid secundogeniture under Roman sovereignty.

after 72 An invasion by the Alans and the secession of Hyrcania, as well as struggles about the throne after Vologeses's death, plunge the empire into a time of crisis.

114–117 *Osroes*'s illegal intervention in Armenia leads *Trajan* to launch upon an expedition against Parthia: *Armenia*, *Mesopotamia* and *Assyria* are established as provinces. Trajan is defeated at *Hatra*, but captures *Ctesiphon*. Rebellions in Mesopotamia. Death of Trajan.

after 117 *Hadrian* gives up the newly acquired territories. The Euphrates again becomes the border. In *Mesene* a ruler who is not dependent on the Parthians maintains himself until 151.

161–165 An initially successful Parthian attack on *Armenia* and *Syria* under *Vologeses IV* is thwarted by *Avidius Cassius*. Ctesiphon is captured, northern Mesopotamia including *Dura-Europus* becomes Roman. An epidemic forces the Romans to retreat with heavy losses.

195   Establishment of the province of *Mesopotamia* by *Septimus Severus*.

from 198 Expeditions against the Parthians by Septimus Severus and his son and successor *Caracalla* do not change the shape of foreign policy, but they enable the 'petty kings' in *Persis* to pursue their own aims: The Sasanids *Pabag* and *Ardashir* expand their territory over the entire south-western part of Iran.

28 April 224 Arda
shir (I) defeats the last Parthian king *Artabanus (Ardavan) IV*.

Iran during the Sasanian period

205/06   Beginning of the Sasanian era (rise of Pabag?).

205/06–224 Conquest of the whole of *Persis* and adjacent territories (*Elymais*, regions around *Isfahan, Kirman, north-eastern Arabia* [?]) by *Pabag* and his sons *Shapur* and *Ardashir*. Victory of A. over Artabanus IV (after the latter's refusal to acknowledge him as a new vassal? or in a power struggle for the whole empire?).

224–239/40?   In the reign of *Ardashir I* all the regions of the Parthian empire (except Armenia) become Sasanian. After Persian invasions into Roman territories, campaign of *Alexander Severus* against the Persians with inconclusive results. The Sasanians occupy *Nisibis* and *Carrhae* (235/6) and attack Dura (239).

239/40–271/72   Under the reign of A.'s son *Shapur I*, wars against Rome with variable results: conquest of *Hatra* (241), defeat of *Gordian III* and peace with *Philip the Arab* (244); conquest of *Armenia* (252); campaigns against *Syria* and *Asia Minor* with successes (occupation of *Antiochia* 252 or 253 [?] and/or 256 [?]; conquest of *Dura* 256; capture of *Valerian* 260) and defeats (counteroffensive by the Palmyrean prince *Odaenathus*).

277   *Mani* dies in prison.

after 277   'Fratricidal (?) war' between *Bahram II* and *Hormizd* leads to Roman victories under *Carus* (283) and the political rise of the mobad *Kirdir*. Conclusion of peace between V. and *Diocletian* (287).

297/98   Treaty of *Nisibis* between *Narseh* and Diocletian after a pre-emptive attack by the Sasanians against Armenia (defeat of *Galerius* 296) and a successful Roman counteroffensive: Narseh has to give up *Mesopotamia* and *Armenia* as well as territories east of the Tigris.

before 309   Unsuccessful campaign by *Hormizd II* against Rome.

309–379   After prolonged wars, H.'s son Shapur II regains large portions of the territories lost in 298, having beaten back the emperor *Julian* before Ctesiphon and concluded peace with his successor *Jovian* (363). These wars give rise to *severe persecutions of Christians*, who christologically share the faith of their Western co-religionists and are thus looked upon as Roman partisans after Constantine's conversion.

387   The eastern part of *Armenia* becomes Sasanian again.

after 400   The *Hephthalites* invade Iran and subsequently become the greatest enemies of the Persians.

465/484   King *Peroz* is dealt two crushing defeats by the Hephthalites. During his reign, *Nestorianism* becomes the characteristic form of the Christian faith in Iran.

488–579   The heavy losses caused by the wars, as well as tributary dependence on the Hephthalites and famines, lead to popular risings which, influenced by Mazdak's demands of equal distribution of ownership, are primarily directed against the (landowning? or lower?) aristocracy. After initial support from King *Kavad I*, leading to his temporary deprivation of power (496), the rebellions are cruelly suppressed by K. and his son

> *Khosrow I.* H. takes advantage of the weakness of the aristocracy to introduce fundamental *social, economic* and *military reforms*: cadastral surveys of landed property and a stable land tax instead of fluctuating revenue taxes; census and a newly established poll-tax (differentiated according to wealth); division of the empire into four military districts, equipment of 'cavaliers' at public expense and organization of frontier defence garrisons; creation of a new court and office aristocracy as well as promotion of the lower landowning aristocracy; infrastructure and frontier safety provisions.

540   Kh. breaks the 'eternal peace' concluded with emperor *Justinian* in 532: he destroys *Antiochia* and deports its inhabitants.

c. 560   Destruction of the Hephthalite kingdom with the help of the *western Turks*.

562   Renewed peace treaty with Byzantium for 50 years (the payments of tribute to the Sasanians already agreed upon in 532 are raised).

571   Conquest of *southern Arabia* and expulsion of the Axumites (Ethiopians) allied with Byzantium.

after 579   Under Kh's son *Hormizd IV*, renewed conflicts between the king and the aristocracy. Heavy battles against the Turks.

590–628   H.'s son *Khosrow II* puts down the rebellion of the pretender *Bahram VI Chubin* with the aid of eastern Rome, conquers large portions of *Asia Minor* and *Syria* from 604 on, occupies *Egypt* in 619 and lays siege to *Constantinople* (together with the *Avars*) in 626. In 614 the Cross is removed from Jerusalem to Ctesiphon. The counterblow by *Heraclius* (626–628) forces the Sasanians to give up the conquered territories. Khosrow is overthrown by a revolt of the aristocracy and killed.

632–651   After a period of anarchy with frequently changing rulers, *Yazdgird III* is raised to the throne by the aristocratic party of Rustam. The empire is weakened by wars and private interests, and the king is not in a position to defend it against the Muslim armies. After defeats at *Qadisiyya* (636) and *Nihavand* (642), Y. retires to eastern Iran, where he is murdered. The Sasanian empire becomes part of the Caliphate.

DYNASTIES AND KINGS

THE ACHAEMENIDS

Cyrus (Kurush) II (?) the Great	*c.* 558–530 BC
Cambyses (Kambujiya) II	530–522
Gaumata/Bardiya	522
Darius (Darayavaush) I	522–486
Xerxes (Khshayarshan) I	486–465
Artaxerxes (Artakhshaça) I	465–424
Xerxes II; Secyndianus	424–423
Darius II	423–404
Artaxerxes II	404–359
Artaxerxes III	359–338
Arses	338–336
Darius III	336–330

THE SELEUCIDS

Seleucus I Nicator	305–281 BC
Antiochus I Soter	281–261
Antiochus II Theos	261–246
Seleucus II Callinicus	246–225
Seleucus III Soter	225–223
Antiochus III the Great	223–187
Seleucus IV Philopator	187–175
Antiochus IV Epiphanes	175–164
Antiochus V Eupator	164–162
Demetrius I Soter	162–150
Alexander Balas	150–145
Demetrius II Nicator	145–141
Antiochus VI Epiphanes	145–142
Antiochus VII Sidetes	138–129
Demetrius II Nicator	129–125

THE ARSACIDS

Arsaces I	*c.* 247/38–217 BC
Arsaces II	*c.* 217–191
Phriapatius	*c.* 191–176
Phraates I	176–171
Mithridates I	171–139/38
Phraates II	139/38–128
Artabanus (Ardavan) I	128–124/23
Mithridates II	124/23–88/87
Gotarzes I	91/90–81/80
Orodes I	81/80–76/75
Sinatruces	*c.* 78/77–71/70
Phraates III	71/70–58/57
Mithridates III	58/57
Orodes II	58/57–38
Phraates IV	38–3/2
Phraates V	2 BC–2 AD
Orodes III	4–6
Vonones I	8/9
Artabanus II	10/11–38
Vardanes	38–45
Gotarzes II	43/44–51
Vonones II	51
Vologeses (Valakhsh) I	51–76/80
Pacorus	77/78–108/09
Vologeses II	77/78
Artabanus III	79–81
Osroes	108/09–127/28
Vologeses III	111/12–147/48
Vologeses IV	147/48–191/92
Vologeses V	191/92–207/08
Vologeses VI	207/08–221/22 or 227/28
Artabanus IV	213–224

THE KINGS OF CHARACENE
(datings largely based on coinage evidence only)

Hyspaosines	*c.* 127–122/21 BC
Apodacus	110/09–104/03
Tiraius I	95/94–90/89

Tiraius II	79/78–49/48
Artabazus	49/48–48/47
Attambelus I	47/46–25/24
Theonesius I	c. 19/18
Attambelus II	c. 17/16 BC – AD 8/9
Abinergaus	c. 10/11; 22/23
Orabazes I	c. 19
Attambelus III	c. 37/38–44/45
Theonesius II	c. 46/47
Theonesius III	c. 52/53
Attambelus IV	c. 54/55–64/65
Attambelus V	c. 64/65–73/74
Orabazes I	c. 73–80
Pacorus (II)	80–101/102 (Parth. interregnum)
Attambelus VI	c. 101/102–105/06
Theonesius IV	c. 110/11–112/13
Attambelus VII	c. 113/14–117
Meredates	c. 131–150/51
Orabazes II	c. 150/51–165
Abinergaus II (?)	c. 165–180
Attambelos VIII	c. 180–195 (?)
Maga (?)	c. 195–210
Abinergaus III	c. 210–222

THE KINGS OF ELYMAIS

(datings largely based on coinage evidence only)

Kamnaskires I Soter	c. 147 BC
Kamnaskires II Nicephorus	c. 145–139
Okkonapses	c. 139
Tigraios	138/37–133/32
Kamnaskires III	82/81–75
Kamnaskires IV	62/61 or 59/58 and 56/55
Kamnaskires V and successors	36/35
Orodes I	2nd half of 1st century AD
Phraates	end of 1st/beg. of 2nd century
Orodes II	1st half of 2nd century
Kamnaskires–Orodes III	2nd half of 2nd century
Osroes (?)	2nd century

THE KINGS OF PERSIS

(datings largely based on coinage evidence only)

Baydad	end of 3rd/ beg. of 2nd century BC
Ardashir I	1st half of 2nd century
Vahbarz	1st half of 2nd century
Vadfradad I	mid-2nd century
Vadfradad II	c. 140
'Unknown king I'	2nd half of 2nd century
Darev I	end of 2nd century
Vadfradad III	1st half of 1st century
Darev II	1st century
Ardashir II	2nd half of 1st century
Vahshir	2nd half of 1st century
Pakor I	1st half of 1st century AD
Pakor II	1st half of 1st century
Nambed	mid-1st century
Napad	2nd half of 1st century
'Unknown king II'	end of 1st century
Vadfradad IV	1st half of 2nd century
Manchihr I	1st half of 2nd century
Ardashir III	1st half of 2nd century
Manchihr II	mid-2nd century
'Unknown king III'	2nd half of 2nd century
Manchihr III	2nd half of 2nd century
Ardashir IV	end of 2nd century
Shapur	beg. of 3rd century

(Baydad and Ardashir I as sub-Seleucid, Vadfradad I and his successors as sub-Parthian dynasts; Shapur is the brother of the first Sasanian, Ardashir I.)

THE SASANIANS

Ardashir I	AD 224–239/40 died 241/42
Shapur I	239/40 (241/42?)–270/72
Hormizd I	270/72–273
Bahram I	273–276
Bahram II	276–293
Bahram III	293
Narseh	293–302

Hormizd II	302–309
Shapur II	309–379
Ardashir II	379–383
Shapur III	383–388
Bahram IV	388–399
Yazdgird I	399–421
Bahram V Gor	421–439
Yazdgird II	439–457
Hormizd III	457–459
Peroz	459–484
Valakhsh	484–488
Kavad I	488–496; 499–531
Zamasp	496–498
Khosrow I Anoshirvan	531–579
Hormizd IV	579–590
Khosrow II	590–628
Bahram VI Chubin	590–591
Kavad II	628
Ardashir III	628–630
Shahrbaraz	630
Khosrow III	630
Puran	630–631
Azarmigdukht	631
Hormizd V	631–632
Khosrow IV	631–633
Yazdgird III	633–651

INDEX